THE PELOPONNESIAN WAR

Sir Nigel Bagnall was born in India in 1927. He joined the British Army in 1945 and served in Palestine, Malaya, Borneo, the Canal Zone, Cyprus, Singapore and Germany. He ended his distinguished military career as Chief of the General Staff in London. He was an Honorary Fellow of Balliol College, Oxford, and is the author of *The Punic Wars: Rome, Carthage, and the Struggle for the Mediterranean*. He died in April 2002.

Also by Nigel Bagnall

*The Punic Wars: Rome, Carthage, and the
Struggle for the Mediterranean*

The

PELOPONNESIAN WAR

*Athens, Sparta,
and the Struggle for Greece*

Nigel Bagnall

THOMAS DUNNE BOOKS
St. Martin's Press ⚏ New York

THOMAS DUNNE BOOKS.
An imprint of St. Martin's Press.

www.thomasdunnebooks.com

www.stmartins.com

Library of Congress Cataloging-in-Publication Data

Bagnall, Nigel, 1927–2002
    The Peloponnesian War / Nigel Bagnall.
       p. cm.
    Includes index.
    ISBN-13: 978-0-312-34215-9
    ISBN-10: 0-312-34215-2
    1. Greece—History—Peloponnesian War, 431–404 B.C. I. Title.

DF229.B34 2006
938'.05—dc22

2006040193

First published in Great Britain by Pimlico

First U.S. Edition: August 2006

10 9 8 7 6 5 4 3 2 1

CONTENTS

LIST OF MAPS

TO THE BRITISH ARMY

ACKNOWLEDGEMENTS

My husband completed this book in February 2002. He died un-expectedly two months later.

I know he would have wished me to thank those who so gener-ously gave their time and expertise to help him. Foremost is Professor Jasper Griffin who read the manuscript as the book progressed. I think also, especially, of our neighbour, Roger Hebblethwaite, who patiently found much information on the internet.

I am sure there are others I should thank. They will know who they are and I thank all of them warmly for him.

My husband took great pride in the professionalism of the British Army, and cared so much for its members and their wellbeing. I also know, therefore, that he would have wished to dedicate *The Peloponnesian War* to them, and so I now do this on his behalf.

Anna Bagnall
June 2004

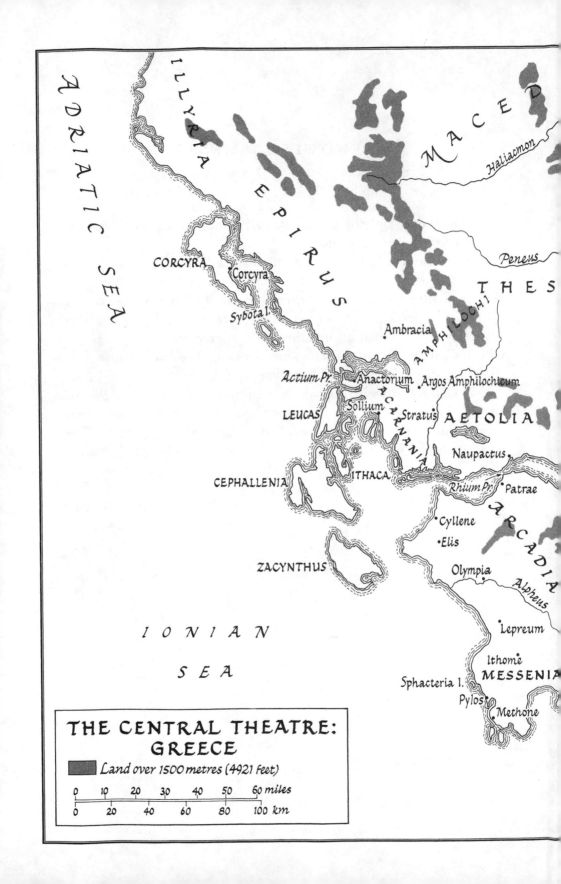

THE CENTRAL THEATRE:
GREECE

Land over 1500 metres (4921 feet)

0   10   20   30   40   50   60 miles
0   20   40   60   80   100 km

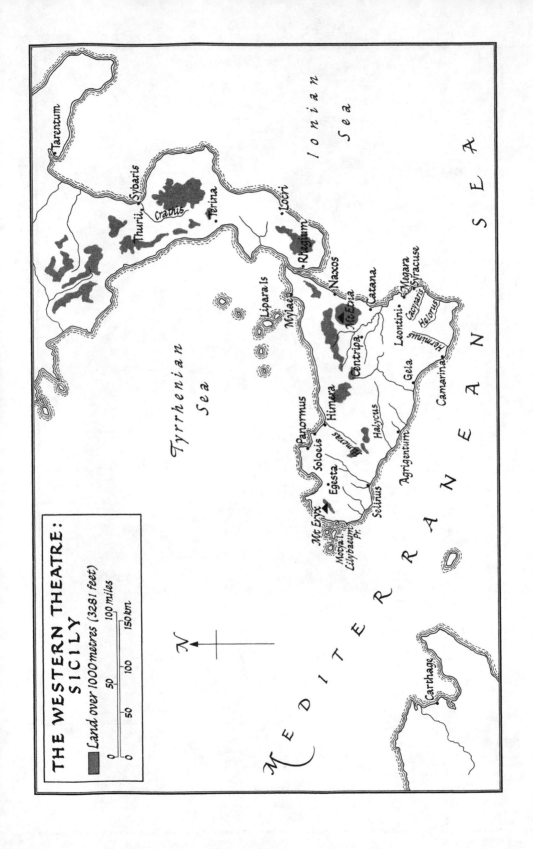

THE WESTERN THEATRE: SICILY

■ Land over 1000 metres (3281 feet)

0   50   100   150 km
0   50   100 miles

N

Tyrrhenian Sea

Ionian Sea

MEDITERRANEAN SEA

Carthage

Tarentum

Sybaris

Thurii

Cratus

Terina

Locri

Rhegium

Naxos

Catana

Megara

Syracuse

Cyparis

Helorus

Leontini

Hermimus

Centripa

Mt Etna

Mylae

Liparals

Panormus

Solocis

Himera

Himeras

Halycus

Egesta

Mt Eryx

Motya I.

Lilybaeum Pr.

Selinus

Agrigentum

Gela

Camarina

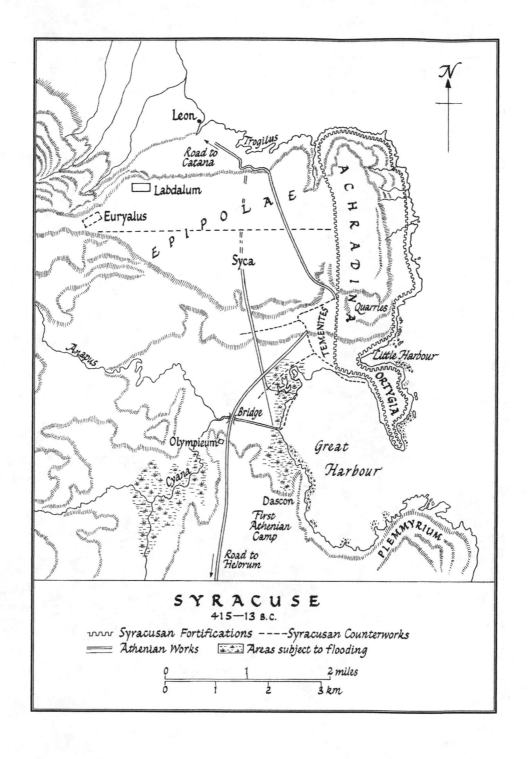

SYRACUSE
415—13 B.C.

ⅿⅿⅿ Syracusan Fortifications   ----Syracusan Counterworks
═══ Athenian Works   ⁙⁙⁙ Areas subject to flooding

0 .... 1 .... 2 miles
0 .... 1 .... 2 .... 3 km

THE EASTERN THEATRE: ASIA MINOR

BLACK

THRACE

Doriscus

Aenus

Selymbria Byzantium
Perinthus   Chalcedon

Bosphorus

PROPONTIS

Cardia   Proconnesus

IMBROS   Sestos   Lampsacus   Cyzicus

LESBOS   Abydos

Hellespont   Elaeus

Sangarius

Scamander

Rhyndacus

Mt Ida   Antandrus

Methymna

Eresus   Mytilene   Caïcus

LESBOS

Arginusae I.   LYDIA

Magnesia   Hermus

CHIOS   Erythrae   Smyrna   Sardis

Clazomenae

Teos   Colophon   PHRYGIA

Notium   Ephesus   Maeander

SAMOS

ICARIA   Priene

Mt Mycale   CARIA

Miletus

Iasus

Halicarnassus   Aspendus

Cos   Caunus

Cnidus   Phaselis

Cynossema Pr.

RHODES

CARPATHOS

CRETE

MEDITERRANEAN   SEA

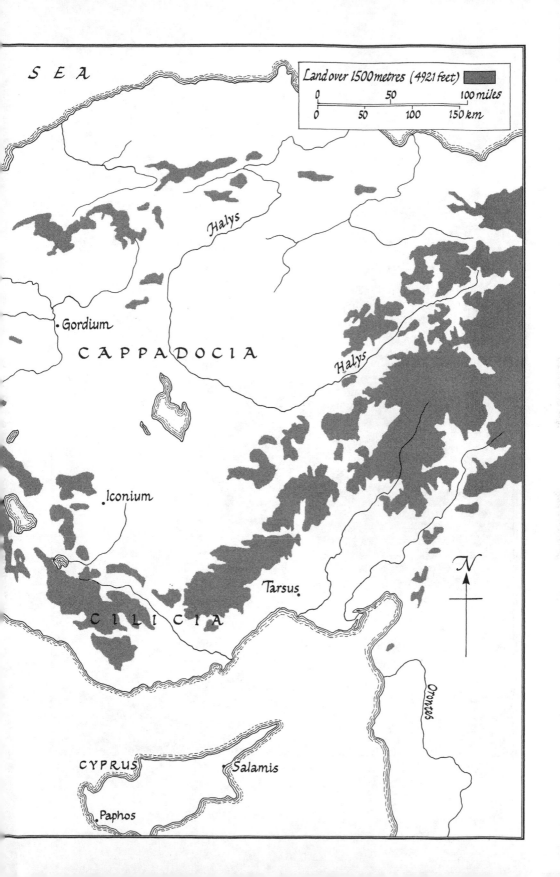

S E A

Land over 1500 metres (4921 feet)

0   50   100 miles
0   50   100   150 km

Halys

•Gordium

C A P P A D O C I A

Halys

•Iconium

Tarsus
•

C I L I C I A

Orontes

N

CYPRUS   Salamis

•Paphos

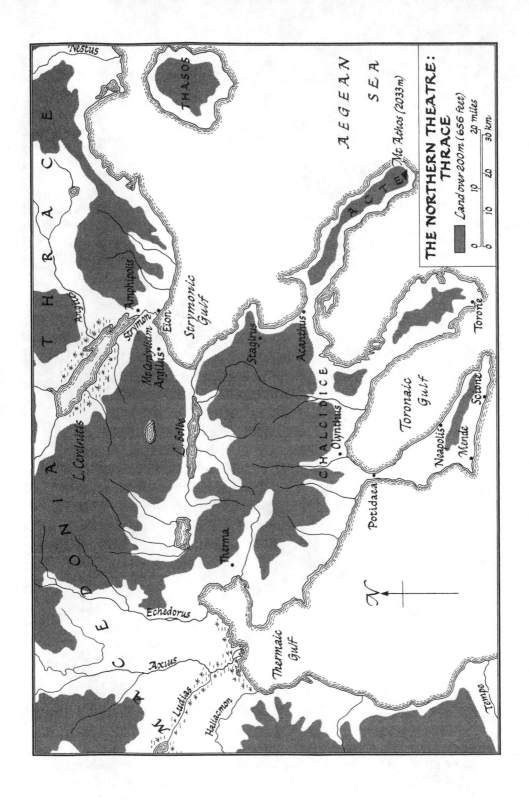

THE NORTHERN THEATRE: THRACE

Land over 200m (656 feet)

0   10   20 miles

0   10   20   30 km

Nestus

THASOS

AEGEAN SEA

Mt Athos (2033m)

ACTE

T H R A C E

Argilus

Amphipolis

Strymon

Mt Cerdylium Argilus

Eion

Strymonic Gulf

L. Cercinitis

L. Bolbe

Stagirus

Acanthus

M A C E D O N I A

Echedorus

Therma

CHALCIDICE

Olynthus

Toronaic Gulf

Acanthus

Potidaea

Neapolis

Mende

Scione

Torone

Axius

Ludias

Haliacmon

Thermaic Gulf

Tempe

N

Principal Characters

ALCIBIADES Athenian statesman and general, aristocratic, glamorous and dissipated, who was largely responsible for launching the ill-fated Sicilian expedition in 415 BC. When summoned back to Athens to stand trial for sacrilege, he fled to Sparta where he turned traitor; but, after seducing King Agis' wife, he was forced to take refuge with Tissaphernes, Persian satrap (governor) of Ionia and Caria, whom he advised to play Athens and Sparta off against one another. He was called back by the Athenians, but lost their confidence; so once again he sought refuge with the Persians, this time with Pharnabazus, satrap of the Hellespont, where he was finally assassinated.

BRASIDAS Spartan general who in 424 BC, with a handful of hoplites (heavily armed foot soldiers) and Helots (serfs), marched some 800 miles from the Isthmus of Corinth to Thrace, where he captured nearly all the Athenian cities, including Amphipolis, the most important of them all. When the Athenians under Cleon tried to retake Amphipolis in 422, he won a major victory, but was mortally wounded and died shortly afterwards.

CIMON Athenian aristocrat, statesman and general, who played a leading role in transforming the Delian League, an equal and free association of states, into the Athenian Alliance, demanding recognition of Athenian domination. Between 476 and 464 BC he consolidated the Athenian hold throughout the Aegean, pursuing a policy of hostility to Persia and friendship with Sparta. A truly pan-Hellenic figure, he died in 449 while campaigning in Cyprus.

CLEON Athenian statesman and general who dominated Athenian policy after the death of Pericles. In 425 BC, following the capture of

Pylos by Demosthenes, he rejected the Spartan offer of peace and friendly relations. In 422 he commanded an expedition to try and recover Thrace, but through poor generalship was defeated and killed at the battle of Amphipolis by Brasidas, who was himself mortally wounded.

CYRUS In 407 BC he was sent by his father, King Darius II, to Sardis as governor of the three Maritime Provinces, the Hellespont, Ionia and Caria, with instructions to give the Spartans all the assistance they required. With the wealth of the Persian Empire now placed decisively behind Sparta, the eventual outcome of the war was no longer in doubt.

DARIUS I The Persian king who invaded Greece in 490 BC. His army landed at Marathon in Attica, where it was defeated and withdrew.

DARIUS II Persian king who seized power in the dynastic struggle following his father's death, and whose reign saw a series of uprisings. He sent his son, Cyrus, to govern the Maritime Provinces in 407 BC.

DEMOSTHENES Athenian general who led an abortive expedition into Aetolia in 426 BC, but thereafter proved himself to be an outstanding commander. He captured Pylos in 425, then took part in fighting at Megara and Thrace in 424. He was sent out in joint command of the relief force to Syracuse in 414, but came under the command of the incompetent Nicias on arrival. In 413, when the Athenian expedition was destroyed, he was put to death after being taken prisoner.

GYLIPPUS Spartan general who was sent out to Syracuse in 414 BC and through his vigorous and skilful leadership saved the city by defeating the Athenians the following year. After such an outstanding performance, it is strange that he then apparently disappears off the military scene.

LYSANDER Spartan admiral who took command of the Peloponnesian forces in the Eastern Theatre in 407 BC. He annihilated the Athenian fleet at Aegospotami in 405, so cutting off Athens' grain supplies through the Hellespont and starving her into surrender the following year. He was killed when leading an army against Thebes in 393 BC – long after the Peloponnesian War had ended.

MARDONIUS The son-in-law of Darius I. He commanded an early Persian attempt to invade Greece in 493 BC, but his fleet was destroyed in a storm when trying to round the Mount Athos promontory. He took part in Xerxes' invasion in 480, and when the Persian fleet was defeated at Salamis the same year, causing Xerxes to withdraw, Mardonius was left behind to continue the land campaign. He was killed at the battle of Plataea in 479.

MILTIADES Athenian governor of the Chersonese on the European side of the Hellespont. He accompanied Darius I on his Scythian campaign in about 525 BC and afterwards was recalled to Athens to account for his stewardship as governor. Having been exonerated, he commanded the Athenian army at the battle of Marathon, where he defeated the Persians in 490 BC. His end was unfortunate. Taking an expedition to the island of Paros for personal reasons, he was injured while trying to rob the temple of Demeter and died from gangrene.

NICIAS Athenian statesman and general, who succeeded Pericles after his death in 429 BC. He commanded a number of ineffectual expeditions, which included one to the island of Melos in 426, and to Tanagra the following year. In 421 he negotiated a truce with Sparta, which was irrevocably broken in 415 BC when the Athenians mounted their ill-fated expedition to Syracuse – an undertaking he had opposed as a statesman, then found himself commanding as general. He was put to death by the Syracusans after surrendering to Gylippus in 413. A thoroughly decent man, a fine statesman, damagingly superstitious and a useless soldier.

PAUSANIAS Spartan general who defeated the Persians under Mardonius at Plataea in 479 BC. He was given command of a fleet in 476 to evict the remaining Persian garrisons on the fringes of the Aegean. The success of Plataea and his campaign in the Hellespont went to his head, and he conceived the idea of becoming the ruler of Greece, which led to his being relieved of his command and eventually being put to death for treason.

PERICLES The great Athenian statesman who dominated Athenian policy for some thirty years, 462–429 BC. With his public building works he turned Athens into a city of outstanding splendour, which was matched by the creative achievement of the Athenians themselves. But his grandiose ambitions for Athens, together with his anti-Spartan policy, led to the Peloponnesian War and the downfall of the proud city. He died in 429, only two years after the war had broken out.

PHARNABAZUS Satrap governor of the Hellespont province who, when the struggle for the Hellespont began in 411 BC, supported the Spartans. His policy was then in accord with that of Cyrus, whose father, Darius II, appointed Cyrus governor of the Maritime Provinces.

THEMISTOCLES Athenian statesman and general who founded the fleet, so making Athens the supreme maritime power; fortifying the city and connecting it to the port of Piraeus, he made her invulnerable to attack by land. He saved Greece and thus embryonic Western civilisation by defeating the Persian fleet at Salamis in 480 BC. Ostracised in about 472 for greed and ambition, he either died or took his own life in Persia, where he had taken refuge and found high favour with the king.

TISSAPHERNES Satrap of Ionia and Caria who, advised by Alcibiades, when the war shifted to Asia Minor in 413 BC, encouraged the Athenians and Spartans to wear one another out, after which they could both be evicted. He was marginalised when Cyrus was appointed governor of the Maritime Provinces with instructions from his father, Darius II, to pursue a pro-Spartan policy.

XERXES Son of Darius I. He bridged the Hellespont to invade Greece in 480 BC, but when his fleet was destroyed at Salamis he withdrew, leaving Mardonius to do what he could on land.

Introduction

With only one short break, the Peloponnesian War lasted for twenty-seven years, from 431 to 404 BC; but this relatively short span cannot be considered in isolation, since the events that preceded it largely determined what was to follow. This is especially clear with the Persian War, which at the practical level resulted in the eventual division of Greece between Athenian- and Spartan-led alliances. Even more significant, however, was the survival of Greece as a whole against what seemed an overwhelmingly powerful Eastern autocracy, so permitting an as yet embryonic Western civilisation to develop into full maturity.

This book is a companion volume to my account of *The Punic Wars*. It is presented in much the same manner, by examining the different campaigns sequentially, each in its entirety, rather than giving an across-the-board chronological account. There are advantages and disadvantages to both methods, but I have again chosen the former because I consider that any difficulty in interrelating events occurring at the same time in the different theatres of war is far outweighed by the ability to follow through the developments of each separate campaign in an unbroken sequence. I have tried to reduce the disadvantage of this approach by mentioning the more important events taking place in other theatres, whenever this appeared to be helpful.

There is considerable similarity between the Punic and Peloponnesian Wars. Both were struggles for supremacy between what were initially a maritime and a land power: Carthage and Athens ruled the seas, while Rome and Sparta dominated the central land mass. There is, however, one significant geographical difference that affects the presentation. Whereas the Punic Wars were comparatively easy to follow, since they took place in well-known and clearly identifiable areas such as Sicily, Spain and Italy, this ready identification does not apply to the Peloponnesian War. That fact, together with the many mainland states, independent cities and numerous islands, can make the course of events difficult to follow. I have therefore written an Historical Survey that is intended to ease this problem, while eliminating the need for interruptive explanations when these places are encountered in the main text. The survey, then, acts as an orientating landmark, which the reader can refer back to if necessary.

As with my account of the Punic Wars, in analysing the various campaigns I have considered them at the three levels of war:

- *The Strategic* The definition of strategic objectives to be achieved in fulfilment of government policy.
- *The Operational* The planning and execution of military operations to achieve stated strategic objectives.
- *The Tactical* The planning and conduct of battles in pursuit of the operational aim.

I have also included a short introduction to some of the principal characters to help with their identification when encountered in the main text.

It may be asked: what relevance has a war that took place nearly 2500 years ago for our present age? Herodotus gives no reason for writing his *History* other than saying that he wished to preserve the memory of the past. Thucydides goes further, telling us that he wanted to give an understanding both of the past and of what is likely in the future; but some 300 years later Polybius offered an explanation for his account of the Punic Wars, which has a timeless relevance: 'There are only two sources from which any benefit can be derived: our own misfortunes, and those which have happened to other men.' Again, as I did with the Punic Wars, I have therefore written a short Epilogue, pulling together the various lessons and deductions that can be drawn, and showing their contemporary relevance. For the moment all that needs to be said is that, had the Romans and Carthaginians studied the Peloponnesian War, they might have avoided repeating many of the same mistakes.

I must stress that I am writing as a professional soldier endeavouring to clarify and analyse existing material. I am not attempting to conjure up new revelations, which is the field of academics; a fraternity to which I am unqualified to belong.

I am again deeply indebted to Professor Jasper Griffin for his corrections, helpful comments and encouragement; without his profound knowledge and unstinted help, this book would have been all the poorer. Finally, my sincere thanks are due to Pimlico of Random House, for publishing this companion volume to their edition of *The Punic Wars*.

An Historical Survey
The Central Theatre

Mainland Greece

Acarnania

In spite of being regarded as a backward state, whose inhabitants lived in villages and subsisted largely on piracy, most of Acarnania joined the Delian League in 478 BC. No doubt in order to cement the alliance, when the Peloponnesian War broke out in 431 BC, Athens gave Acarnania the Corinthian town of Salium, which she had recently captured. The following year Athens tried to enlist the support of Acarnania, together with the western islands of Corcyra, Cephallenia and Zacynthus, for the encirclement of the Peloponnese. At the suggestion of the Corinthians, the Spartans with some allied troops invaded Acarnania in an attempt to detach her from the Athenian Alliance which, it was considered, would bring important consequences. First, Cephallenia and Zacynthus would be easily conquered, so preventing the Athenians from sailing round the Peloponnese to raid the west coast; and second, such an achievement offered the prospect of capturing the important Athenian base at Naupactus on the north coast of the Corinthian Gulf. But both the invading land forces and the Corinthian fleet, which was to have supported them, were severely mauled, and the survivors were forced to make a hasty withdrawal.

The Acarnanians played an active part in the campaign that lasted from 427 to 425 BC, during which the Athenians invaded Aetolia and, after being badly mauled, appealed to the Acarnanians to help defend

Naupactus when it was threatened by the Peloponnesians – Naupactus was an important naval base on the north coast of the Corinthian Gulf. The Acarnanians then played a leading role in destroying this force when it marched off to attack Argos Amphilochicum, in the north of the province. In 415 BC the Acarnanians took part in the fateful Athenian expedition to Sicily, either out of goodwill or more probably as mercenaries, but following the surrender of Athens in 404 BC they became subservient to Sparta.

Aetolia

Lying to the east of Acarnania, Aetolia dominated the western and southern sea passages. Not being a member of the Delian League, it constituted a threat to the Athenian base at Naupactus. Not dissimilar to the Acarnanians, the Aetolians were a warlike, backward people who lived in unfortified and widely dispersed villages, so they were slow to mobilise. In 426 BC, five years after the outbreak of the Peloponnesian War, an Athenian contingent, augmented by allies, attempted to force a passage through Aetolia in order to invade Boeotia, which lay further to the east; but they were so mauled by the lightly armed and mobile Aetolians that the broken survivors were fortunate to make their way back to Naupactus, on the northern coast of the Corinthian Gulf. In 415 BC an Aetolian contingent took part in the expedition to Sicily, where, as Thucydides says, they fought under compulsion against their fellow Aetolians who had sided with Syracuse. Like Acarnania, following the defeat of Athens in 404 BC, Aetolia was dominated by Sparta.

Athens

As Athens, like Attica, will figure prominently throughout the main text, only a brief introduction to the city is given at this stage, apart from its political developments during the 6th century, which are best recorded here. It was under the great statesman Pericles, who was born in 493 and died in 429 BC, that the amazing achievements of Athens occurred. From a population that has been variously assessed, but which probably numbered about 200,000 (including slaves), arose architects, sculptors and dramatists who produced works that remain unsurpassed to this day. The slaves filled many public appointments, such as clerks, attendants on officials and custodians of state archives, extending far beyond their usual association with domestic and agricultural serfdom; others worked as skilled artisans, employed by contractors undertaking Pericles' public building works.

Militarily, it was the Athenians who defeated the first great Persian invasion of Greece by Darius' troops at Marathon in 490 BC. But in spite of all these glories, by the end of the 5th century Athens was ignominiously humbled by Sparta in the Peloponnesian War and came close to being destroyed by her victorious enemies.

In about 560 BC Pisistratus, an aristocrat, had risen to a dominant position in Athens by means of a *coup d'état*. But, like so many of those labelled as 'tyrants', his domestic policy was actually to advance the well-being of the ordinary people, which he did by introducing far-reaching reforms. Though Solon, the great lawmaker, had earlier in the century freed agricultural labourers from what amounted to serfdom, Pisistratus now gave them smallholdings of their own. His foreign policy was designed to ensure the security and prosperity of Athens by establishing friendly relations with her neighbours, while extending Athenian power further afield. Recognising that the growing population of Attica would entail an increasing dependence on the import of food from the Greek settlements that fringed the Black Sea, he recaptured Sigeum, on the south coast of the Hellespont (Dardanelles) opposite the Thracian peninsula of Gallipoli. That was an act of imperialism, however, that probably entailed having to acknowledge the suzerainty of the Persians, who were now overlords of the coast of Asia Minor. Although Sigeum does not figure prominently in any of the subsequent wars, its recapture from Mytilene, the principal city of Lesbos, indicates the extent of the antagonism between Athens and Mytilene, which will be mentioned again later. Even more significant, however, is that Sigeum was recaptured because Pisistratus, apparently unlike any of his successors, recognised the critical importance of the Hellespont – a matter that will be considered in due course.

When we come to look at the Athenian constitution, it should be remembered that 'tyrants' often introduced practical reforms that benefited the ordinary people, not infrequently at the expense of the aristocracy, as did Pisistratus. Any hard, condemnatory division, except as a matter of principle between tyrants and democrats, should then be treated with some reservation. In times of unrest or grave danger, an all-powerful leader may be essential for survival. So it was with Rome's imperium, and, in a watered-down version, with the authority bestowed on Churchill in the Second World War; the difference being one of accountability, an inconvenience not tolerated by tyrants.

When Pisistratus died in about 521 BC, his son Hippias succeeded him and continued his policy of careful neutrality; but the endemic squabbling of the Greek states changed the scene. Sparta's attitude had hardened, so it was decided to remove Hippias and replace him with his exiled rival, Cleisthenes, who would then be in thrall to his deliverers. In 511 BC a contingent of Spartans landed in the Bay of Phalerum, immediately east of Salamis, but were routed by the Thessalian cavalry, who were fighting alongside the Athenians. To revenge this humiliation, the Spartans returned in force the following year, forcing Hippias to capitulate and retire to Sigeum. Cleisthenes now returned but, almost at once, found his authority being challenged by his rival, Isagoras – 'a man of reputable family' as Herodotus describes him – who appealed to the Spartans for support. The arrival of a small Spartan force under one of their kings, Cleomenes, forced Cleisthenes to leave Athens. The people, however, rose up in his support and the Spartans, together with Isagoras, took refuge in the Acropolis, where they were blockaded and eventually had to capitulate. Back in power, Cleisthenes set about his reforms of the Athenian state, including the reorganisation of the citizens into ten new artificial tribes, and the banning of prominent citizens considered to pose a threat to the state. It seems that the object of this strange constitutional contrivance was to provide a safeguard against the possible rise of a new tyrant.

Fearing that the Spartans would revenge the humiliation they had suffered, as they had done after their defeat at Phalerum, Cleisthenes appealed to Darius for aid. But when the Athenian envoys were called upon to signify their submission by the usual offerings of earth and water, there was a change of mind. Meanwhile, as suspected, Cleomenes had been assembling an army, and in concert with the Boeotians, who were to attack from the north, he marched across the Isthmus. But dissension amongst the Spartan allies, and between the two Spartan kings, led to the whole operation being called off. The Spartans now decided to consolidate their position in the Peloponnese before trying to establish their hegemony over mainland Greece. So, in about 494 BC, Sparta attacked Argolis, the territory of the city of Argos, the capital, her rival for leadership of the Peloponnese.

Athens' successes in thwarting Spartan ambitions and defeating the Boeotians imbued the newborn democracy with such a sense of confidence that it ensured the continuation of a democratic government for the next century.

Attica

The district surrounding Athens was slightly smaller than Gloucestershire; the soil was poor but, according to Thucydides, the people were remarkably free from political diversity, which he attributes to their racial homogeneity. Herodotus, however, refers to civil war in the past between the coastal villages and the inland settlements. But whatever the internal situation may have been, when Athens prospered and the population grew, Attica became too small to sustain such numbers – the age-old problem of *Lebensraum* – and found relief in the colonisation of Ionia on the west coast of Asia Minor. In the first seven years of the war, only two years passed without the Spartans invading Attica and, by ravaging the countryside, they hoped to draw the Athenians out from behind their city's fortifications.

Boeotia

About the same size as Attica, which lay on her eastern border, Boeotia (meaning 'cow land') had rich pastoral plains, which, apart from providing grazing for cattle, enabled the Boeotians to breed horses and so maintain a cavalry arm. The state was divided into ten polis, or cities, which were normally in alliance with the capital, Thebes. Being predominantly oligarchic, Boeotia was a natural ally of Sparta and an enemy of the democratic Athenians, who referred to its inhabitants as 'Boeotian pigs'. Thebes illustrates the divided loyalties of both cities and states, whose political parties generally schemed for their own advancement, totally devoid of any wider sense of loyalty. When Xerxes invaded Greece in 480 BC, the few powerful families who governed Thebes were instrumental in bringing the Persians into Boeotia. Though the oligarchs – aristocrats referred to as tyrants – were removed after the Persian defeat in the following year, they remained a powerful faction that infiltrated itself back into power, especially in the north. Thespiae, a relatively small town some ten miles west of Thebes, provided a 700-strong contingent for the defence of Thermopylae, who were the only Greeks who volunteered to remain and die with the Spartans – an act of heroism that has received scant recognition.

In 457 BC a Peloponnesian army under Spartan leadership, after settling affairs in Phocis, entered Boeotia. Here the Spartans sought to make an ally of Boeotia to counterbalance Athenian influence, so Thebes was restored to its former supremacy as leader of the Boeotian League; a situation that the Athenians were not prepared to tolerate. The two armies clashed at Tanagra, not far from the border with Attica, and after a protracted battle, with heavy casualties on both sides, the Athenians were defeated. But the battle cannot have been decisive as the Spartans made no attempt to interfere with the construction of the walls at Athens, but contented themselves with withdrawing unimpeded back over the Isthmus. The Athenians were then free to re-establish their control and put an end to Theban supremacy.

The battle of Tanagra was the first open conflict between the Athenians and the Spartans since before the Persian Wars, and represented a step in that fatal progress that was to divide Greece. Eight years later, in 449 BC, the Boeotians, encouraged by the Spartans, revolted against the Athenians, who had remained in virtual occupation of their country ever since the Persians' withdrawal, and drove them out. As will be recounted later, through dabbling in the muddy waters of Greek political intrigue, Thebes was one of the sparks that ignited the powder trail leading to the Peloponnesian War in 431 BC. The oligarchic government was bitterly opposed to Athens throughout the Peloponnesian War, even opposing Sparta's desire to make peace with Athens in 422 BC, and urging the destruction of the city in 403 BC.

The small Boeotian town of Plataea, near the Attic frontier some ten miles south-west of Thebes, deserves a special mention. It had a democratic government that had friendly relations with Athens, and they were the only Greeks who helped Athens to defeat the first Persian invasion, under the direction of Darius, at Marathon in 490 BC. After Xerxes' attempt to crush Greece in 480 BC, the part of his army that he had left behind after his naval defeat at Salamis was annihilated at Plataea in 479 BC by a combined force of many Greek states, headed by Athens and Sparta. As will be related later, Plataea was to play a less distinguished role when, through treachery, she helped spark the Peloponnesian War in 431 BC. The town was besieged by the Peloponnesians in 429 BC, and after a heroic resistance was starved into surrender two years later.

Locris

A small state on the east coast, opposite the island of Euboea, Locris was divided into two distinctly different districts: the Opuntian Locrians in the east, who had continuously raided Euboea, and the Ozolian Locrians in the west, who were equally piratical but specialised in armed land robbery. When the state submitted to Athens in 459 BC the oligarchs were exiled, but after the Boeotians had expelled the Athenians in 446 BC, the Locrians took advantage of finding themselves behind the substantial buffer state of Boeotia, so declared their independence and the exiles returned. Thus, at a blow, Athens' effective northern frontier was precipitously removed from Thermopylae back to her border with Boeotia, some seventy miles to the south. When the Peloponnesian War broke out in 431 BC, Locris provided cavalry rather than infantry to fight as an ally of Sparta, though why this should have been so is not clear, especially as there is no further mention of the Locrian cavalry.

Megara

Lying across the Corinthian isthmus that separates mainland Greece from Peloponnese, Megara held a key and exposed position. Although an ally of Sparta, she was attacked by another member of the Spartan Confederation, Corinth, which was seeking to extend her control over the Isthmus. Receiving no help from Sparta, in about 464 BC Megara turned to the Athenians, who not only came to her assistance, but constructed a long wall to connect their hilltop city to its harbour at Nisaea, nearly a mile away. This was a valuable acquisition for the Athenians, which they at once secured with their own troops, as it gave them access to the western sea approaches and blocked the passage of any Peloponnesian invasion across the Isthmus. So, according to Thucydides, began the burning hatred of Corinth for Athens, which, as will be related later, was to contribute to the outbreak of the Peloponnesian War.

Rather than treating Megara as an ally, the Athenians clearly behaved as an occupying power, concerned solely with maintaining the strategically important position they had gained. So oppressive must Athens' occupation have been that the Megarians eventually revolted in 446 BC to side with Sparta. Megara then let a Corinthian force cross the Isthmus in 432 BC, to march to the relief of Potidaea, in Thrace, when it was under siege by Athens. This resulted in an Athenian decree, which banned Megara from trading with Athens or her allies; a ban that become one of the factors leading to the Peloponnesian War. Megara, together with Boeotia, was to oppose the Spartan proposal to make peace with Athens in 422 BC.

Xenophon records how the Megarians continued to play an active part in the closing years of the war with both naval and land forces. In 410 BC three ships they were crewing for King Agis of Sparta were sunk in the Hellespont, and in the following year their contingent in the garrison of Byzantium, a city that had been founded by Megara, was made prisoner when it fell to the Athenians.

Phocis

Another small state in central Greece that lay between Aetolia and Boeotia, Phocis was at one time a willing ally of Athens, but the once-proud state had been devastated during the first great Persian invasion by Darius in 490 BC. The Phocians had been the only people who had not gone over to the Persians in this part of Greece, but Herodotus, perhaps rather cynically, ascribes this loyalty to their hatred of Thessaly, which had welcomed the Persians. The Thessalians had always been on bad terms with the Phocians, especially since a few years before the Persian invasion the Thessalians had themselves invaded Phocis and suffered two humiliating defeats. By white-washing themselves and attacking at night, the Phocians had first terrified and then routed the Thessalian infantry. Not satisfied with one such trick, they next dug a large ditch across a neck of land, covered it over again and broke the subsequent mass cavalry charge.

The Thessalians now made sure that the Persians spared nothing when they overran Phocis, for everything was devastated; towns and villages were burned and some of the women raped successively by so many Persians that they died. After the bulk of the Persians had withdrawn to Asia following the defeat of their fleet at Salamis in 480 BC, a strong force had been left to continue the war on the Greek mainland under Mardonius. Some of the Phocians now found themselves forced to serve alongside the Persians, but others, who had taken to the hills around the foothills of Mount Parnassus (Lyakour-eia), continued to harry the Persians until the last of them withdrew from Europe following their defeat at Plataea in 479 BC.

Thinking that the Athenian garrison in Megara would prevent the Spartans from crossing the Isthmus, in 457 BC the Phocians attacked the Dorian communities that lived around the foothills of Mount Parnassus, and captured one of the towns. But the Spartans, because of their traditional connections, crossed the Corinthian Gulf without being detected, marched through Boeotia and restored the captured town. They then returned to Boeotia where, as will be remembered, they drew the Athenians into the battle of Tanagra and, after defeating them, marched back home.

In about 448 BC the Spartans crossed the Isthmus and expelled the Phocians from the temple at Delphi, which, since it formed a part of Phocis, they claimed the right to control. But as soon as the Spartans had withdrawn, the Athenians reinstated the Phocians. Though the incident, which was dignified by the name of a Sacred War, had no consequences, it could have been otherwise. Two years previously Athens and Sparta had entered into a five-year truce, and though neither of them had broken the truce, their actions could easily have brought them into conflict.

At the outbreak of the Peloponnesian War in 431 BC, Phocis joined the Spartan Confederation and, like Boeotia and Locris, provided a cavalry contingent. Throughout the period, with only one brief interruption, Phocis controlled Apollo's prestigious oracle at Delphi, on the slopes of Mount Parnassus, which was consulted by Greeks of all cities before undertaking any controversial enterprise, so bringing the Phocians considerable distinction and no little wealth.

Thessaly

The most northern of the Greek states, Thessaly, possessing a particularly fertile soil, attracted numerous settlers and so saw many changes in her population. On an even greater scale than Boeotia, Thessaly was able to rear large numbers of horses and maintain a formidable cavalry arm that dominated the open battlefield, giving them the ability to manoeuvre almost unimpeded, when not engaged in close or broken country. As has been related, the Thessalians had attacked Phocis a few years before Darius invaded Greece in 490 BC, but had been outwitted. Now, when news of Xerxes' impending invasion reached the Thessalians in 480 BC, they sent envoys to the conference being held by those Greek states intending to resist the Persians. The Thessalian delegates made it quite plain that, though they were ready to join the common cause, the defence of Greece must begin on their own borders, otherwise they would come to terms with Persia. So it was agreed to send a strong force by sea, to defend the pass that ran between Mount Olympus and Mount Osa at Tempe, but though this was done, the troops were withdrawn after only a few days. The reason for this withdrawal will be discussed when we consider the various factors determining where the defence of Greece should begin. The result, however, was that the Thessalians now cooperated wholeheartedly with the Persians.

Though Thessaly had been abandoned, the willing assistance she provided to the Persians may have also been because she lacked a homogeneous population; so she felt neither any particular loyalty to Greece as a whole, nor to any individual state. Yet in spite of Thessaly's seemingly traitorous conduct, the Athenians made an ally of her in 459 BC, just as she did with Argos, who had also not rallied to the Greek cause, though for different reasons that will be explained later. Only two years later, however, at the battle of Tanagra in Boeotia, the Thessalian cavalry deserted the Athenians to side with the Spartans and Boeotians. Generally, however, despite these hiccups, Thessaly had maintained good relations with Athens, particularly in the southern part of the state, but the nobility – the class between the dominant oligarchic families who owned vast estates and the common people – was more inclined towards Sparta. This divided sense of belonging, Thessaly's disparate population and her relative remoteness on the periphery of mainland Greece probably explain why she played no part in the Peloponnesian War.

The Coastal Islands of Mainland Greece

Aegina

Lying almost midway between Athens and the northern coast of the Peloponnese, Aegina occupied a position of considerable strategic importance. The Aeginetans were Dorians from Epidaurus, on the north-east coast of Argolis just across the straits, against whom they rebelled, and from whom they gained their independence. But they were soon in conflict with Athens as commercial and maritime rivals. The trouble started in 505 BC when the Aeginetans raided the coast of Attica, which brought about sporadic fighting until Darius' invasion in 490 BC, when there was a temporary cessation to hostilities, brought about by Spartan intervention at the request of Athens. But once the danger was past, the fighting broke out again with renewed vigour, each of the cities ravaging the coast of the other as an opportunity presented itself. But at the time of the second Persian invasion, thirty of the Aeginetans' best ships fought on the Greek side at the critically important battle of Salamis, just to the west of the Athenian port of Piraeus; this, as will be related, led to Xerxes withdrawing from Greece.

While the Athenians were occupied with an expedition to Egypt in 453 BC, Aegina took the opportunity and renewed her war with Athens, and, though the Aeginetan fleet was virtually annihilated, because of the support given by the Corinthians and others of Aegina's allies the island was not captured, remaining autonomous but having to pay tribute to Athens. When the Peloponnesian War broke out in 431 BC, the Athenians were quick to secure Aegina because of its strategic position. The population was expelled and resettled on land provided by Sparta, an act of magnanimity that was partly due to Aegina's hostility towards Athens, and partly in recognition of the support she had given Sparta during the Helot revolt and after the devastating earthquake in 463 BC. The Aeginetans having been evicted, the island was then occupied by Athenian colonists, but they in their turn were displaced at the end of the war when the rightful owners returned.

Cephallenia (Kefalonia)

Lying off the west coast of mainland Greece, Cephallenia initially did not respond to the Athenian attempt to enlist her support against Sparta in 430 BC, and she remained neutral until the following year when, to quote Thucydides, an Athenian fleet 'won them over' without having to use force. Possession of Cephallenia was important to Athens, because it provided a base for her fleet when harrying the Peloponnese after war had broken out with Sparta, while at the same time preventing the Peloponnesians from using it to obstruct the free passage of Athenian shipping along the west coast.

Cephallenia took part in the ill-fated expedition to Sicily, though, as Thucydides concedes, 'they had little choice'. It will be recalled that, at the outbreak of the Peloponnesian War, Sparta had invaded Acarnania to detach her from the Athenian Alliance and so, most importantly, simplify the capture of Cephallenia.

Corcyra (Corfu)

North of Leucra, off the west coast of the Greek mainland, Corcyra will figure prominently both as one of the causes of the Peloponnesian War and later serving as a staging post and the mounting base for the Sicilian expedition. The island then only requires a brief introduction at this stage. Corcyra is first mentioned by Herodotus, when he relates how the Corinthians were in charge of transporting 300 boys belonging to the leading Corcyraean families to Sardis, in Asia Minor, where they were to be castrated and, one presumes, later employed as eunuch guardians in the harems. On the way the Corinthians put in at Samos, an island off the coast of Asia Minor, and when the Samians learned of the boys' fate, they gave them protection and later returned them to their homes.

When Greece was threatened with being overwhelmed by the Persian invasion under Xerxes, envoys were sent to Corcyra to seek support. The Corcyraeans, whose fleet was second in strength only to that of Athens, promised support, but when the invasion came in 480 BC, its fleet never got beyond the Peloponnese, where it hung about off Pylos in the belief that a Persian victory was inevitable. Should this occur, seeking better treatment than the other Greek states, the Corcyraeans could then say that they had refused to oppose the Persians. But when the Persians were repulsed, they claimed that they had sent sixty ships, but were prevented from getting round the southern cape by an unfavourable wind.

Nearly fifty years afterwards, in 435 BC, Corcyra became involved in a dispute with Corinth over the colony of Epidamnus – a dispute that later resulted in Athenian intervention and was to become one of the principal factors leading to the outbreak of the Peloponnesian War in 431 BC. When the war started, the Corcyraean fleet supported the Athenians in raiding the Peloponnese, but four years later a vicious civil war broke out between the oligarchs, who supported Sparta, and the democrats, who sided with Athens; a split that exemplifies how the rival political parties divided the Greek states, cities and families. According to Thucydides, it was in Corcyra that civil war first brought about a breakdown of law and order within a Greek community, though by 415 BC the situation appears to have improved, as the Corcyraeans participated in the Sicilian expedition and, as just mentioned, the island served as its mounting base. So the Corcyraeans, who were not only Dorian but Corinthian in their origin, found themselves at war with the Corinthian colonists in Sicily, including the Syracusans with whom, according to Thucydides, they were racially connected.

Epidamnus

A colony had been established on the Illyrian coast at Epidamnus by Corcyra in 625 BC, though the leader of the emigrants actually came from Corinth. The colony was important to Corcyra because it secured her trade with the interior of Illyria and Epirus. Under its oligarchic government, Epidamnus rapidly became a wealthy and populous town. In about 435 BC, the people succeeded in driving out the oligarchs and establishing a democratic form of government. Not prepared to accept defeat, the exiled oligarchs enlisted the aid of the Illyrians and set about plundering the property of their opponents. So severe was the damage that the Epidamnians were finally compelled to turn to Corcyra for assistance. Their request, however, was treated with indifference, so, after consulting the oracle at Delphi, the Epidamnians appealed to Corinth, the home of their founder, where they received a ready response. Here we will leave Epidamnus since, as will be related in due course, what happened subsequently was one of the causes of the Peloponnesian War.

Euboea

A long, lozenge-shaped island lying off the eastern coast of mainland Greece, Euboea was one of the original members of the Delian League, with at least 5000 Athenians later settling there. These colonists were known as lot holders, and did not cease to be Athenian citizens, but were provided with plots of land at the expense of the Euboeans. No doubt this colonisation strengthened one strand of loyalty to Athens, but it must have weakened another – that to the indigenous population. In spite of Thucydides' claim that Euboea was a faithful ally of Athens for more than thirty years, such high-handed behaviour can only have caused deep resentment and been a major cause for the unsuccessful revolt that occurred in 445 BC. Though one modern historian attributes the uprising to the machinations of the oligarchic party in Boeotia, it seems more likely that this was no more than a contributory, if important factor.

There were two principal cities in Euboea, Chalcis and Eretria, which had been age-old rivals, so perhaps partly explaining their different attitudes towards Athens. Both cities took part in the Sicilian expedition as tribute-paying allies in 415 BC, but while Chalcis seems to have remained loyal after the disastrous defeat inflicted on Athens, in 411 BC Eretria betrayed the Athenians who had been sent to defend Euboea, and the island passed into Spartan hands. Earlier, in 490 BC, Eretria had been destroyed by Darius when on his way to Marathon for the invasion of Greece.

Leucas

Just north of Cephallenia, Leucas sent ten ships to help the Corinthians in 433 BC during their dispute with Corcyra over Epidamnus, a Corcyraean colony about 100 miles north of the island on the coast of Illyria. The dispute became one of the causes of the Peloponnesian War two years later, when Leucas had joined the Spartan Confederation. With its good port, it served as an assembly place for the Peloponnesian fleet on a number of occasions, for instance in 429 BC, when the Spartans mounted an expedition against Acarnania, the coastal province opposite the island – a campaign for which Leucas provided ships. As will be described later, Leucas was attacked by the Athenians in 426 BC, but though their land was laid waste, the city was not taken. A ship from Leucas was in the Peloponnesian fleet which the Athenians defeated at the battle of Cynossema in 411 BC. The thinly populated island never played a significant role during the Peloponnesian War, but its geographical position made it a near-continual thorn in the Athenians' side.

The Peloponnese

Achaea

Achaea lay on the north-west of the Peloponnese and was populated by successive waves of immigrants: Ionians, Achaeans and finally Dorians, who drove out the Ionians to settle along the coast of Asia Minor and, it would seem, give it its name, Ionia. Such great heroes as

Agamemnon, Menelaus and Achilles, who figured so prominently in the siege of Troy, were referred to by Homer as 'brown haired Achaeans', whose successors later founded four colonies in Italy. Achaea was confined to a comparatively narrow plain along the southern coast of the Corinthian Gulf. In a conflict with Sparta in the middle of the 6th century BC, Athens had captured Achaea, but as a part of the Thirty Years Truce made in 445 BC, they handed it back. Initially Achaea played no part in the Peloponnesian War, trying to maintain friendly relations with both sides, but gradually she became involved and in 419 BC took part in a confrontation with Argos, when Sparta was asserting her authority throughout the Peloponnese. Now seemingly fully committed, eight years later Achaea was providing ships for operations in the Aegean.

Arcadia

Herodotus says that the Arcadians were indigenous to the Peloponnese, and, according to Homer, the ships they provided for the siege of Troy were supplied by Agamemnon of Achaea, though since Arcadia was centrally placed, with no obvious access to any port of consequence, it seems a bit odd that the crews for a fleet were available. Arcadia was the proverbial agricultural and rural community, which later on was imagined to be idyllic, but in reality practised many barbaric customs that were accompanied by a multitude of fertility cults and superstitions. Thucydides describes the Arcadians as being ready to march against any enemy who was pointed out to them, and, when in the service of Athens, Arcadians were quite prepared to regard their fellow citizens in the Corinthian service as their enemies, just as much as anyone else. But however aggressively disposed they may have been, the Arcadians were clearly fearful of Spartan domination, and they were prominent amongst those who saw little justification for the Spartan Confederation once its original purpose of restraining Argos had been fulfilled.

Tegea, some thirty miles north of Sparta, merits a special mention: it was the most prominent city in Arcadia, and had defeated the Spartans' attempts to conquer it during the middle of the 6th century BC. But by the turn of the century the Tegeans had become stalwart allies of Sparta, fighting alongside them with distinction at Plataea in 479 BC.

Though in about 427 BC Arcadia fought Sparta, like Argos she remained neutral for most of the Peloponnesian War, restricting herself to providing mercenaries for both sides. Only at the very end of the war did she join Sparta and the other Peloponnesian states (except Argos) to participate in the final downfall of Athens. As a point of interest, Polybius, the great historian of the Punic Wars that began in 264 BC, was born in Arcadia around 200 BC.

Argolis

On the north-east of the Peloponnese, Argolis jutted out into the Aegean Sea and, as the most independently minded of the Peloponnesian states, became Sparta's greatest rival. When Xerxes invaded Greece, and Athens was urging her fellow Greeks to cooperate in resisting him, the Argives refused on the grounds that in about 494 BC the Spartans had set out to humble them. This was, as has been mentioned, when the Spartans, after their fourth attempt to intervene in Athenian affairs, decided to establish their supremacy in the Peloponnese, before venturing across the Isthmus again. Though when invading Argolis there had been no attempt to take Argos, the capital, the Spartans had killed 6000 Argive men in the fighting. It was because of this rivalry that the Spartan Confederation had been called into existence in the first place; but after Argos' eclipse and until Athens was perceived as a threat, the Confederation came to be regarded by the other Peloponnesian states as little more than a tool for their suppression, a view that was to cause considerable unrest and trouble for Sparta.

There was initially a period of quiescence after the Argives' control over the greater part of the north-east Peloponnese and their looser authority over the whole of the long eastern coastal strip had been ended. Even when the Helots, or serfs, revolted against Sparta in 464 BC, Argos did not take advantage of the situation to settle old scores; but four years later Sparta's apparently random and ill-directed aggressiveness in the Peloponnese drove Argos into an alliance with the Athenians, who – overlooking the Argives' refusal to cooperate in resisting the Persian invasion – willingly associated themselves with a state traditionally hostile to Sparta.

When the Peloponnesian War broke out, Argos (like Achaea) remained neutral, but ten years later following the Peace of Nicias in

421 BC, and then Sparta's alliance with Athens, she tried to forge a defensive alliance with any independent Hellenic state that would join her. The spreading unrest in the Peloponnese broke out into open fighting when Sparta made a determined effort to stamp it out in 419 BC. In the following year there was a large, indecisive battle near Mantinea, after which a fifty-year treaty of peace was made between Sparta and Argos, but it only endured a year before intermittent fighting was resumed. Mantinea was some twenty miles north-west of Argos, and in 421 BC it had been the first to respond to Argos' offer of a treaty, leaving the Spartan Confederation the same year. As the war drew to a close in 405 BC, Argolis was the only Peloponnesian state not to join with the Spartans and march into Attica to besiege Athens.

Corinth

Whereas Megara, which dominated the northern approaches to the Isthmus, was primarily a land power, Corinth at the southern end was a maritime one and a great commercial centre. Originally her trade had been more by land than sea, but as her wealth grew, and Corinth built a fleet, it became increasingly seaborne. At that period she possessed the largest navy in Greece, rivalled only by Aegina, and had been the first to build triremes, the workhorses of the Peloponnesian War. In 453 BC, when Athens was occupied with her Egyptian expedition and Aegina had taken the opportunity to attack her, Corinth sent a small force to help the Aeginetans, but to no avail; so, thinking Athens was fully occupied, she seized the passes of Mount Geraneia, which divide Megara and Corinth, and then invaded Megara. But the Athenians hastily raised a force composed of old and young men, and in the second of two engagements defeated the Corinthians.

But by the time the Peloponnesian War broke out, Athens had surpassed Corinth to become the leading maritime power. As has already been mentioned, in 435 BC Corinth was in dispute with Corcyra over Epidamnus, a Corcyraean colony on the Illyrian coast further up the Adriatic, and clashed with the Athenians who had come to the islanders' assistance. Three years later another dispute arose with the Athenians who were besieging the Corinthian colony of Potidaea, on the isthmus of Pallene in Thrace. Claiming that such acts of aggression demonstrated Athens' imperialistic ambitions, the Corinthians persuaded Sparta to take the lead in checking this expansion before it was too late and, as will be seen later, they played a full part in the Peloponnesian War that followed.

Elis

A comparatively small state on the west coast, Elis had helped build a wall across the Isthmus against Xerxes, which cannot have greatly endeared it to the Athenians who, somewhat naturally, wanted to repel the Persians before they had overrun Attica. In 435 BC Elis provided money and ships to help Corinth in her dispute with Corcyra and had her port, Cyllene, burned by the Corcyraeans in revenge. Shortly after the Peloponnesian War broke out, the Athenians spent two days ravaging the Elean countryside, defeating a picked body of men who had sallied out from the Elis, the capital, to hinder them. Ten years later Elis accepted the offer of an alliance by Argos to counter growing Spartan domination, using the pretext that the Spartans had broken a truce, and in 419 BC she fought alongside the Argives when the Spartans began trying to suppress unrest in the Peloponnese. In 405 BC, however, she was back in the Spartan ranks again, helping to starve Athens into submission.

Olympus was at Elis, well south of the mountain identified as the abode of Zeus (Jupiter), the remote and terrifying king of the gods. Every four years the Olympic games and a great festival were held in his honour, during which a truce was declared – the truce which the Eleans alleged the Spartans had broken. The Olympic games had already been in existence for some 300 years when the Eleans, the guardians of Olympia, decided to build a temple to Zeus in the middle of the holy precinct. The temple was completed in 456 BC, but lacked a statue of the god, until Phidias of Athens, the great sculptor of ancient Greece, was commissioned to erect one twenty years later. The result of his work, completed in about 430 BC, was one of the Seven Wonders of the World identified by Antipater of Sidon. Plates of gold and ivory, representing the god's drapery and bare skin, covered the wooden frame of the forty-two-foot-high statue. After standing for some 800 years, the statue was removed to Constantinople by the Christian emperor, Theodosius, where it was destroyed by fire fifty years later in AD 476.

Laconia

Lying at the southern extremity of the Peloponnesian peninsula, the greater part of Laconia had been controlled by Sparta from about 715 BC. Laconia's history is so tied up with that of Sparta, which will be covered in the main text, that only a brief introduction is given here. All the land belonged to the state but, in order to be free for military training, none of it was cultivated by the Spartans themselves. Instead Helots, or enslaved serfs, worked the land which, except for the estates of the aristocrats, was divided into lots with one or more for each adult Spartan. These plots of land, like the Helots themselves, could not be sold, but were passed on from father to son. The Helot who cultivated the lot provided the landowner with a fixed amount of grain, wine and fruit, retaining any surplus. To many fellow Greeks the structure of the Spartan state, with its simplicity and orderly organisation, seemed far nobler than their own conditions, if less comfortable. Even Plato thought the Spartan state represented the nearest approach to the ideal that could be devised, a belief that has prevailed in some quarters until quite recently. Hitler's 'Strength through Joy' camps – magnificent barracks furnished with every facility, where the finest young Germans were brought together to breed a master race – must have had their roots in a distorted version of the Spartan myth.

Messenia

On the western coast of the Peloponnese, Messenia had sustained Sparta's military system ever since about 715 BC, when the original inhabitants were reduced to serfdom. Their descendants, the Helots, were a brave and hardy race who tilled the soil in remote farms and hamlets owned by the Spartans – to whom, as has already been described, they gave a fixed quantity of their produce. Resentful at their loss of independence, they were always ready to revolt, which, taking advantage of a huge earthquake that destroyed much of Sparta, they did in 464 BC. Retiring into a mountain stronghold, they waged a guerrilla war against the Spartans until coming to terms eleven years later, when they were exiled from the Peloponnese. They were settled at Naupactus, on the north shore of the Corinthian Gulf, which was to play an important part during the early years of the Peloponnesian War, as well as later when the Messenians joined the Athenian expedition to Sicily in 413 BC; as did those living in Pylos, on the coast of Messenia about forty-five miles west of Sparta. Pylos was separated from the mainland by a narrow isthmus, so it occupied a naturally strong position, which in turn gave protection to a good harbour on the landward side. Pylos had been seized and fortified by the Athenians in 425 BC and, with the help of the Helots and Messenians from Naupactus, had then resisted a determined attempt by the Spartans to take the city by storm.

In a treaty that was agreed between Athens and Sparta in 421 BC, in return for Spartan concessions the Athenians withdrew the Messenians and the Helot deserters from Laconia and settled them on Cephallenia, leaving just an Athenian garrison. Thucydides, however, records that in 419 BC some of them were sent back to carry out raids into Laconia, while four years later the Athenians from Pylos plundered Spartan territory; even then the Spartans did not renounce the treaty, but merely issued a proclamation stating that anybody who wished to was free to raid Athenian territory. Only the Corinthians took the opportunity to settle some private quarrels, with the rest of the Peloponnese staying quiet. Later, when the war had been resumed, Messenians from Naupactus and Pylos took part in the Athenian expedition to Sicily in 413 BC.

The Coastal Islands of the Peloponnese

Cythera (Kithera)
According to Herodotus, Cythera – though lying on the southern extremity of the Peloponnese – belonged to Argos. When Xerxes was planning his next move after breaking through the pass at Thermopylae, he was advised to seize Cythera and use it as a base from which to threaten Laconia. The Spartans would thus be drawn south to defend their own homeland, and the rest of the Greeks could then be crushed, leaving Sparta isolated and in a hopeless position. The suggestion that, without the Spartans, the rest of the Greeks would be incapable of serious resistance, is somewhat surprising since it was the Athenians, not the Spartans, who defeated Darius' troops at Marathon. But leaving that aside, it had once been said that it would be better for the Spartans if Cythera were to sink below the sea, for it would provide such an opportunity for a hostile force to threaten Sparta as was now being proposed to Xerxes. But in the event, the

alternative plan of concentrating the army and the fleet in an overwhelming assault across the Hellespont was adopted.

By 425 BC Thucydides was reporting that the population was Spartan, though they belonged to a semi-independent class. A garrison was maintained on the island since its port was of great importance for merchant ships from Egypt and Libya, while it served to protect Laconia, the whole of which jutted out into the open sea. Yet in spite of these precautions, when the Athenians were raiding the Spartan coast after the outbreak of the Peloponnesian War, they rarely met with any opposition and had no difficulty in occupying Cythera in 424 BC. But instead of using it as an assault base, they contented themselves with removing the more suspect citizens, and putting to death the Aeginetans who had been taken prisoner, for no better reason than the implacable hatred that existed between the two peoples. The rest of the inhabitants, however, were allowed to resume their normal life, but had to pay a tribute to the Athenians. Neither the Athenians nor the Spartans appear to have been very enterprising, and that is the last we hear of Cythera.

Zacynthus (Zakinthos)

Opposite Elis on the west coast, Zacynthus – together with Corcyra and Cephallenia – was persuaded by the Athenians in 431 BC to join them as allies, so that the war could be carried on all round the Peloponnese. The inhabitants were colonists from Achaea, which was also fighting alongside Athens. Hoping to detach Zacynthus from the Athenian Alliance, in 430 the Spartans and their allies mounted an expedition against the island, but after laying waste most of the countryside, they sailed back home again. As will be recalled, the Spartans planned to crush Acarnania, after which Zacynthus and Cephallenia could be seized, so making it difficult for the Athenians to sail their fleet round the Peloponnese. But the expedition into Acarnania achieved nothing, and the Confederation's fleet, which was to have seized the islands, was destroyed before it even got under way. When, as has been described, the Athenian garrison in Pylos held firm against the Spartan attempt to retake the city, it was the fleet from Zacynthus that brought relief and a defeat for the Spartans not far distant from the heart of their homeland. In 415 BC Zacynthus joined the Athenian expedition to Sicily as an independent power, though, like Cephallenia, it probably had little choice.

The Northern Theatre

Thrace and Macedonia

Although distinctly separate, the history of these two countries, during the period with which we are concerned, is so entwined that it would make little sense to try and deal with them separately. Moreover, except in the most general terms, we will not be treating either of them as an entity, since it is only their coastal regions that served as a battleground, and even this battleground possessed little coherence. As Herodotus wrote, the population of Thrace was greater than that of any other country and, had they united, they would have been the most powerful nation on earth; but they remained divided and thus weak. Herodotus could have said much the same about Macedonia as well during this period; it was a country riven by dissent and it took Alexander the Great to show in the next century what it was capable of when united under a powerful leader. To give even an abbreviated account of the kaleidoscopic scene when the Athenians and Spartans contested for supremacy in this Northern Theatre would result in repetition of the main text, so at this stage only a brief introduction will be given, together with two of the more significant events that occurred, before taking a look at the island of Thasos.

Some modern historians claim that the Northern Theatre was of importance to Athens because her grain imports came through the Hellespont, but whether Thrace was really the best place to prevent a hostile power from intercepting the free passage of her merchant ships, and so imperil Athenian security, will be discussed later. Moreover, it is questionable whether Athens' real interests were not economic more than military; but, however motivated, in 465 BC Athens had tried to establish a colony on the River Strymon at a place that was then known as the Nine Ways. Only two years later, however, the colonists were massacred by the Thracians, and it was not until another twenty-five years had passed that a second attempt was made, resulting in the founding of the important city of Amphipolis. Sited on a position of great natural strength, Amphipolis lay on the only place where the Strymon could be readily bridged, so it dominated the route that Xerxes was to take when marching from the Hellespont to Greece in 480 BC. Below the city, the river was too wide; while above, the river extended into Lake Cercinitis, the shores of which were marshy and tractless.

To strengthen their position in the Northern Theatre, in 432 BC the Athenians made the Corinthian colonists in Potidaea – strategically placed astride the Pallene isthmus protruding from Chalcidice – dismantle their fortifications and sever all links with Corinth. Such unmasked high-handed behaviour was one of the causes of the Peloponnesian War and, more immediately, it brought about Macedonian intervention, initially hostile, but – after some opportunistic Athenian footwork between the two contenders for the throne – the reigning brother changed tack and sided with Athens. In 424 BC the Spartans marched through Thessaly to counter this Athenian expansion; but here we will leave matters for now, though they will be picked up again in the main text.

Thasos (Thassos)

Lying off the southern coast of Thrace, Thasos played no significant part either before or during the Peloponnesian War. The island had been conquered by the Persians in 492 BC, but after the defeat of Xerxes twelve years later, Thasos joined the Delian League until it revolted in 465 BC. The uprising, however, seems to have been directed more against Thrace, because of a dispute about markets and a mine on the mainland that was under Thasian control. But, seeing an opportunity to restore her position, Athens despatched a fleet to Thasos two years later and retook the island; that, at least in part, must have compensated them for their unsuccessful attempt to establish a colony on the River Strymon at the Nine Ways in the same year. In 411 BC the democrats in Athens had been temporarily displaced by an oligarchy, which soon set about ousting democratic governments, including that of Thasos. But, according to Thucydides, these measures had the opposite effect to what the Athenians had anticipated; as soon as the oligarchic government was installed, it declared its independence. Xenophon, however, says that the Spartan governor and the pro-Spartan party, which would have been oligarchic, survived only a year before being driven out. He then goes on to relate how, in 407 BC, the Athenians went to the Thracian coast and reduced all the places that had revolted and gone over to the Spartans – amongst them 'Thasos which, what with war, revolutions and famine, was in a very miserable condition'.

The Western Theatre

Sicily

It was the Sicels who came from Italy and gave Sicily its name and, according to Thucydides, were the earliest inhabitants; but archaeological excavations during the last hundred years have shown that there had been waves of earlier settlers, the first dating back to 5000 BC. In about 1300 BC a series of disasters appear to have occurred, resulting in a dark age that was not ended until 500 years later when a new wave of migrants arrived, this time the Phoenicians. To quote Thucydides:

> There were also Phoenicians living around Sicily, who occupied the headlands and the small islands around the coast and used them for trading with the Sicels. But when the Greeks began to come by sea in great numbers, the Phoenicians abandoned most of their settlements and concentrated on the towns of Motya, Soloeis and Panormus, where they lived with the neighbouring Elymians, partly because they relied on an alliance with them, and partly because the voyage from here to Carthage is the shortest.

From this account, and the archaeological evidence, it seems that the Phoenicians were not forcibly evicted by the Greeks, but merely abandoned what were no more than trading posts. It was not until they were settled in the towns mentioned by Thucydides that any permanent construction was carried out. The first Greeks to arrive were also no more than traders, but as reports of the island's natural wealth filtered back to the over-populated and relatively barren mainland, Greek immigrants began to establish flourishing agriculturally based settlements both in Sicily and southern Italy. Although in many cases these new communities had originally been sponsored by a Greek mainland city, they were politically independent, retaining only ties of heritage and sentiment. Nor did they have any sense of collective loyalty to one another, but all remained fiercely independent. Yet, like the great majority of Greek cities wherever located, this independence did not result in their seeking security through cohesion within their individual communities. They were as divided internally as they were in their external relationships: factions and classes schemed and fought with one another for power, and had no hesitation in betraying their communities to outsiders, if this offered the prospect of bettering their own cause.

In broad terms the south and east coasts of Sicily were settled by the Greeks – starting from the west – with their cities of Selinus, Agrigentum, Gela and Camarina; and on the east coast with Syracuse, which possessed the south-eastern cape and the southern portion of the eastern coast, then Leontini, Catana, Naxos and Messina. The centre of the island and much of the northern coast was occupied by the non-Hellenic Sicels and Sicans, though Himera on the north coast was Greek. Between Himera and Lilybaeum, on the west coast, were the Hellenised cities of Egesta and Eryx, whose inhabitants, according to Thucydides, escaped from the Archaeans when Troy fell. There were also the Carthaginian sea ports, of which Panormus (Palermo) was the most important. The Greeks founded some fifteen cities in Sicily, in which – though originally aristocratic – the constitutions gradually became despotic, as power-seeking individuals (later to be described as tyrants) seized control in most of them. By the 5th century BC, Doric Syracuse had become the dominant power under Gelon, the tyrant of the Rhodian settlement of Gela on the south coast, who had been installed in Syracuse during a period of factional rivalry. When the Persian invasion of Greece seemed imminent, envoys were sent to Gelon in 481 BC seeking his assistance. According to Herodotus, Gelon would agree to help only if he were appointed to supreme command; when this was not accepted, he refused. Herodotus has perhaps placed over-much emphasis on personalities in this dispute: Sparta, Athens and Syracuse were the three great imperial cities of Greece, and recognition of the pre-eminence of a mere colony may well have been more than either the Athenians or the Spartans could stomach.

As it was, almost immediately afterwards Gelon found himself under attack from the Carthaginians, who invaded Sicily in 480 BC. A major battle was fought in the same year at Himera, on the north coast, when the Carthaginians were soundly defeated, so effectively removing their influence from Sicily for seventy years. According to Diodorus Siculus, Xerxes had sent an embassy to the Carthaginians urging them to join him and, by making a vast pincer movement, exterminate the Greeks. As has been argued by J. F. C. Fuller and others, this was quite probable for two reasons: first, because the Phoenicians were both subjects of Persia and blood relations of the

Carthaginians; and second, because each invasion would clearly assist the other.

In 427 BC, four years after the Peloponnesian War had broken out, the Athenians sent in twenty ships to Rhegium, lying on the toe of Italy, which they then used as a base to help their allies, the Leontinians, who were at war with Syracuse, some twenty miles further down the east coast. The real reason for the Athenian intervention, however, was to assess the possibility of preventing corn being brought to Sparta and her Peloponnesian allies by gaining control of the whole island. Nothing came of this preliminary survey until nearly ten years later, when, in 416 BC, Athens agreed to come to the help of Egesta, an inland city that had found herself at war with Syracuse. Such was the pretext for Athenians to mount a huge expedition, with contingents from all her allies, to secure the whole of Sicily and starve the Peloponnese into submission. As the story of this expedition will be fully related when we come to look at the conduct of operations in the Western Theatre, for the moment we must leave Sicily.

Magna Graecia

Magnia Grecia, 'Greater Greece', as the Greek settlements in southern Italy were called, did not play a prominent part in the Peloponnesian War, so only requires a brief mention. Although some of its cities fought alongside both the Athenians and the Syracusans, the war did not spread onto the Italian mainland. Tarentum (Greek Taros, modern Taranto) with its magnificent harbour, and because it was the first city to be reached when crossing over from Greece, was the most important of the Italian settlements. Although it was not much more than an irritating inconvenience, it was unfortunate for the Athenians that Tarentum was a Doric city, which (like Locri near the toe of Italy) refused to replenish their ships after they crossed the Ionian Sea from their mounting base on the island of Corcyra (Corfu).

The Eastern Theatre

The Hellespont

Though geographically the Hellespont forms a part of Thrace, and so should have been considered when we were looking at the Northern

Theatre, operationally it falls into the Eastern Theatre, serving as a hinge between the two. As with Thrace and Macedonia, only a brief introduction will be given at this stage, or there will be a danger of repetition in the main text. By 600 BC both sides of the Hellespont were fringed with Greek cities, both on the European and Asiatic sides of the Chersonese, or Gallipoli peninsula.

As has already been mentioned, Athens was vulnerable to any prolonged disruption to the supply of grain that flowed through the Hellespont from the Black Sea, and as the Persians had bridged the narrows twice when invading Greece, it is strange that the Athenians did not accord the security of the Hellespont a higher priority. According to Plutarch, when Pericles led an expedition to the Chersonese in 447 BC, he brought with him a thousand Athenian colonists to strengthen the Greek settlements there, while securing the neck of the isthmus with a fortified line stretching from sea to sea. This defensive line certainly helped keep the Thracians out, but it achieved little else. The supreme importance of the straits called for the establishment of a powerful base in the immediate area. Yet Pericles, who must have been aware of the need for protection – especially after having taken a large fleet beyond the Bosphorus in 445 BC to flaunt the power of Athens – appears to have done no more than leave thirteen ships and a small land contingent in the area. Not until the closing years of the Peloponnesian War did the Hellespont receive the attention it should have had from either of the belligerents. As we will see in due course, it was not until 410 BC that King Agis of Sparta belatedly recognised the need to cut the supplies of grain flowing into Athens from the Black Sea. But even then, he only sent an ineffectual force of fifteen ships to the Bosphorus; three of which were sunk by the Athenians before they even got there.

In 405 BC Lysander, the Spartan admiral in command of the Eastern Theatre, seized Lampsacus, on the Asiatic coast of the Hellespont, and then, at Aegospotami, annihilated the Athenian fleet that had followed him. It was a blow from which Athens had no hope of recovering and spelled the end of the war.

Ionia

In the 6th century BC the Asiatic Greeks were under no central authority and their disunity eventually led to their enslavement by the great Persian Empire lying to their east. There were eighteen

Greek cities in Ionia, of which Miletus was the most southerly and the most important of the twelve Ionian settlements strung along the northern sector of the Asiatic coast; below Miletus were the six Dorian cities. Herodotus describes Miletus, which had been established in about 1000 BC, as being the pride of Ionia, enjoying great prosperity. The city, however, suffered a considerable decline after wars with Croesus and Cyrus in the 6th century BC, although it later staged a recovery when winning the friendship of Darius, whom Miletus had assisted during his Thracian and Scythian campaigns. This happy relationship, however, proved to be short-lived, turning to oppression when Darius became suspicious of Miletus' ambitions after it had tried to obtain a site on the River Strymon in Thrace, an area rich in timber and mines. As will be recounted in more detail later, in 499 BC Miletus rose in revolt and, in answer to the city's appeal for support, Athens sent twenty warships together with a strong contingent of troops to ravage the coast further north. After doing considerable damage, but achieving nothing of consequence, the Athenians fell back on Ephesus, where they were soundly defeated.

Ephesus, the only city that rivalled Miletus in importance, was the site of another of the Seven Wonders of the World: a temple dedicated to the goddess Artemis (Diana), the virgin huntress, made of gleaming white marble, standing on a high stepped podium some 250 feet wide and 400 feet long, nearly twice the size of the Parthenon at Athens. Like Zeus' statue at Olympia, Artemis' temple stood for over 700 years: from near the outbreak of the Peloponnesian War until its destruction was ordered by the patriarch of Constantinople in AD 401.

But to return to the fighting around Ephesus. After their ignominious reverse, the Athenians withdrew their support from the rebellion, which had spread to all the other Ionian cities, so leaving them to fend for themselves. Having gone so far, there was little the Ionians could do but continue with the uprising, which achieved some initial success: Byzantium was captured and support obtained from most of Caria, the district extending inland from Miletus. The odds, however, were too great, so the revolt was crushed within a year and Miletus fell, thus ending its long history as a free city-state.

In Herodotus' estimation, the Athenian intervention provoked the Persians into invading Greece shortly afterwards, though he had previously claimed that it was the capture of Troy, many centuries earlier, which first made the Greeks the enemies of Persia. Whatever the causes of this antagonism, following the defeat of the two Persian invasions by Darius and Xerxes, Miletus obtained only a shadowy freedom after joining the Delian League in 479 BC, though she was permitted to retain her oligarchic government. In spite of both Miletus and the island of Samos being members of what by then had become the Athenian Alliance, they went to war in 440 BC over the small town of Priene on the Asiatic mainland, but Athens intervened and suppressed the Samians, who were gaining the upper hand. As tribute-paying subjects, Milesian troops joined the disastrous Athenian expedition to Sicily in 415 BC, but with Spartan influence gaining ground in the Eastern Theatre, Miletus revolted against Athens in 411 BC and successfully resisted an Athenian landing, though the Spartan general commanding the garrison was killed. Later in the year, however, the Athenians defeated the Peloponnesians and Milesians in a battle outside the city, which led to its recovery.

According to Plutarch, in his *Life of Lysander*, when the Spartan admiral returned to take command of the Peloponnesian fleet in 408 BC he found that Ephesus had enthusiastically espoused the Spartan cause. So he made the city his base, turning it into a great commercial centre, with the harbour full of shipping, warships under construction and the markets bursting with activity. If this really was so, then Ephesus contrasted with the other Greek Asiatic cities, which, following the suppression of their revolt against Persia, never regained their former prosperity.

The Aegean Islands (starting at the north with those on the coast)

Imbros

Lying off the west coast of the Gallipoli peninsula, Imbros has an unusual history. According to Herodotus, both Imbros and Lemnos were still occupied by the Pelasgians when, in about 514 BC, they were captured by the Persians during their westward expansion. Then, in about 500 BC, Miltiades, an Athenian who had campaigned alongside Darius and established his own domain around the Hellespont, secured both islands. After the Persians had suppressed the Ionian revolt in 494 BC, Miltiades returned to Athens, where he was promptly arrested, although he was acquitted on presenting the Athenians with the islands of Imbros and Lemnos. Shortly afterwards, however, both islands fell under Persian domination when Darius, following his troops' defeat at Marathon in 490 BC, secured the whole coastal strip between the two continents to place himself within easy reach of the Greek homeland. After Xerxes' invasion had been defeated ten years later, the inhabitants of Imbros and Lemnos were exiled and the islands settled by Athenian colonists. They served two purposes: first, to relieve the pressure of an expanding population at home by emigration; and second, to secure these two strategically important outposts. Such close racial ties with Athens naturally brought both islands onto her side when the Peloponnesian War broke out, and thereafter the Imbrians and Lemnians remained loyal allies, supporting Athens against Mytilene, the chief city on the island of Lesbos, when it revolted in 428 BC, and taking part in the Sicilian expedition in 415 BC. When Athens finally surrendered, the peace terms stipulated that Imbros, together with Lemnos and Skyros, should be returned to their exiled owners. As a matter of interest, Imbros was a major British support base during the Gallipoli campaign of 1915. It was here that Patrick Shaw-Stewart, a Balliol scholar who was killed in action in 1917, wrote during a brief break from the trenches:

> Was it so hard, Achilles,
>   So very hard to die?
> Thou knowest and I know not –
>   So much the happier I.
> I will go back this morning
>   From Imbros over the sea;
> Stand in the trench, Achilles,
>   Flame-capped and shout for me.

Lemnos (Limnos)
As has been seen, so closely was the history of Lemnos tied in with that of Imbros that they are virtually inseparable. Thucydides refers to them as though they were one – which, given their close racial connections and geographic proximity, is only natural. All that then needs to be said now is that, lying some twenty miles south-west of Imbros and about thirty miles from the coast of Asia Minor, Lemnos

occupied a commanding position on the approaches to the Hellespont, through which flowed the vital supplies of corn that sustained
Athens, the heartland of the Delian League.

Lesbos

Lesbos was originally settled by the Aeolians, who also established
themselves along the north-west coast of Asia Minor. Thucydides,
however, says that the inhabitants of Mytilene, which became the
principal city, were related to the Boeotians, particularly those from
Thebes, but it would seem that they arrived considerably later. This
Boeotian connection may have accounted for the latent hostility that
existed between Mytilene and Athens, which, in about the middle of
the 6th century BC, led to Mytilene taking Sigeum, the Athenian
settlement on the Asiatic coast opposite the tip of the Gallipoli
peninsula. But, as has been mentioned, Sigeum was recaptured by
Athens to secure her grain supplies passing through the Hellespont.

The Persians took Lesbos at the same time as Imbros, during their
western expansion in about 492 BC, but lost it to the Athenians after
Xerxes was defeated some dozen years later. Lesbos then joined the
Delian League and, like the islands of Samos and Chios, was allowed
to retain its fleet when Athens took over all the ships of her newly
acquired allies. In 430 BC, the year after the Peloponnesian War had
broken out, Lesbian ships took part in raids along the Peloponnesian
coast, but only two years later the Lesbians (except for the city of
Methymna) revolted in protest at Athenian domination. Like the
Spartan Confederation in the Peloponnese when Argos no longer
posed a threat, the Delian League had lost its original purpose
following the defeat of Persia, and it had become a tool for the
suppression of Athens' allies. Although Mytilene was in revolt against
her loss of independence, this did not deter her from trying to make
the whole island into a single state under her domination. Though the
Athenians quickly intervened, they lacked the strength to do more
than blockade the city. Envoys, however, managed to evade the
blockade and reach Sparta, where their appeal for help received
willing acceptance, and Lesbos was promptly declared an ally. The
following year the Spartans and their allies attempted to relieve the
pressure on Mytilene by invading Attica and sending a fleet to
Lesbos, but neither endeavour achieved anything and in 427 BC
Mytilene was starved into submission.

Feelings in Athens were very bitter following the revolt and, after a protracted debate, a trireme was despatched with instructions to the Athenian commander on Lesbos to put to death all the Mytilenians immediately. The next day, however, there was another debate during which the monstrosity of killing the entire population, regardless of their guilt or innocence, brought about a change of feeling. So another trireme was despatched in all haste some twenty-four hours later and the crew, by eating their meals of barley mixed with wine while still at their oars and by taking it in turns to sleep, arrived shortly after the decree of death had been read and just as it was about to be implemented. Though the population as a whole had narrowly escaped annihilation, the new terms were still harsh enough: more than a thousand of the ringleaders were executed, the fleet taken over, the fortifications destroyed and the land – except that belonging to the loyal Methymnaeans – distributed to Athenian shareholders. The shareholders were sent out to Lesbos and, with their agreement, the Lesbians worked the land paying a fixed rent to the shareholders, much as the Helots paid the Spartans. As will be recounted later, however severe the reprisals, they were lenient enough in comparison to the fate that befell the citizens of Melos when they refused to accept Athenian suzerainty.

In 415 BC Lesbos provided ships for the expedition to Sicily, though, as with many others, they probably had little choice. In 411, when the war had turned decisively against Athens, the Spartans made an unsuccessful attempt to secure Lesbos, but four years later they returned and took Methymna by storm, bottling up the Athenian fleet in Mytilene by blockading the city. Under cover of darkness, however, two triremes slipped out of the harbour, and one of them escaped to bring news of the blockade to Athens. After debating the matter, the Athenians voted to send a relieving force of 110 ships, putting aboard all the men of military age they could muster, whether slaves or free. After thirty days the preparations were complete and the fleet made for the island of Samos, where forty more ships were collected before it sailed up the Ionian coast to Lesbos.

On learning of the Athenian approach, the Spartans left some fifty warships to continue the blockade of Mytilene, while the main force of 120 Spartan and allied ships set out to face this new threat. At dawn the following day the two fleets clashed and, after a hard-fought battle, the Peloponnesians were routed and fled in disarray to the island of Chios, some forty miles to the south. Lesbos now remained in Athenian hands until after their disastrous defeat in the Hellespont at Aegospotami in 405 BC, when Lysander, the victorious Spartan admiral, sailed to Lesbos, where – to use Xenophon's words – 'he settled matters'.

Chios

The rock-bound island of Chios had been settled by Ionians, who provided 100 ships in support of the Ionian revolt, fighting on bravely at the battle off Miletus, even after being deserted by the Lesbians and Samians and so facing inevitable defeat. After the fall of Miletus, Chios was occupied by the Persians in 492 BC and held until after the defeat of Xerxes twelve years later, when it was freed and joined the Delian League, paying no tribute but, like Lesbos and Samos, undertaking to provide her fleet when required. When war broke out between Athens and Sparta, the Chians took part in the raids against the Peloponnesian coast in 430 BC, but six years later they were made to demolish their fortifications, because the Athenians suspected them of wishing to revolt. Thucydides makes no attempt to substantiate this suspicion, merely claiming that the Chians secured the most reliable guarantee possible, that Athens had no intention of altering the existing state of affairs; which sounds a bit hollow, especially as Chios had an oligarchic government.

As a so-called independent ally, the island provided fifty ships for the Sicilian expedition in 415 BC, but during the general unrest amongst Athens' island allies following the expedition's catastrophic defeat, Chios was ready to revolt and the oligarchic party, without informing the people, entered into a secret alliance with Sparta. Fearing that the Athenians would learn what was afoot, the Spartans were urged to send some visible signs of support and so, after being reinforced by a number of Corinthian ships that had been dragged across the Isthmus, a thirty-nine-strong Peloponnesian fleet sailed for Chios. It was by now 411 BC and the Athenians had learned of the plot; so they despatched a fleet of their own which, though slightly smaller, drove the Peloponnesian ships into an uninhabited harbour where most of them were destroyed. So disheartened were the Spartans by the failure of their first venture into the Eastern Theatre of war that, at least for the time being, they abandoned the idea of doing anything more. In spite of these developments, however, the oligarchic party in Chios openly revolted against the Athenians who, seriously alarmed at being deserted by the greatest city amongst their allies, took resolute action and landed on the island. But after defeating the Chians who tried to oppose them, the Athenians were unable to take the city itself, which later served as a Spartan base during the final years of the war.

Samos

The 500-year-old Ionian settlement on Samos was incorporated into the Persian Empire by Darius in about 518 BC, when he was securing the frontiers of his recently inherited empire. The Samians joined the Ionian revolt in 499 BC, but when they saw that it was doomed to failure, they shamefully deserted at the critically important naval battle off Miletus. Though the islanders saved their skins from Persian retribution after the revolt had been crushed, Samos fell under Persian domination until, like the other islands, it was freed after Xerxes' invasion of Greece had been defeated in 480 BC, when it joined the Delian League.

Although Thucydides refers to Chios as being the greatest of the allied cities, it seems that Samos was really the most powerful, surpassing both Chios and Lesbos and, like them, paying no tribute money but furnishing ships and men when called upon, while being allowed to retain its oligarchic government. But in the same way as Lesbos and others, feeling that Persia no longer posed a threat and that the Athenians were treating it as a subject state, Samos also revolted in 440 BC and promptly went to war with Miletus. Like most of the islands near the Asiatic coast, Samos possessed some territory on the mainland, and it was here that there was a dispute with Miletus over the small town of Priene which, after Miletus had been defeated, fell into Samian hands. Athens then intervened and, after Samos' appeal to Sparta for assistance had been declined (rather surprisingly, and mainly because of Corinthian objections), the island was retaken in 439 BC. According to Plutarch in his *Life of Pericles*, it was during this operation that siege engines were used, which were then impressive innovations. Through having revolted, the Samians lost their right to keep a fleet and became tribute-paying subjects, who were later to join the disastrous expedition to Sicily in 415 BC.

Four years later the people rose against the ruling classes who, in cooperation with the Athenians, were either executed or exiled. Confident that the Samians would remain loyal, the Athenians gave them their independence shortly afterwards. In 411 BC, when the oligarchs in Athens seized power, the army on Samos remained staunchly democratic and prevented an oligarchic coup on the island. So Samos served as the principal Athenian naval base for the remainder of the war, and was the only ally of Athens to remain loyal after her defeat at Aegospotami in 405 BC; finally being forced to surrender after being blockaded by the victorious Spartan admiral Lysander.

Rhodes

Lying off the south coast of Asia Minor, Rhodes had been settled by the Dorians whose three cities formed a league with the island of Cos and two mainland cities, Halicarnassus (Bodrum) and Cnidus. This Dorian association may have contributed to the unity of Rhodes itself, which, unlike so many of the Greek states and islands, experienced no warring city rivalry.

Another of the Seven Wonders of the World was to be found at Halicarnassus: the mausoleum of Mausolus, satrap of Caria from 377 to 353 BC. The mausoleum was a three-tiered tower: first, there was a massive rectangular base, approximately 100 feet square and 100 feet high, over half the height of the whole monument. Above this was a colonnade of fluted Ionic columns, each about thirty feet high, supporting the stepped, pyramidal roof, which was surmounted by a marble chariot. After being ravaged by Alexander the Great in 334 BC, and severely damaged again by the Arabs when they sacked Halicarnassus in AD 655, the monument was finally destroyed by the Knights of St John, who used the remains to build their nearby castle in 1494. Some surviving sculptured slabs and statues were excavated by Sir Charles Newton in the mid-19th century and shipped to the British Museum.

To return to Rhodes: the island became a prosperous commercial centre trading throughout the eastern Mediterranean, later establishing settlements in Sicily, most noticeably Gela on the south coast; but the Rhodians became subject to Persia in about 540 BC, only gaining their freedom after Xerxes' defeat and joining the Delian League in 478 BC. Rhodes provided fifty ships and a contingent of 700 slingers for the Sicilian expedition, where they found themselves fighting their own settlers. Four years later in 411 BC, after the expedition's crushing defeat, the oligarchs who governed Rhodes revolted against Athens and sided with Sparta, which thus acquired a naval base, together with a seafaring population and not inconsiderable wealth at no cost to themselves. Though the Spartans were able to mount naval operations from Rhodes up as far as the Hellespont, they were constrained by the Athenian fleet based on Samos until it was destroyed at Aegospotami in the final year of the war.

Before leaving Rhodes, although it lies outside the period we are considering, brief mention must be made of the Colossus of Rhodes: the giant 100-foot statue of the sun god Apollo (Helios), another of Antipater's Seven Wonders of the World. The statue allegedly straddled the entrance to the harbour, permitting ships to pass between its legs; an impossible feat in fact, as the harbour mouth is some 100 yards wide at its narrowest point. Work began on the white marble base in 292 BC, and when this was finished it took twelve years to complete the statue itself, with its internal stone and iron framework, which was then covered with bronze skin. But after standing for only some sixty years, the Colossus was brought down when its knees gave way during an earthquake.

Naxos

The important island of Naxos in the Cyclades lay in the middle of the Aegean, almost midway between the Peloponnese and Asia Minor. But in spite of their central position, the Cyclades never figured prominently, either in peace or war. The islands were too separated from one another to form a federation or undertake any coordinated action. According to Herodotus, Naxos was the richest island in the Aegean and had been settled by Ionians, originally of Athenian blood, but the usual Greek fractiousness divided the islanders. The people's party forced a group of the more prominent citizens to seek refuge in Miletus and, as will be recounted more fully later, through trying to return, they had become involved in the Ionian revolt. At the beginning of the uprising in 499 BC, the Persians attempted to seize Naxos, but were forced to relinquish the siege – a humiliation that was not forgotten by Darius nine years later when, on his way to the invasion of Greece at Marathon, he landed on the island, burned the capital city and took into slavery all those who were captured. The majority of the population, however, escaped by fleeing into the hills, and were fortunate that Darius had more pressing business to attend to than delaying to round them up.

Though evidently not occupied by the Persians, Naxos was clearly under their domination, since when Xerxes invaded Greece in 480 BC, the Naxians were ordered to assist by providing ships; however, instead of joining the Persians, these sailed to Salamis, where they took part in the great naval battle that brought about the Persian defeat. In 476 BC the Naxians revolted and left the Delian League, but were forced back again, offering but weak resistance as, since they had become tribute-paying subjects, they lacked a fleet of their own and the associated military skills. Naxos was the first city to be enslaved by fellow Greeks, and had little option but to be classed as an Athenian ally at the outbreak of the Peloponnesian War. Later, however, though Thucydides refers to Naxos in Sicily, he makes no mention of the island of Naxos when listing those of Athens' allies who joined the fateful expedition to Sicily in 415 BC; nor does Xenophon make any reference to Naxos when relating the final stages of the war. It seems then that the Naxians were left in peace to quarry their beautiful coarse-grained marble and enhance their school of sculpture.

Melos (Milos)

Some forty miles south-west of Naxos, Melos was a 700-year-old Spartan colony, which, unlike nearly all the other islands, had refused to join the Delian League and which, when the Peloponnesian War broke out, attempted to remain neutral. In 426 BC, however, the Athenians tried to force the Melians into joining the alliance, laying waste their land without being able to make them submit or pay the assessment of tribute made against them in the following year. Such temerity eventually brought the full wrath of Athens against them, and in 416 BC an expedition arrived on the island; but before doing any harm, the Athenians sent representatives forward to negotiate. The Melians did not permit them to address the people, but invited them to explain to the governing body exactly what it was that they wanted.

Thucydides sets out the political and moral issues at stake in an historically unconvincing formal dialogue held between the Athenians and Milesians, which aims to establish the position in analytical terms. There is, however, no attempt to justify the Athenian demands;

the Melians are just bluntly told that it is intolerable that they should remain outside the alliance, because this would lead to others trying to do the same. The Melians are therefore urged to be realistic: there will be no help coming to them, and they are too weak to resist on their own, so they must accept the situation and surrender. When the Melians refused, they were besieged and, after making a number of spirited sallies, eventually surrendered as a result of treachery within. Without comment, Thucydides then goes on to relate how all the adult males were slain, the women and children sold into slavery and the island repeopled with Athenian settlers. There was little sign of the relative magnanimity displayed to the Mytilenians of Lesbos, though, according to Xenophon, there must have been some survivors, as he says they were able to return to Melos at the end of the war. Partly, no doubt, because of Thucydides' elaborate treatment, the sack of Melos continued in the 4th century to be a matter for anti-Athenian propaganda and Athenian self-defence.

Delos

Delos was a geographically insignificant island some twenty miles north-west of Naxos but, being Apollo's birth place, one of great religious importance, serving as the spiritual and, for a short time, the political heart of the Delian League. According to Herodotus, so revered was Apollo's temple that, as an act of purification, all the graves within sight of the holy precinct were dug up in about 560 BC and the bones buried elsewhere on the island. Thucydides takes the purification measures a step further; stating that, no doubt because of some oracle, all the tombs of those who had died in Delos were dug up in 426 BC, and it was proclaimed that in future no deaths or births were to be allowed on the island. Between these two events, after they had left Naxos to continue on their way to the invasion of Greece in 490 BC, the Persians sailed to Delos, where they found that the inhabitants had fled on receiving warning of their approach. The islanders, however, were later induced to return after being assured by the Persians that they had no desire to harm them, or their sacred island. Within a few years following the defeat of the Persians at Salamis in 480 BC, with no external threat to unify them, the Greeks divided into two halves. The first move was made by the Dorian cities of the Peloponnese, who withdrew their contingents from the united Greek fleet, then joined the Spartan Confederation. The Athenians for their part incorporated their allies into a league, with political decisions being taken in the Synod at Delos, to which every city – great or small – sent a deputy who had an equal vote. It was in the Synod that the various contributions were also decided, with some cities providing military contingents and others money, the latter being collected by the Athenians but placed in Apollo's temple for safekeeping. As will be recalled, these two alliances were initially not directed at one another: the Spartans saw Argos as posing a threat, and the Athenians Persia. Only much later did they confront one another as enemies.

After the defeat of the Athenian expedition to Egypt, in about 450 BC Delos lost its place as the centre of the league when the Treasury was transferred to Athens, with dues being paid to Athena as the presiding deity, and not to Apollo. Additionally, the Delian Synod had faded into obscurity, with power passing to the Athenian Assembly, where all important decisions were taken with total disregard for the opinions of others. With the demise of the Delian League arose the Athenian Alliance, into which the former league members were forcibly incorporated as allies.

Skyros

Lying in the northern Aegean aloof from the clutter of islands to the south, Skyros was strategically important to the Athenians because it lay across the sea route bearing corn through the Hellespont from the Black Sea. There was also another reason for the Athenians wishing to secure the island: it had become a haven for pirates, who were not over-concerned about whose shipping they plundered. To mask their real motives for securing Skyros, Cimon, the leading Athenian statesman at the time, claimed that the Delphic oracle had instructed him to bring back from the island the bones of Theseus: a hero of Attica who had slain the Minotaur and conquered the Amazons, but who, tired of the political strife raging in Athens, had retired to the tranquillity of Skyros. So in 476 BC Skyros was seized, the inhabitants expelled, the land settled by Athenian colonists, the bones and armament of a suitably statuesque warrior located and borne back to Athens in triumph. All of which brought much credit to Cimon.

As we have already seen, colonisation had long acted as a safety valve for over-population, but it had also been given the task of securing strategically important outposts such as Skyros, Imbros and

Lemnos. No longer were there just loose ties linking colonies to their mother city, but firm bonds of unquestioning loyalty, secured through the colonists who retained their Athenian citizenship and paid no tribute. Probably because of its small population, who would have been required for its defence, Skyros seems to have played no part in the Peloponnesian War.

As a matter of interest, in 1915 Skyros provided anchorage for the hospital ships assembled for the Gallipoli campaign, and it was on one of these that Rupert Brooke died. His grave lies in the south-west corner of the island and is inscribed with Brooke's most famous poem, 'The Soldier'. To quote from the first three lines:

> If I should die, think only this of me:
> That there's some corner of a foreign field
> That is for ever England.

Cyprus and Crete

Though Cyprus and Crete both lay on the southern edge of the war zone, where they divided the Greek archipelago from Egypt and Libya, neither of them became directly involved in the wide-ranging Peloponnesian War. The Cypriots had volunteered assistance during the Ionian revolt as they were themselves already in rebellion against Persia, but, after enjoying a year's freedom, they were once again conquered and obliged to contribute a hundred ships when Xerxes invaded Greece in 480 BC. Some twenty years after the Persian defeat, the Athenians – who, as Thucydides laconically says, 'happened to be engaged in a campaign in Cyprus' – abandoned it when their attention was drawn to Egypt. The much fought-over island was subjected to yet another campaign in 449 BC, which was called off after the death of Cimon. The death of Cimon marks an epoch in the history of Athens; he was the last of the great generals who thought it the mission of Hellas to be at war with Persia; for the next fifty years it was to be Sparta.

More isolated than Cyprus and so not occupying such an obvious strategically important position, Crete had been settled by Greeks who had then remained aloof from the discord raging around them. Being a maritime power, it was only natural that Athens should have maintained relations with Crete, but though an urgent appeal was made to support the common cause in resisting Xerxes' attempt to crush Greece, the islanders refused to help, and in the Peloponnesian War did no more than permit Athenian ships to put in at their ports and provide some mercenaries for the Sicilian expedition in 415 BC. There was no attempt by Athens to coerce Crete into joining the Delian League, probably because of the island's sheer size, while its remoteness made it indifferent to the league's original purpose of containing Persia.

I

The Greeks and Their Background

The Origins

This is no more than a short introduction to the origin of the Greeks, about which there have been many interpretations in the past, though recent archaeological discoveries have started to fill in some of the gaps and correct earlier opinions. In about 1200 BC, Mycenaean Greece was disrupted by invaders from the north, who came down in several waves, the most powerful calling themselves 'Dorians'. The great centres of population, like Mycenae, Thebes and Pylos, were destroyed, and most of Greece was captured and settled by the Dorians. The earlier inhabitants managed to defend the citadel of Athens and its surrounding country of Attica, though Thucydides suggests that it may have been because of Attica's poor soil that no newcomers wanted to settle there. Attica then remained remarkably free from political disunity, through always being inhabited by the same race of people (referred to as Pelasgians by Herodotus), who had never been displaced. Thucydides' theory as to why Athens rose to notoriety is worth quoting:

> it was because of migrations that there were uneven developments elsewhere; for when people were driven out from other parts of Greece by war or by disturbances, the most powerful of them took refuge in Athens, as being a stable society; then they became citizens, and soon made the city even more populous than it had been before, with the result that later Attica became too small for her inhabitants and colonies were sent out to Ionia.

It was then from this Attican stronghold that a large number of people emigrated to the Aegean islands and to the western seaboard of what is now Turkey, calling themselves 'Ionians'; a name that already occurs in Homer. Both Ionians and Dorians thought of themselves, and each other, as 'Hellenes' – what we, following the Romans, call 'Greeks'. But they were always aware of the distinction between the two groups, who spoke and wrote clearly distinct dialects of the Greek language. In the 5th century BC there are frequent traces of rivalry, and sometimes hostility, between Dorians and Ionians, which, in the Peloponnesian War, crystallised into a conception of Greece as divided between a Dorian alliance, headed by Sparta, and an essentially Ionian one, led by Athens.

Since we have reached the stage when Athens and Sparta have clearly begun to develop in very different ways, and so need to be considered separately, we will end this short survey of their common origins. There are, however, two additional aspects of commonality, which must first be examined: their religion and their broadly similar military organisation.

Religion

When we speak of religion, we instinctively visualise an established church, possessing its own hierarchy, beliefs and moral code. But for the Greeks there was nothing of the sort: there was no church, creed or articles of faith, without which there could be no individual conscience to define between right and wrong. Nor were there any worthy saints, interpreting priests, venerable martyrs or witches to hunt and heretics to incinerate. The only religious crimes were acts, or attitudes, that caused public resentment; like Socrates' conduct, for which he was prosecuted and condemned to death in 399 BC. The charge against him read: 'Socrates is an evil-doer and a curious person, searching into things under the earth and above the heavens; and making the worse appear the better cause, and teaching all this to others . . . and not recognising the gods that the city recognises.'

What then was Greek religion all about? What was the purpose of worshipping the gods? One reason was clearly practical: Poseidon (Neptune) could ensure the safe return of mariners, and Demeter (Ceres) an abundant harvest, while Athena (Minerva), with her temple on the Acropolis, was the guardian of selected heroes and the patroness of Athens. But more fundamentally, the gods explained the seemingly inexplicable: storms, thunder, lightning, earthquakes, rain, the growth of crops and the fertility of life itself. It was not, however, just natural phenomena that could be attributed to the gods, but also human passions: love, violence, inspirational heroism and wanton abandon. Though proud of their own prowess, the Greeks recognised that much lay beyond their control, and this was the area that belonged to the gods. It was important then to establish a close relationship with them and enlist their support. This made the Greeks feel at home in the world; they were in communication with gods who, though immortal and residing on the heights of Olympus, resembled them and behaved much as they did themselves. The gods too had their petty jealousies, fights, favourites and amours. One of the more engaging stories, from *The Odyssey*, tells how Ares was caught making love to Aphrodite under a net cast by her husband, Hephaestus. In case the Latin names of the three actors in this little comedy are more familiar, they are Mars, Venus and Vulcan.

The gods being capricious and unpredictable, there was no knowing what they actually wanted, so an elaborate system of sacrifice and divination had to be devised and practised. Though it was open to individuals to make their own interpretations, there were officials, or seers, who performed these functions on state and other important occasions; but they exercised no overriding authority, and it was up to the individual to decide whether or not to accept their divinations. It was the same with the oracles, who invariably proffered advice that was open to a variety of interpretations, thus preserving their reputation, irrespective of what occurred subsequently. Perhaps the most famous example of such ambiguity occurred when Athens was threatened by the Persians in 480 BC. The Delphic oracle advised the Athenians to 'put their trust in the wooden walls', which was understood by the officials to mean that the Athenians should seek safety behind their city walls. But Themistocles, who will be properly introduced later, argued against the officials, maintaining that the gods were referring to the fleet; it was ships that would provide their salvation, not walls.

According to Herodotus, actual battlefield decisions could also be influenced by divination, as occurred at Plataea in 479 BC, when the Greeks were facing the Persians (those left behind by Xerxes) after the defeat of his navy at Salamis the previous year. The official diviner, whom the Spartans had brought along with them, declared that the omens for the Greeks were favourable, provided they fought a defensive action; but unfavourable, should they attack. For Mardonius, the Persian commander, who used the Greek ritual to get his omens, the prediction was similar: good for the defence, bad if he yielded to his eagerness to attack. For ten days the two armies faced one another in masterly inactivity, until, on the eleventh, Mardonius' patience broke; he would ignore the omens and engage in battle in the good old Persian way – which he did, and lost. Three other examples will serve to show how operational decisions could be affected by divination. The Spartans, with some undefined intent, marched out in 419 BC to Leuctra, a frontier town that was probably near their northern border. The result of the sacrifices for crossing the border, however, were not favourable; so they marched back again. In the same year Epidaurus, on the north-east coast of the Peloponnese, was under attack by the Argives, and when the Epidaurians appealed to their allies for help, they were refused on the grounds that it was the sacred month. But the most fateful example, which will be recounted later, occurred when the Athenians decided to abandon the siege of Syracuse in 413 BC; but, just as they were about to set sail, they were deterred by the eclipse of the moon.

There was another, and sometimes darker, side to Greek religion which, though largely held in check, would occasionally erupt in passionate outbursts; as though in revolt against what was, for that period, a restrictive, sober and orderly society. To the man or woman who, by convention or compulsion, is more civilised in behaviour than in feeling, there must be a safety valve, and for the Greeks this was provided by the cult of Dionysus (Bacchus), which was centred on Athens. The worshippers of Dionysus were renouncing prudence; by casting away everyday preoccupations and restrictions, they escaped into a world free of care, one offering a renewed intensity of feeling and freshness of perception. Today Dionysus is almost entirely associated with drunkenness, lewdness and bawdy behaviour, but during the period we are discussing the disreputable god's rituals also brought about spiritual intoxication – permitting him to enter into his worshippers, who then believed they had become one with the god. These 'enthusiasms', as they were termed, sound remarkably akin to today's stimulated bouts of 'ecstasy', without the religious element.

This highly personalised conception of the gods, with their many human failings, owes a great deal to the influence of poetry, especially that of Homer. Everyone read these poems as a part of their schooling and was constantly aware of them; so they tended to squeeze out the more impersonal, and often more serious, aspects of religion. Hence Plato's hostility to these myths: they were destroying the religion.

The Armies

As the Athenian and Spartan military organisation, tactics and equipment are broadly similar, they can be considered together, and any differences between them brought out as we proceed. The reason for this similarity is that the Greeks had mainly fought amongst themselves, so developing military characteristics relevant to the conditions under which their encounters took place. There were, however, exceptions; such as when the Athenians attempted to force a passage through Aetolia in 427 BC, but were subjected to furious flank attacks by light troops. Not having any light troops with them, the Athenians had no means of countering the hit-and-run tactics employed, so they were forced to withdraw. Much the same happened to the Spartans at Pylos in 425 BC when, encumbered by their heavy body armour, they could not get to grips with the light troops provided by Athens' allies and, after being trapped, in a very uncharacteristic manner, finally surrendered.

The heavy infantry, or hoplites, were by far the most important arm: partly because Greece's mountainous, broken terrain and many islands limited the employment of cavalry, and partly because, as we have seen when discussing the different states, only two of them (Thessaly and Boeotia) possessed the pasture land upon which horses could be bred and reared in any number. Horses also cost money: they had to be fed, equipped and cared for, an expense which their limited employability hardly justified. So the basic fighting man was the hoplite: the citizen foot soldier, organised into a close, massed formation (the phalanx) and equipped with a helmet, body armour, greaves, shield and a thrusting spear, or pike. Some historians suggest that, since the hoplites had to provide their own equipment, they were recruited from the moderately well-to-do, while the less well endowed served as auxiliaries, or rowed in the fleet. But it seems unlikely that the hoplites had to provide their own equipment during the 5th century BC, especially in view of Athens' wealth at the time, and during the Persian and Peloponnesian Wars resident aliens and slaves would have served as hoplites. The former were lured by the promise of citizenship when demobilised, and the latter by freedom. There were, for example, 3000 resident alien hoplites in the Athenian army that invaded Megara at the end of the first year of the Peloponnesian War. While there is no recorded evidence, with the recruitment of slaves in an emergency, and the absence of a conspicuous number of light troops, it is not improbable that many of them served as hoplites.

But to return to the phalanx. When advancing, the pikes of the first five ranks were held forward, and were of such length that even those of the fifth rank extended beyond the leading soldiers. In the succeeding ranks, the pikes were rested on the shoulders of the men in front, with their points slanting upwards, so affording some protection against enemy missiles. According to Plutarch, the Spartans had their own procedures when battle was about to be joined: a she-goat would be sacrificed, garlands put in place, the 'Ode to Castor and Polydeuces' (Pollux) played by the pipers and, roaring out a swelling paean, the solid, unbroken phalanx would begin its terrifying advance. Perhaps it should be explained that Castor and Polydeuces were the twin sons of Zeus and the patrons of the Spartan army.

Since the shield played such an important part in determining the actual conduct of close-quarter fighting, it requires a special mention. Well before the outbreak of the Peloponnesian War, the earlier shoulder-strap, single-grip shield had been discarded in favour of one with a double-grip. The disadvantage of the old shield was that, in actual combat, its whole weight had to be taken by the wrist. Now, through bearing the weight of the new shield on the forearm, it was much easier to carry, so it could be enlarged. It had, however, one disadvantage. As the hand-grip was now much nearer the rim of the shield, if the right arm was to be used effectively, half the shield projected to the left. Thus, if the hoplites stood shoulder-to-shoulder, their exposed side could only be protected by the half shield of the man to the right. But through trying to seek this protection, there was a tendency to edge to the right. Clearly there was then a great deal of interdependence within the phalanx; each man relied on his neighbour not to expose him, either by breaking ranks or merely moving his shield. The shield then became a symbol of honour which, as Plutarch says, a man carried 'for the sake of the whole line'. Hence the injunction of Spartan mothers to their sons to come back with their shields, or on them.

Normally a phalanx, or at any rate an Athenian one, seems to have been deployed eight shields deep, but the number varied greatly. Thucydides says the Thebans were twenty-five deep at the battle of Delium in 424 BC, while their allies were of varying depth, and their enemy, the Athenians, eight deep. Nine years later, just outside Syracuse, the Syracusan phalanx was sixteen deep, while that of the Athenians was once again eight. There could be several reasons for these variations: for example, at Delium the Thebans on the right wing clearly intended to turn the Athenian left by pushing it back through sheer weight of numbers, which they succeeded in doing; while at Syracuse, the Athenians' numbers may have been influenced by their perceived need to deploy half their army in a hollow square to the rear, also eight shields deep, to protect their baggage train and non-combatants, while providing a reserve. Later, Xenophon says that near Piraeus, in 404 BC, the Athenians 'formed into a line of battle, so as to fill the road . . . their line was not less than fifty shields deep and, when they had taken up their position, they advanced up the hill'. This, however, sounds more like a massed column than a phalanx; but whether or not these formations and figures are accurate, clearly tactics, available numbers and terrain all influenced shield depth.

The Spartans were the past-masters of hoplite fighting, not only because of their vigorous training (which we will take a look at later), but because their field force, of whatever size, was organised into manageable tactical units, not greatly dissimilar to today's battalions, companies and platoons. Such an organisation permitted greater flexibility, certainly before battle was joined, as the phalanx could be subdivided to permit a considerable degree of internal flexibility, without destroying its cohesion. For example, the distance between the rows of shields and individuals within the rows could be increased to permit turning and even counter-marching. The Athenians, on the other hand, appear not to have had any sub-unit below the approximate size of a battalion, numbering several hundred men.

The Spartans also organised their army into age groups, and Xenophon refers to Pausanias, the Spartan commander, at the end of the civil war in Athens in 403 BC, ordering the twenty-to-thirty age group to follow a cavalry charge, while he, with the older part of the army, would follow on more sedately. Such a system not only allowed greater flexibility on the battlefield, but provided an equally flexible means of mobilisation: whole units, or just sub-units and certain age groups, could be called up according to the numbers required. Finally, nothing can better illustrate the Spartans' attitude towards fighting than to quote the assessment of them given to Xerxes by Demaratus, an exiled Spartan king who had taken refuge with Xerxes:

> Fighting singly, they are as good as any, but fighting together they are the best soldiers in the world. They are free – yes – but not entirely free; for they have a master, and that master is Law, which they fear much more than your subjects fear you. Whatever this master commands, they do; and his command never varies: it is never to retreat in battle, however great the odds, but always to stand firm, and so conquer or die.

But however brave and fearful of the Law, the Spartans were not superhuman and sometimes failed. At Thermopylae they stood and died, but after a hard fight at Pylos in 425 BC, 292 prisoners were taken from the original force of 400. It becomes clear, then, that the Spartans were outstanding soldiers who did nothing but train for war, while the Athenians had great arts, and also proved themselves to be good soldiers, as at Marathon.

The Athenians' attitude is summed up by Pericles who, in the famous funeral speech that he gave in 431 BC, said: 'We also differ in our military institutions from our opponents . . . we prefer to rely on our valour in the field and not upon secret military preparations. In education, again, we leave it to our opponents to cultivate manliness by laborious training from their tender years upwards, while we, with our undisciplined life, are as ready as they to face every reasonable danger.'

As will be seen, the Athenians fought as bravely and successfully as the Spartans, and kept a balance in their attitude towards professionalism. Such a balance is not always easy to obtain. Over-emphasis on professionalism can produce officers who are too narrow-minded, while affected amateurism breeds ignorance and costs lives. Battles are not won by officers only knowing how to die gallantly, but by those who have also studied their profession and trained hard. For far too long there were those in the British army who prided themselves on their amateurism, regarding their commands as private fiefdoms, and orders as little more than debating points. As General von Mellenthin wrote in his book *Panzer Battles*, 'we could not have resisted an attack by the 8th Army. We now know that on 4 July [1942], Auchinleck gave an order for such an attack, but as happened so frequently in the desert, he could not stir his corps commanders into action.' It was not just the fault of the corps commanders, for others down the chain of command were equally to blame. But all this ended when Montgomery arrived; he was far from being the only professional, but he was at the helm and made the fact clear to everybody.

All the Spartan innovations we have been discussing were, wittingly or unwittingly, later incorporated into the Roman legion, with its cohorts, chequerboard pattern and three maniples, each of which comprised soldiers of different age groups. It was through renouncing any flexibility within the individual legions, and then massing all eight of them together to form a vast phalanx designed to smash through the Carthaginian centre, that the Romans suffered an annihilating defeat by Hannibal and the Carthaginians at Cannae in 216 BC.

But to return to the Athenians: it should not be thought that they were wedded solely to the hoplite phalanx. Being prosperous, they could afford to hire mercenaries, who brought different skills; for example, the archers from Crete and slingers from Rhodes. When continuing with his account of how the Athenians advanced up the hill near Piraeus fifty shields deep, Xenophon goes on to say that there were 'a large number of slingers, since this was the district where they lived'. Whether they were Athenian citizens or resident mercenaries is not clear – a point that will be discussed when considering the light troops as a whole.

Light Troops

Probably because light troops played a secondary role to the decisive, battle-winning hoplites, they do not figure prominently in any of the ancient historians' accounts of even the larger engagements. They are, however, mentioned frequently enough for their role on the battle-field to be defined, but before doing so, let us first look at the light troops themselves. Except for Xenophon's statement about slingers, there is no mention of Athens or Sparta providing light troops from amongst their own citizens. In his exhortation to the Athenians at the outbreak of the Peloponnesian War, Pericles refers to archers, but he does not tell us whether they were Athenian citizens or enrolled from amongst the resident aliens; and except for the Aetolians and Boeotians there is no mention of another Greek state specifically providing them. This, however, is almost certainly an omission, for two reasons: first, there were states like Acarnania, which were unlikely to have been able to afford the cost of equipping heavy infantry, even if they needed them in the first place; and second, and even more compellingly, Thucydides specifically mentions that there were 800 archers fighting alongside the Athenians at Pylos in 425 BC, and that there were 480 of them available for the Sicilian expedition in 415 BC, of whom eighty were Cretans (leaving 400 unaccounted for). When recounting the first major engagement between the Athenians and their allies against the Syracusans, Thucydides mentions that stone-throwers fought alongside the slingers and archers; but he does not tell us to whom they belonged, nor where they came from. He then goes on to say that two years later, when reinforcements arrived from Athens, they included 'a great force of javelin-throwers both from Hellas and from outside, and slingers and archers'.

While there is then considerable uncertainty about the provision of the Athenian light troops, it is quite clear that no Spartan would serve other than as a hoplite. Although there were 35,000 lightly armed troops fighting alongside the Spartans at Plataea, they were all Helots. Similarly, when Brasidas marched up to Thrace, although he took 700 Helots with him who had been enrolled as hoplites, the 300 peltasts (lightly armed infantry) who later augmented his force were all Chalcidians. The Greeks regarded the great hoplite battle as being really all that mattered, for those outside the phalanx were of peripheral importance and thus held in low esteem.

Now let us look at the light troops' equipment and roles. All the light troops were armed with missiles: bows and arrows, slings and javelins. Though we are told nothing about their capability, it seems reasonable to suppose that sling technology is unlikely to have advanced greatly in the 140 years separating the Peloponnesian and Punic Wars, so the Balearic Island slingers can serve as an example. These Carthaginian mercenaries were armed with two types of sling: one for long-range engagements against a densely packed enemy, and the other for close-quarter, individual targets. Their delivery of stones could penetrate a helmet or light protective armour, while matching contemporary archers' rate of fire and accuracy. They were trained to whirl their slings about their heads and hit a bundle of straw or faggots at 600 feet. Without wishing to suggest any further comparison with the Athenian slingers, the Balearic Islanders were savage fighters, who were often paid in women rather than gold or silver.

It is clear then that the light troops engaged the enemy at long range, fighting as individuals in a loose, open formation; and, unless the heavy infantry was severely disadvantaged, avoiding any close-quarter engagement with them. In a set-piece battle, the main role of the light troops would have been to act as skirmishers in advance of the massed hoplites, escaping as best they could before the opposing phalanxes clashed. From Herodotus' account of the battle of Plataea in 479 BC, we know that the Persian light troops were positioned behind the heavy infantry, from where 'they were shooting arrows in such numbers that the Spartan troops were in serious distress'. Though we do not know whether this was the case with the Greeks; after the light troops had fulfilled their task as skirmishers, they could then be redeployed behind the heavy infantry, so continuing to play an important part in the battle.

Apart from their role in the set-piece battle, light troops could be used to harass an enemy's advance or withdrawal, as occurred when the Athenians advanced into Aetolia in 427 BC, and when they made their final withdrawal from Syracuse in 413 BC. They could also be used against an enemy who had been thrown off balance, as occurred when the Corinthians were withdrawing from an unsuccessful attempt to seize Megara in 479 BC. Part of the retreating army lost its way, becoming trapped in a cul-de-sac enclosed by a ditch. Seizing the opportunity, the Athenians quickly blocked the Corinthians' retreat, then encircled them with light troops, presumably slingers, since all who were inside were 'stoned to death'. The only mention made of the Spartans employing light troops is in 424 BC, when they were trying to counter Athenian raids along the Peloponnesian coast. According to Thucydides, the Spartans then raised 'a force of 400 cavalry, and a force of archers – something quite at variance with their normal way of doing things'. But he tells us nothing about their employment, or how successful they were. Finally, in 418 BC, the Boeotians sent 5000 light troops to support the Spartans when attacking Argos, as well as 500 dismounted troops trained to operate with the cavalry. It is a pity that Thucydides tells us nothing more about these dismounted troops, who were clearly antecedents of the German *Panzergrenadier*, or the mechanised infantry of Britain and other countries who operate closely with tanks.

Cavalry

For the reasons already discussed when we looked at the different states, most of the cavalry were provided by the Thessalians and, to a lesser extent, the Boeotians, and even they played a very subordinate role. In the exhortation to the Athenians that Pericles made at the outbreak of the Peloponnesian War, he refers to 1200 cavalry, including mounted bowmen, but tells us no more than that some of them were Thessalian. As with the light troops, none of the ancient historians gives a coherent account of the cavalry, so once again we will have to build up a picture of their role by examining cavalry tactics in three battles: Phalerum, Plataea and Delium.

Herodotus describes how the Thessalians used their cavalry against the Spartans at Phalerum, on the east coast some ten miles from Athens, in about 500 BC. The ground around Phalerum was cleared of trees to give the horses freedom of movement, and the advancing Spartans were then routed by the charge of a 1000-strong cavalry troop. Since it is inconceivable that a head-on cavalry charge could break up a well-disciplined phalanx, any more than Napoleon's cavalry could could break into Wellington's infantry squares at Waterloo in AD 1815, the Spartans must have been caught on the move, or in the process of deploying.

Following the battle of Plataea in 479 BC, when the defeated Persian army fled, the Boeotian cavalry in particular kept in close contact with the pursuing Greeks, acting as a screen between them and the fugitives. Finally, at Delium in 424 BC, the Theban hoplites, drawn up twenty-five shields deep, forced back the Athenian left wing of only eight shields deep. But on this occasion the cavalry also played a significant part; though the Athenian left wing was in considerable difficulty, their right wing had defeated the Boeotians opposite them and was carrying out an encircling movement. But at this near-victorious stage, two squadrons of Boeotian cavalry, which had moved round out of sight behind a hill, suddenly appeared beyond the Athenian right flank. Imagining that this was another army bearing down on them, the Athenians fled, being saved from total disaster only by nightfall, which, according to Thucydides, prevented the pursuing Boeotian cavalry from continuing to cut them down.

So, from these battles, four roles emerge for the cavalry: a massed charge to overwhelm an ill-prepared enemy; covering a withdrawal; manoeuvring to a flank to gain surprise – a fundamental battle-winning factor; and pursuit, to complete defeat. These roles remain as applicable today for armoured formations as they were for horsed cavalry some 2500 years ago – a clear demonstration of ancient history's relevance. As for weapons, since the fleeing Athenians were being cut down, the Boeotian cavalry must have carried slashing swords. Additionally, as stirrups had not yet been introduced, the horses would have been small enough for the riders to get a firm leg grip; otherwise there is no way they could have remained seated when charging into heavy infantry, even if not fully deployed.

As was mentioned when discussing light troops, the Spartans raised 400 cavalry in 424 BC, to counter Athenian raids against the Peloponnesian coast, but we know no more than that.

The Navies

When we talk about navies, we really mean that of the Athenians, since initially the Spartans did not even possess a fleet, and when they did, they introduced nothing innovative. Although Thucydides says that it was the Corinthians who built the first trireme, probably during the 8th century BC, some historians attribute its construction to the Phoenicians of Sidon, who had a long naval tradition. The Phoenician cities on the Syro-Palestinian coast all had warships and, as they did not have a fleet of their own, it was these that the Persians employed. The composition of the Persian fleet, as it is sometimes misleadingly called, will be examined more fully in the next chapter. A Phoenician ship, and most probably a Greek one, was commanded by three officers: the captain, his second-in-command, and the navigator, who was held in great esteem because of his experience. According to Plutarch, in his *Life of Themistocles*, the Greek ships at Salamis carried fourteen hoplites and four archers to fight from the decks, while the ships themselves were lighter and lower in the water than those of the Persians, with their high sterns and raised decks. Again, in his *Life of Cimon*, Plutarch says that the triremes ordered by Themistocles were constructed for speed and manoeuvrability; but Cimon had them widened, and provided each of them with a bridge connecting the decks, so that with a large complement of hoplites, they would be more effective in any close combat with the enemy. In his *Life of Pericles*, Plutarch talks of fifty ships carrying 5000 heavy-armed men aboard, but many of the ships must have been troop carriers.

On a trireme there were about 150 rowers, arranged in three banks, while some thirty sailors handled the sails and worked on deck. As will be seen, when we come to examine the equipment of the crews provided by the Greek colonists, which, according to Herodotus, 'were armed in the Greek fashion' – wearing helmets, body armour and carrying thrusting spears (or in some cases riphooks) – they thus resembled hoplites. In addition to the crews, all the ships carried some infantry, which, according to Plutarch, included a few archers; while in the case of the Greek colonists, the infantry were Persians or Medes.

Between the 7th and 4th centuries BC the trireme dominated the seas, but it was later displaced by the Carthaginian quinquereme. This larger vessel had 300 rowers, arranged in a single bank, with five of them to each oar. Not only was the quinquereme faster and heavier, and therefore potentially more lethal, but as it lay lower in the water it was also more stable. The early merchant ships seem to have been relatively small: the stone bases for such a ship dating from about 600 BC, found on Samos, suggest that it was only some sixty feet long and six feet wide; and a late 5th-century wreck of much the same dimensions, found in the straits of Messina, is thought to have had a thirty-ton carrying capacity. Professor Tod, writing in *The Cambridge Ancient History*, says that during this period much larger ships were introduced, some of them with as much as a 250-ton capacity. Another wreck, discovered at Alonnisos, an island some twenty miles to the north-east of Euboea, is calculated to have been able to carry some 126 tons. With the introduction of larger ships, coastal navigation was giving way to ocean-going ventures, conducted over greater distances and with greater speed.

Sails were used by both merchant vessels and warships, for normal travelling, but when approaching the battle area the masts would be lowered and the ships rowed. The Phoenician ships had two masts: the central mast provided the propulsion, and the smaller one, mounted on the prow, allowed the ship to be manoeuvred in a cross-wind. Tactics varied greatly. Herodotus describes the battle off the northern tip of Euboea in 480 BC, when the Greek fleet formed a close circle with their bows pointing outwards. After letting themselves be encircled by the greatly superior Persian fleet, the Greeks suddenly went on the attack, throwing the Persians into confusion and capturing thirty of their ships. A year later, at Salamis in 479 BC, the Greeks executed a minor Cannae; the centre of their line back-paddled, and their two wings enveloped the Persians. And Thucydides, when describing the battle between the Corinthians and the Corcyraeans off Corcyra (Corfu) in 433 BC, says that the fighting was somewhat old-fashioned, with both sides having a number of hoplites, archers and javelin-throwers on board. The two fleets formed into line, and after clashing together, the ships remained motionless, while the hoplites fought it out on the decks. All three of these battles will be put into context later.

Battles normally took place near the coast, where the ships could be handled in relatively calm water and there was some hope for the shipwrecked. The opposing fleets nearly always deployed in line, and as the intention was to ram the enemy's ships, when the signal to attack was given they advanced at maximum speed. The subsequent tactics depended on the enemy's dispositions. If there was sufficient space, the ships would steer between those of the enemy and then, by suddenly turning, ram them amidships. If there was not enough room to operate in this manner, the ships would pass through gaps in the enemy line and, after turning sharply about, take them in the rear. But this was not necessarily the end of the action, for the enemy ships often had to be boarded and taken into captivity, while sometimes the battle area was so restricted that, as in the great harbour of Syracuse in 413 BC, manoeuvre was virtually precluded and, as off Corcyra, desperate hand-to-hand fighting ensued. As we will be looking at the battle in the harbour at Syracuse in some detail later on, all that needs to be said now is that both the Corinthians and the Syracusans, who were less adept at manoeuvre than the Athenians, greatly strengthened the bows of their ships, so making them suitable for ramming their enemy head-on. In much the same way, during the Punic Wars, to compensate for their inferior seamanship, the Romans also reverted to turning naval engagements into little more than a land battle. They introduced the *corvus*, a boarding bridge, at the end of which was a large metal spike, which, when dropped onto the decks of the more mobile Carthaginian ships, grappled them and allowed the legionaries to storm aboard.

There appears always to have been a sharp distinction between the skills required for the actual handling of individual ships and their employment in battle. The former required professional seamen: the ship's officers, the navigator and deckhands; but no nautical skills were required of the fleet commander who was a general, exercising command on either sea or land as the situation required. Equally, the rowers were not purely seamen; they certainly had to be trained for their primary task, but, this completed, they were then expected to fight as soldiers. When the Spartan Gylippus landed at Himera, on the north coast of Sicily, in 413 BC, he left his ships there and marched to the relief of Syracuse with his sailors. Moreover, though there were special transport ships, it is clear that amphibious operations were undertaken without them. For example, in 411 BC, when the Athenians were conducting amphibious operations against Chios after it had revolted, they called up a number of hoplites who, Thucydides says, 'were compelled to serve as marines'. Which, as we will see, they did very successfully. Likewise, in 409 BC, when the Athenian fleet sailed to Samos for operations in Ionia, Xenophon says that 5000 of the sailors were equipped as peltasts, so that they could also fight as light infantry.

From Thucydides' and Xenophon's accounts of the considerable naval activity between 412 and 404 BC off the Ionian coast, a fairly clear picture emerges of the routine. Movement was nearly always by day, taking place within sight of the coast, where the many

distinguishable features made navigation relatively easy. Unless there
was an element of urgency, meals were often taken ashore, even if this
meant beaching the ships. Though there were occasions when nights
were also spent in this manner, it was more usual to make for a secure
harbour or safe anchorage. Even deep-sea navigation was mainly
conducted from one prominent coastal reference point to the next,
but when this was not possible, direction was kept from the stars,
particularly the Ursa Minor constellation, which was known to the
ancient world as the Phoenician Star.

Finally, it should not be overlooked that those who manned the
triremes also fulfilled an important political role. Since most of the
sailors came from the poorest class of citizens, their military
importance acted as a balance in maintaining Athens' democratic
institution: the rich could not claim that they were bearing the main
brunt in time of war.

The Athenian Constitution

The reforms of Solon in 594 BC resulted in the first positive steps
towards the establishment of democracy in Athens, and those of
Cleisthenes in 508 BC took the process a stage further. Let it not be
forgotten, however, as was mentioned earlier, that 'tyrants' also made
a contribution to reform; as did Pisistratus, coming between Solon
and Cleisthenes, with his distribution of land to agricultural workers.
But that apart, Athens continued to be governed by archons, or
rulers, who were elected annually from selected noble families by the
citizens' Assembly. After a year in office, the archons became
members of the ancient Council of the Areopagus, on the Hill of Ares
(Mars), just north-west of the Acropolis, upon which stands the
Parthenon. Membership of the Areopagus had been for life, and it
embodied the administrative experience of its time. Since the archons
had been elected by the free choice of the Assembly, it could be
argued that the Council represented the will of the people, but this
did not prevent it from being virtually swept away in 462 BC. The
change was one of great significance in the constitutional history of
Athens, and is said to have removed the last serious check on the
development of democracy. The word democracy, as understood by

the Greeks, needs to be defined, since it varied considerably from the meaning we ascribe to it today.

Athens was not a democracy, if we mean the participation of all the *adult population* in the government, since – having no vote – women, slaves and resident aliens were debarred, much as they were in England until the 18th-century Reform Acts and the franchise reforms of the 20th century. If, however, we mean participation of all the *citizens* in the government, then Athens was a democracy; since, by definition, only those qualifying for citizenship had the right to vote. If this sounds like hair-splitting today, it was not so with the Athenians, who regarded citizenship as equivalent to membership of a family of kinsmen, standing distinctly apart from the rest of the population. A further complication is introduced into the meaning of democracy by the political theorists, notably Plato and Aristotle, who interpreted it as meaning *government by the poor*, an anarchical inverted form of oligarchy.

Pericles played a major part in furthering the steps towards democracy, though the measures had been proposed by Ephialtes, who was later assassinated for his trouble, probably by a member of the aristocracy. The changes Pericles introduced were justified on the grounds that the Council of the Areopagus was undemocratic: the members held office for life, and were not accountable to any higher authority for the way they discharged their duties. This lack of accountability contrasted with the rule that every other official had to abide by: he was not released from his office until he had rendered a satisfactory account of his doings. As we will see, the Council of the Areopagus resembled the Spartan Council of Elders; which may have commended it to the many admirers of Sparta, but not to Pericles.

Under the reforms, the Assembly, consisting of every adult male citizen over the age of eighteen, became all-powerful. These mass meetings were usually held once a month, but were specially convened to settle matters of importance; for example, when the fate of the Mytilenians was debated. As will be recalled, the Assembly at first decided to put the entire population of Mytilene to death for having revolted, but after a change of mood there was another debate the following day. Thucydides records what happened, when Cleon and Diodotus had finished speaking: 'When these two motions, each so opposed to one another, had been put forward, the Athenians, in spite of the recent change of feeling, still held conflicting opinions, and at a show of hands the votes were nearly equal. However, the motion of Diodotus was passed.' So the second trireme was despatched in all haste, to cancel the order for execution. Such debates may have been very democratic, but it is notoriously easier to stir the emotions of a crowd than convince a few sceptical individuals; and obviously, much depended on the speakers' oratorical skills. Thucydides brings this point out when he describes the opening of the second debate: 'Cleon spoke again. It was he who had been responsible for passing the original motion for putting the Mytilenians to death. He was remarkable amongst the Athenians for the violence of his character, and at this time he exercised far the greater influence over the people.' We will come across further such examples in due course.

Most of the Assembly's work, however, was less emotionally charged. It was the sole legislative body and exercised considerable control over administration and judicature – the legislature and executive judiciary not being separated, as they would be in any of today's true democracies. Any citizen could speak and, within bounds, put forward proposals. But so large a body was too unwieldy to deal expeditiously with everything that arose; so a subordinate Council of Five Hundred was formed, to filter out some of the work. Selection to the Council was made annually, by ballot, so there was never any danger of its members developing a corporate spirit and overshadowing the Assembly. But as the Council of Five Hundred itself was too large to make an effective executive committee, and could not be in permanent session anyway, there was an inner council of fifty members, which remained in session for some thirty or forty days a year. Every day the chairman was elected by ballot, and if there was a meeting of the Assembly, he presided for twenty-four hours, during which time he was titular head of state.

The driving force justifying all this amateurism was the belief that a man owed it to himself and to his city to participate in all its activities. There was no room for the professional; every citizen took his turn at being a soldier, a judge and an administrator. Such individualism could only be realised in a relatively small community; hence the Greek ideal was the city-state, or polis, which should multiply so that none of them was oversized, each of them was independent, yet all of them cooperated harmoniously. Like most human ideals, however, the practice was very different. In the 6th century BC the Greek cities in Asia Minor were certainly of modest size, and independent, but, as has already been mentioned, a latent hostility smouldered between the Ionians and the Dorians; while the search for autonomy resulted in a lack of cohesion, making the cities easy prey for their great Asiatic neighbour. As for Greece itself, the cities were generally under the hegemony of some centralising power: Sparta in the Peloponnese, Thebes in Boeotia, and Athens more generally.

The Spartan Constitution and Educational System

Few would disagree with Bertrand Russell when he says that the constitution of Sparta was complicated, but his clarification will serve us well. There were two kings, belonging to different families and succeeding by heredity. After the humiliation Sparta had suffered when its two kings' disagreement had led to the fiasco before Athens, only one or other of them was permitted to command the army in time of war. In times of peace their powers were limited, though, perhaps in compensation, at communal feasts they got twice as much to eat as anyone else, and there was general mourning when one of them died. The kings were members of the Council of Elders, the Gerousia, which, as was mentioned earlier, resembled the Athenian Council of the Areopagus. The Gerousia consisted of the two kings and twenty-eight aristocrats over the age of sixty, who were chosen for life by all the citizens. The Council tried criminal cases and prepared matters that were to come before the Assembly. The Assembly differed from the Athenian one in two significant ways: first, all the men had to be over thirty, instead of just eighteen; and second, nobody could initiate anything – participation was restricted to voting on the proposal under consideration. The system of voting was also different; whereas the Athenians' approval was shown by the raising of hands, the Spartans indicated theirs by acclamation, the loudest cheers carrying the motion. The reason for this was probably because the raising of hands was a sign of surrender: an act of such despicable cowardice that its use was precluded for any other purpose. Finally, no law could be enacted without the Assembly's consent; but this in itself was not enough, for the elders and magistrates, quite separately, had to proclaim the decision before it became valid.

In addition to the kings, Council of Elders and Assembly, there was a fourth branch of the government, peculiar to Sparta: the five ephors. These were chosen out of the whole body of the citizens by lot, and represented a democratic element in the constitution, apparently to balance the kings. Every month the kings swore to uphold the constitution, and the ephors then swore to uphold the kings, so long as they remained true to their oath. When one of the kings went off to war, two ephors accompanied him to watch his behaviour. The ephors were the supreme civil court, but over the kings they had criminal jurisdiction. One of the reasons for the admiration felt for Sparta was its political stability; all the other Greek cities had revolutions, but this mixed Spartan constitution remained unchanged for centuries, except for a gradual increase in the powers of the ephors, which occurred legally and without violence.

The Spartan constitution was supposed to have been due to a legislator, Lycurgus, who is said to have promulgated his laws in 885 BC. Lycurgus is a remote, shadowy figure, and the antiquity of his legislation has been greatly exaggerated. Like most political systems, Sparta's constitution developed empirically, crystallising into the form just described in about the 6th century BC. Bertrand Russell dismisses Lycurgus out of hand as being a mythical person, perhaps originally a god originating from Arcadia, whose name meant 'wolf repeller'. The Delphic oracle also proclaimed that it was not sure whether Lycurgus was a god or a man. However much of a myth Lycurgus may have been, when writing his life, Plutarch tells us a lot about Spartan customs and education.

Selection for the Spartans began at birth; children belonged to the state, not to the parents, and to ensure that its future citizens only came from the best stock, they were examined by the elders and, if found wanting, despatched by exposure on a nearby mountain. The fit and healthy were left with their mothers until they were six, when they joined up with other boys and started an education that lasted until they were twenty. The emphasis was on the endurance of hardship, a general toughening up and strict discipline.

Had a Spartan youth been placed in an English boarding school, at any rate until comparatively recently, he would have recognised certain similarities, though badly distorted. Music, for example, though taught, no longer serves a purpose; whereas in Sparta it would enable him to march in time with the pipers and, in roaring unison, sing his phalanx's battle paean. He would have considered the attention paid to reading and writing excessive since, as Plutarch drily comments, Spartan boys only received 'as much as they would need to get by with'. As for the Spartan emphasis on manliness in preparation for war, he would have found a sadly watered-down version; though had he attended the author's preparatory school, he would at once have recognised a familiar figure: the classicist, battle-scarred headmaster, with his connoisseur's collection of assorted canes. But in contrast to what is sometimes imagined, his final discovery would have come as a surprise: an absence of homosexuality. In Sparta, on the other hand, homosexual relations between older and younger boys was a common practice, with the elder 'lover' serving as a guide and mentor. The boys were taught to steal and, if caught, were thrashed – not for stealing, but for having been stupid enough to be caught. As Plutarch relates, a boy's conduct reflected on his lover; if a boy cried out when hurt during a fight, the lover was fined for his boy's cowardice. As will be seen when we come to consider the relationship between Socrates and Alcibiades, not dissimilar attitudes also existed amongst the upper classes in Athenian society.

Spartan education did not end with adolescence. When adults, Spartans continued to take their meals in common messes, where only carefully prescribed food was served. In this manner they were prevented from ruining themselves, both morally and physically, by over-indulgence at home. Outside the messes and communal dormitories, life in the city resembled that of a military camp, with its disciplined, orderly routine and shared common tasks. All of which, it should be remembered, was only made possible because of the Helots who sustained the whole system. But in spite of this indispensable function, if the story really is true, the Helots were treated abominably. Rather like the Japanese, who used live prisoners for bayonet practice to harden their soldiers, young Spartans would go out at night and murder any Helots they could find. Against this must be set the fact that thousands of Helots served loyally alongside the Spartans; as has been mentioned, there were 35,000 of them at the battle of Plataea in 479 BC, many of whom were killed in action. So much for the upbringing and training of the young Spartan male; as Plutarch observes, with all this demanding, closely controlled activity, it was hardly surprising that war was a more restful occupation.

Young women had their part to play as well, urging the young men on and, by participating naked in athletic competitions, encouraging marriage; as Plato puts it, 'because the young men were drawn by sexual rather than logical reasons'. Marriage, when it came, was a furtive affair. The bride-to-be would be handed over to her so-called bridesmaids who, having performed the customary rituals, left her lying on a straw mattress in total darkness. Later the groom would enter the room, locate the girl, who somehow seems to have become his wife, pick her up and place her on a bed. Then, having done what was expected of him, he would return to the young men's dormitory. For the next few years the marriage would continue to be a clandestine affair, while it was perfectly permissible for others to fulfil the husband's role, especially if he were past his prime – the procreation of healthy children being all that mattered.

To end this introduction to the Spartans, let us leave the last word to Plutarch: 'Lycurgus thought that happiness in the life of a whole city, was due to the same factors as in the life of an individual, namely virtue and internal harmony, and so the point of all his arrangements and institutions had been to enable the Lacedaemonians to be free, autonomous, and self disciplined for as long as possible.'

2

The Persians and Their Background

As the Persians figure so prominently in the history of Greece – especially their two invasions, which threatened to stifle the nascent Western civilisation – they merit attention. Our story can begin with Croesus, the King of Lydia, who reigned between 560 and 546 BC; his name passing into posterity through the expression 'as rich as Croesus'. But Croesus' wealth did not save him from Cyrus, who took him prisoner shortly after a battle near Sardis, the capital of Lydia, in 547 BC. According to Herodotus, Cyrus – curious to see whether any divine power would save Croesus from being burned alive – placed him on a great pyre, which, when lit, was extinguished by a sudden downpour after he had offered a prayer to Apollo. But the Assyrian chronicles say that he was killed by Cyrus, which sounds more probable. For the rest of his life Cyrus continued to devote himself to conquest; in 539 BC he captured Babylon, the great city on the Euphrates some forty-five miles south of Baghdad, and the following year he gave permission for the Jewish captives to return home. He finally died in battle against the Scythians, near Lake Aral, in about 528 BC.

Cyrus was succeeded by his son Cambyses, who conquered Egypt in 525 BC, with Ethiopia having a narrow escape. When he died four years later – from an accidentally self-inflicted wound – the Persian Empire stretched from the Aegean to the borders of India, and from Libya through Egypt up to the Caspian Sea. Greece was just an insignificant dot on the periphery of this vast, as yet undigested conglomeration; probably it would have gone unnoticed, had it not been for the revolt of Miletus in 494 BC, which, it will be remembered, led to Athenian intervention. Herodotus thought it was this ineffective foray that provoked the Persians into invading Greece four years later in 490 BC. The delay was caused by Darius having to impose order, and organisational coherence, within the sprawling empire he had inherited. Moreover, since his right to the throne was questionable, Darius also had to establish himself as Cambyses' undisputed heir. In spite of having innumerable wives (including a couple of his own sisters), when Cambyses died, he left no children. There is no need to go into the details of how Darius came to inherit the throne, other than to say that, even after some neat dynastic footwork, he had found it necessary to assassinate his immediate predecessor, an alleged impostor posing as the brother of Cambyses. Having secured his inheritance, Darius then turned his attention to wider issues.

The first organisational change that Darius made was to divide the empire into twenty satrapies, or 'protectors of the realm', each under its own governor who was responsible for its administration, and for the security of its communications, and who was the highest judicial authority within the province. Darius also built a network of roads; the most important being the royal road linking his capital at Susa, some 400 miles south of the Caspian Sea, with Sardis, the capital of Lydia, about 1500 miles to the west; posting stations and inns were established every fifteen miles, thereby enabling instructions and reports to be rapidly relayed throughout the Empire. Though much administrative authority was decentralised, ultimate power rested at the centre, where all major decisions were taken. According to some historians, roads were not all that Darius had constructed. About a century previously, an attempt had been made to dig a canal from the Red Sea to the Mediterranean, but it had been abandoned. Darius now completed this work, not by following the course of today's Suez Canal, but by linking the Red Sea to the Nile, so gaining access to the Mediterranean.

Appreciating the need for a fleet, Darius raised one from amongst the Phoenicians, while the army was organised into what equated to divisions, each 10,000 strong, with ten battalions of 1000 men, further subdivided into ten companies of ten sections. There was also a Household Division, the king's 10,000-strong personal bodyguard, known as the Immortals, because they were always kept up to strength. The Persian cavalry, allegedly for reasons of expense, was recruited from the nobility, with a 1000-strong elite regiment of

Household Cavalry. But because of the open plains and abundant pasture, horses were found throughout the Empire, so it seems highly improbable that cavalry were really restricted to the wealthier classes. For at least a part of the population, the ownership of horses must have been essential for the conduct of everyday life; especially for some of the nomadic tribes, like the Sagaritians, who provided one of the two cavalry contingents which, according to Herodotus, accompanied Xerxes when he invaded Greece. Given abundant pasture land, horses could be a source of wealth, not just a financial burden.

Having put the Empire onto a war footing, Darius next turned his attention to securing his frontiers. In about 518 BC he captured the important island of Samos, off the coast of Asia Minor, before turning east to lay siege to Babylon, which, it will be recalled, had been captured by Cyrus, but had then revolted. To save rations while under siege, most of the women in the city were strangled; each man, however, could spare his mother and – rather ominously for troublesome wives – one other woman to bake his bread. According to Herodotus, the city walls were fifty-six miles long, eighty feet thick and 320 feet high, with equally strong inner walls, though without being so thick; and rising above the city soared the Tower of Babel, which seemed to reach to the heavens. Even if archaeologists have reduced Herodotus' figures, the wall being only ten miles long, the city must still have seemed impregnable. As siege weapons had not yet been developed, well-fortified cities could only be taken through starvation, treachery or trickery, and it was through the last that Babylon finally fell.

Strangely enough, Herodotus does not mention the Hanging Gardens of Babylon, another of the Seven Wonders of the World, built during the reign of Nebuchadnezzar II (604–562 BC). Diodorus Siculus describes the scene: 'The approach to the Garden sloped like a hillside, and several parts of the structure rose from one another, tier on tier ... on all this, the earth had been piled ... and was thickly planted with trees of every kind that, by their great size and other charm, gave pleasure to the beholder ... the water machines raised the water in great abundance from the river, though no one outside could see it.' He goes on to say that the gardens were about 400 feet square, but the German archaeologist, Koldewey, who spent some fourteen years on the site, reduces the gardens' size by nearly two-thirds – hardly big enough to contain Diodorus' 'thickly planted trees'. So perhaps, on reflection, it is not so strange that Herodotus does not mention the gardens.

But to get back to Darius, who next set off to invade Scythia, north of the Black Sea, which Herodotus describes as 'having few really remarkable features, except its rivers, which are more numerous, and bigger than anywhere else in the world ... and the vast extent of its plains'. A feeling for the extent of these plains is given by Field Marshal von Manstein in his book *Verlorene Siege*: 'The horizon appeared like a shimmering wave, behind which lay a luring Paradise: but there was never anything, the emptiness just extended further and further.'

After bridging the Bosphorus in about 515 BC, Darius sent the Ionian fleet, together with the other Greek ships from Aeolia and the Hellespont, to bridge the Danube and await his arrival. Though Herodotus, when referring to the Ionian fleet, only mentions the contingent from Mytilene, there must also have been one from Miletus, since, as was mentioned earlier, it was this Ionian city that had won favour with Darius, because of the assistance to him during the Scythian expedition. Darius himself marched through eastern Thrace to join the fleet, subduing the tribes through whose territory he passed. He then crossed the Danube, leaving the Ionians to guard the bridge; but after fruitlessly attempting to close with the evasive, mounted Scythians, he decided to call off the expedition and withdraw. He was lucky to escape. Once the Scythians realised his intentions, they tried to persuade the Ionians to break the bridge and seize the opportunity to free themselves from the Persian yoke. Miltiades, whom we have already met at Imbros, and will meet again at Marathon, commanded one of the Ionian contingents and urged his compatriots to follow the Scythian advice; but he was outvoted, and Darius was able to escape over the Danube.

The expedition had been a major blunder. If Darius' aim had been to secure Persia's northern frontier, rather that just indulging in aimless conquest, this would have been best achieved by utilising the natural frontier provided by the Danube. Darius was fortunate not to have suffered a major disaster, but he now left his most able general, Megabazus, to subdue the Greek settlements on the Hellespont that had refused to accept Persian domination, then to secure Thrace and demand the submission of Macedonia. Having given his orders for

the establishment of a substantial European bridgehead, Darius set off
on his return to Sardis.

Since, at this stage, Athens had not enraged Darius through her
intervention in the Ionian revolt, it is unlikely that he had given
serious thought to invading Greece. But when this did occur, and his
strategic aim became the conquest of Greece, the acquisition of
Thrace had clearly been a sound operational move – providing a
springboard should he wish to invade by land, or alternatively
ensuring flank protection, and anchorage for his fleet, should he
decide to mount a seaborne assault. The successful military operations
in Thrace, however, were not matched politically when it came to
Macedonia. High-level envoys were sent to demand earth and water,
the traditional signs of submission, which were granted. But at the
celebratory banquet that followed, the envoys over-indulged themselves and, inflamed by wine, started to fondle the young Macedonian
women. Enraged by this spectacle, but not wishing to cause a
disturbance in public, the Macedonians tactfully suggested that the
women should take a bath, before retiring to the Persians' beds, a
suggestion that was readily accepted. So the women withdrew, but
instead of returning themselves, they were replaced by some beardless
youths, who, when the Persians got into bed and started making
groping advances, stabbed them to death. And that, as Herodotus
laconically observed, was the end of the Persian envoys.

Whatever one may think about this entertaining story, there had
been three important consequences resulting from Megabazus'
campaign. In spite of the envoys' fate, Macedonia had recognised
allegiance to Darius. This in itself might not have meant very much,
had it not been for the fact that a substantial Persian bridgehead had
been established in Europe, stretching from the River Strymon
(Struma) to the Sea of Marmara. For the Persians to have acquired the
allegiance of Macedonia, lying to the north of this European
foothold, greatly strengthened their position. But, historically, the
most significant consequence was that East and West had clashed for
the first time, issuing in a struggle that, with varying fortunes and
under different guises, has lasted throughout the centuries. With
Israel representing a European state established to the east of the
Hellespont, the struggle cannot yet be said to have ended; at least not
in the eyes of the Arab world. After Darius had left Megabazus to
reduce Thrace, he first travelled to Sardis, where he must have given

orders about his future policy, which was clearly to further Persia's western expansion. Having given his instructions, Darius then continued his journey to his capital at Susa. It was now about 512 BC, and in compliance with his orders the governor promptly conquered the islands of Imbros and Lemnos.

In 499 BC the Ionian revolt against Persian domination broke out and lasted for five years. Although Herodotus gives a full account of what occurred, he does so as a series of unconnected episodes, which makes it difficult to present the revolt in a coherent sequence. What is clear, however, is that before the revolt started there had been little antagonism between the Greeks and the Persians. The Greek cities had accepted Persian domination without any serious resistance, and afterwards the Persians had left them to conduct their affairs without interference. The extent of Persian tolerance is illustrated by what occurred at Sigeum which, it will be remembered, was a Greek settlement on the Asiatic coast of the Hellespont. Not long after Megabazus had fulfilled Darius' order to subdue the Greek cities around the Hellespont, ostensibly for not having supported his expedition against Scythia, Athens recaptured Sigeum from Mytilene. Greek claims to ownership were evidently inconsequential – submission to Persia was all that was required.

According to Herodotus, this state of peaceful coexistence was ended as a result of yet another internecine quarrel amongst the Greeks, which, in the normal course of events, would have been unlikely even to have attracted Persian attention. But Aristagoras, tyrant of Miletus, broadened the canvas by bringing about Persian involvement. Aristagoras was persuaded by a group of political exiles from Naxos to reinstate them on the island. Seeing an opportunity to secure Naxos for himself, but lacking the means, Aristagoras approached the Persian governor of Lydia, Artaphrenes, the brother of Darius. By conquering the Cyclades, and Naxos in particular – so argued Aristagoras – the Persians would have established a base from which they could then secure Euboea, the large prosperous island off the Greek mainland, which would be easy to take. The proposed plan was welcomed by Artaphrenes, who sought Darius' agreement to its execution. Once royal approval had been received, a fleet of 200 ships, under the command of Megabates, a relation of Darius, set sail for Miletus where they were to pick up Aristagoras, who would then take command of the expedition.

But during the voyage a quarrel broke out between Megabates and Aristagoras, over the former's disciplining of a lax ship's captain. Getting the worst of the disagreement, Megabates took his revenge by warning the Naxians of the coming assault. Forewarned, Naxos held out, and the expedition had to be called off when both stores and funds were nearly exhausted. Having damaged Persian prestige and squandered Persian money, Aristagoras feared for his life, so he turned to rebellion as offering the only means of escape. His first step was to conciliate public opinion throughout Asiatic Greece by disposing of the tyrants of the various cities; all of whom, as supporters of Persia, had joined the expedition and were still together, as the fleet had not yet dispersed. Thus Aristagoras managed to spread support for the revolt throughout most of Ionia and, at the same time, obtain possession of a large part of the Persian fleet.

Persian response was slow, and Aristagoras had time to try and enlist the support of first Sparta, and then Athens. He was ignominiously turned out of Sparta by the king, Cleomenes, with whom he had had a personal interview, but he was more successful in Athens, where he had been able to address the Assembly. A squadron of twenty Athenian ships sailed to Miletus, where they joined up with the Ionians before proceeding to Ephesus. Here the troops disembarked and marched on Sardis, which they burned to the ground, but when threatened by an advancing Persian army they hurriedly withdrew to Ephesus. As has already been related, it was at Ephesus that the Athenians and Ionians were decisively defeated, which resulted in the surviving Athenians sailing for home and leaving the Ionians to their fate.

Though other Ionian cities joined the revolt after the daring raid on Sardis, there was no hope of their being able to resist the overwhelming strength of Persia. Cyprus, which was already in open revolt, had joined the uprising; but though the Ionian fleet won a resounding victory against the Phoenicians off Cyprus, the Cypriot army was routed and the Persians recaptured the island in 497 BC. In the same year the Persians struck at the Hellespont, before turning south to subdue the Aeolian settlements. Probably in the following year the southerly advance was continued, reaching as far as Cyme, midway down the western seaboard. The next move was against Caria, which offered the prospect of opening up the road to Miletus, the centre of the revolt. Here tough resistance was encountered, but after winning two battles, rather than trying to suppress the whole province, in 494 BC the Persians turned their attention on Miletus. A new Phoenician fleet, replacing the one lost off Cyprus, took its revenge by winning a crushing victory near Miletus, largely brought about by the Samians deserting, and the Lesbians, seeing their flank exposed, fleeing – a double loss, which even the tenacious courage of the Chians could not redress. Hemmed in by land and sea, it was not long before Miletus was taken by storm; elsewhere, the last embers of the uprising in Caria were extinguished, all the remaining cities and islands eventually being retaken.

After some vengeful bloodletting, the process of reconciliation and reconstruction began. The cities of Ionia never recovered their earlier prosperity, but fourteen years later Xerxes was confident enough in their loyalty to include a number of Asiatic Greek contingents amongst the host he assembled for the invasion of Greece in 480 BC. It had been a revolt that lacked not only the resources to succeed, but the necessary cohesion to mount coordinated operations under a joint command. This disunity, inevitably bringing disarray, may well have been the cause of Athens withdrawing her active support for the revolt; whatever the reason, abandoning the Ionians after a single reverse suggests that there were divided views in Athens about her foreign policy. The initial decision to intervene had been taken by the Assembly. As Herodotus comments: 'Apparently it is easier to impose upon a crowd than upon an individual, for Aristagoras, who had failed to impose upon Cleomenes – the Spartan king – had no difficulty with 30,000 Athenians.' But as had occurred before in the case of Mytilene, wiser counsels seem to have prevailed as to where Athenian interests really lay. Athens was a maritime power, possessing neither the means nor the prospect of gaining any advantages – political, economic or military – to justify her involvement in a high-risk continental war. But however precipitous the Athenians' withdrawal, their participation in the burning of Sardis aroused the fury and implacable hostility of Darius, who now prepared to take his revenge.

3

The Expeditions of Mardonius and Darius
493–490 BC

In about 493 BC Darius superseded all his other generals to appoint his young son-in-law, Mardonius, to command the army and fleet that had been assembled for the conquest of Greece at Cilicia, in south-east Asia Minor. When all was ready, the army set off on its long march to the Hellespont, where it was met by Mardonius who had sailed round the coast with the fleet. Having been ferried across the straits, the army next entered Thrace, which, it will be remembered, had been subdued by Megabazus and seems to have remained tranquil throughout the Ionian revolt. The island of Thasos surrendered to the fleet without resistance, and the army crossed the Strymon without having encountered any opposition. Good progress continued to be made through Macedonia, and the fleet was ordered to sail round the Chalcidic peninsula to join the army in the Gulf of Therma. But having got no further than Mount Athos, lying on the first of the trident-like Chalcidic promontories, most of the fleet was driven onto the rock-strewn shore by a violent northerly gale, with the loss of some 20,000 men. Following the disaster, and with the army coming under attack from hostile tribes, Mardonius decided to withdraw.

In spite of this reversal, Darius remained determined to crush Greece, and while the preparations to raise a new fleet were in hand he sent heralds to a number of Greek islands and mainland cities, to judge the extent of the resistance he was likely to encounter. The usual tokens of submission, earth and water, were demanded, with many encouraging responses, including that of the major maritime

power, Aegina; which aroused Athenian suspicions that the Aeginetans were going to join Persia in mounting a combined attack against
them. This suspicion was aggravated by the fact that, as has been
mentioned, ever since 505 BC a desultory war between Aegina and
Athens had been smouldering away for some thirteen years. The
Athenians now appealed to Sparta, as the leading power in Greece, to
intercede, for the general benefit of Hellas. As the Spartans had flung
the Persian envoys down a well, telling them to take water and earth
from there back to Darius, they were now as committed to opposing
Persia as Athens herself (where the Persian heralds had also been
roughly handled, being cast into a deep ditch).

There now occurred an important development in Grecian relations: the emergence of Hellas as an aggregate body, with Sparta at
the head, a position she held through respect. Sparta was indisputably
the leading land power, and it was now a land threat with which
Greece was confronted; her political stability, it will be recalled, was
the envy of many other Greek cities. In responding to the Athenian
appeal, Sparta was serving pan-Hellenic interests. The security of the
whole of Greece was at stake, not just that of Athens. The ten
eminent Aeginetan citizens whom the Spartans had taken as hostages
and handed over to the Athenians may have helped ensure that
Aegina did not actively support Darius, but there was no question of
her resisting him. The justification given for this stance of neutrality
has already been explained, so need not be repeated here. Such was
the state of affairs when the long-threatened Persian invasion finally
materialised.

Not wishing to risk a repetition of the disaster that had overtaken
the fleet off the Chalcidic peninsula three years earlier, the Persians
chose to cross the Aegean. Not only would this keep them well away
from an area notorious for its sudden storms, but it would settle
accounts with Naxos, which had successfully resisted an earlier
attempt to capture it during the Ionian revolt. As Herodotus says,
'the capture of Naxos was now their first objective in the war'. The
army had again assembled in Cilicia, the province in south-eastern
Turkey, where it was embarked: the cavalry horses on transports, and
the troops in ships of war. Mardonius having been relieved of his
command, the orders that had been given by Darius were to the new
commander, his nephew Datis, who was to 'reduce Athens and
Eretria to slavery and bring the slaves before the king'. Though there

was no mention of Naxos in these admirably brief and clear orders, the significance of specifying Eretria will be brought out later.

When all was ready, the fleet of 600 assorted vessels followed the coastline to Samos, from where it set sail for the Cyclades, a convenient halfway stepping stone. Here, as has already been recounted, Naxos was reduced, Delos treated with piety and the other islands pressed into providing troops for the expedition. From the Cyclades, the Persians next assaulted two cities on the island of Euboea, Carystus (Karysto) on the southern tip and Eretria on the west coast. Eretria had appealed to Athens for help, but none was forthcoming. A number of complex reasons have been put forward to account for this failure, but the explanation was probably simply a military one. The Athenians would not have wished to risk fighting a decisive battle under unfavourable conditions. Almost inevitably there would be a major fleet engagement, conducted while the army was still embarked there; if surviving this encounter, the troops would have to make what could have been an opposed landing, all without the slightest hope of receiving any allied support. Only a lunatic would have risked such an unpromising enterprise.

What is more puzzling is why the Persians seemingly wasted so much time on Euboea. There was no need to secure any part of the island before landing at Marathon, while the delay provided more time for the Greeks to complete their defensive preparations. Although Herodotus cannot bring himself to accept the possibility, one explanation is that there were traitors in Athens only too ready to betray the city for their own political ends. The plan was to lure the Athenian army away to Eretria, and then for the Persians to make a second landing at Phalerum, a few miles south of Athens, which would spark a revolt. Athens would then be carried by treachery rather than storm. All this is perfectly plausible: the Persians had an Athenian with them, the ejected tyrant Hippias, who had been exiled from Athens and taken refuge in Asia, where he had consistently urged the Persians to subject Athens, then install him as a subject of Darius. It is not unreasonable to suppose that it may have been Hippias who had helped conceive this plan, which would also explain why Darius specifically included the reduction of Eretria in his orders to Datis. As for the plan itself, this was thoroughly sound, incorporating both deception and surprise; but its success was dependent on the Athenians being lured to Eretria. When this did not occur, and the Persians eventually landed at Marathon, only some twenty miles separated the battlefield from Athens, so the landing at Phalerum served no purpose; any revolt could wait upon the outcome of the contest at Marathon.

A few days after the destruction of Eretria, the Persians sailed for Attica, with everybody on board in high spirits, confident that Athens would also soon be destroyed. The part of Attica providing the best ground for cavalry to operate was at Marathon, so this is where the exile Hippias directed the invading army. As soon as the news reached the Athenians, they hurried to counter the landing, sending a messenger to Sparta – rather strangely only one, who was not even mounted – urging the Spartans to come to their assistance. But though sympathetic, the Spartans would not move because it was the ninth day of the month, and they could not take the field until the moon was full in about ten days' time. As already mentioned, the observance of religious laws frequently affected the conduct of operations, though seldom so critically as on this occasion. Meanwhile the Athenians, under the command of Miltiades, had been joined by the Plataeans, who came with every available man the little town possessed. This voluntary march of the whole 1000-strong Plataean army to Marathon is as moving a story as that of the Newfoundland Battalion, also 1000 strong, which was decimated on the opening day of the battle of the Somme in the First World War. The Plataeans' readiness to come to the assistance of the Athenians was commemorated in public prayers and the granting of civil rights as Athenian citizens; the Newfoundlanders were commemorated by the planting of a small wood and the erection of a monument where they fell.

But to get back to Miltiades, whom we have already met at Imbros and on the Danube, but who now needs a fuller introduction. He was an Athenian who had established himself as the governor of the Chersonese, on the European side of the Hellespont, and had accompanied Darius at the head of the Chersonese contingent during his Scythian campaign. As will be remembered, when the Ionians were left to guard the crossing over the Danube, it was Miltiades who had urged them to break the bridge and prevent Darius withdrawing. Then, during the Ionian revolt, he had helped expel the Persian garrisons from the islands of Imbros and Lemnos; so when the

uprising was crushed and a Phoenician fleet approached the Hellespont, he had little option but to flee for his life – not, however, before
he had loaded five triremes with his personal property. Once back in
Athens, at the instigation of his political enemies, Miltiades was
prosecuted for his unconstitutional and despotic government in the
Chersonese, but was acquitted. By popular vote, he was then
appointed to command of the army, just at a time when it would have
been known that the Persians were approaching.

Although Miltiades was the commander, his authority was heavily
circumscribed by the nine other generals, all of whom had a vote
before any major decision was reached. Now, confronted with the
prospect of a battle that would decide the fate of Athens, opinions
were divided: five felt that facing the Persians without Spartan
assistance would be suicidal, while the other five, including Miltiades,
urged action. The issue was resolved by the Polemarch, or War
Archon, who held a casting vote, which he used to support Miltiades.

The 10,000 Athenians, together with the Plataeans, deployed on the
high ground in an extended line. But either through endeavouring to
cover the whole Persian front, or intentionally, they thinned their
centre (probably to four ranks), while the wings were maintained at
the usual eight. Below them, on the plain about a mile away, the
Persians were drawn up with their backs to the sea and their ships
behind them. Herodotus says that the Athenians advanced at a run,
but for this to have happened from the outset seems highly
improbable. Encumbered with body armour, shields and pikes, the
hoplites would have quickly lost formation and arrived winded. Nor
was there any necessity to run the full distance; only when entering
within range of the Persian archers – about 200 yards – would there
be any need to close as quickly as possible.

The advance would then have begun in slow time, the terrifying
battle hymn sung, the line steadied, and the last hundred yards or so
covered at the double. Whether intentionally or unintentionally, the
two wings got ahead of the centre, with the result that the Greek
front became concave and probably disjointed, enabling the Persians
to at least hold their ground, if not actually advance. But as the
Persian front became convex and so shortened, the Athenians on one
wing and the Plataeans on the other were able to wheel inwards and
take the Persians in the flank. Confusion resulted, and the Persians
made a precipitate withdrawal, though some order must have been

preserved on the shoreline. Only seven vessels were taken, and the Persians confidently set sail for Athens, which they hoped to reach before the Athenian army could return. But through diverting to pick up the Eretrian prisoners, whom the Persians had disembarked on the islet of Aegina, they found the Athenians ready to receive them a second time. After riding at anchor for a while to assess the situation, they eventually decided against risking another defeat, so they unfurled their sails and returned to Asia. No mention is made of the Athenian fleet, which, had it intervened while the Persians were trying to escape, could have turned what was a costly defeat into an annihilating disaster. Perhaps, in spite of the hostages they held, the Athenians still feared that the Aeginetans might seize the opportunity to attack Athens, should both their fleet and army be engaged at Marathon.

But the strangest thing about Herodotus' account of the battle is that, having said that the Persians chose to land at Marathon because the ground favoured the use of cavalry, he makes no mention of them. One can only conjecture that, though the ground may have been suitable for the deployment of cavalry, it was far too small a space to accommodate more than the estimated 15,000 Persian infantry. Only about a mile deep and a mile wide at its mouth, the valley could not possibly have allowed room for the cavalry to manoeuvre before the infantry had cleared the battlefield. So probably the cavalry had not even been disembarked. Herodotus does, however, mention – and emphasise – that a pre-arranged signal was made to the Persians when they were approaching Athens, which lends weight to the view that treachery was intended to deliver Athens into their hands.

Again according to Herodotus, 6600 Persians were killed, and only 192 Athenians, while the Eretrian prisoners, when paraded before Darius, were, surprisingly, spared their lives and settled on some land he provided for them, far away in Asia. Marathon resembled a minor Cannae, except that the Persians were able to escape by retreating to their ships, whereas the Romans were trapped when Hannibal's heavy cavalry, having defeated that of the Romans, encircled them. Marathon was not a decisive defeat for the Persians, but it was the first they had ever suffered from the Greeks in the field. As for the Greeks, according to Plato, Marathon gave them the confidence and resolution to face the far greater threat that was to come in ten years' time. For the Spartans, Marathon must have come as a blow to their pride; after waiting for the full moon, 2000 of them made a forced march to join the Athenians, but by then the battle had been won, so they had to content themselves with inspecting the Persian dead. Then, after congratulating the Athenians, they marched back home.

After the victory at Marathon, the already high reputation of Miltiades was greatly increased, so when he asked for a fleet of seventy ships, together with troops and money, for an undisclosed expedition that would enrich Athens, his request was readily granted. Miltiades then set sail for the island of Paros, just to the west of Naxos, to settle what was no more than a personal score. The expedition was a total failure. Other than destroying the crops, nothing was achieved, and not a penny gained, and Miltiades badly injured his thigh when trying to meddle with, if not rob, the shrine of Demeter. Back in Athens he was charged with fraud and fined; but he died shortly afterwards from gangrene. Such was the nemesis of overweening hubris: a great man brought low through arrogance.

When Darius learned about the Persian defeat at Marathon, he immediately started to prepare for an even greater expedition, sending out couriers to every part of his empire to raise the necessary troops. For three years the preparations continued, but then Darius suffered two serious checks: Egypt revolted and a quarrel arose over succession to the Persian throne. Though Darius wished both to crush the Egyptian revolt and simultaneously revenge Marathon, Persian law decreed that the king could not march with his army until his successor had been nominated. As was related earlier, Darius' right to the throne had been open to doubt; and now, with seven sons from two wives to choose from, he found it difficult to make up his mind. Eventually Darius nominated Xerxes, the eldest son of his second marriage, on the grounds that he had not been on the throne when the three sons of his first marriage were born. It was a timely decision, because barely a year later in 486 BC, after a reign that had lasted for thirty-six years, Darius died, and Xerxes was able to succeed him without an internecine struggle.

Initially Xerxes showed no interest in invading Greece, thinking only of completing the preparations for the campaign in Egypt. At length, however, he was persuaded by Mardonius, who was his cousin, that, once he had dealt with the Egyptians, he should mount an expedition against Greece. The revolt in Egypt was ruthlessly suppressed in the year following Darius' death, which reduced the country to a state of servitude even worse than it had experienced before. Leaving his brother, Achaemeneis, to govern this wayward province, Xerxes now turned his attention to Greece. First, he held a high-level conference for an exchange of views, which at one stage resulted in his announcing the cancellation of such a hazardous undertaking. The following day, however, he changed his mind, and the preparations, which were to last for four years, were vigorously pursued. Every corner of the empire was ransacked for troops: provisions and equipment were assembled in Cappadocia (approximately in the middle of modern-day Turkey), while supply dumps were established by sea throughout the length of the march, even beyond Eion on the River Strymon and into Macedonia itself. Then, when all was ready, at the head of his enormous army Xerxes ordered the march to begin.

4

Xerxes Invades
480 BC

Herodotus gives a full description of the forty-seven different infantry contingents that made up the Persian army, but only a few will be mentioned here, in order to give an impression of the miscellaneous host that had been assembled. Some of the infantry contingents, such as the Medes, the Cissians and the Persians themselves, carried light wicker shields and were armed with short spears, powerful bows shooting cane arrows, and daggers swinging from belts beside the right thigh. They had no body armour, only embroidered tunics; no helmets, but soft felt caps; and no greaves, but only linen trousers. Other contingents, like the Sarangians, wore brightly coloured clothes and high boots reaching to the knees; while the Ethiopians wore leopard skins and lionskin skirts. It all sounds most decorative, but not very effective against the Greek hoplites with their long thrusting-spears, heavy shields, metal helmets, corslets and greaves. The description Herodotus gives, however, needs to be treated with considerable reserve.

Professor M. Rolin, late Principal of the University of Paris, quotes a number of authors in his *Ancient History*, to give an alternative account:

The ordinary arms of the Persians were a sabre, or scimitar; a kind of dagger, which hung at their belt on the right side; a javelin, or half pike, having a sharp pointed iron at the end. It seems that they carried two javelins, one to fling and the other to fight with. They made great use of the bow and of the quiver in which they carried their arrows. The sling was not unknown amongst them; but they did not set much value by it. It appears from several passages in ancient authors that the Persians wore no helmets, but only their common caps ... yet the same authors, in other places, make mention of their helmets ... The foot for the most part wore cuirasses made of brass, which were so artfully fitted to their bodies, that they were no impediment to the motion and agility of their limbs: no more than the vambraces, or other pieces of armour, which covered the arms, thighs, and legs of the horsemen. Their horses themselves for the most part had their faces, breasts, and flanks covered with brass. These are what are called barbed horse – less spirited than a pure blooded Arab and clearly heavy cavalry. Authors differ very much about the form and fashion of their shields. At first they used very small and light ones: only made of twigs of osier. But it appears from several passages that they also had shields of brass, which were of great length ... The light armed soldiers, that is the archers, slingers etc, composed the bulk of the armies amongst the Persians and Medes. Cyrus (who died about fifty years before Xerxes' invasion) who had found by experience that such troops were only fit for skirmishing, or fighting at a distance, and who thought it most advantageous to come directly to close fight, made a change in his army, and reduced these light troops to very few.

This passage is important, as it contradicts the not uncommonly held belief that the Persians' forthcoming defeats can, to a large extent, be attributed – as they are by Herodotus – to their inferior weapons and lack of body armour. Moreover, as will be put in context later, Herodotus tells us that when he was unhorsed, the Persian cavalry commander proved difficult to kill, because he wore armour, a corslet of gold scales, *under* his scarlet tunic. Appearances were clearly very deceptive. The Persians, especially the infantry, could of course have discarded their body armour in view of the long march ahead, but this seems most unlikely. The Greek hoplites, and later the Roman legionaries, covered enormous distances. For instance, the Spartans made a forced march of more than a hundred miles in three days, when trying to join the Athenians at Marathon; and during the Second Punic War, according to Polybius, when it was learned that Hannibal had crossed the Alps, the Roman legions at Lilybaeum were ordered back to central Italy and averaged more than

twenty miles a day. During such marches, conducted out of contact
with the enemy, there is no reason why the hoplites, or legionaries,
should have remained fully clad; the more cumbersome items could
well have been carried.

But to return to Herodotus, who says that all the national
contingents he mentions could have provided cavalry, though only
the native Persians and Sagaritians – the nomadic tribe that has
already been mentioned – were called upon to do so. The Persian
cavalry contingent was armed in the same way as the infantry, most
noticeably with powerful bows, which, as we will see, were used to
good effect at the battle of Plataea in 479 BC. The 8000 Sagaritians had
a novel way of fighting: once in contact, they would lasso their enemy
and haul towards them whatever they had caught, horse or man. The
victim would then be despatched with the only metal weapon they
carried, a dagger; from Rolin's description, probably a scimitar.
Unfortunately, Herodotus makes no further mention of the Sagaritians, which, if there were really as many of them as he says, is
perhaps surprising.

Herodotus is quite specific in confirming that Persia was not a sea
power, but relied mainly on the Phoenicians, who were used to
support land operations – either by landing troops, as at Marathon,
or, as occurred when Cambyses marched along the Palestinian coast
to invade Egypt, supplying the army by sea. Moreover, when listing
the composition of Xerxes' fleet, Herodotus makes no mention of
Persian ships, but says that, apart from the Phoenicians, there were
Egyptians, Cypriots and Greek colonists: Peloponnesian Dorians –
who must have been from Rhodes, Cos and Halicarnassus – together
with Ionians, Carians, Aeolians and Aegean islanders. These fleets
together provided some 1200 triremes – a conjectural estimate, but
comparable to the figure given by Aeschylus in *The Persians* for the
battle of Salamis.

The crews of these ships, again according to Herodotus, 'wore
body armour' and, except for the Carians who carried riphooks and
daggers, 'were armed in the Greek fashion'. So, as was mentioned
earlier, the mainland Greek crews must also have been equipped like
the hoplites: wearing helmets and body armour, carrying shields and
armed with some form of pike. They, and the Greek colonists serving
in the Persian fleet, were then capable of fighting at sea or on land,
constituting a truly amphibious force. Some of the crews of the other

ten nations contributing ships, noticeably the Phoenicians and Egyptians, had helmets like the Greek ones, and some were armed with shields; all of them carried javelins, swords or bows. The crews of the Persian fleet were thus far better equipped for a land battle than was the army; which makes Herodotus' account of the Persian infantry's equipment all the more improbable.

All the senior fleet commanders were Persian; but since the actual handling of the fleet, as opposed to the individual ships, was not so greatly different from conducting a battle ashore, they (like their Greek counterparts) were expected to be able to act as both admiral and general. The two roles were interchangeable. Finally, all the ships carried some soldiers – Persians, Medes or Sacae (Scythians) – who stood on deck ready for immediate action; so buying time for at least some of the crew to drop their oars and arm themselves for close-quarter fighting.

While the army was on the march, two bridges had been constructed across the Hellespont from Abydos, opposite about the middle of the Gallipoli peninsula, where it is some 1500 yards wide. One of the bridges was constructed by the Phoenicians using flax for the cables, and the other by the Egyptians using papyrus; but after they had been completed they broke up in a storm, so the work had to start afresh. Galleys and triremes were lashed together to carry the bridges: 316 vessels for the one on the Black Sea side, and 314 for the other. The ships were joined by cables, and moored by heavy anchors, so that they were at right angles to the bridge they supported. This time each bridge had a mix of flax and papyrus cables, which were hauled taut by wooden winches ashore. Planks were then laid on the cables and, after being bound together, were covered – first with brushwood, then with earth, which was trodden down. Finally a paling was constructed along each side, high enough to prevent the horses and mules from seeing over and taking fright at the water.

The army had wintered in Sardis, and in the spring of 480 BC it marched to Abydos and the crossing started, with the cavalry and infantry using the bridge nearer the Black Sea, while the pack animals and camp followers used the other. The crossing continued by night and day, taking a week to complete, before the whole army was safely across onto the European shore. When reaching Doriscus, on the Thracian coast about fifty miles west of the neck of the Gallipoli peninsula, Xerxes decided to count his army; so the opportunity was taken to dry out the ships, which were hauled ashore on an adjacent beach.

The counting of the army was done by first packing 10,000 men as close together as they could stand; then, after a circle had been marked out around them, they were dismissed and a waist-high fence constructed, into which successive groups of troops were marched. In this way the grand total (excluding the sailors) amounted to 1,700,000. The figure seems improbably large, as do most of Herodotus' figures, except when it comes to Greek casualties, but it would be sheer conjecture to offer any alternative. It was here, at Doriscus, that the description Herodotus gives of the different national contingents was actually made, but as where it took place is irrelevant, it seems more logical for this to be done at the start; not least because the various contingents, even if they had joined during the march, would have remained together after their arrival, and not, as one historian says, all jumbled up until being sorted out at Doriscus.

After reviewing the army, Xerxes had the fleet launched, and he sailed along the line of anchored ships before the advance was resumed. As will be recalled, Thrace had been conquered by Megabazus, and Macedonia made tributary to Persia by Mardonius; so, as he passed through, Xerxes swelled his ranks still further with the enforced enrolment of additional troops from the inland cities and ships from the coastal ones. Not only were the subject towns and Grecian colonies stripped of their manpower in this manner, but, in spite of the pre-positioned supply dumps, they were brought to near ruin by having to feast Xerxes and provide for his army. As the Persians continued their locust-like progress across the forty-mile-wide Chalcidice peninsula to Therma, at the head of the Thermaic Gulf, the fleet rounded the three trident-like promontories that protrude into the Aegean Sea. Once reunited at Therma, the army spread along the coastline, while Xerxes called a halt and planned his next move. Both Herodotus and Thucydides say that, to avoid a repetition of the disaster that had overtaken Mardonius' fleet when rounding the Mount Athos promontory, Xerxes had had a canal dug across its neck. This does, however, seem improbable; there were still two further, equally hazardous, promontories to be rounded, and in his *Ancient History* Rolin says that a French traveller could find no trace of the canal in the early sixteenth century. On the other hand, Professor J. A. R. Munro, writing in *The Cambridge Ancient History*, claims that vestiges were still visible at the beginning of the 20th century.

Until now the Persians had been conducting no more than an approach march, but having reached the Thessalian frontier they faced the prospect of encountering opposition. Although some mention has already been made of the courses open to Xerxes, let us now try and assess them and, having done so, consider those open to the Greeks. As has already been stated, Xerxes' strategic aim was the conquest of Greece. At the operational level, he had two ways of achieving this: either by advancing into Greece with his force concentrated; or by executing a pincer movement by dividing his force. There were three advantages to keeping the army and the fleet concentrated: overwhelming and coordinated force could be brought to bear by land and sea; amphibious landings could be made in strength down the Grecian coast to outflank opposition – in the same way as the Allies did in Italy during the Second World War with landings at Salerno and Anzio; and the resupply of the army would be assured. The only disadvantage was that, lacking any element of surprise at the operational level, the Greeks would be able to anticipate the course of events and act to counter them.

There were also three advantages to executing a wide pincer movement: if the Persians landed on the island of Cythera, the Spartans would look to their own security and return home, almost certainly taking the other Peloponnesians with them; the Athenians would be left practically alone, and so powerless to withstand a land assault; and finally, all this could be achieved by merely posing a threat from Cythera. There would be no need to do anything more, at any rate initially. The disadvantages were: first, until naval supremacy had been won, dividing the Persian fleet ran the risk of being defeated in detail; and second, the problems of resupplying two widely separated forces would be greatly increased. So Xerxes, supremely confident in being able to overwhelm any resistance, even if the Greeks could anticipate his intentions, saw no reason to run the risks inherent in dividing his force.

As we have seen, the Greeks had received long warning of the Persians' intentions and, following the conference under the presidency of Sparta, held at the Isthmus of Corinth in 481 BC, a number of pan-Hellenic initiatives were taken. The quarrel between Athens and Aegina was settled, at any rate for the duration of the Persian threat; and efforts were made to enlist the support of the Cretans and the powerful tyrant Gelon of Syracuse, but these came to nothing. Though the Corcyraeans promised assistance, in the event they reneged. The Greeks were then left on their own to counter the Persian invasion, but there was no unanimity of view as to how this should be achieved. The dilemma facing the Greeks was similar to that facing NATO nearly 2500 years later during the Cold War. Should the operational concept be to defend forward, irrespective of the ground, or in depth using some major natural obstacle? Except for those whose frontiers were directly threatened – as was the case respectively with Thessaly and with Germany – the other Greek states and NATO countries were sceptical about the practicability of holding an overwhelming force on ground that did not lend itself to defence. Amongst the Greeks, Sparta and the other Peloponnesians then favoured defending the Isthmus of Corinth, while the Athenians preferred the pass at Thermopylae, and the Thessalians the defile at Tempe. Within NATO, the British, who commanded the Northern Army Group, originally favoured holding back on the River Weser. The Americans, who commanded the Southern Army Group, were less geographically specific; they just wanted to trade space for time, so avoiding the early use of tactical nuclear weapons, which could escalate into a strategic exchange. After rearming and joining NATO, the Germans, who were represented in both army groups, wanted to hold every inch of their border. For political reasons the Germans won their case, and NATO adopted the twin strategy of Forward Defence and Flexible Response. Militarily, they were uneasy bedfellows; but let us leave aside NATO and consider more fully the three possible positions for the defence of Greece.

The Spartans wanted to hold back on the Isthmus of Corinth. That was clearly unacceptable to all but the Peloponnesians, and it is surprising that they ever thought it possible. Apart from abandoning Athens and the rest of Greece, all of which might have come to terms with Xerxes, there would have been no need for the Persians to attempt to break through the fortified Isthmus; possessing complete maritime superiority, all they would need to do was bypass the Isthmus and land elsewhere. On the other extreme, the Thessalians wanted to hold well forward. As will be recalled, following their appeal, 10,000 Athenian and Spartan hoplites had been sent to secure the defile at Tempe, which wound its way between Mount Olympus and Mount Ossa, through which flowed the Peneius river. The coast road from Macedonia into Thessaly could then be easily blocked, but the position was found to be untenable. During the summer another route was open, which led over the mountain range of Olympus; though this could probably also have been held, should the Persians land further down the coast, the whole position would be turned. Moreover, the Thessalians, whatever their envoys had said, do not seem to have been wholehearted in their determination to oppose Xerxes. Herodotus only refers to some Thessalian cavalry reinforcements at Tempe who, other than acting as a forward screen or covering the rear, would not have been of great value.

Finally, according to Herodotus, Alexander of Macedonia (though hardly in person) advised the Greeks to withdraw, or they would be trampled to death. As his advice seemed sound and was clearly offered in a friendly spirit, we can assume that it was not so simplistic as it sounds. Most probably Tempe was abandoned because, if it were not to be outflanked, the Persian fleet would have to be brought to battle on the open sea, where the full weight of its numerical superiority could be exercised. So the hoplites re-embarked and Thessaly, as she warned she would, came to terms with Xerxes, who by then was at Abydos preparing to cross the Hellespont.

To divert momentarily from the main theme. The shadowy appearance of Alexander has an historical replay of greater substance. After the Prussians' defeats at Jena and Auerstadt in 1806, they had been divided in their loyalties. Some had sided with Napoleon, while others (like von Clausewitz) had chosen to oppose him by joining the Russians. When Napoleon was conducting his ignominious retreat from Moscow in 1812, the Prussians formed the advance guard of the pursuing Russians and the rearguard of the retreating French. It was then that Clausewitz crossed the lines to try and persuade his fellow countrymen to abandon the French and, with him, to declare Prussian neutrality – a move that was agreed by the officers on the spot and, without much option, ultimately confirmed by those who ruled in Prussia. But to return to the more distant past.

The Greeks now held another conference at the Isthmus to decide what to do next. But before recounting what occurred, Themistocles needs a proper introduction. We have already met him briefly, when discussing the Delphic oracle's prophecy that Athens should trust her defence 'to her wooden walls', which Themistocles interpreted as meaning her fleet. After Miltiades, the victor at Marathon, had died in disgrace, Themistocles emerged as the greatest Athenian leader of the period. His major achievement, which altered the course of history, was to persuade the Athenians not to share out the newly found wealth from the silver mines of Laurium, but instead to construct a fleet. The enemy at the time were seen as the Aeginetans with whom, it will be recalled, there was a smouldering war, until the threat of Xerxes' invasion temporally damped it down. In this way Athens became a major maritime power, which was to prove her salvation at Salamis, where Themistocles commanded the Athenian fleet. But here we must leave him for the moment, or we will be running too far ahead of events.

At the Isthmus conference it was decided to hold the Persians at Thermopylae. Here the narrow pass, and the restricted channel that separates the island of Euboea from the mainland, would severely restrict the deployment of the Persian troops and fleet. Additionally, the nearly 100-mile-long island would make it difficult to turn the position by landing further down the coast. This could, of course, be done, but it would entail conducting two widely separate battles, which – even if eventually successful – would initially have little impact on one another.

Herodotus gives a very disjointed and tangled account of the fighting at sea, so the picture has to be pieced together. The Greek plan was to hold the Persian advance at Thermopylae and block the Euboean Straits by positioning a fleet of some 270 warships at Artemisium, on the northern tip of the island. In this way they would hold the interior lines, while preventing any close cooperation between the Persian army and fleet. The Persian plan was to force the pass of Thermopylae, and destroy the Athenian fleet by confronting them at Artemisium, while sending 200 ships round Euboea to seal the southern passage, thus preventing their escape. When still off the coast of Magnesia, however, the fleet was caught in a sudden storm: those ships that were lying inshore were safely beached, but those standing further out to sea were driven onto the rocks around the foot of Mount Pelian, where they were smashed to pieces. Herodotus says that, at the lowest estimate, 400 ships were lost. But even if this is an exaggeration, after having sent 200 ships round Euboea the fleet facing the Greeks at Artemisium must have been greatly reduced.

Eurybiades, the Spartan admiral commanding the Greek fleet, had learned not only of the storm but, from a deserter, of the Persian intentions. So, after sending a detachment to secure his rear at Chalcis, where the Straits narrow into a slim waist, he decided to take the offensive himself. Sailing out into the mouth of the Straits, the Greeks formed into a close circle with their bows pointing outwards, whereupon the Persians left their moorings and, being numerically superior, were able to encircle them. But no sooner had they done so than the Greeks suddenly launched themselves into the attack, capturing or destroying thirty Persian ships. It was not a decisive engagement, and with the approach of night both fleets withdrew to their respective stations. Another storm then completely disrupted the Persian plans, leaving the main Persian fleet in a state of disorganisation, while completely destroying the 200 ships making their way round Euboea to the south. Now that it was no longer necessary for the Greeks to cover their rear, the fifty-three Athenian ships from Chalcis were ordered back to reinforce the main fleet.

After recovering from the storm, the Persian fleet sailed out in a great crescent, as though to engulf the Greeks off Artemisium, but after some severe fighting, during which they both suffered heavily, the indecisive engagement was broken off. The two fleets then returned to their moorings, where they took stock of the situation. The Greeks had been so roughly handled, with half the remaining Athenians ships being damaged, that they considered their position untenable. The decision was then taken to withdraw, but hardly had this been agreed when news of what had occurred at Thermopylae reached them. With no purpose now being served by remaining at Artemisium, the Greeks got under way, sailing down the Euboean Straits, with the Corinthians leading and the Athenians bringing up the rear.

While all this naval activity had been going on, at Thermopylae the Greeks had secured the pass, though with no more than what amounted to an advance guard. The move of the main force was delayed by two festivals: that of Carneia, which prevented the Spartans from taking the field, and the Olympic games, which delayed all the others. As has been related, military operations were frequently hampered by the need to observe religious ceremonies, and we now have this truly amazing example. The whole future of Greece was at stake, yet these venerated festivals could not be cut short, no doubt because to do so would be to enrage the gods and lose their indispensable support at this critical moment.

The Greek force that was then available for the defence of Thermopylae consisted of 300 Spartans and some 5000 others, including 400 from Thebes as a test of their loyalty, all under the command of Leonidas, one of the two Spartan kings. Leonidas had chosen the Spartan contingent from middle-aged men who had living sons; perhaps because, having passed their youthful prime, and bred the next generation to fill the ranks, they were regarded as being more readily expendable.

When Xerxes learned that his advance was going to be contested, he paused for four days, according to Herodotus, waiting for them to withdraw, not believing that such a small force would be so foolhardy as to try and bar his way. This sounds unlikely. Herodotus says that a Persian scout, who had gone forward and watched the Spartans preparing for battle, could not see the whole Greek army. Moreover, for Xerxes to have kept his host waiting, because of resistance he contemptuously expected to be able to brush aside, makes no sense. There is a more probable explanation. When Xerxes reached Thermopylae, his fleet was still making its way down the coast off Magnesia, near Mount Pelian, about twenty-five miles north of the Euboean Straits, when, as will be recalled, it was caught in a storm that lasted for three days. Only after it had ended did the fleet continue down the coast, round the southern point of Magnesia, and turn into the mouth of the Euboean Straits. Xerxes would not have wished to precipitate the Greeks' fleet into withdrawing from Artemisium by prematurely bursting through at Thermopylae; so he waited for his fleet.

When the Persians did attack at Thermopylae, first with the Medes and later with the Immortals themselves, they were unable to bring their larger numbers to bear, made no progress and finally withdrew. The next day the Persian attacks were renewed, but the Greeks, by rotating their front-line contingent, were able to replace their losses with fresh troops. Only the Phocians took no part in the two days of fighting; instead, they had been posted to guard a small track running over the mountains, which bypassed Thermopylae. Now, just after the Persians had called off their attacks for the second time, the existence of this track was revealed to Xerxes, and as dusk fell a Persian force started to follow its winding course up into the hills. By dawn it had reached the crest where the Phocians were holding, but they, almost unbelievably, had seemingly failed to position an outpost further down the track. They were surprised and, being caught still arming themselves, took refuge on one of the nearby peaks. Here the Persians disdainfully left them, and pressed on along the now descending track with all possible speed.

Deserters had come in during the night warning the Greeks of the Persian move round their flank, and as day was breaking their lookout men came running down the hillside to confirm the Persian movement. After a quick conference, the Greeks split. Most of them withdrew before being cut off, but Leonidas with his 300 Spartans and 700 loyal Thespians (Thespiae was in Boeotia) remained, together with 400 Thebans who were given no choice.

Perhaps because Leonidas knew that his small force would inevitably be crushed whatever he did, he decided to move forward onto a wider stretch of the pass to meet the Persian attack. Here the Spartans and the Thespians stood and fought, until those Persians who had been following the mountain track started to close in from the rear. They then withdrew to the narrow neck, where, in a single compact body, they made their final stand on an adjacent hill, before being finally overwhelmed. Meanwhile the Thebans, who had been compelled to make some display of resistance, as soon as the Spartans and Thespians had withdrawn, went forward to surrender. Advancing with outstretched arms, they pleaded that they had been the first to submit to Xerxes by willingly giving earth and water, and had been forced against their will to join the Spartans at Thermopylae. Uncertain as to their intentions, the Persians killed some of them as they approached, but though the rest were spared, beginning with their commander, they were branded with the royal mark to show that they were untrustworthy slaves.

So ended the Greek attempt to check the Persian advance; but had it not been for the storms, or if preferred the intervention of the gods, their fleet would not have escaped to fight again at Salamis. Xerxes had spent four days waiting and three days fighting, while his fleet had been storm-bound for three days, sailing for one, and scrapping for three; which confirms that the breakthrough at Thermopylae occurred almost simultaneously with the Greek decision to withdraw from Artemisium. According to Herodotus, it was now that Demaratus advised Xerxes to seize the island of Cythera, so drawing the Spartans back to defend their homeland. Perhaps this was so, but it was far too late to have put forward such a proposal. Following their victory, no major obstacle now stood between the Persians and Athens, a mere 100 miles away – a fraction of the enormous distance that had already been covered. Moreover, until reaching the border of Attica, only the Phocians would be likely to offer any resistance, all the other Greeks having submitted. The way ahead was clear, so after Xerxes had finished burying his own dead, and displaying the slain Greeks to impress his followers, the advance was resumed.

After devastating Phocis, Xerxes marched with the main body of the army through Boeotia to Athens, while a small contingent made for Delphi, skirting the foothills of Mount Parnassus, which it kept to its right. As the Boeotians had already submitted, Xerxes reached Athens without encountering any resistance. The detachment of Persians tasked with robbing the temple at Delphi was not so fortunate. As they approached the holy sanctuary, they were struck by thunderbolts from the sky and swept away, as two great pinnacles of rock came crashing down the slopes of Mount Parnassus. The more sceptical may think that the Persians had been caught in a landslide, possibly of their own making, but whatever the cause, the result was the same: those who survived the rockfall were despatched by the good people of Delphi. Here we must leave the Persians for the moment, in order to see what the Greeks had been doing after the Thermopylae–Artemisium position had been lost.

Herodotus says that, instead of the Peloponnesians withdrawing to defend the Isthmus, the Athenians had expected them to concentrate their full strength in Boeotia, where the Persian advance would be held. Very understandably, this is what the Athenians wanted; but could they really have expected it, when they had played no part in the defence of Thermopylae? Their absence seems inexplicable, especially when they had so much more to lose than Peloponnesian cities like Sparta, Tegea and Mantinea, which had all sent contingents. Moreover, the Peloponnesians had only renounced defending the Isthmus in response to the Athenian appeal to hold the pass, and all had been equally involved with religious ceremonies. Nor was there any other position that the Athenians could have been preparing; their city now lay open and was being hurriedly evacuated.

The Greeks had, however, agreed to assemble the fleet at Salamis, from where it would be well placed to counter any Persian move into the Saronic Gulf and, as Herodotus emphasises, it could help with the evacuation of Attica. Shipping most of the population to Troezen, on the coast of Argolis, with others going to Aegina and Salamis, was certainly a major task, but it was unlikely to have been the determining consideration for choosing Salamis. There were some Athenians, however, who refused to be evacuated, preferring to take refuge in the Acropolis: here, persisting in their literal interpretation of the Delphic oracle's pronouncement about 'the wooden wall not being taken', they erected a stockade of timber. But after a spirited resistance the Persians broke in, butchered everybody they found and destroyed everything they could by fire. Three months after crossing the Hellespont, Xerxes was master of mainland Greece, and Athens was in ruins; all that needed to be done was to finish off the Peloponnesians.

The Greeks now held a council of war to decide what to do, and Eurybiades, having stipulated that the next fleet action must take place in some part of Greece still under their control (which therefore excluded Attica), called for suggestions. The majority voted for sailing to the Isthmus, and when the conference broke up that night they returned to prepare their ships for departure. Themistocles, however, went to see Eurybiades and put squarely before him the consequences of the decision, which were much the same as those that made the Greeks abandon Tempe, in favour of Thermopylae and Artemisium.

Fighting at the Isthmus would involve doing so on the open sea, where the Greeks' smaller numbers and slower ships would be gravely disadvantaged. Moreover, Salamis, Megara and Aegina would be lost, and the Persian army drawn south to the Peloponnese. Finally, there was the danger that the miscellaneous Greek fleet would disintegrate, seeking to disperse to its various homelands, rather than rallying at the Isthmus. On the other hand, fighting in a confined space would largely redress the disadvantages of having fewer and slower ships, while keeping the Persians away from the Peloponnese. Finally, Themistocles told Eurybiades that, should he withdraw to the Isthmus, the Athenian families would be embarked and the fleet would sail to Italy, where Athens already had a number of established settlements. Appreciating that without the 180 Athenian ships it would be impossible to oppose the Persians, Eurybiades agreed to stay and fight at Salamis. At any rate, this is the account Herodotus gives, but it is hard to believe he got the issue right.

Salamis is only a few miles from the Isthmus, so the fleet was already well placed for its defence; while to have withdrawn in order to defend the Isthmus still more closely would have risked being boxed in against the shoreline, with no room for manoeuvre. More probably, what concerned the Peloponnesians was that, if it were decided to remain at Salamis and fight in the Straits, the Persians might not take the bait, choosing instead to wait until necessity drove the Greeks out onto the open sea, while they assaulted the Isthmus or landed elsewhere. Far better, then, to prevent the Persian fleet from reaching the Isthmus, by engaging them well forward in the Saronic Gulf. This, however, was not to be. But before relating what occurred, a short topographical introduction might be helpful.

The island of Salamis is approximately five miles long, approached from the west and east by two narrow straits, one between Salamis and Megara, and the other between Salamis and the mouth of the Piraeus. The latter is divided by the island of Psyttaleia into two channels, the western one being about half a mile wide and the eastern one a little more than three-quarters of a mile. Both channels lead into the spacious Eleusis Bay, which provided a natural harbour. On a much smaller scale, the geographical setting is then similar to that at Euboea, though tactically, this time, the Greeks actually wanted the Persians to try and bottle them up. Some of what Herodotus has to say about the fighting sounds more legendary than historical, but a number of facts can be drawn from Aeschylus, who took part in the battle and wrote his account in *The Persians*, some eight years later. From what Herodotus says, it was Themistocles who addressed the fleet, presumably to explain his plan, and then gave the order to embark. Eurybiades may well have accepted that, as the Athenian contingent was by far the largest, and the plan was Themistocles', he should explain its execution. To avoid the danger that the Persians would not try and block the Straits, Themistocles proposed that they should be misled into believing that the Greeks were going to abandon Salamis, and should thus be drawn into trying to prevent them. This audacious ruse was accepted by Eurybiades; so a trusted messenger was sent to pass on this misinformation, which seems to have contained no details as to where the Greeks intended to go, thus making it all the more imperative to concentrate on trapping them at Salamis.

The Persian fleet was at Phalerum, some ten miles due east of Salamis, and it was here that Xerxes was informed of the Greeks' intentions. After holding a conference with his admirals, he gave the order, in the words of Aeschylus, to 'range the main body of our fleet threefold, to guard the outlets and the choppy straits'; one group to block the western exit, and the other two to take station either side of Psyttaleia, the small island that divides the sound into two channels. At the same time, the island was to be secured, assuring its availability for shipwrecked Persian crews, while denying it to the Athenians. A number of ships were also posted round Salamis, presumably to facilitate communications and watch out for the unexpected. Once darkness had fallen, the three groups moved to their positions, with the Egyptians (who were deploying to the western, or Megarian, channel) moving first, then the Phoenicians and last of all the Ionians, who were closest to the Attic coast. The Greeks only learned that their ruse had succeeded when Themistocles' exiled political rival Aristides, who had sailed from Aegina and eluded the Persian blocking force, came to offer his support.

The Corinthians, who, since they only had sixteen ships, must have been supported by others, were sent to hold the Megarian channel. The main fleet moved due east along the coast, emerging at daybreak from behind the finger-shaped eastern promontory, to close the mile-wide mouth of the Straits. The Persians immediately surged forward to meet them, passing on either side of Psyttaleia, to flow together again and concentrate against the Greek centre; which, Herodotus says, back-paddled until they almost grounded, against what can only have been the Attic coast. The wings then wheeled inwards to develop a sack, into which the Persians now poured. As Aeschylus, talking as a Persian, says: 'The enemy came round us in a ring and charged.' It was a naval replay of what happened to Darius at Marathon, and what would happen to Varro at Cannae: assaulted on the flanks, checked in the centre and fouling one another in the crush, all coordinated resistance ended. But the trap was never fully closed, permitting at least half the Persian fleet to escape. According to Herodotus, who gives no account of the losses, some 380 Greek ships were present at Salamis, nearly all triremes. And Aeschylus writes:

Three hundred vessels made the total Hellene strength,
Not counting ten picked warships, Xerxes had, I know,
A thousand at his command, the vessels built for speed
Numbered two hundred and seven, so stands the count.

Even if Aeschylus' numbers are correct, not all the Persian fleet was at Salamis; some, for example, were at Cythnos, an island about 160 miles south-east of Salamis. Moreover, the thousand vessels to which Aeschylus refers must have included a considerable number of transport and supply ships, and it seems that about one-third of the warships had been sent to block the Megarian channel; certainly far more than the Greeks would have sent as a rearguard. So the Persians probably did not have greatly superior numbers at the main fleet action, though, according to Diodorus, they suffered far more heavily, losing 200 ships as opposed to the Greeks' forty. Salamis was not an annihilating victory – a fact recognised by the Greeks who, after retaking Psyttaleia and salvaging what they could from the flotsam and jetsam of battle, prepared themselves for a further assault.

Mardonius, who, it will be remembered, had commanded the first Persian attempt to invade Greece, now proposed two alternative plans to Xerxes. The first was to attack the Peloponnese: the army was still intact and had only been let down by the Phoenicians, Egyptians, Cypriots and others who comprised the fleet. Alternatively, if Xerxes wished to return to Persia then he, Mardonius, should be left behind with 300,000 picked troops to continue the campaign. Why Xerxes chose the second option and called off the expedition remains something of a mystery. Various reasons have been put forward: pusillanimity, anxiety about what was occurring in the rest of the Empire, or news of the recent Carthaginian defeat in Sicily. As will be remembered, there was an alleged treaty between the Carthaginians and Xerxes, whereby the Greeks would be eliminated by a vast pincer movement: the Carthaginians seizing Sicily and southern Italy, while Xerxes occupied Greece. If this were so, then with one arm of the pincer irreparably broken, and the tip of the other blunted, Xerxes may have felt that by destroying Athens he had exacted sufficient revenge for the Athenian burning of Sardis. Additionally, the army would now be confined to unsupported land operations and cut off from its external source of supplies. But whatever the reasons, by deciding to depart, Xerxes turned a tactical victory into a major strategic one with consequences that still affect our lives today.

Having reached his decision, Xerxes gave orders for the fleet to leave Phalerum and sail to the Hellespont, where it was to guard the bridges, while Mardonius was authorised to select his stay-behind force. When the Greeks learned of the Persian fleet's withdrawal, their first reaction was to set sail for the Hellespont and break the bridges. But Eurybiades persuaded them that it would be better to let Xerxes escape, arguing that if he were cut off, he might renew the campaign – an improbable eventuality. The Greeks are more likely to have realised that there was more important business to be done at home: Athens was in ruins, the Athenian families dispersed, the crews needed resting and the ships repairing, winter was approaching, and there was plunder to be gathered. So the Greek fleet turned back, and the Persian army began its departure, accompanied by Mardonius as far as Thessaly, where he proposed to spend the winter. On leaving Greece, the Persians were beset by hunger and disease, and assailed by those whom they had treated so haughtily when passing through the other way; they were forced to abandon their sick and wounded, all of whom received short shift. Then, when the army reached the Hellespont, they found that nature had undertaken the work of the Greeks – the bridges lay broken. There was no question of Xerxes returning to renew the campaign; instead, the remains of his once-proud army, which had taken seven days and seven nights to cross the Straits some eight months previously, were ferried ignominiously back again by the fleet.

Mardonius at Plataea

Before looking at what Mardonius had been doing, we will round off the character sketch of Themistocles, which had taken him as far as Salamis. After the last of the Persians had been driven out of Greece, Themistocles devoted himself to the rebuilding and fortification of Athens, while developing Piraeus as a port. According to Plutarch, 'Themistocles, however, did not, as Aristophanes the comic poet puts it, knead the Piraeus on to the city; on the contrary, he attached the city to the Piraeus and made the land dependent on the sea.' The result was to increase the influence of the common people at the expense of the nobility. The fêted, and increasingly indispensable, crews of the triremes now exercised a powerful influence in determining policy. But Themistocles, after emerging as the hero of Salamis – even being awarded special recognition by the Spartans – destroyed his high standing through greed and unbridled ambition. As a result, in about 472 BC the Athenians decided to banish him, making use of ostracism to humble his great reputation and authority. Though there were suggestions that Themistocles had been hedging his bets with the Persians, it is still somewhat surprising that he eventually sought refuge at Susa. Here, according to Plutarch, rather than comply with the royal command to serve Persian interests at the expense of his fellow countrymen, he committed suicide. Thucydides, however (rather more prosaically but certainly with greater authority, since he lived far closer to the times), says that Themistocles died a natural death, adding that 'some people' say he killed himself, in despair at being unable to fulfil his promises to the king.

In the spring of 479 BC Mardonius left his winter quarters in Thessaly and, accompanied by those Greeks who had gone over to the Persians, marched on Athens. As the story of the Phocians has already been told, it will not be repeated here. Once again the Peloponnesians failed to assist the Athenians, preferring to continue with the fortification of the Isthmus. But after much recrimination 5000 Spartans, under the command of Pausanias, each of them attended by seven Helots, eventually set out from Lacedaemonia for the Isthmus. Here they were joined by other Peloponnesians and, after receiving favourable omens from the sacrifice, crossed over to meet up with the Athenians.

When Mardonius heard that the Spartans were on the march, he destroyed what little there was left of Athens and withdrew to Boeotia; choosing a piece of ground that favoured the use of cavalry, with the friendly and fortified city of Thebes to his rear. Following their entry into Boeotia, the Greeks kept to the high ground. When they showed no intention of descending onto the plain, Mardonius recklessly launched his cavalry into the attack. Charging in successive squadrons, the Persians succeeded in pressing back a part of the Greek line; but when their commander, Masistius, was killed and a final desperate attempt to recover his body failed, they withdrew, loudly lamenting their loss. As was mentioned earlier, Herodotus did not believe that the Persians wore body armour, and later says that this was one of the causes of their defeat. But in his account of how Masistius died, he clearly states that he was wearing 'a corslet of golden scales *under* his scarlet tunic, upon which no blow had any effect'. The Greeks now decided to give up their position, seemingly at night after the day's fighting, and move onto lower ground just north of Plataea, which, though only broken by the occasional low hill, was afforded some protection by the River Asopus to their front, while a nearby spring provided a plentiful supply of badly needed water. Maybe it was the need for water that made Pausanias decide to move; but there is another possible reason that will be discussed later. When Mardonius learned of the Greeks' move, he shifted his own position to the north bank of the Asopus, from where he faced the Greeks on the opposite bank.

According to Herodotus, the Greek army numbered 110,000, which included 69,500 lightly armed auxiliaries and 1800 Thespians who, for some undisclosed reason, were not armed. The Spartans were positioned on the right flank, the Athenians on the left, with the seventeen other contingents filling the centre. As for Mardonius' 300,000-strong army – if Herodotus' figure is any guide – the Persians were posted on the left flank, opposite the Spartans, and on the right flank were the Boeotians, who faced the Athenians. In the centre were a host of contingents, drawn from all over the Empire, possibly including as many as 50,000 Greeks. Mardonius seems to have made a strangely assorted choice when selecting those to remain with him, but perhaps more homogeneity would not have resulted in greater operational effectiveness; so all should have a share in the anticipated victory or fear-laden gamble.

As has already been recounted – when we were looking at the Greek attitude to religion – for eight days the two armies faced one another, until at last Mardonius received a favourable omen from the repeated sacrifices. He then sent his cavalry round the Greek position to a pass running over the hills, through which reinforcements and provisions were arriving. Here the cavalry caught a long supply column of 500 laden mules; most of the unfortunate animals were then slaughtered on the spot, though some were driven back to the Persian lines. After a further two days of inactivity, Mardonius decided to ignore the unfavourable prophecies and attack forthwith. The cavalry was ordered forward to within missile range of the Greeks, then to shower them with arrows and javelins, which caused heavy casualties. At the same time the Persians choked up and fouled the spring, from which those on the Greek right wing had been drawing their water; then, by using their missiles to cover the Asopus, the Persian cavalry denied its water to the rest of the Greeks.

With his supply route interrupted and water unobtainable, Pausanias ordered a night withdrawal onto a piece of ground about a mile further back, which, as it was never occupied, need not concern us. After dark the night move began, and, as anybody who has taken part in such a manoeuvre will not be surprised to learn, it had its problems. First, according to Herodotus, the greater part of the Greek force, which had been under attack all day, decided it had had enough and fled to Plataea. Maybe; but they could just have lost their way and, finding a good track to follow, ended up at Plataea. Then there was trouble with the Spartans. One commander held it to be a dishonour to his country to run away from the enemy, so he refused to move, until finally prevailed upon to do so at dawn. Meanwhile the Athenians had waited to see that the Spartans were really on the move, before they too abandoned their position. So it was not until daylight that the two contingents got under way: the Spartans, together with their loyal Tegeans, keeping to the high ground so as to avoid the Persian cavalry; while the Athenians took the risky decision to keep down on the plain. It did not take long for Mardonius to discover that the Greeks had once again slipped away during the night, and to set out after them in all haste. For those interested in tactics, these two Greek undetected moves portray the importance of remaining in close contact with the enemy. Two similar incidents occurred in the Gallipoli campaign when, under the very noses of the Turks, first the Australians and New Zealanders, then the British, were able to evacuate their separate positions on the peninsula without suffering a single casualty. Mardonius did not learn the lesson after the Greeks' first night move, any more than the Turks did from that of the Australians and New Zealanders. There is a lot to be learned from the study of military history, even if it is some 2500 years old; so let us go back to see what was happening at Plataea.

As the Athenians had been concealed from view by some low hills, they had initially remained undetected; but when the pursuing Persians caught up with the Spartans, and the Athenians turned to help them, they came under attack from the Boeotians, whom they eventually defeated. In the meantime, the Spartans and Tegeans were being hard pressed. Sheltered behind a barricade of wicker shields, the Persians showered the Spartans with arrows, which they stoically withstood while awaiting more favourable results from a second sacrifice. But the Tegeans' patience had expired, so they sprang into the attack, followed shortly afterwards by the Spartans. The fighting that followed was bitter, but when Mardonius was killed, Persian resistance began to crumble and finally broke, and the defeated army fled to its palisaded base camp. Here the Spartans were joined by the Athenians, and when a breach was made, all organised resistance ended, with first the Tegeans, then the Spartans and Athenians, fighting their way in, sparing only a meagre 3000 of those who had sought refuge in the camp. But not all the original 300,000 Persians were present for this final massacre: some 40,000 had earlier marched off the battlefield under their disgruntled commander, Artabazus, who had always opposed Xerxes' decision to leave Mardonius behind in Greece; then there were the Boeotians who, after being defeated by the Athenians, had withdrawn to Thebes; finally there was the cavalry, whose disappearance is not explained. Though only 159 Greeks fell (ninety-one Spartans, sixteen Tegeans and fifty-two Athenians), this does not include those killed earlier, or the casualties suffered by the other contingents.

It was unfortunate that there was no Aeschylus present, as Herodotus' account of the battle is incomplete and lacks an authentic ring. A number of questions present themselves. No mention is made of the part played by the many thousands of Helots, yet when it came to clearing the battlefield, the Helots were interred in one of the three Spartan mass graves. The practice of repeating sacrifices until favourable results were obtained makes the ten days of inactivity seem inexplicable. Why was the cavalry sweep not developed, then or later, into an attack on the Greek rear, like Hannibal's Spanish and Gallic cavalry at Cannae? The disobedience of a subordinate Spartan commander sounds out of character. The abandonment of the battlefield by all the Greeks, but for the Spartans, Tegeans and Athenians, may have occurred; but if so, that they then formed up again at Plataea, instead of decamping completely, makes it look more like a mistake than an intent to desert. In sum, it seems as though Herodotus had been solely dependent on Attic sources, since he gives the impression that, by blaming all the other Greeks for letting the Athenians down, he is covering up for some major failure on their part – perhaps a failed attack across the Asopus, which in itself presented no great obstacle.

Finally, what were the reasons for the Greeks' ultimate victory? Herodotus gives three: the Persians were deficient in armour, untrained and greatly inferior in skill. The Persian deficiency in armour has already been discussed and requires no further comment. That they were untrained and inferior in skill is just two ways of saying the same thing, and is indisputable. But there were other, less clearly definable reasons. The Greeks were fighting for their homes, their families and their very survival, while the majority of the Persians were devoid of any sustainable incentive, other than perhaps plunder and rape. Greece being much smaller than the sprawling Persian Empire, in spite of their many disparities and squabbles the Greeks were far more homogeneous, and therefore cohesive, so they were able to identify themselves as a common race. But in the end Herodotus got it right when he said it was training that accounted for the Greeks' superiority. The exhortation 'train hard in order to fight easy' is as valid today as it was then, and will always remain so.

The Aftermath

There are two matters to be related before closing this account of the Persians: the withdrawal of Artabazus and the battle of Mycale, on the Ionian coast nearly opposite Samos, in 479 BC. As will be recalled, Artabazus left the battlefield disgruntled with the whole campaign, taking 40,000 men with him. That he should have waited to do this until battle had been joined seems unlikely; more probably he had departed after Mardonius had rejected his advice to retire within the fortifications of Thebes, from where they could bribe most of the Greeks into accepting submission. The only trouble with this story is that it would have been impossible to have crammed 300,000 men into a town the size of Thebes; which indicates that either the proposal was never made, or Herodotus' figures are grossly exaggerated. Anyway, Artabazus made it back to Asia, partly because news of the Persian defeat was not yet generally known to people along the route, and partly because, when it was, the resistance he met was not pressed home.

At Mycale, to avoid a naval engagement with a Greek fleet from

Delos, the Persians had beached their ships and constructed a defensive rampart around them, surrounded by an outer ring of stakes. When the Greeks landed further up the coast, the Persians, who wanted to be rid of the untrustworthy Ionians, sent them to guard some tracks leading up to the heights behind. But instead of then fighting from behind their palisade, the Persians formed a defensive line with their interlocking, wicker shields. As the Greeks advanced to the attack, a rumour spread through the ranks that the Persians had been defeated at Plataea that very morning. Inspired by this news, they went into the attack: the Athenians directly along the beach, with the Spartans making a detour through the heights, evidently without meeting the Ionians. Assaulted from two directions, the Persians fought stoutly from behind their line of shields, but were eventually driven back into their stockade, so closely pursued by the Greeks that they had no opportunity to re-form. The barricade was soon breached, whereupon most of the Persians fled, leaving only the native Persians to fight on until they were overwhelmed.

We should not be too quick to discount the possibility that somehow the Greeks did intuitively believe that Mardonius had been defeated at Plataea; there have been other similar incidents. Constantine is said to have seen a cross in the sky when marching on Rome, while Joan of Arc was directed by heavenly voices to save France; and more recently, when the British 3rd and 4th Divisions were nearly overwhelmed while withdrawing from Mons in 1914, their survival is attributed to the appearance of an angel with a flaming sword, symbolically holding back the advancing Germans. Nonsense, one can say; but, for those present at the time, imagery became a living reality.

Mycale, like Plataea, poses a number of questions. Herodotus gives no indication as to the numbers involved, but the fact that the Persians at first fought outside their stockade suggests they were there in considerable force. Nor does Herodotus explain what the purpose of the battle was, though it seems clear that after Plataea, the Greeks' strategic aim was to secure the Aegean. At the operational level, this meant driving the Persians back from the coast of Asia Minor, and in so doing liberating the Greek Asiatic colonies. Whether intentional or not, as Herodotus says, Mycale sparked a second Ionian revolt against Persian domination, with the victorious Greek fleet then sailing to liberate the Hellespont, before returning home. This task was evidently not fully completed, since the following year, as we will see, another combined Greek fleet had to return to capture Byzantium. Moreover, as will be recounted in the following chapter, if Plutarch is correct, it was not until Cimon's sea and land victories at Eurymedon that the Persian power in Ionia was finally broken.

What had started as a seemingly hopeless defensive war for the Greeks finished with an offensive victory that ended the Persian threat and, except for the Thracian seaboard, secured the whole of the Aegean, which increasingly fell under Athenian domination. Tragically, however, once the Persian threat was clearly seen to have receded, and Athens' imperium became unbridled, Greek unity started to fall apart, eventually resulting in a fearful, self-destructive war.

Lessons

Let us now see what lessons can be drawn from the Persian Wars, considering them under the three levels of war that have already been defined: the Strategic, the Operational and the Tactical. Not, however, that such distinctions would have been made at the time.

The Strategic Level

The first thing to note is that both the Persians and the Greeks had reasonably balanced forces, with their fleets and armies working together in close cooperation under a single, joint command, in pursuit of clear strategic objectives. Their strategic thinking was then not limited to land or sea warfare; they had the capability to project power so long as, in the case of the Persians, their hold on the Empire did not weaken, and in the case of the Greeks, the alliance held together. Darius' strategic aim was the conquest of Greece, while that of Xerxes appears to have been the elimination of the Greeks as a Mediterranean power.

As for the Greeks, their initial strategic aim was to defend their homeland, and not until this had been achieved did their aim change to securing the Aegean. But even then, if only because they lacked the resources to do otherwise, the Greeks' aim was strictly limited, and there was never any question of their offensive developing into a major land campaign. The need to have a clear strategic aim is illustrated by Darius' near-disastrous campaign in Scythia, when he launched himself into a vast wilderness with no purpose other than unlimited conquest. Napoleon and Hitler would have done better to reflect on the strategic lessons of the Persian Wars, rather than try and emulate Alexander the Great and Genghis Khan.

The Operational Level

Darius' plan for the conquest of Greece was straightforward and well founded. Possessing maritime superiority, he would sail to the Greek mainland, disembark his army where he chose and capture Athens. Surprise would be achieved through the uncertainty of when he would set sail, and where he would land. We do not know what Darius' subsequent intentions were; nor may he have formulated any, preferring to keep his options open, waiting to see which of the Greek states would submit, before deciding what needed to be done. Although we cannot be certain, Xerxes' operational plan for the elimination of the Greeks as a Mediterranean power seems to have been on a much wider and more ambitious scale. While he undertook the conquest of Greece itself, the Carthaginians would deal with the Greek settlements in Sicily and Italy. Within this overall concept, Xerxes' plan was to bring overwhelming power to bear by land, while using his naval superiority to sustain his army and, if necessary, to outflank any Greek opposition by landings to their rear. Confident in his ability to crush any opposition, Xerxes rejected the suggestion that he should achieve surprise by dividing his huge force, one arm continuing by land and the other sailing to Cythera, so as to draw off the Spartans and the other Peloponnesian states.

It was fortunate for the Greeks that they had several years' warning of Xerxes' intentions, as it took them an inordinately long time to decide on how to defend their homeland. As will be recalled, the Thessalians wanted to hold forward on their northern boundary at Tempe, while the Spartans wanted to secure the Isthmus. In the end, the Athenian plan to hold at Thermopylae was adopted, with the fleet utilising Euboea to provide flank protection. When the Persians broke through at Thermopylae, all was staked on wrestling maritime superiority from them; so confining their army to unsupported land operations, and cutting it off from external resupply.

The Tactical Level

A number of tactical lessons have already been brought out, but only the more important will be mentioned now. The single most decisive battle-winning factor is surprise. Darius attempted to achieve this by first landing on the island of Euboea, so as to lure the Athenians to its defence. Their army could then be cut off from Athens by a landing at Marathon and, if necessary, by a further one at Phalerum, leaving the isolated city to be taken by pre-arranged betrayal from within. It was a masterly piece of deception, but the Athenians refused to be drawn and, after defeating the Persians at Marathon, they stood ready to confront them again at Phalerum, so negating any uprising.

Surprise was achieved at Marathon and Salamis by the Greeks through manoeuvre. On both occasions the centre gave ground and the wings, specially strengthened at Marathon, then closed round the exposed Persian flanks. Neither battle resulted in the complete success that Hannibal was to achieve at Cannae, when he annihilated eight Roman legions, but the tactical defeat of the Persian fleet at Salamis – however incomplete – had an enormous strategic consequence: the withdrawal of Xerxes and the bulk of his army. At Plataea, through the Persians not maintaining close contact, the Greeks were able to achieve surprise by withdrawing unobserved during the night; as did the British, Australians and New Zealanders at Gallipoli, when the Turks made the same mistake. While at sea off Artemisium, the Greeks – by letting the Persians surround their circle of ships so as to make it look as though they were preparing to fight a defensive battle – suddenly took the offensive and threw the Persians into utter confusion.

Finally, as Herodotus pointed out, it was the superior training of the Greeks that was largely responsible for their victory. It is a lesson that should never be forgotten; that said, training has to be purposefully directed, which is not always the case. Moreover, the need for training does not suddenly stop at a certain rank, for it is a continuous process. Those weak-kneed individuals who seek to know what is going to happen on an exercise, claiming that in this way they can concentrate on training their subordinates, need to be given short shrift.

Here we must leave Herodotus and turn to Thucydides. With the change in historians, there is also a perceptible change in style and

presentation. Whereas Herodotus intersperses his history with diversionary tales, Thucydides is concerned only with recording the
military and political events that occurred. Though one can only
admire his single-mindedness, for better or for worse intrusions will
continue to be made in giving this account.

5

The Inter-War Years
480–431 BC

All major wars bring in their wake enormous changes: political, social, commercial and military. So it was with the Greeks after their defeat of the Persians, though it was some time before they realised just how complete their victory had been. For some years afterwards they feared there would be another onslaught. But even before the threat had receded, a new era was clearly discernible. Though for a short time the wartime alliance held together, it was an unquiet peace, marked by an uneasy relationship between Athens and Sparta. But it was not just between the two major protagonists that tension existed. In northern Greece there were those who had aided the Persians, like Thessaly and Thebes, and in the Peloponnese there was Argos, which had remained neutral – acts of disloyalty that it was not easy to forget, let alone forgive. As for Asia Minor, the situation had radically changed, and that brought about a shift in the balance of power. Before the Asiatic Greeks' total subjection to Persia following the Ionian revolt, they had enjoyed a commercial and cultural standing that exceeded that of Greece itself. Now, however, the centre of gravity shifted across the Aegean, and Athens entered into the commercial and intellectual inheritance of the eastern Greeks. Emerging from the war with a much-enhanced reputation and authority, while remaining an ally, Athens no longer needed to accept Spartan predominance and leadership in Greek affairs; she could steer her own course with increasing confidence.

As we have seen when introducing Themistocles, the internal political scene in Athens had also undergone considerable change. After the battle of Salamis, the aristocrats' near-monopoly over the directing of policy was to be curtailed by the democratic voice of the newly esteemed trireme crews – a voice that was to be nourished and sustained by the growing importance of Themistocles' maritime policy; epitomised by Plutarch's account of how the aristocrat Cimon dedicated his bridle to Athena, as a token of his recognition that Athens depended not upon her cavalry, but upon the sea. The result was that the citizens as a whole came to exert a far greater influence in the Assembly, not only over policy, but administration generally. But while these political developments were taking place, Athens had to be rebuilt and, once this task had been completed, Themistocles turned his attention to its future security. Piraeus was fortified and its three natural harbours developed, not only for use by the greatly enlarged fleet, but also adapted for commercial purposes with the construction of quays and warehouses.

As has already been described, Athens and Piraeus were then connected by a near-impregnable wall which, when completed in spite of Spartan protests, enabled the Athenians to follow a new strategic direction. As Athens lacked the manpower both to field an army capable of resisting a major attack, and simultaneously to maintain a fleet large enough to win her maritime supremacy, her security would rest on her ships and fortifications. It is best described as a strategy of sword and shield, whereby Athens would dominate the Aegean militarily and commercially, while assured of her security at home. Almost inevitably, as the Persian threat receded and Athenian power grew, this maritime and commercial supremacy led to domination. The free association of states and cities, believed to number some 150, which formed the Delian League was slowly turned into an Athenian Empire with, as will be remembered, the Treasury being moved from Delos to Athens. Tribute money was no longer used solely for common defence, but was diverted by Pericles into his ambitious schemes for the prestigious enhancement of Athens.

As Pericles is going to figure so prominently from now until his death in 429 BC, he requires an introduction. The date of his birth is uncertain, but is thought to have been about 495 BC, so he would have been a boy of thirteen when the Persians were finally expelled. Plutarch implies that one of Pericles' teachers was the Ionian philosopher factor Anaxagoras, but though Pericles was greatly influenced by him, it was only after he had reached manhood.

Anaxagoras was intelligence personified – his nickname was *Nous*, 'The Mind' – and, cutting through superstition, he sought a cause for physical phenomena, maintaining that the seeming confusion of things could only be given a sense of order by intellect. It was through Pericles' close association with Anaxagoras that he not only acquired knowledge that put him above the superstitions of the time, but learned how to compose himself, maintaining a natural dignity whatever the circumstances.

That is one side of the coin. The other is that, being the scion of an aristocratic family, Pericles had a chilling air of superiority, being disdainful and arrogant in the way he spoke to people, and proud, supercilious and contemptuous of others. Because conviviality and familiarity broke down even the most majestic demeanour, Pericles never attended social events, even going so far as to refuse his friends' invitations to dinner. He also distanced himself from the ordinary people, only occasionally addressing them, and declining to involve himself in what he regarded as inconsequential matters, reserving himself instead for matters of importance or great occasions.

He was certainly disliked by Plato, but this was probably because of his political views; though an aristocrat, Pericles was the leader of the People's Party, the democratic rabble, whom Plato held in scant regard. Thucydides characterises Pericles' administration as being distinctly aristocratic: 'democracy in name, but in practice, government by the first citizen'. Others give Pericles credit for allotting land to the Athenians that belonged to subject people; not unlike the British colonisation of Australia, New Zealand, the New World and parts of Africa, which would be regarded with opprobrium today. Pericles also funded public festivals and paid for public services; today, in another reversal of perceptions, this would be regarded as a good thing, but at the time it was condemned by many people (including Plato) for encouraging extravagance and raising expectations, at the cost of frugality and self-sufficiency. Pericles can then be viewed as either a noble, inspirational ruler or a vain, opportunistic demagogue. There is no telling, but the truth probably lies somewhere between the two extremes.

However, one thing is quite certain: he plunged Athens into an unnecessary war, so he bears ultimate responsibility for her suffering and downfall. This is, of course, a disturbing judgement to make about a man when many feel that the flawless splendour of his public buildings must somehow reflect his character, and that he would be incapable of holding anything but the noblest political ambitions. This was no doubt right as far as Athens was concerned, but Pericles' policy was the creation of a magnificent city, with imperialism and art going hand-in-hand. It is then not a great step for such a proud, disdainful man to regard it as no more than an extension of his policy to subordinate Sparta. But here we must leave him for the moment and return to earlier days.

At the end of the Persian War, not only had the commercial prominence of the Ionian Greeks been diminished, but also that of Euboea, with its two important cities, Eretria and Chalcis. There were then only three contestants ready to exploit the new opportunities for expanding trade: Corinth, Aegina and Athens. Geographically, Corinth was well placed, with ports on both sides of the Isthmus, giving her access to markets as far afield as Syracuse and Ionia. But other considerations were not so favourable, the ill-will that existed between Corinth and her foundling settlement, Corcyra, if not posing a serious threat to the western sea routes, doing nothing to ease the inherent difficulties of the long journey from the Corinthian Gulf to Sicily; while to the east, Corinthian trade across the Aegean had never been very great and, perhaps because of the Athenians' increasing domination of the Saronic Gulf, she seemed uncertain about trying to establish anything of significance now. Aegina, possessing enterprising people but inadequate fertile land, had long since turned to trade, developing a large navy and mercantile marine, so she was well placed to extend her activities. But commercial rivalry with Athens had resulted in smouldering hostility, ending with a protracted blockade that left Aegina autonomous, but made her a tributary member of the Delian League. As developments within the Peloponnese during this period have already been related, they will not be repeated here; so we will now turn to see what was happening elsewhere.

After the defeat of the Persians in Asia Minor at Mycale, while the Athenians had remained to secure most of the Hellespont, Herodotus says that the Spartans sailed for home. But in 476 BC the Greeks sent a fleet under the command of Pausanias, the victorious Spartan commander at Plataea, to complete the eviction of the remaining Persian garrisons on the fringes of the Aegean. According to Herodotus, first Cyprus was freed from Persian domination: a great claim, but one without much substance since, barely a year later, the

Persians had reasserted their authority. The fleet then sailed to the Hellespont, where Byzantium was captured, and the straits opened for the restoration of grain supplies from the Black Sea cities, while Persian communications with their garrisons in Thrace were cut. Clearly, freeing Cyprus from Persian domination was of secondary importance, and the ill-executed endeavour brings out an important military lesson: never have a double aim. The Athenians' priority was to open up the Hellespont for the restoration of trade, and no diversion of secondary importance should have delayed this. Ending Persian domination of Cyprus – however valuable the island was as a forward operating base for the Phoenician fleet – was not of immediate concern, and should have been achieved later.

The success of his campaign in the Hellespont, coming on top of his victory at Plataea, evidently went to Pausanias' head, and he conceived the idea of becoming the ruler of Greece, perhaps as a satrap of Xerxes, since he needed the Great King's help in realising his ambitions. His conceit, his arrogance and his affectation of wearing Persian dress soon alienated the other Greeks, especially the Ionians, who had only recently regained their freedom from Persian domination. Reports of Pausanias' scheming eventually reached Sparta, and he was recalled to face charges of conspiracy. Although acquitted of actual betrayal, Pausanias was convicted of a number of lesser offences and relieved of his command, which then passed to the Athenians.

The next task facing Athens and her allies was the expulsion of the isolated Persian garrisons from the Thracian seaboard. A new charismatic figure now arises: Cimon, the son of Miltiades – an aristocrat who, it will be remembered, as a token of his support for Themistocles' maritime policy, had dedicated his bridle to Athena; moreover, he had received public acclaim by returning what were alleged to be Theseus' bones to Athens from Skyros. Plutarch describes Cimon as being admirable and noble, as brave as Miltiades and as intelligent as Themistocles, and more honest than either of them. After Cimon had replaced the disgraced Pausanias, his natural authority and relaxed, genial manner soon won over Athens' allies. But behind his affability lay a steely determination, and it was under his direction that the Delian League was gradually transformed into an Athenian Empire. Rather than trying to coerce those of the allies who were reluctant to provide ships and troops, Cimon accepted payment in money instead, so enabling him to keep the Athenians under arms in pursuit of Athens' interests. According to Plutarch, Cimon trained the Athenians hard, turning both their fleet and army into more disciplined and cohesive forces. In this way the allies came to fear the Athenians and seek their favour, gradually becoming tribute-paying subjects instead of allies and, in so doing, losing not only their freedom but also their ability to defend themselves.

Though the few isolated Persian garrisons in Thrace posed no threat, since the original strategic aim of the Delian League had been to secure the Aegean, it was easy enough for Cimon to adapt the League's policy and transform it into a purely Athenian aim: domination of the Aegean. A league of political equals had become an Athenian Alliance, into which the former's members were coerced as allies by different degrees of persuasion. As will be discussed shortly, the purpose of this domination had more to do with economics than security, and was ultimately directed against fellow Greeks. So, intent on furthering Athenian interests, Cimon sailed to the Strymon in 476 BC and began the subjugation of the Persian garrisons. The only two cities to offer any serious resistance were Doriscus and Eion, though this may have been because the other garrisons had deserted or joined the withdrawing Persian army as it passed through.

In spite of repeated attempts, Doriscus (on the mouth of the Hebrus) held out, and so never formed a part of the Athenian Empire. Eion was taken, but only after Cimon had cut off all supplies to the town. Even then the governor Boges, rather than surrender, set fire to a great pile of timber, then killed his wife, children, concubines and servants, whose bodies were thrown into the flames. Having collected together all the gold and silver in the town, he then scattered it from the walls into the Strymon, before leaping into the funeral pyre himself. Whether this massacre and self-immolation is to be regarded as an act of heroism or fanaticism depends upon where one stands. So it is with some of today's acts of terrorism; in the Persian court, Boges' memory was certainly highly honoured.

Cimon's next move was to clear Skyros of pirates in 476 BC, and though his name is not specifically mentioned, it seems probable that he also suppressed the revolt in Naxos in the same year. In 465 BC the attempted colonisation of what was to become Amphipolis took place, while in the same year Thasos revolted; though it was not until two years later that the island was forced back into the Delian League.

Since these events have already been related, there is no need to repeat the details now. This record of forceful suppression, however, does not sit very easily with Plutarch's assertion that Athens' allies had acquired the habit of fearing and currying favour with the all-powerful city.

Hand-in-hand with imposing Athenian authority over the Aegean islands, operations against Persia had been actively pursued. In about 468 BC Cimon won two major victories at Eurymedon, a river in south-east Asia Minor, where he first defeated a large Persian fleet and then disembarked his hoplites to rout a numerically greatly superior Persian army. Not content with this double achievement, he at once turned on a Phoenician fleet of eighty triremes, which had been trying to join up with the Persians, and practically annihilated it.

Four years later in the Peloponnese, Cimon answered a call for help from the Spartans during the Helot revolt, but after he had arrived at the head of a considerable force the Spartans had second thoughts. Fearing that the Athenians might take the opportunity to stir up the revolt even further, the Spartans abruptly dismissed them, telling them that the task they had been asked to undertake – the reduction of the Helot stronghold of Ithome – was no longer necessary. Deeply resentful of this offhand treatment, on their return the Athenians renounced the treaty of alliance they had made with Sparta at the time of the Persian invasion, and instead made one with Sparta's rival, Argos. The first positive signs of mistrust, if not antagonism, between the two principal Greek powers had now been given open expression – a situation that was further aggravated when, as has been related, because of a frontier strife with Corinth, Megara joined the Delian League. The Athenians then built them long walls connecting the city to its port, as Athens had been connected to Piraeus, and provided an Athenian garrison; all of which, according to Thucydides, earned them the hatred of the Corinthians. A hatred which, no doubt, had its roots in the commercial and maritime rivalry that already existed between them and which, as we will see later, was to spill over into Thrace.

It was, however, not only the near-elimination of the Persian garrisons from Thrace that the Athenians achieved. They also acquired the gold and silver mines that abounded in the province, together with an abundant supply of timber for shipbuilding. The capture of Eion provided Cimon with a good port, together with fertile land along the banks of the Strymon and, in the adjoining region, rich mines; while on the south-eastern side of the island of Thasos, Herodotus says that 'a whole mountain has been turned upside down in the search for gold'. This rich and fertile province was ready for exploitation by colonisation, which is exactly what the Athenians did, though it was not always successful. As will be remembered, the first 10,000 colonists who tried to establish a settlement at what was later to become known as Amphipolis, some three miles further up the Strymon beyond Eion, were mostly slaughtered by the Thracians in 463 BC. It was not until twenty-five years later that a second, and this time successful, attempt was made to colonise this important site.

During the thirteen years we have been discussing, between 477 and 464 BC, the Athenians seem to have been almost entirely occupied with consolidating their position in the Aegean, with nothing of consequence being recorded as occurring in mainland Greece itself. On the opposite coast of the Mediterranean, however, the Athenians had become involved in Egypt, which had been a Persian province since 525 BC. Xerxes had been murdered in 465 BC and was succeeded by Ataxerxes, to whom Athens sent envoys in 461 BC seeking a restoration of normal diplomatic relations. Having driven the Persians out of Asia Minor, secured the Hellespont and reduced their garrisons in Thrace, Athenian domination of the Aegean was now complete. It was therefore important to ensure the neutrality of their still-powerful Asiatic neighbour, before the growing tension with Sparta broke into open hostility. Though this stage had not yet been reached, the treaty made with Argos in 462 BC had widened the breach and increased the possibility of war. Not altogether surprisingly, the Athenian approach to Ataxerxes was rebuffed, so when the Egyptians revolted shortly afterwards and appealed to the Athenians for help, they received a willing and prompt response.

In 460 BC an Athenian and allied fleet of 200 ships was engaged in a campaign against the Persians in Cyprus, and though Thucydides tells us nothing more, abandoning the campaign in this manner displayed another serious misappreciation of priorities. On arrival in Egypt, the Athenians sailed up the Nile to Memphis where, with the help of their new Egyptian allies, they captured most of the city and confined the Persian garrison to the citadel. Ataxerxes' first move was to send an embassy to Sparta, offering a substantial bribe if they would invade

Attica, so compelling the Athenians to recall their fleet. But having accepted the bribe, the Spartans declined to invade. So in 456 BC Ataxerxes despatched a relief expedition to Egypt which, after freeing Memphis, drove the Athenians onto an artificial island, formed by a canal linking two branches of the Nile. After a prolonged siege, the Persians succeeded in diverting the water from the canal, thereby stranding the Athenian ships and enabling them to storm the island. Only a few determined survivors managed to escape and then make their way across the Libyan desert to Cyrene. Shortly afterwards, a fleet of fifty Athenian ships, which had been sent to relieve the original expedition, and in ignorance of what had happened, sailed into the mouth of the Nile, where most of them were cut off and captured.

Although Thucydides gives only a brief account of the Egyptian expedition, which lasted for six years, the scale of the disaster should not be under-estimated. The Athenians and her allies had lost nearly 250 ships (about half their total fleet) and perhaps as many as 50,000 rowers and hoplites; losses that were not to be surpassed until the fateful Sicilian expedition in 415 BC. It had been a reckless adventure. The campaign against the Persians in the strategically far more important island of Cyprus was abandoned, and instead support was given to an uprising which, even if successful, would have achieved no strategic or operational advantage. Detaching Egypt from the vast Persian Empire would not have materially altered the balance of power, while its remoteness from the main theatre of operations made a near irrelevancy of its possession. The only tangible advantage would have been economic: the granaries of Egypt would have become available to Athens, but, other than as an insurance against an interruption of her supplies from the Baltic, the need for an alternative source of grain did not justify such a high-risk adventure.

With a reversal of geographical positions and roles, the British response to the German invasion of the Balkans in 1941 displayed a similar misjudgement at the operational level. Forces were sent from Egypt to defend Greece, an undertaking that was wildly beyond British resources to achieve, let alone sustain across the Mediterranean while under constant air attack. The result was a disaster, which so weakened the British in the Western Desert that, had Hitler reinforced the Africa Corps instead of turning on Russia, Egypt and much else besides would have been lost. But to return to the Greeks in Egypt.

Shortly after returning from the fiasco of going to help Sparta during the Helot revolt, Cimon had been ostracised in 461 BC for being too pro-Spartan, so he had played no part in the Greek involvement with Egypt. But when he did return to Athens in 451 BC, he had to bear the consequences. The danger was that, after expelling the Athenians so ignominiously from Egypt, Persia would feel confident enough to try and recover her other lost possessions; while the humiliation that Athens had suffered must have lowered her standing and encouraged her allies to defect, especially as the cost of the campaign had obliged her to impose heavier financial contributions on them. To maintain its authority, an enhanced Athenian presence in the Aegean was now called for, which meant that any danger of conflict with Sparta must be removed. Cimon then overturned Pericles' democratic anti-Laconian policy, which he had been ostracised for opposing in the first place, and made a five-year truce with Sparta, though this was only achieved by the renunciation of the alliance with Argos – an alliance dear to the hearts of the democrats, since it kept a Peloponnesian rival to Sparta in play. Having removed the danger of an immediate threat from Sparta, Cimon persuaded the Assembly to give him command of a 200-strong fleet for the resumption of the war against Persia. Once again the Athenian objective was Cyprus. But though a naval victory was subsequently won against a Phoenician fleet, before Cimon could achieve anything he died in 449 BC and the campaign was abandoned. Cimon had been as genuinely pan-Hellenic as any Greek could be, and with his death all hope of a lasting reconciliation between a divided Greece came to an end. But that was not all. His death also signalled an end to the campaigns against Persia, and the beginning of a new, though militarily less glorious, epoch.

From the lists of tribute paid by members of the Delian League between 446 and 440 BC, which have been preserved in inscriptions on stone, it is clear that the amount Athens received had been considerably reduced. Some cities had left the alliance, while others just did not pay their tribute. It seems that the cessation of operations by Athens to contain Persia left the Asiatic Greek cities feeling particularly exposed; if Athens was not going to protect them, what was the purpose of the Alliance with its demand for tribute? To flaunt their attachment to Greece, under these circumstances, would only serve to aggravate Persia. So, not surprisingly, a number of Athens' allies decided to defect.

Given this weakening of Athens' position, when her five-year truce with Sparta expired in 445 BC, it was of even greater importance to maintain good relations with Sparta and her allies. So the Thirty Years Truce was concluded, with Athens renouncing all her possessions in the Peloponnese: the two Megarian ports of Pegae and Nisaea, together with Achaea and Troezen in Argolis, while Sparta recognised the Athenian Empire in the Aegean. As will be remembered, it was to Troezen that many of the Athenian families had been evacuated at the time of Xerxes' invasion. To strengthen their position in the Saronic Gulf by the acquisition of a good port, the Athenians had captured Troezen in 459 BC. What is surprising is that Sparta agreed to Athens keeping Naupactus, which dominated the entrance to the Corinthian Gulf, and retaining Aegina as a tributary ally, which gave her control over the Saronic Gulf. Athens' two principal commercial rivals at the end of the Persian War had now been reduced to near impotency. It was a positive indication that Sparta sought a settlement with Athens through compromise, even if it meant straining her relations with Corinth and leaving Aegina in thraldom.

Athens' major foreign-policy decisions having been implemented, the principal preoccupations of the Athenians for the next ten years were domestic politics and their control over the empire. After the death of Cimon, his kinsman Thucydides (not the great historian) had assumed the leadership of the oligarchic party, but he was overshadowed by the rise of Pericles. For many years Pericles had provided subsistence for the poorer citizens through three state-funded enterprises: extensive colonisation, massive expenditure on public building works, and maintaining the fleet at a high state of readiness. Though the income from tribute had fallen between 446 and 440 BC, it seems that the slide had at least been halted, while the cessation of hostilities with Persia had resulted in a substantial surplus being accumulated. As has been mentioned, much of this was now devoted to the embellishment of Athens, turning the city into a workshop and giving employment to untold thousands. Magnificent buildings arose, such as the Parthenon, the great temple on the Acropolis dedicated to the city's goddess and protector, Athena. But even though the danger of war had receded, for eight months in the year Pericles kept sixty ships at sea, thus providing further employment and creating a reserve of trained crews. Pericles had thus made the state the paymaster of the poorer citizens and, in so doing, virtually emasculated the oligarchs. This happy domestic situation, however, did not extend to the Empire, where there was unconcealed anger amongst the allies that their tribute for common defence should be so flagrantly misappropriated for the benefit of Athens.

Some ten years after his death in 449 BC, Cimon's policy of imperialistic expansion was abandoned and replaced by that of Pericles, which sought consolidation. There was a lot to consolidate. On land, Athens controlled the Greek mainland from Thermopylae to the Isthmus. In the Peloponnese, Argos was her ally, and near the mouth of the Corinthian Gulf she held Naupactus. Her empire extended from Byzantium to Phaselis, on the south coast of modern Turkey, some 100 miles east of Rhodes, and across the Aegean from Euboea to Ionia. Linking all this together was her fleet, which, following the humbling of Aegina in 453 BC, had no rival. The situation was not unlike that of the British Empire when, after the French were defeated at the battle of Trafalgar in 1805, the Royal Navy also had no rival. The other similarity was that the hubs of both empires were vulnerable to a direct threat.

Neither Athens nor Britain had the resources to maintain the security of their empires and face a land power on their very doorsteps: Sparta and Germany respectively. Fortifications were the Athenian solution; an alliance with France was the British. Much praise has been showered upon Pericles for his curbing of Athenian ambitions, but it should be recognised that his revision of policy was born of necessity rather than wisdom. Although the details of the unrest were given when we considered the Greek states and islands, they will be summarised and consolidated here. In 457 BC the Athenians defeated the Boeotians at Oenophyta (meaning 'vine-yards') near Tanagra, and for ten years controlled Boeotia, until the Boeotians revolted and ousted them in 447 BC; the Spartans expelled the Phocians from control of the oracle of Delphi in 448 BC, but they were reinstated by the Athenians; Aegina continued to be a source of conflict; Megara revolted in 446 BC, Euboea in 445 BC and Samos in 440 BC. In an attempt to exploit the allies' discontent, Thucydides and his fellow oligarchs brought a case for ostracism against Pericles in

444 BC; but the attempt misfired, and it was Thucydides who was exiled. Though Pericles may have secured his position as the undisputed leader of Athens and her empire, it made him ultimately responsible for the disaster that was to follow.

Athens took two steps that made war virtually inevitable. First, her participation in the dispute over Epidamnus and Corcyra; then her siege of Potidaea. As the origins of these disputes have already been related, they will only be summarised now. Epidamnus had been founded by Corcyra (Corfu) on the Illyrian coast in 625 BC. When the oligarchs were driven out of government by the democrats in 435 BC, they set about plundering the property of their opponents, who appealed to Corcyra for assistance. When this was not forthcoming, they turned to Corinth and received a ready response. The story can now be taken forward.

There were two reasons for the Corinthians' favourable response: first, since Corcyra itself was a colony of Corinth, they regarded Epidamnus as belonging to them just as much as to Corcyra; and second, because they disliked the Corcyraeans for not showing them the respect due to a mother city, and for boasting about their naval superiority. In fact the Corcyraeans did have a considerable navy – 120 triremes – and to avoid the risk of being intercepted by them, a force of Corinthian troops and settlers that was sent to Epidamnus marched there. On learning of the Corinthians' arrival, the Corcyraeans sent a fleet to Epidamnus, accompanied by the oligarchic exiles, whom they demanded should be reinstated. They also demanded that the Corinthians should be sent back to Corinth. When both demands were refused, they laid siege to the city, a task simplified by the fact that Epidamnus lay on an isthmus.

When the Corinthians heard about the siege, they raised a relief force, calling for support from a number of allied cities. These measures led to both disputants demanding the recall of each other's troops and ships, accompanied by an offer by Corcyra to go to arbitration. As none of these conditions was acceptable, the Corinthians declared war and despatched a fleet of seventy-five ships, together with 2000 hoplites, to Epidamnus. The Corcyraeans responded by putting to sea with eighty ships, the other forty being at Epidamnus, and intercepted the Corinthians. The result of this engagement was a decisive victory for the Corcyraeans, with fifteen Corinthian ships being destroyed.

The same day, however, Epidamnus was forced to surrender; the terms being that, pending a final decision, Corinthian citizens would be held as prisoners of war, but all foreigners would be sold into slavery. When the Corinthian fleet withdrew, somewhat surprisingly, the Corcyraeans made no attempt to retake Epidamnus, contenting themselves instead with ravaging a number of Corinthian cities and those of her allies. Forced to counter this havoc, the Corinthians despatched another fleet, but neither of the opponents was prepared to risk a trial of strength, so they restricted themselves to confronting one another, but only from fortified ports. Eventually, after a year of sabre-rattling, both fleets retired to their home bases.

A further year passed while the Corinthians prepared for another expedition, thus giving early warning of their intentions to the Corcyraeans, who decided to try and join the Delian League and obtain the protection of Athens. The core of their case was that, since a war with the Peloponnese was now imminent, the Athenians should give careful consideration to their position. There were three considerable naval powers in Hellas: Athens, Corcyra and Corinth. If Athens permitted the Corinthians to acquire the Corcyraean ships, she would have to fight the combined fleets of Corcyra and the Peloponnese; but if she received Corcyra into the alliance, her ships would join those of the Athenians. The Corinthian delegates then put their case, arguing that the Athenians already had treaty obligations towards Corinth, whereas they had never even had a peace treaty with Corcyra. Moreover, when the Athenians were fighting Aegina, Corinth had provided twenty warships; so Athens should either remain neutral or join forces with Corinth.

At first the Athenians inclined towards the Corinthian argument, but in a second debate, accepting that war with the Peloponnese was bound to come, they made an alliance with Corcyra, and ten ships were immediately despatched to the island. The Corinthians responded by sending 150 ships, sixty of them from their allies, which included Megara and Elis, and reinforcing their troops on the mainland. As the Corinthians approached, the Corcyraeans sailed out to meet them with 110 ships and battle was joined. Neither of the fleets was handled with much skill, and it was more like a land battle than a naval engagement, with both contestants relying mainly on their hoplites, who fought it out on the decks, while most of the ships remained motionless.

Initially the Athenians restricted themselves to helping the Corcyr-aeans only when they were hard pressed, and not openly joining the battle, as this would have been contrary to the instructions they had received from Athens. But when it looked as though the Corcyraeans were heading for defeat, they joined in wholeheartedly, but without being able to tip the scales. So the Corinthians emerged as the victors. But the unexpected appearance of a further twenty Athenian ships brought about a Corinthian withdrawal, and darkness put an end to any further fighting. The next day another engagement was avoided when the Athenians sailed to the harbour of Sybota, where the Corinthian fleet lay at anchor. Here they told the Corinthians that, so long as they did not sail against Corcyra, they were free to go where they liked; which, as far as the Corinthians were concerned, was back home. So off they went, taking with them 800 Corcyraean prisoners, most of whom were sold as slaves; but, with a significance that will be seen later, 250 oligarchs were treated with great consideration, in the hope that they could be returned to Corcyra and win over the island to Corinth. The dispute was then not overlooked by the Corinthians, but before it could be used as a justification for the Peloponnese going to war with Athens, something more tangible was required to reinforce their plea – a requirement the Athenians were to provide the following year.

As we have seen, Potidaea, the Corinthian colony in Thrace, was strongly placed astride the Pallene isthmus, which protruded south from Chalcidice. In 432 BC, to consolidate their domination of the Aegean, the Athenians turned on their fellow Greeks, demanding that the Corinthian colonists in Potidaea, who were allies of Athens in the tribute-paying class, should dismantle their fortifications. They were also to send hostages to Athens and to banish their Corinthian magistrates. Though these demands were seemingly harsh, they were not without considerable justification.

With good reason Athens feared that not only the Corinthians, but also the Macedonians, were inciting Potidaea to revolt, so sparking a general uprising amongst the other allied cities in Thrace. The political scene was highly complex. Quite apart from the mixed loyalties within and between the Greek settlements, Macedonia had encroached into former Persian territory in Thrace and was initially hostile to the Athenians' growing presence. But, as will be remem-bered, after some opportunistic footwork, Athens secured the support of the reigning monarch in return for upholding his right to the throne against his rebellious brother. We need not concern ourselves further with Macedonia's involvement in Thrace; but it should not be forgotten that it remained a complicating factor.

Thirty Athenian ships had been despatched to intervene in the Macedonian dispute, but when they arrived they found that the situation had changed dramatically. In Thrace, Potidaea and several other cities were in open revolt, posing a serious threat to Athens' hold on the province with the consequential loss of its wealth, while ultimately – though hardly envisaged at this stage when short-term economic considerations would have predominated – providing a stepping stone to threaten the Hellespont, through which flowed Athens' corn supplies. Historically nothing has changed. It is always the unexpected that occurs, bringing the most improbable scenarios, so nobody would have foreseen the threat that would be posed by the Spartans in 424 BC, any more than we have foreseen the crises that have arisen in our day. But to return to the situation in 432 BC.

After taking stock of the situation after their arrival, the Athenians decided that their force was too small to do more than adhere to their original task. But their cool-headed realism brought an unfortunate consequence. A Corinthian relief column of 1600 hoplites and 400 light troops, who were partly Corinthian volunteers and partly Peloponnesian mercenaries, had marched up from Corinth and was now securely installed in Potidaea. Luck, that fickle factor which so often decides the fortunes of men, had bestowed a second favour on the Corinthians. Their relief column had reached Potidaea just in time; shortly afterwards a further forty Athenian ships and 2000 hoplites arrived, tasked with laying siege to the city. So by the autumn of 432 BC, the Ionian Athenians were attacking a Dorian city, partly garrisoned by Peloponnesian volunteers under a Corinthian general, which had been incited to revolt by Macedonia. All of which came on top of a quarrel with Megara.

As will be remembered, fourteen years previously Megara had revolted and massacred the Athenian garrison; a traitorous act in the eyes of the Athenians, which had gone unavenged. Then, during the dispute over Corcyra the previous year, Megara had provided the Corinthians with eight ships. Now, when the Corinthians set off for Potidaea, the Megarians permitted them to cross the Isthmus and pass through into mainland Greece. The Athenian reaction was prompt and severe. They barred the Megarians from all the ports throughout their empire, as well as from the market of Athens itself. The reason for this draconian decree has been given two interpretations: it could be regarded as a deliberate act of provocation to bring the simmering crises to a head, or it could be seen as a deterrent to others contemplating hostility to Athens. Maybe; but, in either case, why should Corinth not also have been debarred? More probably, then, the decree was taken for a number of complex reasons; amongst which could have been the settling of old scores, and anger that Peloponnesian access to mainland Greece should have been permitted by a constituent state. Clearly the Athenians could not proclaim their true reasons, but their justification was sadly unconvincing: that the Megarians had been cultivating consecrated ground and land that did not belong to them, while giving shelter to slaves who had escaped from Athens.

Adding all the events of the last two years together, it made a heady mixture, so it is small wonder that there was an explosion shortly afterwards. Over the previous fifty years Sparta had seemingly remained imperturbable as the Athenians extended their empire, enormously enriched themselves, fortified their city and constructed a fleet that enabled them to project their power wherever they chose. Then, as though these predominantly military developments were not enough, Athens had established herself as the intellectual and cultural centre of the Greek world. Respected and admired, yet feared and even hated, Athens had largely recovered her position after the debacle of the Egyptian expedition and must have looked, and probably felt, virtually unassailable. All this the Spartans had accepted, but now that Athens had turned on two of their allies, they were shamed into reacting.

Sparta called a conference of all her allies in 432 BC, to decide whether or not there should be a declaration of war. All the representatives put forward their views and aired their many grievances. Megara claimed that the economic sanctions that Athens had imposed on her were a breach of the Thirty Years Truce, while Aegina complained that the autonomy she been granted under the same treaty had been infringed by the restrictions preventing her from trading with Megara. But it was the Corinthians, speaking last amongst the Peloponnesians, who made the most telling point. In a barely veiled threat they declared that, if the Spartans would not stand by her allies, Corinth would look to some new alliance to provide for her security. The Athenian delegates, who were in the Peloponnese on some other business but had been permitted to attend the conference, now spoke. Having justified the origin and working of the Athenian Empire, Sparta was urged not to be carried away by the invective of others, but to give calm consideration to the dangers of taking an irrevocable step, bringing unforeseeable consequences. Rather than break the truce, it would be better to settle their differences by arbitration, as Athens was prepared to do, and for which the truce provided.

The Athenian delegates were then dismissed, and the vote was taken, city by city, irrespective of size or status; and when the final count was made, the majority had voted for war. But as time was needed to prepare, no offensive was to be opened for about a year. During this time Sparta undertook some seemingly inept diplomacy. First, she tried to undermine Pericles' position by demanding that the tainted house of the Alcmaeonidae, to which his family belonged, should be expelled. But Pericles' standing was too great to be affected by such a dated gambit; so the Spartans then demanded autonomy for the Greeks: an indefinable requirement, which would have been impossible to monitor, while leading to a morass of legalistic wrangling. Other than perhaps wanting to keep the negotiations in play, so as to avoid, or at least delay, the necessity for war, it is difficult to see what Sparta was hoping to achieve. Finally, however, she came up with three unambiguous demands: the siege of Potidaea must end, Aegina's autonomy must be respected, and the decree against Megara must be repealed. None of them was acceptable to the Athenians, so that was the end of Spartan diplomacy, perhaps never their strongest point.

A variety of causes can be ascribed for the breakdown of a negotiated settlement: Athenian intransigence, Spartan refusal to submit to arbitration, the accumulation of grievances – however slight and inadequate to justify a war – the arrogance of Athens, the Helot fiasco, the treaty with Sparta's rival Argos, Pericles' anti-Spartan policy, the frustrated anger of Corinth and Megara, and the seemingly near-fatalistic acceptance that war was inevitable. All these disparate factors brought about a drift into disaster – a drift that Pericles, the principal player, aggravated rather than tried to arrest. Cimon would almost certainly have averted war with Sparta, but he was no longer around to do so.

The military lessons can be briefly summarised. The Athenian strategy was initially an allied one, to eliminate the Persian threat. At the operational level, this meant driving the Persians back from the Aegean seaboard, while ensuring the security of Athens itself, a task that was undertaken with a clear sense of priorities and achieved with tactical skill. With no need for an allied strategy, it was replaced by an Athenian one: domination of the Aegean; which, at the operational level, meant removing the last traces of Persian influence, and the relegation of free and equal allies into a state of subordination – a task that was accomplished at the tactical level by a combination of direct intervention and persuasion. But Athenian strategy (if it can be dignified by such a name) then lost its focus, becoming no more than hostility to Persia. It was implemented at the operational level by freeing Cyprus, but this was quickly abandoned in favour of an opportunistic adventure in Egypt. The need for a clear strategic aim, which is then adhered to, could hardly be better demonstrated.

With the rise of Pericles, Athenian strategy was declared to be one of consolidation; her commitments were extensive enough already, and they were not to be enlarged. Though this policy was applied to overseas theatres, it was contradicted in Greece by Pericles himself. He was continually trying to wrong-foot Sparta, obliging her to break the Thirty Years Truce and to open hostilities. His strategic aim then must have been to subordinate Sparta to Athens; so enabling her to become the capital of a pan-Hellenic empire, a role for which he had already adorned her.

6

The Central Theatre
431–423 BC

The Central Region

Almost as an anticlimax, when war came in 431 BC, it was not brought about by some grand offensive, or even provocation, on the part of Sparta or Athens, but by a typical Greek act of treachery. Plataea was an ally of Athens, but the oligarchic party in the city hoped to obtain power by betraying it to Thebes, the capital of Boeotia and an ally of Sparta. After the negotiations had been completed, the gates were opened during the night, and a force of 300 Thebans marched into the city to the market place. Here, rejecting the request of the oligarchs to seize their political opponents, the Thebans grounded arms and called upon all those who were willing to join the Boeotian League to come forward. Initially overcome by surprise, and unaware of the relatively small number of the Thebans, the Plataeans made as though to comply, but when they came to appreciate the situation, they changed their minds.

The Thebans appear to have been over-trusting, and certainly not nearly alert enough, as during the night the Plataeans blocked the streets with carts and, by making breaches through the connecting walls of their houses, were able to assemble in force. While it was still dark they suddenly attacked, and though the Thebans resisted stoutly, being outnumbered and subjected to a hail of tiles and masonry from the women and slaves thronging the roofs, they eventually broke and fled. Lost amongst the unknown streets, often blocked by the barricades and pursued by the Plataeans, there was no escape for the majority, who were either killed or taken prisoner. A further Theban force was on its way, but having been delayed by heavy rain and the swollen Asopus – the river across which the Greeks and Persians had faced one another before the battle of Plataea – it arrived too late to intervene.

As the Theban attempt to seize Plataea had been made without a declaration of war, the Plataeans had been caught unaware, and so a great deal of their property was out in the fields – possessions which they now tried to recover. Seeing all this activity, the Thebans first thought that it presented an opportunity to seize some prisoners, who could be exchanged for their own men; but when the Plataeans told them that, if they withdrew, the prisoners they held would be released, the Thebans desisted and retired. At any rate, that was the Theban story, which the Plataeans denied, claiming they had only undertaken to release the prisoners if there was an agreement after negotiation.

Whatever the understanding, once the Plataeans had gathered in all their property, they immediately put the 180 prisoners to death, returning the bodies to Thebes under a truce. They had previously sent a messenger to the Athenians, telling them what had happened, but saying nothing about their intentions towards the prisoners, which may well not yet have been decided. Then, as Thucydides cryptically says, 'in their own city, they took whatever measures seemed best to them in the existing circumstances'. After the arrival of the messenger, the Athenians immediately arrested all the Boeotians in Attica, and told the Plataeans not to decide on the fate of the prisoners until they had given the matter more thought. If Athens did not want war, which is far from being certain, then the prisoners could be released, the incident played down, and Thebes, which had taken no part in the Athenian–Spartan negotiations, possibly isolated and condemned. But after the prisoners had been executed, whatever the Athenians' intentions may have been, there was no turning back. So they marched to Plataea, stocked it with provisions and, after leaving some of their own troops to stiffen the garrison, returned to Athens, taking all the Plataean women and children with them.

Athens' strategy for the war was the maritime encirclement of the Peloponnese, so embassies were sent to muster her allies, especially Corcyra, Cephallenia, Zacynthus and Arcarnania, upon which she would be particularly dependent for operations against the Peloponnesian western seaboard. As for the Spartans, they sought to widen support by sending embassies to Persia and to all the uncommitted Hellenic states, while enlarging the alliance's fleet. The Doric settlements in Italy and Sicily had already been ordered to start building more ships, but they were now told to increase the numbers, as well as provide additional money in proportion to their size. The Spartan intention was to create a fleet of 500 triremes; but until the preparations were complete, the settlements were to remain neutral, though no Athenian ships were to be allowed to enter their harbours. Even if Thucydides' figure is only approximately correct, it gives a clear indication of Spartan strategy. Though a land power herself, Sparta saw that, following the fortification of Athens, the only way the city could be taken and the Athenians defeated was by starving them into submission, and this could only be achieved by gaining maritime supremacy herself. Since this is exactly how the Peloponnesians won the war twenty-seven years later, we must search for reasons why it took so long to achieve. If none can be found, it suggests that either the shipbuilding programme was too ambitious, or Thucydides was mistaken in his figures. If it was the latter, then clearly Sparta never intended to challenge Athens' naval supremacy, thus leaving her without a strategic aim.

Thucydides lists the states and cities involved in the war. The principal ones allied to Sparta were: all the Peloponnesian states except Argos and Achaea, which remained neutral, and outside the Peloponnese, Megara, Boeotia, Locris, Phocis and the island of Leucas. The combined strength of their fleet at this stage has been assessed as no more than 100 ships, not all of which were in a state of good repair. Athens' principal allies were: most of Acarnania, Corcyra, Zacynthus, Thrace, the Hellespont, the Ionian and Carian coastal cities and most of the Aegean islands, and, of course, little Plataea. The island of Cephallenia, important for the maritime encirclement of the Peloponnese, did not join the alliance until some months later.

Immediately after the affair at Plataea, the Spartans had sent instructions to their allies, telling them to prepare troops and supplies for the invasion of Attica and, at the appointed time, to assemble with two-thirds of their total force at the Isthmus. Shortly before midsummer in 431 BC the expeditionary force was ready under its Spartan commander, Archidamus, one of the Spartan kings. Archidamus was an intelligent and moderate man who, in the great debate, had tried to dissuade the Spartan Confederation from going to war. Now he told the assembled army that they must not fall short of their fathers' standards, but live up to their own reputation, warning them against over-confidence by reminding them that they faced a formidable enemy. After making this speech, he made one final effort to avert war by sending a prominent Spartan to Athens, instructing him to see whether the Athenians were any more likely to come to terms, now that they saw that their enemies were already on the march. But he was refused admission into the city, Pericles having ordered that no Spartan herald or envoy was to be permitted entry, once the Spartans had marched out of their own country. Which hardly suggests that Pericles had any desire other than to make war inevitable.

Rebuffed in his attempt to find a way out of the confrontation with Athens, Archidamus advanced into Attica, where he was joined by a Boeotian contingent, which included cavalry, while a further Boeotian force had been sent to devastate the land around Plataea. As for the Athenians, as had always been intended after the fortification of Athens, those living outside its walls were told to abandon their homes and take refuge in the city. While they could bring their household goods with them, and even the woodwork of their houses, their sheep and cattle were sent over to Euboea and other coastal islands. But though the huge influx that now occurred had been foreseen, no preparations had been made. A few fortunate families had relatives or friends with whom they could stay, but most of the refugees found themselves in a strange city with nobody to turn to for help, being left to fend for themselves. Some erected shelters on what open ground remained, while others took over the shrines, though many of these (like the Acropolis itself) were barred to them on religious grounds, or because of superstitions stemming from oracular pronouncements. It was complete chaos, though some semblance of order was later restored when room was found in Piraeus and along one section of the fortifications. The human misery that this lack of foresight brought to country people, herded together with inadequate sanitation, was bad enough in itself, but it was nothing compared to what was to follow. Whatever the origins of the plague may have been, when it struck the following year, the consequences were disastrous.

Meanwhile everything was being put onto a war footing, with 100 ships being made ready for an expedition against the Peloponnese, while Pericles called upon the Athenians to be prepared to make great sacrifices, though they should be confident in ultimate victory. Adhering to his old maxim that war was mainly an affair of money, he reminded them of Athens' wealth and reviewed the forces available to her. There were 16,000 heavy-armed infantry, recruited from amongst the older and younger men, who were responsible for the defence of Athens and a few outlying strongholds; with a further 13,000 hoplites of military age, 1200 cavalry, including mounted bowmen, and 1600 foot archers. Then there was the fleet, which had 300 triremes immediately ready for active service, quite apart from those of the allies. It was an imposing array of wealth and military capability, and Pericles' call for confidence was not without foundation.

After all the tension, proclamations and military preparations, the first year of the war was something of an anticlimax, with no great clash of arms. The Peloponnesian army left the Isthmus and marched north-east through Megara into Attica, where they laid siege to Oenoe, an Athenian frontier town on the border with Boeotia. By leaving the ripening corn untouched, Archidamus hoped to inspire the Athenians to make some conciliatory gesture. But when nothing occurred, and an assault on Oenoe failed some three months after the affair at Plataea, and with his army losing patience, he opened his campaign in earnest. By devastating the land and burning the houses he hoped to provoke the Athenians into leaving their fortifications and facing him in the field. Although there were many in Athens, particularly the young men, who urged Pericles to do something to hinder the Peloponnesians from their work of devastation – felling their slow-growing olive trees and uprooting their vines – he would not be deflected from his defensive stance, doing no more than permitting the occasional cavalry foray when the Peloponnesians approached too near the city.

As for the Spartans, they persevered with their work of destruction, moving from region to region, until their supplies began to run low. Then, with no supply chain, and isolated amongst a desolate and barren land of their own making, they withdrew back over the Isthmus. Once they had gone, the Athenians ventured out in force and invaded Megara. This large-scale operation, involving some 10,000 hoplites (3000 of whom were resident aliens), was seemingly sanctioned by Pericles for two reasons: first, to act as a safety valve for the bottled-up emotions brought on by inactivity while their homes were being burned; and second, to take it out of the Megarians for having, yet again, let the Peloponnesians march through their territory. The Athenians also established a number of new outposts, which they intended to hold throughout the war. It is difficult to see what purpose they served; should the Peloponnesians invade again, such strong points would not stem their advance, while they offered little prospect of being able to do more than defend themselves. As we do not hear of them again, Pericles may only have been trying to show that he was not just callously abandoning the countryside. It is sometimes necessary to act against one's better judgement for reasons of morale, but this is only justified if the stakes are not too high.

While remaining on the defensive in Attica, the offensive element in Pericles' operational concept had been under way. It was now that the inhabitants of Aegina were expelled, accused of having been largely responsible for starting the war, but in reality to enable the Athenians to secure the importantly placed island and settle it with their own colonists. At about the same time, thirty triremes were sent up the Locrian coast, opposite the northern part of Euboea, where two towns were sacked. The uninhabited island of Atalanta, which lay within the straits, was occupied and fortified, and a permanent garrison installed. There was a clear purpose to this measure: to provide protection against the raids of privateers from Locris against Euboea.

Meanwhile a fleet consisting of 100 ships, with 1000 hoplites and 400 archers on board, had set sail to raid the Peloponnesian coast. Probably after rounding the southernmost capes, this force was reinforced with another fifty ships coming from Corcyra and other allies. A landing was made at Methone (Modon), on the south-west coast of Messenia; this is when we first hear of the Spartan, Brasidas, who was later to distinguish himself on other battlefields, particularly those in the Northern Theatre. The small garrison at Methone would have been overwhelmed, had not Brasidas, at the head of 100 men from a neighbouring post, cut his way with great dash through the Athenians and relieved the town. After re-embarking their troops, the Athenians then sailed northwards, stopping to raid the coast at various points until they reached Sollium, a Corinthian settlement on the coast of Acarnania, which they captured and handed over to the local people. After enrolling the neighbouring town of Astacus as a member of their league, the Athenians crossed over to Cephallenia and, as has been related, persuaded the islanders to join them as an ally. The fleet then returned to Athens, where they heard that the army had invaded Megara, so they sailed over to join in the work of devastation and plunder.

What had Pericles' twin strategy of the defensive in Attica and the offensive elsewhere actually achieved in its first year of war? The defensive element had fulfilled its aim: the Spartan invasion had posed no threat to Athens, and there had been no disruption to the free movement of shipping in and out of Piraeus. But the Athenian offensive element had done no more than acquire two relatively small allies, hand over a Corinthian settlement (which was recovered shortly afterwards anyway), secure Euboea from attacks across the straits and harry the Peloponnesian coast. The strategic objective, the maritime encirclement of the Peloponnese, had been fulfilled, but what thereafter?

One can but assume that the aim was to detach Sparta's allies, so leading to the break-up of her Confederation. There was, however, no operational-level concept as to how this could be achieved; certainly not by mounting a series of tactical-level raids. But to have done more would have entailed mounting a campaign in the Peloponnese, so contradicting the land strategy of avoiding giving battle. The deficiency in Pericles' strategic thinking is then exposed: there could be no effective maritime operations against the Peloponnese. The offensive element of his strategy in the main theatre of war just did not exist. The same criticism can, of course, be levelled at the Spartan land campaign. But it should not be forgotten that, according to Thucydides' figures for their shipbuilding programme, the Spartans' strategic aim was to achieve maritime supremacy. Meanwhile their operations on land were mere time-fillers.

The Athenian custom of bringing back the bones of those who had died on active service gave Pericles the opportunity to address the Athenians assembled for the burial ceremony. Thucydides uses Pericles' oration, from which a short extract has already been quoted, to survey Athenian life and institutions, spelling out the advantages of democracy, while dwelling on the greatness of Athens and what she provided for her citizens, before praising those who had died in her service and consoling those who had been bereaved.

In the spring of 430 BC the Peloponnesians under Archidamus again invaded Attica, and it was only a few days later that the plague broke out. Thucydides says it had been reported in the neighbourhood of Lemnos and elsewhere, but it was not so virulent there, nor did it cause so many deaths. Maybe; but it is strange that the plague, except when exported from Athens, did not occur elsewhere, suggesting that it originated from the conditions prevailing in Athens itself. The symptoms were a sudden burning feeling in the head, eyes becoming inflamed, with bleeding from the throat and tongue, accompanied shortly afterwards by coughing and then vomiting. There was no known remedy. Gripped by an unquenchable thirst, some unattended victims plunged into the water-tanks, which must have had fatal consequences for others. The imminence of death, striking indiscriminately at rich and poor alike, and when no one expected to live long enough to stand trial, brought unprecedented lawlessness; while, since it seemed to make no difference whether one worshipped the gods or not, the observance of religious rites was replaced by a search for more immediate pleasures. Money and life appearing equally ephemeral, it was better to buy pleasure while one was still alive to enjoy it.

But there must have been some stalwart souls, otherwise Athens would have dissolved into chaos, and the prosecution of the war would have been abandoned. The plague continued until 428 BC, and then after easing off for a year broke out again in 427 BC; during which time one-third of the population died, including 300 of the 1000 Athenian cavalry, and some 4400 of the 16,000 hoplites. The losses did not only have an immediate effect on fighting strength, but also greatly reduced the number of new recruits reaching military age each year. The army shrank to about the same strength as that of the Boeotians, and while maritime superiority was maintained, the shortage of rowers meant that a smaller number of ships could be put to sea. It is important to remember Athens' manpower shortage when we come to review her conduct of the war later in this chapter.

The Peloponnesians, meanwhile, were extending their work of systematic destruction beyond the plains around Athens, to which they had largely restricted themselves the previous year, continuing as far south as the silver mines of Laurium; though, once again, they found the countryside deserted. Fear of the plague, however, caused them to withdraw earlier than they would otherwise have done. In spite of the ravages of the plague, or perhaps before it had got a hold, Pericles himself commanded another expedition to raid the Peloponnesian coast. Some old vessels were converted into transports, carrying cavalry for the first time – 300 of them, as well as 4000 citizen hoplites. After being joined by fifty ships from Chios and Lesbos, the fleet sailed along the coast of Argolis, where four landings were made; but though the country was laid waste, no towns were taken. A fifth landing was made on the Laconian coast, where an insignificant town was destroyed. After the fleet returned to Athens, as will be related later, it was immediately sent north to Thrace to take part in the siege of Potidaea.

Once again nothing of consequence had been achieved, and when Pericles left the fleet and entered Athens, though he found that the Peloponnesians had withdrawn, a more significant occurrence was his discovery that there had been a change in the Athenians' mood. The plague raged within the city, the land outside had been laid waste, and now Pericles, who had been the cause of all their suffering, had returned with nothing to show for his expedition. It was time to end this pointless war and come to terms with Sparta, before things became even worse. With this in mind, embassies had already been sent to Sparta to seek peace, but the Spartans – no doubt fortified by the plight in which the Athenians found themselves – rejected their overtures, and the embassies returned empty-handed. The prevalent feeling was that, if Pericles could not find a way to end the war, he should give up the command.

Faced with this wave of discontent and near-despair, Pericles summoned an assembly and, as Churchill was to do in 1940, gave a great wartime speech to rally the people. He claimed that he had warned them of the hardships they would have to face (other than the plague, which could not have been foreseen); if they had been right in deciding upon war in the first place, they were wrong in now wanting it to be discontinued just because the going was a bit rough. He then reminded them of their greatness, pointing out that it was their freedom that mattered, and not material losses, which could be replaced; they had a responsibility to maintain the great empire their ancestors had founded. Only great leaders, gifted with the power of oratory, can sway the mood of the people on such occasions, which is exactly what Pericles achieved, while masking his responsibility for edging Athens into war and for having failed to prepare for the influx of refugees, the probable cause of the plague.

But it was a transient recovery. The people may have accepted Pericles' continuing leadership, but his political opponents did not. They brought a charge of embezzlement against him which, though it could not be proved, was believed by most of the population. So he was found guilty, fined and removed from office. But such was the misfortune of the Athenians that the democratic party, who were in favour of the war, yet opposed to Pericles, must have proved stronger than the oligarchs, who would have combined his overthrow with negotiations for peace. After fifteen years of uninterrupted power, of which more than two had been during the war, Pericles was out of office. A year later, however, there was a reaction in his favour, and he was re-elected in 430 BC; but, broken in health, and overwhelmed by the loss of his two sons in the plague, he died the following year.

With the death of Pericles, there was a divergence of opinion within the democratic party, brought about by economic considerations. In broad terms the richer classes, who bore the main financial burden of the war, and the farmers, who had lost their livelihood and property, wanted peace. But the sailors, craftsmen and traders, who had found employment and profit without great danger, were happy enough for the war to continue. Nicias, who had succeeded Pericles, steered a cautious course between these two currents of opinion and, in so doing, lost the initiative.

The North-Western Region

The offensive now passed to the Peloponnesians, who shifted the war's centre of gravity to north-western Greece. Here, as will be remembered, they had sent a 100-strong fleet to try and detach Zacynthus from the Athenian Alliance, but, though their land was ravaged, the Zacynthians stood firm and the Peloponnesians withdrew. Further north, Amphilochian Argos, inland from the northern extremity of Acarnania, was attacked by the Ambraciots – a troublesome Hellenic people allied to Sparta, living over the border in Epirus, whom we will meet again – and, as Athens was an ally of Acarnania, she was appealed to for help. An expedition of twenty ships was accordingly sent to Naupactus under the command of

Phormio who, having assisted Argos in resisting an earlier attack, was well known in the area. Although it will be running slightly ahead of events elsewhere, for the sake of continuity the victories of Phormio between 429 and 428 BC will be related now.

The Spartans had sent a Peloponnesian fleet and 1000 hoplites to Acarnania, with the object of capturing the whole of the country, after which it was considered that Zacynthus and Cephallenia could easily be subdued, and even Naupactus captured. Thus, by making it far harder for the Athenians to send their fleet round the Peloponnese, the whole of western Greece would be detached from her alliance, and the sea routes to Sicily and Italy secured. It must have seemed an attractive prospect, but unfortunately for the Spartans, Phormio was to disrupt their plans. Without waiting for the Corinthian fleet, which was to tie down the Acarnanians on the coast, so preventing them from reinforcing their countrymen in the interior, the Spartans set off. Marching with their allies into Acarnania, they advanced towards Stratus, the biggest town in the province, hoping that its capture would lead to the submission of the rest of the country.

Seeing the invaders advancing in three widely separated and uncoordinated columns, the Acarnanians seized the opportunity to try and destroy them in detail. They first ambushed the most advanced column, consisting of local tribesmen, as it was approaching Stratus, and completely routed it. The survivors fled back to the two Hellenic columns, which then closed together and waited to be attacked. But the Acarnanians kept their distance, using their slingers to such effect that, when night came, the Peloponnesians withdrew behind the River Anapus, some nine miles from Stratus. Receiving none of the expected reinforcements, the expedition was eventually abandoned, the troops either withdrawing or dispersing to their various homes.

Meanwhile the Corinthians and their allies had set sail for the Acarnanian coast with forty-seven ships, including a number of troop transports. Initially Phormio with his twenty ships from Naupactus did no more than shadow the Corinthians as they kept to the coast, but when they tried to make the crossing from Patrae, on the Peloponnesian coast, to Achaea on the mainland, he intercepted them in mid-channel. The Corinthians adopted the same formation as had the Greeks off Euboea at the time of Xerxes' invasion: they formed a tight circle, with their prows facing outwards. All the light craft, and five of the fastest and best-equipped triremes, were positioned inside the circle: the former for their protection, the latter to act as a reserve, ready to reinforce the circumference should this be required. The Athenians sailed round them, continually threatening to attack, and so gradually edging the Corinthians back until they began fouling one another, with orders and curses being shouted from one ship to another and adding to the confusion. This was the moment when Phormio gave the order to attack, whereupon the Athenians broke into the circle and destroyed every ship they came across. Resistance was minimal, with those who could fleeing to Patrae and Dyme in Achaea, hotly pursued by the Athenians, who captured twelve ships with most of their crews. It had been a significant victory and a clear demonstration of the Athenians' superior seamanship, while bringing out the importance of offensive action. As will be remembered, when the Athenians had been surrounded by the numerically superior Persian fleet off Euboea, instead of shrinking their circle, they had suddenly attacked and scattered the Persians.

When the Spartans heard of this disaster they sent out three commissioners, one of whom was Brasidas, whom we have already met, to advise their fleet commander, Cnemus, who – perhaps surprisingly – had not been sacked. Preparations now went ahead for the assembly of another fleet, causing Phormio, who had received no support from Corcyra, to ask Athens for reinforcements. Twenty further ships were despatched, but incomprehensibly, in view of the obvious urgency, were ordered to Crete to undertake a subsidiary task of no consequence. Bad weather then delayed the Athenians further and so, through not adhering to their priority aim, the Athenians came near to suffering a humiliating defeat, one that was only averted by the skill of Phormio.

The Gulf of Corinth narrows between two headlands, about a mile apart and both confusingly called Rhium, before it gives way to the open sea through a wide channel. Some seven miles to the east lay Naupactus, the important Athenian port where the Messenians had been settled in about 455 BC. The Athenians took up station off the northern headland, just outside the entrance to the Gulf, whereupon the Peloponnesians moved to a position off the southern headland. Here they faced one another for six or seven days, at a loss as to how to obtain the tactical advantage they both sought. While Phormio wanted to keep to the open sea, where he could manoeuvre and exploit the Athenians' superior seamanship, Cnemus and Brasidas wanted to fight within the Gulf, where the restricted space would enable them to conduct the battle as though it were on land and their numerical superiority would prove decisive.

Eventually the Peloponnesians decided to lure the Athenians into the Gulf, so they formed up in four lines and sailed towards Naupactus, which – as the Messenians had moved along the coast to support Phormio – was virtually undefended. Seeing the danger, Phormio set off in single file at all speed for Naupactus. This is exactly what the Peloponnesians wanted; suddenly changing front, they brought their whole line, four deep, to bear against the Athenian flank. The eleven leading ships managed to escape, but the remaining nine were driven onto the shore and captured by the Peloponnesians; though some of them were saved by the timely arrival of the Messenians, who dashed into the water and boarded the ships, fighting on their decks to recover them – an incident that provides a good example of how land/sea cooperation is conducted.

Meanwhile twenty Peloponnesian ships, from their right wing, were in hot pursuit of the eleven Athenian ones that had escaped the trap; ten of which got clean away and formed up at Naupactus to defend the town. One, however, had not been able to keep up, but was now to prove an inspiration. One of the pursuing Peloponnesian vessels, from Leucas, had outstripped the others and was chasing the Athenian laggard, which suddenly saw an opportunity to turn the tables on its pursuer. There happened to be a merchant ship anchored offshore, which the Athenian ship circled right round, emerging to ram the boat from Leucas amidships, sending it to the bottom. Surprised at this sudden turn of events, some of the Peloponnesian ships checked their pursuit and lost way, while others inadvertently ran aground in shallow water. Seizing their chance, the Athenians fell upon them, capturing six of them, before going on to recover their own ships, which the Peloponnesians had taken earlier. It had been a remarkable victory, leaving the Athenians masters of the Corinthian Gulf, while the surviving Peloponnesian ships remained bottled up where they had started, in Panormus.

But even after taking into account the defeat of the Peloponnesian expedition into Acarnania, the situation in the area remained very unstable. The Athenians had failed to exploit their tactical successes, to give them an operational-level dimension by reinforcing the area and completing its conquest. Had they captured the island of Leucas, which was to remain a thorn in their side, their hold on the western seaboard of Greece and the Peloponnese would have been greatly strengthened, the wavering Corcyraeans brought into line, and the sea route to Sicily and Italy secured. As it was, the Athenian tactical successes were in themselves not enough to prevent more trouble arising in the area.

In 427 BC, the year following the series of Athenian victories, civil war broke out in Corcyra: a revolution that had its roots in the naval engagements off Epidamnus in 433 BC. As we have seen, 250 Corcyraean oligarchs who had been taken prisoner by the Corinthians were treated with great consideration, in the hope that they could be returned to Corcyra and win the island over to Corinth. Under a show of ransom, these prisoners were freed, and on returning home they set about gaining power for themselves with a will, while not forgetful of serving Corinthian interests. In spite of their best endeavours, however, when the matter was debated, the people voted in favour of remaining allies of Athens. Corcyra being ostensibly neutral at this stage, Athens and Corinth each had a ship with envoys lying in the harbour, so they were well informed as to the violence between the oligarchs and the democrats that was to follow.

Though the Athenians had passively watched the destruction of Plataea in 427 BC, in spite of a recurrence of the plague it was an active year for them further afield. As will be recounted when we come to look at the Western Theatre, an expedition was sent to Sicily; and in the Aegean the revolt of Mytilene, on Lesbos, was finally crushed, while Athens now became involved in Corcyra when civil war broke out. Having failed to win power by the ballot, the oligarchs next impeached Peithias, the leader of the democrats who looked after Athenian interests in Corcyra, for enslaving the island to Athens. After being acquitted, he then brought counter-charges against five of the leading oligarchs for having obtained vine-props by cutting them down on land sacred to Zeus; tried, found guilty and fined, the oligarchs then attempted assassination. Bursting into the council hall, they killed Peithias and some sixty of his followers, though a few of those present managed to escape to the Athenian ship. Having gained control, the oligarchs then forced through the Assembly a decree declaring neutrality. Next they sent envoys to Athens to explain what had occurred, but on arriving they found that the news had outstripped them and that orders had already been sent to the fleet at Naupactus to intervene. Without further ceremony the envoys were seized, together with any other Corcyraeans who could be found, and imprisoned in Aegina. Meanwhile, Spartan envoys had arrived at Corcyra with promises of help, so the oligarchs decided to force the issue and bring matters to a head.

A force of some 800 mercenaries was brought over from the mainland, but, as the slave population had sided with the democrats, they found themselves worsted in the three days of street fighting that followed. Like their contemporaries in Plataea when the Thebans were driven out of the town four years earlier, the women participated by hurling down masonry and tiles from the rooftops. The mercenaries then set fire to the city – which would have burned to the ground, had the wind not carried the flames away from the buildings – before making their escape back to the mainland. Seeing the way things were going, the Corinthian ship stole away in the night. It was at this stage that the twelve Athenian ships from Naupactus arrived, with 500 Messenian hoplites embarked, and their commander, Nicostratus, managed to arrange a conciliatory settlement between the two parties, provided Corcyra adhered to her alliance with Athens. But just as he was about to depart, the leaders of the democratic party persuaded him to leave five of his ships to see that the settlement was not breached – ships that they would replace with five of their own. A seemingly reasonable arrangement; but the democrats overplayed their hand in nominating their political rivals to crew the five ships they would provide. Somewhat understandably, the oligarchs declined to row themselves into exile in this manner and, as they feared, to delivery to Athens.

In the meantime, the thirty-three-strong Peloponnesian fleet under Alcidas, which had been in the Aegean, was now despatched to assist the oligarchs. As soon as the Corcyraeans learned of the approaching enemy, they hastily manned sixty ships, sending them into battle as they were ready. When the Peloponnesians saw them straggling out in this disorganised manner, they left twenty of their ships to deal with them, while the others went to face the Athenians, but were soon encircled, only being saved by the other Peloponnesian ships leaving the Corcyraeans and coming to their assistance. Though heavily outnumbered, the Athenians kept their enemy at bay until nightfall, so allowing their incompetent allies to return to harbour. Meanwhile the Peloponnesians also withdrew, taking the thirteen Corcyraean ships they had captured with them; but on being informed by fire signals the following night that a second Athenian fleet of sixty ships was approaching, they turned what had been intended to be no more than a limited withdrawal into an urgent escape. At any rate, this is what Thucydides says; but as will be related, he later tells us that the fleet was in fact recalled, when the Athenians seized Pylos.

When the Corcyraean democrats realised that the Athenian fleet was approaching and the Corinthians had gone, they began an orgy of killing. For seven days they hunted down all the oligarchs and their supporters they could find, persuading those who had taken sanctuary in the temples to leave and then putting them to death; and so causing others to commit suicide, rather than be taken alive. Many of those who died had nothing to do with subversion, but were victims of personal vendettas, or died because they were owed money. As Thucydides said when summing up the situation at the end of the year in 427 BC, 'There was death in every shape and form, and as usually happens under these circumstances, people went to every extreme and beyond. There were fathers who killed their sons, men were dragged from the temples or butchered on the very altars; some were actually walled up in the temple of Dionysus and died there.' All this took place under the eyes of Eurymedon and the crews of the forty Athenian triremes on their way to Sicily, who evidently considered that the Athenian cause was being well served.

Thucydides' comment on these events is worth quoting, since it underlines the effect of war on the intensely political minds of the Greeks:

> Later, of course, the whole of the Hellenic world was convulsed, with rival parties in every state – democratic leaders trying to bring in the Athenians, and oligarchs trying to bring in the Spartans . . . It became a natural thing for anyone who wanted a change of government, to call in help from outsiders . . . Family relations were a weaker tie than party membership . . . If pacts of mutual security were made, they were entered into by the two parties only in order to meet some temporary difficulty, and remained in force only so long as there were no other weapons available . . . A

victory won by treachery gave one a title for superior intelligence ... Love of power, operating through greed and through personal ambition, was the cause of all these evils. To this must be added the violent fanaticism which came into play once the struggle had broken out.

Thucydides perhaps goes a bit too far in ascribing the origin of all these ills to the civil war. There were earlier acts of betrayal within cities, for example the attempted betrayal of Athens to Darius, while the oligarchs betrayed Plataea to Thebes in 431 BC, for which they also paid the price. But to return to Corcyra.

Some of the oligarchs had managed to escape to the mainland, and after the Athenian fleet had gone they harried Corcyra, eventually crossing over and seizing Mount Istone, some four miles north of the city. From here they continued to plunder and destroy the surrounding countryside until, in 425 BC, they were forced to surrender when an Athenian squadron from Pylos, which was on its way to Sicily, helped with an assault on their mountain stronghold. Although the oligarchs had been promised a trial in Athens, they were handed over to the Corcyraeans, who promptly executed them; so completing the near-total extermination of the oligarchic faction. Their work done, the Athenians continued on their way to Sicily, where we will pick them up when we come to look at the Western Theatre.

But in this north-western region of Greece it was not only Corcyra with which the Athenians had been occupied. In 426 BC an Athenian fleet commanded by Demosthenes had sailed round the Peloponnese, and after being reinforced by troops from Acarnania, and ships from Corcyra, Zacynthus and Cephallenia, he attacked the island of Leucas, lying off the coast of Acarnania, south of Corcyra. As will be remembered, Leucas had supplied ships to help the Corinthians during their original dispute with Corcyra in 434 BC and had sided with Sparta when war broke out three years later. But Demosthenes failed to keep to his aim and was persuaded by the Messenians of Naupactus to call off the attack on Leucas, when he had done no more than lay waste the countryside. Instead, the Messenians proposed that he should subdue Aetolia, and thus remove any threat to Naupactus from that quarter, while consolidating the Athenian hold on the mainland. Letting his imagination outstrip his resources, Demosthenes visualised adding Aetolean manpower to that of the

other Athenian continental allies and marching through Locris into
Boeotia.

Unsupported by the Acarnanians, who were dismayed at his
breaking off the attack against Leucas, Demosthenes was soon in
difficulty. Assailed on the flanks by the Aetolians – who ran down
the hillsides to throw their javelins and then retire, only to reappear
shortly afterwards and hurl another volley – and unable to respond,
the Athenians and their allies tried to make a hasty withdrawal, still
harried by the fast-moving and lightly armed Aetolians. The main
body then took the wrong road and found themselves ensnared in a
trackless wood, which the Aetolians promptly set alight. What
survivors there were made their way back to Naupactus, where they
were embarked on ships before returning to Athens. Under the
circumstances, Demosthenes undoubtedly made the right decision
not to accompany them, and, as we will see shortly, his reputation
was redeemed by remaining.

One modern historian has suggested that Demosthenes was
intending to link up with Nicias, who, as will be related, was making
an incursion into Boeotia from the east at about the same time. But
this is highly improbable. Thucydides would certainly have mentioned such an ambitious undertaking, but instead he ascribes
Demosthenes' ill-considered excursion to a sudden change of mind.
And since Nicias only remained in Boeotia for some forty-eight hours
before retiring, it hardly suggests that he had any part to play in a
wider, operational-level move. Moreover, given the wide geographical
separation and problems of communication, to achieve the necessary
degree of coordination would have been a near impossibility.

But to return to Demosthenes. Even before he had begun his
operation against the Aetolians, they had appealed to Sparta and
Corinth to help attack Naupactus. So, sometime after the disastrous
Athenian expedition, 3000 Peloponnesian hoplites under the command of the Spartan, Eurylochus, marched through Locris into
Aetolia, where they were joined by a force of Aetolians. They then
entered the territory surrounding Naupactus, and after capturing the
outer part of the city, which was not protected by a wall, continued
towards the main fortifications. Here, however, they were halted.
Hearing of the Spartan approach, Demosthenes had gone to the
Acarnanians and, after overcoming their initial reluctance because of
his retreat from Leucas, he had persuaded them to provide 1000

hoplites, whom he embarked on his ships and brought to Naupactus just in time.

Realising that he now stood no chance of taking the city, Eurylochus marched north to join forces with the Ambraciots, who had tried to take Amphilochian Argos in 429 BC, but had been thwarted by the arrival of Phormio. Now that they were making another attempt, the Acarnanians appealed to Demosthenes to lead their army in defence of Argos; which he did with consummate skill, winning a decisive victory with smaller numbers, killing Eurylochus and, by permitting the Peloponnesian survivors to withdraw, displaying their perfidious nature to those who, hitherto, may have regarded them as reliable allies. After the departure of the Peloponnesians, the Acarnanians practically exterminated the Ambraciots, and could have easily taken Ambracia had they wished. Somewhat cryptically, Thucydides says that they refrained from doing so 'as they feared that if the Athenians occupied the place, they would be even more dangerous neighbours than those they had now'.

After this crushing defeat a truce was declared; and the Acarnanians made a treaty with the Ambraciots whereby they would assist one another in defending their territory, but neither would be expected to assist the other if it involved an attack on their respective allies – the Athenians in the case of the Acarnanians, and the Peloponnesians in the case of the Ambraciots. Having restored his reputation by his energy and skill and having brought affairs to a satisfactory conclusion, Demosthenes now returned to Athens in triumph. But whatever the appearance may have been, the situation was much as it had been before: in spite of a number of tactical victories, the Athenians had failed to develop them into an operational-level achievement. In due course, we will consider the reasons for this failure.

Back to the Central Region

We must now return to central Greece where, during the spring of 429 BC, another Peloponnesian expeditionary force crossed the Isthmus; but this time their objective was Plataea. Seemingly at the request of the Thebans, Archidamus, who was once again in command, called upon the Plataeans to join Sparta as an ally, or at least to remain neutral. As will be remembered, all the wives and children, together with the older men and others unfit to fight, had already been evacuated to Athens, leaving a garrison of 400 Plataeans and eighty Athenians. Rather delicately, Thucydides says that 110 women (presumably slaves) also remained 'to do the cooking'; but in view of their considerable numbers, they probably had other functions to fulfil of a more intimate nature.

On seeking the Athenians' advice, the garrison was urged to adhere to the Alliance, receiving assurances that the town would not be deserted. So the Spartan demand was refused, and the siege began. First a palisade was built around the town, then a mound was constructed against its walls; but the Plataeans undermined it, so that nearly as fast as it rose, it was lowered by removing the material from below. At the same time, they raised the height of the outer fortifications and started the construction of an inner wall. The Spartans then brought forward battering rams, but these were disposed of by the Plataeans dropping heavy beams onto them and so breaking off their heads. Finally, after trying unsuccessfully to set the town on fire, the Peloponnesians prepared themselves for a long siege, encircling the town with a double wall, manned partly by their own troops and partly by Boeotians, while the greater part of their army returned home.

As with the victories of Phormio, which were completed in 428 BC, and the Corcyraean civil war in 427 BC, together with the Athenian expedition against Leucas in 426 BC, we will run slightly ahead of events elsewhere so as not to break this account of Plataea. By the second winter of the siege, the garrison was beginning to run out of provisions, so it was decided to try and escape by forcing a passage through the surrounding wall, and then to strike out for Athens. According to Thucydides, about half the garrison later had second thoughts, finding the enterprise too risky for their liking, which left some 200 of the more venturesome to make the attempt. But as those who stayed behind played an important part in aiding the escape, there may have been sound reasons for their doing so.

Choosing a stormy night, the escapees reached the wall between two of the watch towers, and placed ladders in position. The lightly armed troops gained the summit without being detected; but before the whole party could follow them, the alarm was raised. Thereupon those who had been left behind attacked the encircling wall on the opposite side from where the escape was being made, so confusing the Peloponnesian reserve of 300 men as to where they were required. Fire signals were lit to warn Thebes of an emergency, but the Plataeans had also prepared their own fires on the city's walls, which, when lit, made those of the Peloponnesians unintelligible. In the general confusion most of the escapees managed to cross the second wall and then took the road to Thebes, which they quite correctly thought would throw the Peloponnesians off their track. After having followed the road for about half a mile, they turned off into the hills and were able to make their way safely to Athens. It was a successful and well-coordinated little operation, once again underlining the supreme importance of surprise and deception.

By now the Peloponnesians knew the garrison was so weakened that it could not withstand a determined assault and yet, for political reasons, they were restrained from taking the city by storm. As any peace treaty with Athens would probably require the return of conquests, Plataea must therefore be made to look as though she had abandoned Athens and voluntarily joined Sparta. As it was, it was not long before the garrison was finally starved into accepting the Spartan terms: they would give up their city voluntarily and submit themselves to the judgement of Sparta, on the understanding that the guilty would be punished, but only after a fair trial. But in the event there was no question of a fair trial, largely due to the malice of the Thebans, who pointed out that the Spartans were not judging the heroic Plataeans of the Persian War, but the Plataeans who had stood by Athens and slaughtered the Theban prisoners. No doubt to cement Theban loyalty, the Spartans then asked each prisoner 'Whether he had done any service to the Lacedaemonians or their allies during the present war?' Finding it difficult to do otherwise, each man inevitably answered 'No', whereupon he was taken away and put to death, with no exceptions being made. Some 200 Plataeans were executed in this way, together with twenty-five Athenians, while the women were sold into slavery. After being used for a year to accommodate some political refugees from Megara, Plataea was razed to the ground; this would appear to negate the perceived advantage of not having taken it by storm.

During the entire time that Plataea was under attack, and then under siege, the Athenians made no move to assist her. Clearly, to have discarded Pericles' policy and taken to the field would have ended in disaster, both for Athens and Plataea, but a surprise sally in force to relieve the town would have been another matter. Every year the main body of the Peloponnesian army was withdrawn, and in the first year of the war when this had occurred, 10,000 hoplites had taken revenge on the Megarians for having cooperated with the Spartans. In 427 BC, the year Plataea was starved into capitulation, a Peloponnesian army had not even crossed the Isthmus. Moreover, if 200 audacious men could make their escape from Plataea, then a relieving column ought to have been able to force an entry. Having given the Plataeans solemn assurances that, if the Spartan demands for them to remain neutral were rejected, they would not be abandoned, it was a shameful act of betrayal for the Athenians to have done exactly that. For a considerable time after his death, the Athenian qualities that Pericles most extolled – energy, boldness and versatility – seemingly deserted them.

Returning to 428 BC, with tenacious consistency the Peloponnesians invaded Attica once again under Archidamus, staying to lay waste the land for as long as their supplies lasted, then marching back home again. As on previous occasions, the Athenians for their part contented themselves with sending out their cavalry, tasked with preventing the enemy light troops from marauding over the countryside. Though it had been their intention, for the first time since the outbreak of the war the Peloponnesians did not invade Attica in 427 BC; they had got as far as the Isthmus when a series of earthquakes made them decide to turn back. The earthquakes were clearly very severe; Euboea was hit by a tidal wave that raced ashore, carrying away everything in its path, and on receding it left what had previously been dry land inundated to such an extent that it now formed part of the sea. A number of other places also suffered heavy damage, with fortifications and buildings collapsing or, if near the sea, being swept away.

None of these natural disasters, however, deterred the Athenians from making their annual excursion to raid the Peloponnesian coast and, more significantly, seizing the rocky island of Minoa, which lay at the mouth of Nisaea, Megara's harbour. So they effectively closed the port, which previously had only been possible by the Athenians operating from Salamis on the opposite shore. As will be related, the Athenian possession of Minoa was to prove of importance three years later. Looking further afield, in 426 BC a large expeditionary force of sixty ships and 2000 hoplites, under the command of Nicias, was sent to subdue the island of Melos, some thirty miles south-west of Naxos. Inhabited by colonists from Sparta, Melos stood as an exception to the other Aegean islands in that it had not submitted to Athens, a failing which the Athenians now sought to rectify; but, though there was the usual wasting of the land, Nicias retired without attempting a siege. He then sailed to Oropus, on the north-east frontier of Attica and Boeotia, from where he marched to Tanagra, in Boeotia, some fifteen miles north-east of Plataea.

Here Nicias and his hoplites were joined by a contingent that had marched out from Athens. A day was spent doing as much damage as possible to the land, which seems to have had some effect, since the following day the Boeotians came out from Tanagra and a small battle took place, in which they were defeated. Having evidently completed their work, the Athenians then withdrew the way they had come, with Nicias taking the opportunity to sail northwards and lay waste the coast of Locris. Thucydides does not tell us what the purpose of this expedition was, but as has been discussed, it is most improbable that it had any connection with Demosthenes' ill-considered excursion into Aetolia. Undertaken a year earlier, when the Peloponnesians did not even cross the Isthmus, the combined expeditions could have saved the garrison of Plataea. The abandoning of that unfortunate town becomes all the more incomprehensible.

The following year the first Athenian expedition was against Pylos, but for the sake of geographical continuity we will first consider the expedition led by Nicias. In 425 BC he was given command of eighty ships, which landed 2000 Athenian hoplites and 200 cavalry on a beach just over two miles east of the Isthmus and some seven miles east of Corinth. Having received warning of the expedition from Argos, the Corinthians had assembled an army on the Isthmus, so blocking the route to Corinth; but as the landing took place at night, it went undetected until they were alerted by beacons. Though the Corinthians set off at once, by the time they had arrived, the Athenians had already completed disembarking and stood ready to receive their charge. For a while the battle ebbed to and fro, between an overlooking hill and the water's edge; but largely thanks to their cavalry, the Athenians gained the upper hand and drove the Corinthians back onto the high ground. A lull then occurred in the fighting, which the Athenians used to strip the bodies of more than

200 Corinthians littering the battlefield and to recover their own dead, who numbered rather fewer than fifty. Meanwhile Corinthian reinforcements had started to arrive, so the Athenians withdrew to their ships and, after carrying out the ritualistic torching on the way, they disembarked on the bulb-shaped peninsula of Methana, on the east coast of Argolis some seven miles due south of Aegina, which they then proceeded to cut off from the mainland by building a wall across its neck. Having completed their work, they left a garrison behind, which occupied itself with raiding the adjacent territory of Troezen, to which, it will be remembered, some of the Athenian families had been evacuated at the time of Xerxes' invasion.

Just what Nicias was hoping to achieve with this second expedition remains as obscure as did his one of the previous year into Boeotia. They are, however, not unimportant for us, since they help build up a picture of Athenian commitments, and so they will be of assistance when analysing their conduct of the war. As for the Peloponnesians, they had opened the campaigning season in 425 BC with another invasion of Attica, where they undertook the usual burning and ravaging. They had also planned to send a fleet of sixty ships to assist the oligarchic exiles who were harrying the democrats in Corcyra. It was in response to this threat that the Athenian ships under Eurymedon, en route to Sicily, had been diverted to Corcyra, where they had assisted in the final defeat of the oligarchs. We must now turn to another Athenian expedition, this time to Pylos, which also took place in 425 BC.

The South-West Region

After his successes in the north-west region, Demosthenes had become a national hero. In 425 BC, shortly before Nicias had led the expedition against Corinth, he was entrusted with carrying out a campaign of his own choosing. His plan was to seize Pylos, a naturally strong position on the west coast of the Peloponnese, only about forty-five miles from Sparta. There was a good harbour on the land side and, as the surrounding countryside had formerly belonged to the Messenians, Demosthenes considered that once Pylos was fortified, they would make excellent garrison troops, who could be relied upon to inflict as much damage as possible on the Spartans. Sailing with Demosthenes were forty triremes under the command of

Eurymedon, who, as has been related, was on his way to Sicily but had received orders to divert to Corcyra, where he was to prevent the Corinthians from assisting the oligarchs. Demosthenes now wanted Eurymedon to delay his departure and help him secure Pylos, pointing out its advantages, together with the fact that there was plenty of timber and stone available to improve its natural defences. But Eurymedon, like the soldiers themselves, thought little of Demosthenes' plan and would have made his departure, had not bad weather forced the fleet to seek shelter.

So it was almost by accident that Pylos was secured and then fortified, while its good harbour provided the Athenians with a useful port. When the storm abated and Eurymedon departed for Corcyra, Demosthenes was left to fend for himself with only five ships and a small number of troops. His audacious move, however, led to the immediate recall of the Peloponnesian army in Attica. After joining up with troops mustered from all over the Peloponnese, it marched on Pylos. The Corinthian fleet of sixty ships at Corcyra was also recalled; though, as has already been pointed out, this was not the reason Thucydides gave earlier to explain their abrupt departure.

Demosthenes had been given time to prepare his defences, as well as sending an urgent request to the Athenian fleet at Zacynthus to come to his assistance, which they responded to in all haste.

The peninsula of Pylos was joined to the mainland on the north by a neck of sand, and it was here that the Athenians had built their wall, though there was the danger that it could be outflanked by a simultaneous attack from the sea. The east side of the peninsula, as well as most of the west coast, was well protected by cliffs; though there were rocks, a landing was possible on the south-east corner. A wall had also been built here, but it was weak, and so a landing on the open beach posed a real threat. Demosthenes then placed himself there, together with sixty specially selected hoplites and some archers, who were to oppose any landing at the water's edge. The remainder of the garrison, reinforced by the fortuitous arrival of some sixty Messenian hoplites, held the land wall to the north. At the same time Demosthenes ordered the five triremes that he had been left to be dragged out of the water and protected within a specially constructed stockade.

The Spartan plan, as Demosthenes had foreseen, was to attack from both land and sea, while blocking the harbour entrances with ships, so as to prevent any Athenian vessels from entering to support their garrison from the land side. Brasidas, whom we have already met when he successfully defended Methone and took part in the naval engagements in the Corinthian Gulf, led the assault on the beach where Demosthenes had positioned himself, but he was wounded and the attack was eventually called off. Meanwhile, in the north, two attacks against the wall had been repulsed, and the Peloponnesians had withdrawn to construct some siege engines. It was at this moment that the Athenian fleet of fifty triremes arrived from Zacynthus, but – seeing the mainland and the island thick with enemy hoplites, and their ships showing no signs of sailing out – they withdrew for the night to the shelter of a conveniently nearby island.

The next day they sailed into the harbour and caught the Peloponnesians only half prepared, with some of their ships not yet crewed. Falling upon them, the Athenians won a decisive victory that gave them command of the sea, while stranding some 400 Spartan hoplites, who had been landed on the long, lozenge-shaped island of Sphacteria, immediately south of Pylos. As for the Peloponnesians on the mainland, they appear to have been so shaken by the sudden reversal of fortune that they remained inactive and uncertain what to do next. When news of what had happened reached Sparta, leading members of the government were sent to assess the situation. They quickly came to the conclusion that there was no way of saving the men marooned on Sphacteria, so they proposed sending envoys to Athens to seek an end to the war, while settling for a local armistice. It all sounds very precipitate, so we can only conjecture that the Spartan reluctance to go to war in the first place had been given renewed expression.

The main terms of the local armistice were that the Peloponnesians would hand over all their ships that had taken part in the battle and make no further attempt to recover Pylos; while the Athenians would allow supplies to reach the island, under their supervision, and would not take any further offensive action against the Peloponnese. It was all very reasonable, as were the Spartan envoys' proposals for peace, when they reached Athens in an Athenian trireme: 'Sparta calls upon you to make a treaty and to end the war. She offers you peace, alliance, friendly and neighbourly relations. In return she asks for the men on the island.' But the Athenians, led by the implacable Cleon, demanded the surrender of the Spartans on the island, who would be brought to Athens as hostages for the fulfilment of further demands: the return of Nisaea, Pegae, Troezen and Achaea, places she had given up twenty years ago in the previous peace treaty. Moreover, the Spartans wanted the negotiations to be conducted privately, whereas the Athenians wanted them to be held openly. The significance of the Athenian demands should not be under-estimated; though the restoration of Achaea and Troezen would not have brought any great advantage, the acquisition of the Megarian ports of Nisaea and Pegae was another matter. Quite apart from the embarrassment that open negotiations over the gifting of an ally's territory would cause Sparta, the acquisition of the two ports would bring Athens two significant advantages: her position in the Corinthian Gulf would be greatly strengthened, and her domination of Megara would greatly help her to block the Isthmus to the Peloponnesians. All of which would have been well appreciated by the Spartan envoys, who preferred to return empty-handed rather than concede to the Athenian demands.

The envoys' return spelled an end to the armistice at Pylos. In accordance with what had been agreed in the treaty, the Spartans then asked for their ships back, but the Athenians refused, on what were clearly specious grounds. Hostilities were then vigorously renewed, with the Peloponnesians attacking the wall, and the Athenians closely investing the island of Sphacteria. Conditions were, however, not as unfavourable to the Spartans as the Athenians must have hoped; in spite of their vigilance, supplies were being smuggled onto the island, while the shortage of water in Pylos was causing the Athenians considerable hardships.

As the weeks dragged on with no signs of progress, the mood in Athens changed from over-charged optimism to despondency, manifesting itself in expressions of regret that the peace terms had not been accepted. Recognising his growing unpopularity, Cleon accused those bringing bad news from Pylos of exaggerating the difficulties and not telling the truth – an accusation that rebounded on him when he was told to go and see for himself. Being sent as an inspector, however, would put Cleon on the spot; he would either have to confirm the bad news or, if he tried to deny it, risk being branded a liar. He quickly changed tack. Realising that the Athenians were prepared to send out reinforcements, he told them that if they believed the situation to be as bad as it had been painted, there was no point in just sending out an inspector. What should be done was to send out another expedition: if the commander was a real man like himself, success would soon follow. He then passed the poisoned chalice to Nicias, the man he probably most hated, by proposing that he should be the commander. But Nicias was a match for Cleon, replying that, as far as the generals were concerned, if the task was as easy as Cleon made out, he could take out whatever forces he liked and command the expedition himself. At first Cleon thought this was just a debating point, but when he realised that it was meant in all seriousness, he tried to backtrack, saying that it was Nicias, not he, who was a general. But the Athenians, sensing that they had got him on the run, behaved as people often do on these occasions, shouting at Cleon to stop prevaricating and to get moving without further delay. Unless they were displaying an unbelievable degree of irresponsibility, the Athenians must have had far more trust in Cleon's ability as a field commander than they were prepared to display. That said, by any standards it was an unusual way of selecting a force commander, and probably not one to be adopted too readily.

Hoist with his own petard, and having to accept the inevitable, Cleon assembled the troops he required, all of whom came from Imbros and Lemnos, and then set sail. On arriving at Pylos, he conferred with Demosthenes, whom he had wisely chosen to be his fellow commander. Implementing a plan that Demosthenes had already conceived, the hoplites were embarked on as few ships as possible and landed on both sides of the island of Sphacteria before dawn. Surprising a forward outpost manned by some thirty Spartans, who had regarded the few Athenian triremes as being no more than their usual guard ships, they quickly secured a foothold. As dawn broke, a further 800 peltasts and 800 archers landed, together with the Messenian contingent and a number of other troops who were not required to man the wall. Organised into companies, each of which was about 200 strong, they quickly seized the high ground and, after positioning the light troops well in front, waited for the Spartans to attack.

When the Spartans advanced, weighed down by their cumbersome armour, they were gravely hindered by the close and rocky ground, and though they could drive back the light troops, they could not close with them. Finding themselves being outflanked, and subjected to a hail of javelins and arrows, the Spartans fell back on the fort at the end of the island. Here something of a stalemate set in, with the Spartans able to hold the Athenian assaults, but unable to attack themselves. Eventually the enterprising commander of the Messenians, with some of the light troops and archers, managed to work his way along the steep cliff edge to the rear of the Spartan position, from where he suddenly appeared on the high ground behind them. Caught in the same way as their forebears were at Thermopylae, when the Persians got round behind them, the Spartans prepared to make a last stand. Cleon, however, wanted them as prisoners, not as dead bodies, so that he could take them back to Athens; he therefore stopped the attack and called upon the Spartans to surrender. As an indication of their willingness to do so, the Spartans laid down their shields and waved their hands, whereupon a meeting took place between the commanders. At the Spartans' request, it was agreed that heralds should be brought over to assess the situation, after which the Spartans on the mainland would be asked to give them instructions. When a messenger arrived, he told them that 'The Spartans order you to make your own decision about yourselves, so long as you do nothing dishonourable.' As some 150 of them had been killed in the fighting, after discussing the matter amongst themselves the 300 survivors evidently felt they had done all that could be expected of them, so they surrendered.

Thucydides says that this event caused more surprise than anything else that had happened in the war – it being thought that Spartans would never surrender, whatever the situation. Now the Athenians had nearly 300 of them, whom they sent to Athens to be held in prison until a settlement was agreed. Meanwhile at Pylos a strong garrison was installed, with the Messenians from Naupactus sending some of their best troops back to what, it will be remembered, was originally their own country, until they were evicted by the Spartans in 453 BC. The Messenians now carried out raids into Laconia, causing considerable damage, while arousing Spartan fears of another Helot revolt – a not unlikely possibility as the Messenians spoke the same dialect, and probably found many sympathisers, if not active supporters, amongst the Helots. Without revealing their concern, the Spartans sent envoys to Athens to try and recover both their prisoners and Pylos itself. But Cleon, following his victory, now dominated Athenian policy; the prisoners he had brought back showed that the Spartans were not invincible, and, by threatening to execute them if the Peloponnesians invaded Attica again, he held the Spartans in check. The prestige of Athens rose amongst her allies, and the prospect of victory restored the flagging morale of the Athenians themselves. It was then hardly surprising that the Spartan envoys returned empty-handed.

But was there anything of substance behind the Athenians' optimism? Certainly their string of victories, with their fillip to morale, and the restoration of their standing amongst their allies, with a comparable lowering of that of the Spartans, were of enormous importance. But unless the capture of Pylos had brought some clear advantage to Athens, tipping the scales of the war in her favour, the existing euphoria could prove to be disappointingly ephemeral. So what had been achieved? An additional staging port had been acquired, together with a foothold on the Peloponnesian coast from where Laconia could be raided; but this was, again, no more than another tactical success. There was no connection between the localised and widely separated victories. They were all dead ends, adding to Athens' commitments and a dispersal of her resources, while they proved to be little more than an irritant to the Peloponnesians who, holding the interior lines of communication, could always achieve a rapid concentration of force, should this be required. Unless a clearer strategic aim was pursued, or frustration and suffering intervened, the struggle would continue on its uncertain course.

Although Thucydides has not offered an explanation, by now it was clear that the Spartans' intention to construct a 500-ship fleet capable of challenging Athens' maritime supremacy had come to nothing. The most probable reason was that, coming on top of the additional financial contributions that had been called for, it was just not affordable. Sparta was then left with no strategic aim. The only three offensive measures that she, or her Peloponnesian allies, had undertaken in the Central Theatre were: the annual fire-raising excursion into Attica, the intervention in Corcyra, and the invasion of Acarnania – all three of which had failed to achieve anything. The Athenians refused to be drawn out from behind their fortifications, while the Corcyraean and Acarnanian ventures, though offering the prospect of securing the whole of the north-western region, and being of importance to Corinth, were evidently regarded by Sparta as side shows, calling for only a limited commitment. But before giving further consideration to the overall situation as it affected both Athens and Sparta, we must look briefly at the southern region and then return to the central region.

The Southern Region

In the summer of 424 BC Nicias made another expedition, this time to Cythera, off the southern coast of Laconia. As will be remembered, this was the island that Xerxes had been urged to capture during his invasion of Greece, but he had preferred to keep his forces concentrated and continue his land approach. Now Nicias, with a fleet of sixty triremes, disembarked 2000 hoplites, a few cavalry and a contingent from Miletus. They had little difficulty in routing the inhabitants, who quickly surrendered, on the understanding that their lives would be spared. An Athenian garrison was then installed, some of the more suspect citizens rounded up and taken on board, and after Nicias had spent a few days raiding the Laconian coast, he began his leisurely journey home, stopping off wherever he chose to inflict as much damage as possible.

So the Athenians had won another victory, but what had it achieved? Like the acquisition of Pylos and Methana, it was a boost to their morale and represented a loss of face for the Spartans, which was another positive factor in stiffening Athenian determination. Other than that, it was no more than another tactical victory, which did nothing to advance the Athenian ascendancy in the conduct of the war as a whole, while they had to garrison an island for which they had no purpose, and which tied down manpower badly needed elsewhere. The plague had not only depleted the numbers of those already serving, but also those of succeeding age groups.

Bearing in mind that Cythera was regarded as posing a threat to Sparta, should it fall into enemy hands, one would have expected the Spartan reaction to be to concentrate whatever forces they could muster and take the offensive to recapture the island. Instead they went onto the defensive, dispersing their strength in penny packets along the coast, while more positively, appreciating the need for mobility, they raised a force of 400 cavalry, together with some archers. Thucydides says that the reason for this dispersal of force was that, with the disaster at Sphacteria, the loss of Pylos (he omitted

Methana) and now Cythera, the Spartans feared a Helot revolution. Moreover, they were baffled by the form of warfare with which they were faced: amphibious operations against which they could find no effective response. So, according to Thucydides, their self-confidence ebbed. Maybe; but it does not justify the ineffective penny-packeting of their resources, which should have been concentrated and used offensively, so forcing the Athenians to respond. It is a fine exemplification of the old maxim: 'If you try and defend everything, you will end up defending nothing.'

If Thucydides was correctly informed (which may well not be the case, as he is uncertain as to the evidence), the Spartans now committed a gross act of betrayal. Wishing to keep the Helots in subjugation, they proclaimed that those of them who considered that they had distinguished themselves in battle should step forward; after examination, they would be rewarded by a grant of liberty. In this manner, after a great public and religious ceremony, some 2000 Helots were emancipated, only to disappear without trace immediately afterwards – no one knew how. Perhaps this was so, but it sounds a bit far-fetched and hardly likely to encourage others to seek distinction in the Spartan cause. However, we must now return to the central region.

The Central Region Revisited

Things were not going well for Megara by 424 BC. As has been related, the Athenians revenged themselves for the Peloponnesian annual devastation of their territory by repaying the Megarians in kind. Then, as though this external infliction were not enough, the Megarians were in the grip of that endemic Greek disease, internecine strife. A broadly democratic party was in power, but the exiled oligarchs had seized Pegae, the Megarian port in the Gulf of Corinth, from where they were harrying the democrats. Realising the people felt that, rather than having to contend with enemies on two fronts, it would be better to recall the exiles, the leaders decided that their own interests would be better served by admitting the Athenians. It was then arranged that the Athenians would occupy the walls that linked Megara to Nisaea, the city's port, so preventing the Peloponnesian garrison there from intervening.

The Athenians divided their force into two parties and, displaying an admirable awareness of the importance of security, told only those who had a need to know what was going to happen. After sailing to the small island of Minoa (which, it will be recalled, had been taken by the Athenians three years previously), one party under Hippocrates concealed itself near the gate that was to be opened, while the other – consisting of lightly armed Plataeans, under the command of the indomitable Demosthenes – lay in ambush close at hand. It was a strange sort of ambush as, when the gates were opened, the Plataeans were the first to rush in and secure the gate, so admitting the other party who gained possession of the walls. The Peloponnesian garrison fought back but, being surprised and under attack from some of the Megarians as well, was quickly routed and took refuge in Nisaea.

Though by dawn the walls had been taken, confusion reigned in Megara itself, and an attempt to open another gate for an Athenian force of 4000 hoplites and 600 cavalry, which had marched from Eleusis, some fifteen miles to the east of Megara, was thwarted. Finding themselves surrounded and with no prospect of being relieved, the Peloponnesians accepted the reasonable terms offered to them by the Athenians and surrendered.

At this stage the Spartan Brasidas, who was near Corinth preparing to take an army to Thrace, makes another appearance. Hearing that the Athenians were attacking Megara, he sent a message to the Boeotians to join him as soon as possible, while he himself hastened to reach the city. On finding that it had already fallen, and while the Athenians were occupied with Nisaea, Brasidas appealed to the Megarians to open the gates, but they refused, preferring not to commit themselves while the situation was so uncertain. Having heard what was happening at Megara before receiving Brasidas' message, the Boeotians had already set out, so they arrived unexpectedly promptly. Both armies now formed up for a battle outside the city walls but, for their different reasons, neither of them wished to fight what could be a decisive engagement; so they stood their ground without making a move. This leaves one wondering why the Athenians deployed outside the city walls in the first place.

Eventually they went back to Nisaea, whereupon the oligarchs, thinking that the Athenians were no longer willing to give battle, and seeing that the pro-Athenian party was too paralysed with fear to act, opened the gates to Brasidas. Rather surprisingly, he showed no concern about the Athenians, and once he was assured that the oligarchs were firmly back in power, he returned to Corinth. The oligarchs then picked out about 100 men, a mixture of personal enemies and pro-Athenians, whom they promptly executed.

As for the Athenians, having failed to achieve their primary aim of securing Megara, they evidently saw no advantage in remaining, so they returned to Athens. It was a messy affair, and a sordid little story, though one that was typically Greek from beginning to end. It was a bungled operation on the part of the Athenians: after their praiseworthy start, when they combined security with skilful movement to achieve surprise, they then neglected the other face of security – their own. After being reinforced by 4000 hoplites and 600 cavalry, it seems inexcusable that some of these were not posted to guard the gates, and to watch over affairs in the city while Nisaea was being invested.

The final battle that took place in 424 BC was at Delium, in Boeotia. Demosthenes and Hippocrates, who had been the two Athenian commanders at Megara, now hatched another plot. Demosthenes was to take possession of Siphae, on the northern coast of the Corinthian Gulf, just west of the Isthmus, and Hippocrates was to occupy Delium, on the east coast opposite the island of Euboea. It was expected that both of these Boeotian towns would be betrayed, but on this occasion Athenian security was laxer than it had been at Megara, and the Peloponnesians, warned of the Athenian intentions, quickly occupied Siphae and repulsed Demosthenes' landing. Moreover, there had been a muddle over the dates, so Hippocrates had not even started on his diversionary march to Delium. Undeterred by the reversal at Siphae, Demosthenes mustered every man who could be spared from the defence of Athens and set off for Delium. Having arrived, he then set about fortifying the town, and when this was nearly completed he sent most of the army back towards Athens, remaining behind himself to supervise the organisation of the garrison and complete the work on the fortifications.

Meanwhile the Boeotians had assembled an army at Tanagra, a few miles south-west of Delium, where they waited, undecided what to do. The majority of the commanders were against attacking the Athenian hoplites who, though the light troops had continued on their way, were resting after crossing the border on their route back to Athens. One of the more resolute Boeotian commanders, however, although it was already late in the day, persuaded the others that they must fight for the freedom of their country. Moving into a position behind a hill, which prevented the two armies from seeing one another, they prepared for battle.

When Hippocrates received news of the Boeotian move, he sent orders to the army to form up in line and, leaving 300 cavalry to guard Delium, he joined them shortly afterwards. Meanwhile the Boeotians detached some troops to cover Delium and then moved forward onto the crest of the hill with 7000 hoplites; with the Theban contingent forming a solid mass twenty-five shields deep, and with the others adopting varying depths. The 10,000 light troops and the 1000 cavalry were posted on the wings, and somewhere on the battlefield were 500 peltasts.

The Athenians had about the same number of hoplites, who were drawn up eight shields deep along the entire front, while the cavalry were, like those of the Boeotians, positioned on the wings. Thucydides tells us 'that there were no properly armed light troops present on this occasion, nor did the Athenians have any', explaining that the ones whom he earlier reported as returning to Athens were little more than camp followers, apparently taking the opportunity to enjoy a country outing. They were fortunate to have continued on their way . . .

As the battle has already been described when introducing the Greek cavalry, all that needs to be said now is that, as the Athenians advanced up the hill, the Boeotians came charging down it, clashing at the double. The entire Boeotian left wing was defeated, but on the right the massed Thebans were steadily pushing back the Athenians. It was at this stage that two squadrons of Boeotian cavalry moved round behind the hill, to appear suddenly on the victorious Athenian right wing, which, mistaking them for a fresh enemy army, started to panic. So, with their left wing being forced back, and now their right one breaking, the whole army took to its heels, with Boeotian cavalry in hot pursuit, until they halted as night closed in.

Nearly 500 Boeotians fell in the fighting, together with 1000 Athenians, including Hippocrates. The Athenian cavalry contingent at Delium was then attacked, and after a breach had been made in the surrounding fortifications by an ingeniously constructed flame-thrower, the town was stormed and the garrison either killed or taken prisoner. As for the conduct of the battle itself, one is left wondering what had happened to the Athenian cavalry. If, as Thucydides says, it was posted on the wings, it should have been able to prevent just two squadrons of enemy cavalry from causing such a rout. But before drawing any conclusions about the course of the war as a whole, we must look at the progress of the campaigns being conducted in three overseas theatres: Sicily, Thrace and Ionia.

7

The Overseas Theatres
431–423 BC

It might be helpful to recall the political situation that existed in Athens following the death of Pericles in 429 BC. Though there was as yet little sign of oligarchic opposition to the policies of Periclean democracy, economic considerations tended to divide the population into two broad factions. One wanted peace: the well-off who carried the main financial burden, and the farmers who had lost their homes and livelihood. The other was happy for the war to continue: the sailors, artisans and traders who had found employment and profit at no great risk. Nicias, to some extent Pericles' successor, steered a cautious course between these two currents of opinion, and in so doing lost the initiative. So, as we have seen, the offensive was taken over by the Peloponnesians, who shifted the war's centre of gravity to the north-western region of Greece. It should also be remembered that, as a consequence of the plague, Athens was suffering from a shortage of manpower to undertake her widely dispersed commitments. As for Sparta and her Peloponnesian allies, through a lack of strategic direction and bungled operations they had failed to take advantage of their opportunities. In the diplomatic field, Spartan envoys had attempted to enlist the support of Persia, but they were intercepted by the Athenians and, on being taken back to Athens, were promptly executed.

The Western Theatre

The power of Syracuse had grown rapidly since about 445 BC, and she had been gradually extending her hegemony over the whole of Sicily. But with the construction of 100 new triremes, and the doubling in size of her cavalry in 439 BC, she clearly had wider ambitions. Athens' concern at these developments, and her desire to contain the further expansion of this new power, led her to make a treaty with the two cities most hostile towards Syracuse: Leontini and Rhegium; the former lying some twenty miles to the north of Syracuse, and the latter in the toe of Italy. Though these alliances were going to be of momentous consequence in the years to come, at this stage Athens had no aggressive intentions, and she appears to have been doing no more than signal a warning to Syracuse. The treaties were renewed on identical terms in 433 BC; but since Leontini and Rhegium were by then allied to a number of other cities in Sicily, which were predominantly Ionian in origin, Athens' potential commitments had been considerably extended.

At the outbreak of the Peloponnesian War, Sparta had hoped for at least some naval support from Syracuse, but – probably because the Syracusans considered that their own interests would be better served by remaining neutral – none was forthcoming. Although not prepared to participate in the war, Syracuse and the other Dorian cities remained nominally allied to the Peloponnesians, and certainly gave them moral support. It was not until 427 BC that Athens became involved in Sicily – the year when civil war broke out in Corcyra, Plataea finally fell, the plague recurred in Athens, and a revolt took place in Mytilene, on the island of Lesbos. The ostensible reason for Athens intervening directly was because war had broken out between the Ionian and Dorian cities; as the Ionians were getting the worst of it, Leontini appealed to Athens for help on their behalf. The Athenians promptly sent twenty triremes to Rhegium, from where they cooperated with the Ionians for the next two years. But the real purpose of the ships being sent was to assess the possibility of securing the whole island, so depriving Sparta and her Peloponnesian allies of their corn supplies from the west.

In 425 BC, the year of the Athenian victory at Pylos, the Syracusans and their allies reinforced their ships guarding Messina, on the extreme north-east of Sicily, with the intention of fighting a naval engagement with the Athenians, most of whose fleet was occupied elsewhere. If successful, the Syracusans then hoped to gain Rhegium, on the opposite shore, and so secure control of the Straits. As a matter of interest, Messina and Rhegium are the Scylla and Charybdis, the sea monster and the great whirlpool, between which Odysseus is supposed to have sailed on his epic journey back home after the fall of Troy. But to return to the Syracusan plan: it was intended that Locri, a Doric city on the southern shore of the Italian toe, would synchronise their attack with that of the Syracusans from the sea. Although the Syracusans enjoyed a small superiority – rather more than thirty ships, as opposed to the combined Athenian and Rhegium fleets of twenty-four – they were unable to exploit the fact.

The two naval engagements that took place were scrappy, indecisive affairs; so the Locrians withdrew from Rhegian territory, and the Syracusans returned to Messina. There then followed a number of other contests, both on land and sea, again with inconclusive results, after which the Athenians made no further attempt to intervene, leaving it to the Hellenes in Sicily to fight it out amongst themselves. It had become increasingly clear that the Athenians were primarily concerned with their own interests, so the following year (424 BC) representatives of all the Sicilian states met to air their complaints and discuss the possibility of reaching a settlement amongst themselves.

They were fortunate to have an able, broad-minded delegate from Syracuse, Hermocrates, to direct their discussion and keep the object of the meeting clearly in mind. Parochial differences should be set aside, since they could never be satisfied except at the expense of someone else, a situation that would inevitably bring about a renewal of the fighting at some later date. Instead, they should consider the interests of Sicily as a whole, the benefits of peace and the desirability of ridding themselves of the Athenians. The Sicilians wisely took his advice and agreed to end the war, with each state (with one exception) retaining what it had. The exception was the Ionian city of Camarina, on the south coast, which was to pay Syracuse a fixed sum for retaining what she had acquired.

The Athenian commanders on the spot had little alternative but to agree to the peace terms. Then, having no justification for remaining, they returned home. From what Thucydides tells us, the Athenians had done all that was expected of them. They had actively supported the Ionic cities, but, even with the reinforcements Athens had sent out, they had been able to do little more than hold their own. They had then assessed the situation and correctly concluded that the combination of Dorian cities under the leadership of Syracuse was too powerful to permit the conquest of the island without a major effort; hence perhaps their decision to sit on the sidelines during the last year of the conflict. But when they got back to Athens they received a chilly welcome: two of them were banished, and the third, Eurymedon (whom we first met at Corcyra), was fined. The allegation that supported this uncompromising attitude was that they had all accepted bribes to leave, when, had they so wished, they could have secured the whole island. In other words, the original aim of the expedition, to *assess* whether Sicily could be secured, with a view to denying the Peloponnesians their corn supplies, had been changed to *securing* the island, with a view to . . . and so on. A good example of what is known as mission creep: you are given a limited task, but gradually this is extended beyond your capability, which usually leads to the parsimonious dribbling in of reinforcements, or (like the Americans in Vietnam) to developing what had begun as no more than a support operation into a full-scale war. But Nicias and the other democratic party leaders needed to protect their reputation and positions, so scapegoats had to be found, and who better than the expedition's three commanders? One is left feeling that G. K. Chesterton's epigram on English politicians could equally be applied to the Greeks:

> But they that fought for England
> Following a falling star,
> Alas, alas, for England,
> They have their graves afar.
> And they that rule in England
> In stately conclave met,
> Alas, alas, for England
> They have no graves as yet.

We must now leave Sicily for the time being, and have a look at what was going on in Thrace.

The Northern Theatre

As will be remembered, Potidaea was a Corinthian colony on the isthmus of Pallene, but it was also an ally of Athens in the tribute-paying class. A rather uncertain ally, however, which the Athenians suspected was going to revolt, so they had demanded that the city's fortification should be dismantled and the Corinthian magistrates expelled. On their demands being refused, the Athenians laid siege to Potidaea, which was eventually starved into submission in 429 BC.

Until 425 BC the Northern Theatre had remained something of a backwater, though in that year the Athenian general Simonides captured a town that Thucydides only describes as 'lying in the Thracian area'; but almost immediately afterwards Simonides was driven out with heavy losses by the Chalcidians. Other than this ill-executed venture, the situation had remained surprisingly stable. Unlike events in 432 BC, there had been no uprisings, partly, no doubt, because of the Athenian garrisons and the watchful presence of their triremes. All the while, however, the Athenians – initially with the support of Perdiccas, the king of Macedonia – had been consolidating their position and extending their influence. But in 424 BC the Chalcidians, and then Perdiccas himself, having grown suspicious of Athenian ambitions and concerned at the strengthening of their position, invited the Spartans to intervene. This was the same year that Cythera, the island lying off the southern coast of the Peloponnese, was captured, peace agreed in Sicily, and the Athenians tried to secure Megara.

This was also the year when Brasidas, having thwarted the Athenian attempt to capture Megara, set off on his long march to Macedonia, taking with him 1000 Peloponnesian hoplites and 700 Helots, who had been trained and equipped as heavy infantry. To reach Macedonia and Thrace, Brasidas had to pass through Thessaly, where most of the population were friendly towards Athens, but the oligarchic government and Perdiccas' agents secured him a safe passage. He then marched through Macedonia and across the Chalcidice peninsula to Acanthus on the eastern coast, where he arrived just before the grapes were harvested. As usual, there were the oligarchs in the city who wanted to side with the Spartans, and the majority of the population who did not. Brasidas was eventually admitted into Acanthus on his own and allowed to address the public assembly, which he did with considerable skill: declaring that Sparta was fighting a war to liberate Greece from the Athenians, and that he had made the long march in the belief that he would be welcomed as a harbinger of freedom. He then went on to explain that, should they decide to oppose him, he would have to treat them as an enemy, in which case their grape harvest and much else would be lost. His persuasiveness, and his carefully worded threats, carried the day, so Acanthus was lost to Athens; as was Stagirus, which shortly afterwards followed the lead of her neighbour. The acquisition of Acanthus and Stagirus enabled Brasidas to extend his conquests along the coast to Argilus, where he was welcomed into the city. From Argilus he continued his march as far as the Strymon, where Eion, the important port and trading post, lay at the river's mouth, and Amphipolis, the most important city in the whole region, was to be found only some three miles further upriver.

Here let us draw breath and take stock of the situation. Brasidas had marched some 800 miles since leaving the vicinity of the Isthmus the previous year, and had secured a string of coastal cities, all without having to fight a single battle. He had, however, bypassed the three prongs of the Chalcidice peninsula, where a number of cities allied to Athens were situated, the most important being Potidaea on Pallene, the most western peninsula. More concerned with their own security than anything else, none of these cities posed a direct threat at this stage; but should they be reinforced by the Athenians, Brasidas could lose the cities he had won over. But, putting aside such fears, Brasidas turned his attention to Amphipolis.

Marching through the night with snow falling, Brasidas surprised the small guard posted on the all-important bridge over the Strymon, and with its capture stood poised before Amphipolis. As will be remembered, it was here, at what used to be known as the Nine Ways, that an Athenian settlement was first established in 465 BC, but it had been annihilated by the Thracians, and twenty-five years were to pass before another one took root. Brasidas had expected Amphipolis to be betrayed, but the people had prevented the gates being opened, which allowed time for the Athenian garrison commander to send for help. The general in overall command was Thucydides, the historian, who was with the Athenian fleet based on the island of Thasos, 'about half a day's sail from Amphipolis', as Thucydides himself says. Meanwhile Brasidas, temporarily thwarted in his designs, first let his troops plunder the surrounding land, then camped outside the city walls before deciding his next move. We now have an interesting situation: Thucydides has to explain his own role in the severe reversal that was to follow, so let us listen to what he has to say:

> As soon as he [Thucydides] heard the news, he set sail at once with the seven ships he had with him. His first aim, certainly, was to reach Amphipolis in time to prevent its surrender, and, if he failed in that object, at any rate to secure Eion before Brasidas could get there. Brasidas, meanwhile, was alarmed at the prospect of the naval relief force coming from Thasos . . . he therefore did his best to gain the town as quickly as possible . . . he put forward very moderate terms, making a proclamation to the effect that all who wished to do so could remain in the city, with the possession of their property and full political rights guaranteed to them, and those who did not wish to remain could take their property away with them and leave within five days.

So the Athenian garrison left, and Brasidas was received into the city. Late on the same afternoon Thucydides sailed into Eion, claiming that 'if the ships had not arrived so quickly, it would have been in Brasidas' hands by dawn'. But this does not add up. Thucydides knew about the loss of Acanthus and Stagirus, so what was he doing back at Thasos? Moreover, how could he have sailed the same day as he heard the news, when Brasidas, learning that he was coming, permitted the citizens of Amphipolis five days in which to leave? And his self-congratulation in saving Eion by reaching it so quickly sounds more like an apologia for not having saved Amphipolis. He was clearly caught totally unprepared.

Whoever was to blame, Amphipolis had been lost, and the news caused considerable alarm in Athens. Apart from the loss of revenue and timber for shipbuilding, with Brasidas in possession of Amphipolis and the bridge over the Strymon, Thrace now lay open to him. This was a situation that nobody would have been more aware of than the cities spread along the coast to the east, which, when they heard of the moderate terms being offered by Brasidas, and thinking the Athenians were nearing defeat, sent him messages of welcome and vied with one another to be the first to free themselves. Being taken by surprise at this sudden turn of events, and because it was winter, all that the Athenians managed to do was to reinforce their garrisons

and banish Thucydides for twenty years. As for Brasidas, he asked
the Spartans to exploit his success, but they did nothing – according
to Thucydides, partly out of jealousy, and partly because they were
trying to obtain the release of their prisoners, as well as wanting to
end the war. But the indefatigable Brasidas arranged for the building
of some triremes on the lake higher up the Strymon, and by
constructing a palisade connecting the walls of Amphipolis to the
bridge over the river, he ensured that it would be better defended
than when it had fallen to him. He then set about winning over a
number of small towns to the east of the Strymon, before turning
back to clear up his rear. First he overran the thirty-mile-long Acte
peninsula, the eastern prong of the Chalcidice trident directly south
of Acanthus; before doing the same with Sithonian peninsula, which
forms the middle prong. For the remainder of the winter, Brasidas
occupied himself with consolidating his hold on what he had gained,
and preparing his plans for the future.

Athens' defeat at Delium in Boeotia, and the seemingly unstoppa-
ble successes of Brasidas in Thrace, had led to the temporary eclipse
of Cleon and brought the peace party to the fore; so, after
negotiations that had taken place in the winter, in the spring of 423 BC
a one-year truce was concluded with Sparta. The object of the truce
was to stop the fighting, leaving the antagonists in possession of what
they had gained, until a permanent peace treaty was agreed. Both
Athens and Sparta had strong negotiating hands: Athens held the
Spartan prisoners, together with Pylos, Cythera and Methana; while
Sparta had every prospect of gaining the whole of Thrace, so enabling
her to threaten Athens' corn supplies through the Hellespont.
Brasidas, with a mere handful of hoplites and Helots, had balanced
the negotiating scales for Sparta. Unwittingly, however, he was now
to cause a major disruption and sour the whole peace process.

While the negotiations to secure the truce had been under way,
Scione, a city on the Pellene peninsula, the western prong of the
Chalcidice trident, revolted against Athens. Quick as ever to seize an
opportunity, during the night Brasidas sailed to Scione, where he
made one of his usual conciliatory speeches, praising the citizens for
having the courage to claim their freedom, especially when isolated
like an island by Potidaea, at the neck of the peninsula. Heartened and
completely won over, the Scioneans welcomed Brasidas into the city

and, after crowning him as the liberator of Hellas, enthusiastically threw themselves into the war.

Brasidas next started trying to arrange the defection of the other cities on the peninsula; but just as matters were coming to a head, a trireme arrived with commissioners from both Athens and Sparta, carrying news of the truce. When the terms had been made known, they were readily accepted, with one exception. The exception was Scione, which the Athenian commissioner claimed had revolted after the truce had been agreed – a contention hotly denied by Brasidas, who refused to give it up. When the situation became known in Athens, under the malevolent influence of Cleon, the Spartan suggestion that they should go to arbitration was rejected and preparations to send an expeditionary force were put in hand. Then, to complicate the issue still further, Mende (another city on the Pallene peninsula) revolted and was welcomed as an ally by Brasidas, although it had obviously come over to him after the truce had come into force. Appreciating that his acceptance of Mende's defection made Athenian intervention inevitable, Brasidas made ready to defend both Scione and Mende. All the women and children were evacuated to Olynthus, in Chalcidice at the head of the Toronaic Gulf, and replaced by 500 Peloponnesian hoplites and 300 Chalcidian peltasts. Most commanders, in Brasidas' place, would have wanted to remain at hand to watch over developments and hold themselves ready to intervene. Brasidas, however, had a problem. Were he to remain on the peninsula, with Athenian naval supremacy and their possession of Potidaea, he would have been trapped; but, if he were to position himself outside the peninsula, for the same reasons, he would be unable to gain access. It has been suggested that his force was too small to face the Athenians; but, given the number of new allies he had acquired, this is hardly likely to have been a factor in his considerations.

At first sight what Brasidas did next seems inexplicable: he joined forces with Perdiccas, the Macedonian king, to undertake a remote enterprise of no direct relevance. But, being such an outstanding commander, there must have been some compelling reason for Brasidas to have taken such a step. Most probably he needed to repay the support Perdiccas had given him; so together they launched themselves into the interior to settle some domestic Macedonian business – an expedition that drew off the remainder of Brasidas'

Peloponnesian hoplites as well as the contingents from his local allies, such as the Acanthians and Chalcidians. But things were to go badly wrong. Some Illyrian mercenaries who had been hired by Perdiccas suddenly changed sides; an unsettling development, which caused his army to abandon the field and head for home at best speed. When Brasidas discovered that the Macedonians had vanished overnight, he conducted a skilful fighting withdrawal, but, following in the wake of Perdiccas' flight, his troops took matters into their own hands. Enraged at having been deserted, they unyoked and slaughtered any cattle they came across, while appropriating for themselves the Macedonians' discarded equipment. This was conduct which, according to Thucydides, turned Perdiccas against Brasidas, whom he now regarded as an enemy. So, shortly afterwards, he entered into negotiations with the Athenians. Undoubtedly Thucydides is right in what he says, but Perdiccas must also have felt a sense of shame at what had occurred – a loss of face that would make working with Brasidas embarrassing, and restoring trust impossible. So, better to be shot of the fellow.

In the meantime, the Athenians had arrived at Potidaea with fifty triremes, 1000 hoplites and 600 archers, together with 1000 Thracian mercenaries and some local peltasts, all under the command of two generals, Nicias and Nicostratus. The Athenians then sailed down the coast and, after disembarking, set off for Mende, but on the way they encountered the Peloponnesians and their allies, who had taken up a defensive position on some high ground. The Athenians divided their forces: one contingent mounted a frontal attack, while the other made an outflanking movement; but they became thoroughly disorganised when advancing across the broken ground, and they were easily repulsed. Both sides then withdrew, the Athenians to reorganise themselves, and the Mendeans to retire into their city. The next day when the Athenians circled Mende, burning and plundering as they went, the Peloponnesian commander wanted to make a sortie, but the Mendeans refused. A heated argument followed, which rapidly developed into a free-for-all, with the Mendeans participating on both sides according to their political preferences. In the chaos that now gripped the city, the gates were opened before any terms had been agreed; so the Athenians burst in and sacked Mende, treating it as though it had been taken by storm. It was all very Greek.

The Athenians then turned their attention to Scione. As they approached, the Peloponnesians marched out to meet them, taking up a position on a hill outside the walls; but they were driven off it and withdrew into the city. Feeling unable to carry it by attack, the Athenians settled down to besiege Scione, so they began constructing an encircling wall. This was the situation Brasidas discovered on returning from his Macedonian expedition, and, finding himself unable to recover Mende or relieve Scione, he had to content himself with defending Torone, on the extremity of the middle prong of the Chalcidice trident.

In the meantime Perdiccas had approached the Athenians with his proposals for an alliance. Knowing their man, however, the Athenians demanded some proof that he could be relied upon; so Perdiccas arranged with the Thessalians to prevent the passage of an expected Spartan expeditionary force through their territory. Thucydides says that the Thessalians carried out his request so successfully that the Spartans did not even raise the matter with them. Which does not sound as though the Spartans placed much importance on assisting Brasidas.

Towards the end of the summer the blockading wall round Scione was completed, and, leaving enough troops behind to man it, the two generals and the rest of the army returned to Athens. With the year-long truce still having some ten months to run, the reason for the Athenian departure remains obscure. An enterprising commander, possessing naval supremacy and adequate troops, would have tried to trap Brasidas on the Sithonia peninsula, perhaps driving him into Torone where he could have been contained. But Nicias lacked the drive and enterprise of a successful commander. He was far too cautious and unimaginative.

With the Athenian field army gone, at the end of the year Brasidas attempted to take Potidaea by surprise. Placing scaling ladders against the walls under cover of darkness, he was preparing to mount the assault when they were detected by an alert sentry, leaving Brasidas with no alternative but to call off the operation and withdraw. In spite of all this fighting going on in the Northern Theatre, the truce held in mainland Greece; but with so much recrimination and mistrust, little progress was being made towards reaching a permanent settlement.

In the elections held in the spring of 422 BC, Cleon was chosen as a general and, after the truce had ended, he sailed for the Northern Theatre to repeat his success at Pylos. He had with him 1200 hoplites and 300 cavalry, all of whom were Athenian, as well as a still larger force of allies and thirty triremes. He first put in at Scione, where he collected some of the troops blockading the city, and then crossed over to the Sithonia peninsula, where he disembarked near Torone. On learning that Brasidas was not in the city, and that the garrison was relatively small, Cleon decided to take the city, which he did in a well-conducted little operation. He was fortunate in his timing, however, as Brasidas was marching to the relief of Torone, and was only some four miles away when it fell. Before leaving the area, Cleon posted a garrison in Torone and won back for Athens a number of smaller cities, though he made no attempt to recover Scione, which he clearly thought could be left to starve.

Cleon's next move was to set sail for Eion, which he intended to use as a base for the recovery of Amphipolis. After his arrival he sent messengers to Perdiccas, urging him to come to his assistance, while despatching envoys into Thrace to recruit mercenaries. For his part, Brasidas had been equally active. Taking up a position on Mount Cerdylium, to the south-west of Amphipolis, he assembled a miscellaneous force of some 2000 hoplites, 300 Hellenic and an unknown number of allied cavalry, together with 1000 peltasts and 1500 Thracian mercenaries. Of the total, Brasidas kept 1500 under his personal command on Mount Cerdylium and reinforced Amphipolis with the remainder.

Cleon, finding his army growing restless while waiting for the reinforcements to arrive, decided he must make a move; so he advanced towards Amphipolis and took up position on a hill overlooking the city. As soon as Brasidas saw that the Athenians were on the march, he quickly moved his whole army into Amphipolis. In Thucydides' estimation, the size of the two armies at this stage was about the same, but the Athenians were of a better quality; an assessment that Brasidas shared. As Thucydides says, his army's qualitative inferiority made Brasidas decide to attack in a 'less obvious manner', keeping his troops with their 'rough-and-ready equipment out of sight'. Meeting these two requirements was restrictive enough, but there was also a third: he had to engage the Athenians before they had assembled their full strength, and Cleon's move gave him just that opportunity. Brasidas now explained his plan. With the 150 hoplites whom he had picked out, he would lead a sudden charge, at the double, out of one of the city gates against the Athenian centre. As soon as they were engaged, the rest of the troops were to charge out of another gate and get amongst the Athenians as quickly as possible.

The Athenians, for their part, had seen Brasidas enter Amphipolis and reported the fact to Cleon, who, as every commander should, had gone forward to make a personal reconnaissance. While doing so, he learned that the enemy were massing at the gates, as though preparing to sally out into the attack. Not wishing to risk what could be a decisive battle before his whole army had assembled, Cleon decided to withdraw, so he gave orders for the retreat to be sounded – clearly thinking that if Brasidas did come out to give battle, he would do so in the conventional manner by first forming up outside the fortifications. It must be for this reason that Thucydides says that Cleon thought he had plenty of time to extricate himself. So his instructions were for the army to fall back towards Eion, with the left wing leading the way; he would then wheel the right wing round to follow on behind. When this dodgy manoeuvre got under way, and there was no formed front to oppose him, Brasidas charged out as he had planned and threw the Athenian centre into confusion, where-upon the rest of his troops poured out of another gate into the attack. Taken by surprise and assaulted on an exposed flank, the Athenians panicked and, with the left wing still showing the way, took to their heels.

Cleon made no attempt to stand and fight, but joined in the unseemly flight, only to be overtaken and killed by a Thracian peltast. The hoplites were the one part of the army to try and rally and make a stand, but they suffered heavy casualties from missiles hurled by the Chalcidian cavalry and the peltasts. So eventually even they broke, and the survivors only managed to escape by following various mountain tracks back to Eion. In spite of Thucydides' account of Cleon's death, which has already been given, it does not seem unreasonable to suggest that he may have got it wrong, and in fact Cleon died amongst his hoplites in their last stand; there is no reason for thinking that he was not brave. Only seven of Brasidas' men were killed, as compared to some 600 Athenians. Even if the figures are not

precisely accurate, once again they show that surprise and offensive
action are battle-winning factors. As for the demoralised Athenian
survivors, once they had received back their dead, they delayed no
longer and sailed for home.

But out of this shambles of a defeat came two rays of hope for the
Athenians: Cleon was dead and Brasidas had been mortally wounded.
With Cleon's death, a major obstacle to peace had been removed;
while a vigorous but mediocre general had been despatched to
somewhere he could no longer do any harm. It should be remembered that the Athenian success at Pylos had not been due to Cleon:
he had merely adopted the plan conceived by Demosthenes. With
Brasidas dying from his wounds, the Spartans had lost an outstanding
commander, and the Athenians a matchless opponent: one who, it
will be remembered, had already shown himself to be an able tactician
and a brave, decisive leader – one who was trusted and beyond
considerations of personal gain. Small wonder that he inspired his
men to achieve far more than what could have been expected of them.
He also showed a psychological understanding of what the situation
required, together with an empathy that extended not just to his
soldiers, but to the citizens of the cities he persuaded to join him.

So there we are. According to Thucydides, we have two contrasting
figures: one to admire, the essence of all that is heroic; the other to
despise, the incarnation of all that is contemptible. Like all mortals,
Brasidas must have had his faults, but (except for his disregard of the
truce) they remain unrevealed; while Cleon cannot have been as awful
as he has been portrayed. As a soldier he was certainly no great
tactician, but when he was appointed to command the Athenian force
at Pylos, although Thucydides gives him the most unworthy motives,
he did have the good sense to take with him archers and other light
troops who were far more useful on the rocky, wooded island of
Sphacteria than hoplites. As a politician Cleon was ruthless, demanding the indiscriminate execution of the inhabitants of Mytilene for
revolting, and such an implacable enemy of Sparta that he rejected
any opportunity for peace. But he was not untypical of politicians in
pursuing policies that he saw as being advantageous to himself. It was
his misfortune to meet the hostility of two great writers: the historian
Thucydides and the comic poet Aristophanes, who in his play *The
Knights* launches a merciless attack on Cleon.

The Eastern Theatre

Compared to the turmoil of previous decades, activity in the Eastern Theatre was relatively subdued. The island of Lesbos, except for the city of Methymna, revolted against Athens in 428 BC. As an account of the revolt has already been given, it will only be briefly outlined now. The city of Mytilene, with the support of the Spartans and their kinsmen the Boeotians, was trying to gain complete control of the island. On hearing of this, the Athenians hurriedly sent out a fleet of forty ships, but the Mytilenians refused to obey the orders they brought with them, to dismantle their fortifications. Instead they rose in revolt. The Spartans mounted a particularly devastating invasion of Attica, hoping to distract Athenian attention from Lesbos, so letting the revolt run its natural course, while giving a freer hand to the forty-two Peloponnesian ships going to help Mytilene. But the scheme failed completely. The Athenians were not distracted, and the Peloponnesian fleet displayed so little sense of urgency that Mytilene was starved into surrender before it had even arrived. This occurred in 427 BC, shortly before the fall of Plataea.

The Athenians then debated how the rebel city should be punished for its disloyalty. As will be remembered, Cleon induced them to resolve that the entire population should be put to death, so a trireme was sent bearing this fateful order. The following day there was another debate, when less drastic measures were decided upon; so a second trireme was despatched in all haste, arriving just in time to prevent the slaughter.

In the meantime, the Peloponnesian fleet commanders were undecided as to what they should do. Some were for attacking at once, while the Athenians were dispersed and relaxed after their victory. Others proposed seizing a coastal city and using it as a base for organising a revolt in Ionia; but the fleet commander, Alcidas, found this all too hazardous for his taste, his main concern being to get back home as soon as possible, a concern that was heightened when he was sighted by two Athenian triremes. Weighing anchor as quickly as he could, he fled across the open sea, with the firm intention of not putting in anywhere until he reached the Peloponnese.

Although he was pursued by the Athenians, Alcidas had gained too much of a start, and the chase was called off. But he did not have any respite, for he was at once sent to Corcyra where civil war had broken out.

As a matter of interest, the two Athenian triremes that had sighted Alcidas, the *Paralus* and the *Salaminia*, were the elite of the Athenian navy, kept in service throughout the year for special missions. 'Special forces' have long antecedents.

8

An Unquiet Peace
421–415 BC

Earlier Thucydides told us that the Thessalians, at the request of Perdiccas, had made it so difficult for the Spartans to send reinforcements to Brasidas that they did not even ask them if they could pass through their territory. Now, however, he tells a slightly different story. A Spartan force was actually in Thessaly when it learned that Brasidas was dead and the Athenians had left; so, knowing that their fellow countrymen wanted an end to the war, it turned back. Athenian self-confidence had taken a severe knock following their defeats at Delium and Amphipolis – defeats that could also seriously undermine the resolve and loyalty of their allies. Meanwhile the Spartans, who had never wanted war in the first place, and who ever since had been ready to reach a negotiated settlement, now found themselves confronted with three problems – the last two seemingly intractable, so long as the war continued. However much they might devastate Attica, it was having little effect: the Helots were deserting, and their allies could follow them, while the Athenians still held their prisoners, amongst whom were a number of distinguished individuals with relatives in high places. Both antagonists thus had powerful reasons for wanting peace.

Thucydides tells us that Nicias, because he had not suffered a defeat, was still held in high esteem and carried great authority – a reputation and standing that he wished to preserve before some misfortune overtook him. He personally sought peace. On the Spartan side, King Pleistoanax was equally dedicated to ending the war and, though under attack from his political opponents (because his brother was alleged to have bribed the priestess at Delphi), he was nevertheless much respected and exercised considerable influence. So, with the two most eminent statesmen intent on achieving a settlement, and with the great majority of the people behind them, negotiations were opened and continued throughout most of the winter in 422 BC.

Agreement between Athens and Sparta was finally reached in the spring of 421 BC. A fact that serves to remind us that religion played a vitally important part in the lives of the Greeks, in that the treaty opened with the statement that the pan-Hellenic temples were to be available to everybody for sacrificing, consulting the oracles and attending the sacred festivals; moreover, the temple of Apollo at Delphi was to be administered by the Delphians in accordance with their own laws, taxes and customs. The main points of the treaty that followed were: Sparta would return Amphipolis to Athens and relinquish her connections with the other cities she had taken, though they were not to become allies of Athens unless they so wished, and then only in the tribute-paying class; there would be an exchange of prisoners; and Athens would return Pylos, Cythera, Methone and two towns they had acquired. Finally, the supremacy of Athens and Sparta was underlined by the authority they gave themselves: if difficulties or unforeseen matters arose, they were empowered to amend the treaty as they saw fit. As we will see, this clause was going to cause Sparta considerable difficulties.

The treaty was ratified by the majority of Athens' and Sparta's allies, but there were some important exceptions. Corinth had lost nearly all her dependencies in the north-west, while no restrictions had been placed on the extension of Athenian encroachments in the area; Megara had lost the port of Nicaea, a useful acquisition for Athens, which strengthened her position in the Corinthian Gulf; Boeotia actually had to hand back the frontier fortress of Panactum, lying on the mountainous range between Attica and Boeotia, which she had obtained by betrayal; while Elis refused her assent, not because of the treaty, but because she was in dispute with Sparta over Lepreum, a seemingly insignificant town lying south of Elis.

It fell by lot to the Spartans to make the first move: so they began by releasing all the prisoners and sending representatives to Thrace with orders to implement the treaty. But the envoys met with such a blunt refusal that it could herald a revolt – an opportunistic development that Argos was quick to seize upon. As will be remembered, Argos had remained neutral during the war, but the existing peace treaty she had with Sparta was shortly due for renewal, which the Argives now refused. Faced with this thinly veiled threat, and unable to persuade her allies to conform to the terms of the treaty, Sparta proceeded to make a fifty-year alliance with Athens, which bound them to come to one another's aid if attacked. It was an astute move, since, so long as the alliance held, no other association of states could hope to match the combined power of Athens and Sparta. Argos then seemed to have been marginalised.

The settlement was known as the Peace of Nicias. Plutarch tells us that the reason was that the Athenians believed the peace was the reward of the gods for Nicias' piety. They thought Nicias was responsible for the peace, just as they considered that Pericles had been responsible for the war. With Nicias' reputation at its peak, it is an appropriate moment to pause and consider the character of this man, who has already figured prominently on a number of occasions, and whom we will frequently meet again. Plutarch begins by saying, as had Aristotle, that Nicias was one of the three best citizens of Athens, demonstrating the goodwill and affection of a father to the people; though, following the death of Pericles, he owed his political elevation mainly to the wealthy upper class, who elected him as an antidote to the crass effrontery of Cleon. Plutarch then goes on to say that Nicias was extremely wealthy, owning several silver mines at Laurium, and that he was excessively superstitious, addicted to belief in omens and oracles, while holding safety to be his guiding principle. He was also faint-hearted and lacked self-confidence, but in warfare he overcame his timidity and proved himself to be a successful military commander.

From what we have seen of Nicias' performance so far, Plutarch's assessment of him as a soldier seems to be based more on his avoidance of disaster than on any positive achievement. Moreover, as we will see, though Nicias unwillingly accepted command of the Athenian expedition to Syracuse in 415 BC, he was nevertheless the commander and so carries responsibility for the catastrophic defeat that followed. Though his behaviour in shifting the blame for the unrewarding expedition to Sicily in 427 BC onto the commanders was reprehensible, Nicias otherwise comes over as a thoroughly decent, generous-hearted and self-effacing man, who would have graced any social occasion. But such characteristics are no substitute for the decisiveness, daring and personal magnetism required of a leader in battle. Nor was he a great statesman – who, in addition to the qualities required of a leader, must rise above petty party politics and scorn short-term opportunism. Nicias was a diplomat, clever and cautious, prone to pussyfooting round a problem, and thus unable to cut the Gordian knot when the need arose. He was unfortunate in being born before the diplomatic service was created, so he missed his natural vocation.

But to return to the situation that existed after Athens and Sparta had entered into an alliance with one another. Although, in outright terms, there had been no victor or loser as a result of the ten years of fighting, the Athenians emerged from the war without having suffered any irreparable loss. Their maritime supremacy continued unchallenged, thereby securing their hold on their empire, while Athens itself remained inviolate. Given an enduring peace, Athens' human and material losses, though substantial – the former almost entirely due to the plague – could be replaced. Moreover, Amphipolis was to be returned, together with Panactum, the border town that had been betrayed to the Boeotians, while Athens retained Nisaea, the Megarian port, and her influence in the north-west region; and the restrictions placed on Athens' relationship with the other Thracian cities she was to recover would be unlikely to endure. In return for all this, Athens had only to return the Peloponnesian prisoners (above all the Spartans) and hand back a number of places she had conquered, most prominently Pylos, Cythera and Methana, none of which was of any great importance to her in times of peace.

As for Sparta, in spite of the loss of prestige she had suffered at Pylos, she emerged from the war practically unscathed, and she was still the dominant land power. As has been mentioned, the real losers were Sparta's allies, and it was their resentment that was to cause great difficulty. The trouble started with Corinth, which had lost more than any of Sparta's allies and, feeling injured, now looked for a powerful ally who was prepared to end Spartan hegemony, to pursue Peloponnesian interests and to assume the leadership of a new alliance. With her long-standing hatred of Sparta, who was better qualified than Argos? A Greek city was normally hostile to its nearest neighbour, and indeed such cities were normally at war except when they had a specific treaty of peace, with a set terminal date. So representatives were sent to the Argives suggesting the formation of a new defensive alliance, open to any independent Hellenic state except Sparta and Athens. Thucydides says that there were two principal reasons why the Argives restricted the alliance in this manner: first, now that their treaty with Sparta was on the point of expiring, they saw that war with her was inevitable; and second, they hoped to gain the leadership of the Peloponnese. In view of the fact that it was Argos that had refused to renew the treaty with Sparta, the idea that she should now see war as an inevitable consequence of its termination seems somewhat far-fetched. With their enduring hatred of Sparta for earlier injuries, the Argives' decision not to renew the treaty was more probably taken when they saw an opportunity for revenge. It was this desire to pay off old scores that made war inevitable, not the termination of the treaty itself.

The first to join Argos out of fear of Spartan intentions was Mantinea, lying in the centre of the Peloponnese. During the war Mantinea had occupied a large part of Arcadia, which she now feared Sparta would make her return. Mantinea's abandonment of the Spartan alliance caused considerable disquiet throughout the Peloponnese, with other states attributing her decision to some special intelligence which, though unknown to them, probably made it prudent to follow her lead. It was the clause in the treaty empowering Athens and Sparta to adjust their terms that was the root cause of this concern; so state after state began to edge towards joining the new alliance that Argos was offering.

Realising that this unrest in the Peloponnese was due to Corinth, the Spartans sent envoys to try and dissuade her from joining the alliance she had proposed to Argos in the first place. They reminded the Corinthians that they were already in the wrong in refusing to accept the peace treaty with Athens, when it was expressly laid down that a majority vote of the allies would be binding on them all. The Spartans then went on to say that, were the Corinthians to desert Sparta and join Argos, they would be breaking their oath. Rather than air their personal grievances, the Corinthians replied that, at the time when Potidaea had revolted against Athens, they had sworn a separate treaty with their allies in Thrace, guaranteeing not to betray them; this was exactly what Sparta was doing, and what she now expected them, the Corinthians, to do too. As will be remembered, Corinth and Potidaea had close ties, and it was Athens' attack on the city that had been one of the causes of the Peloponnesian War.

With the exception of Elis, representatives of the other allies who had refused to accept the treaty with Athens, as well as envoys from Argos, were also present at this exchange of opinions. Now, when the meeting was over, the envoys from Argos urged the Corinthians to enter into an alliance with them, but the Corinthians decided to delay a decision, inviting the Argives to attend any future meeting with the Spartans. The Elean envoys now arrived on the scene in a decisive mood, and, after hearing what had taken place, at once made an alliance with Corinth, before going on to Argos to do the same with her. Secession from Sparta was taking place piecemeal, with the Chalcidians of Thrace and the Corinthians now joining the Argive alliance, although the Boeotians and Megarians hung back, thinking that the democratic government of Argos would be less favourable towards their autocratic governments than would that of the Spartans.

Though the Spartan-led alliance was beginning to look as if it was breaking up, there was a self-contradiction in the new one forming around Argos. While Mantinea and Elis had joined because of their hostility to Sparta, without abating her hostility to Athens, Corinth had done so because of her anti-Spartan sentiments following the peace treaty, while the Chalcidians had joined because of their hostility to Athens. The whole situation was inherently unstable, with the web of intrigue becoming more tangled than ever. Tegea, the staunch and loyal neighbour of Sparta, was the next to appear on the scene, when she turned down the request made by Corinth and Argos to join their alliance. Thucydides says this refusal was of such significance that it not only deterred other states from deserting Sparta, but even damped down the Corinthians' anti-Spartan enthusiasm; though this did not deter them from trying to persuade the Boeotians to become an ally of Argos and Corinth herself.

But the Boeotians were not to be drawn – even if they had rejected the peace treaty, they preferred to remain on friendly terms with Sparta; besides, it would be better to wait and see how things developed, before committing themselves. So the Boeotians also refused the Corinthian request to annul their truce with Athens; a request they had made just because the Athenians had declined to extend the truce to include them. In the meantime Sparta, without having enforced the terms of the peace treaty, had withdrawn her troops from Thrace, leaving Amphipolis and the other Thracian towns defiantly refusing to submit to Athens – a defiance that was evidently not tempered by the Athenians' brutal, but not untypical, treatment of Scione. When the city was finally starved into surrender, all the males of military age were executed, with the women and children being sold into slavery.

According to Thucydides, Sparta had repeatedly said that, should her allies refuse to accept the treaty, she would join with Athens in compelling them to do so; but as nothing had been committed to writing, nothing happened. It is difficult not to feel some sympathy for Sparta. The predicament in which she found herself was partly due to her having to make the first move, which she was prevented from completing by a powerful group of her own allies. This failure in turn engendered the hostility of Athens, which, having released the Spartan prisoners, now regretted losing such a powerful bargaining counter; so she refused to hand back Pylos or any of the other possessions she had gained. Perhaps Sparta would not have got herself into such a hopeless position had she heeded Pericles' words in his funeral oration of 431 BC, when he said: 'Acts are foredoomed to failure when undertaken undiscussed.' On the other hand, had Sparta discussed the terms of the peace treaty with her allies, it would have been equally foredoomed to failure. Such is the price to be paid for cobbling together a disparate alliance of self-seeking states.

Towards the end of the first year of peace, the Spartan position hardened when new ephors were appointed, some of whom were opposed to the treaty. A large conference was called, which was attended by representatives from the Spartan Confederation, as well as from Athens, but in spite of a lot of discussion no agreement was reached, and they were all on the point of dispersing when the Spartan ephors – with the knowledge of the Corinthians, but behind their own government's back – advanced a truly Machiavellian proposal to the Boeotians. Boeotia should join the Argive alliance, and then try and bring herself and Argos into an alliance with Sparta. Meanwhile, they asked the Boeotians to hand over Panactum to Athens, which might enable them to recover Pylos and put them in a stronger position for making war on Athens. The plot then thickened.

Quite separately, the Argives themselves now proposed to the Boeotian envoys that they join them in an alliance, as the Corinthians and Mantineans had done, after which they would be strong enough to make war or peace with anyone they wished. Though welcoming this proposition, which accorded with that made by their Spartan friends, the Boeotians first wanted to ensure that the Corinthians, Megarians and Chalcidians would work in concert with them. Once satisfied on this score, all seemed ready to proceed; but the Boeotian government, which had only been brought into the discussions at this stage, refused to agree, fearing that the anti-Spartan policy of Corinth and the Chalcidians would draw them into a conflict with Sparta. So the plot unravelled and came to nothing, though it provides us with an illuminating insight into the Byzantine intricacies of the Greek states' relationship with one another, while giving us a better understanding of the difficulties involved in reaching an enduring peace. Finally, to end the year, the Spartans, persevering with their hope of recovering Pylos, made a final effort to persuade the Boeotians to hand over Panactum to them, so that they could use it as a bargaining counter with the Athenians.

Although the Boeotians abandoned Panactum, they only did so after demolishing the fortifications, and then proceeded to hand it over directly to the Athenians. Two ungracious measures: the former enraging the Athenians, and the latter hardly endearing them to the Spartans.

The year of 420 BC was another year of nefarious diplomatic activity. The attempt to form an Argive coalition having failed, Argos quickly shed her ambitions and instead, fearing that the whole alliance would now go over to Sparta and leave her isolated, hurriedly tried to come to terms with Sparta. Though previously Argos had always thought she could fall back on the support of Athens if things went wrong, she now mistakenly believed that the Athenians were a party to the shifting loyalties that were taking place. Driven by a sense of urgency, the Argive representatives obtained Spartan agreement to a fifty-year peace treaty but, as will be seen, this was overtaken by events before it was ratified.

Unknown to the Argives, Athenian and Spartan relations had in fact been deteriorating. Athens was outraged that Panactum's fortifications had been demolished and that, in contravention of the peace treaty concluded between them, Sparta had entered into an alliance with Boeotia. For their part, the Spartans remained resentful that Pylos had still not been returned to them. To make matters worse, Alcibiades – a well-placed and influential young man, anxious to strike out in an independent and assertive way, who believed that Athens' interests were best served by forming an alliance with Argos

– proposed such a treaty on his own initiative. The Argives now realised how mistaken they had been in thinking that the Athenians had had a hand in the alliance between Sparta and Boeotia, so they quickly did an about-turn. No further instructions were sent to their representatives negotiating the treaty with Sparta, while negotiations were at once opened with Athens.

From now on we are going to come across Alcibiades with increasing frequency, so, even if it is to some extent anticipating the future, a proper introduction is called for. According to Plutarch, he was arrestingly handsome, and the attractiveness and charm of his good looks never left him, while his lisp made his conversation charmingly persuasive. Of noble birth and wealthy, he had a passionate nature, and his most powerful motivation was the desire to compete, and to come first. As has been mentioned, in upper-class Athenian society homosexuality was an accepted practice, with an older man taking a handsome youth as his lover until the boy grew up. In this way Alcibiades became Socrates' 'tent mate' on campaigns – they both fought at Potidaea and Delium – though Plutarch maintains that Alcibiades shunned his rich and eminent lovers in favour of an intellectual and spiritual relationship with Socrates, who kept him free from corruption. As Plutarch goes on to say that Alcibiades 'was cruel and intractable to the rest of his lovers', he evidently does not regard homosexual promiscuity as a form of corruption, which makes one wonder what he had in mind. But to return to Alcibiades' characteristics. He was a fine, persuasive orator – which he put to good use in winning over the ordinary people; clever, vigorous and determined. He had many of the talents that go towards making a great statesman, a national leader who could direct the affairs of Athens with vision and purpose. But he was flawed, a sort of Jekyll and Hyde, being also devious, greedy for fame, a shameless liar, unprincipled, and contemptuous of the worthy, solid character-istics that go to make up the backbone of society, or of a country itself. Let us then watch him in action as Robert Louis Stevenson's Mr Hyde.

At the same time as the delegates from Argos came to Athens to discuss making a treaty, a Spartan deputation also arrived, concerned at the prospect of Athens making an ally of Argos, and asking for Pylos in exchange for Panactum, as well as explaining that the alliance Sparta had made with Boeotia was not directed at Athens. Most importantly, in front of the Council, they made it clear that they had come with full powers to reach an agreement on these and all other matters in dispute. This speech made Alcibiades fear that, should it be repeated in front of the Assembly, the Spartans might win over the people to their side and reject the Argive alliance. He therefore promised the Spartans that if they made no mention to the Assembly of their full powers, he would arrange for the return of Pylos, and for the other points to be settled.

Either from naive gullibility, or charmed out of their senses by Alcibiades' eloquence, the Spartan deputies agreed to his proposal. When they appeared before the Assembly, in reply to a question – and to the astonishment of the senators who had heard them saying exactly the opposite the previous day – the Spartans said they had not come with full powers. Whereupon Alcibiades launched a vicious attack on them, swaying his audience to such an extent that the Assembly would have been prepared to make an immediate alliance with Argos. But before a decision was reached, the tremors of an earthquake caused the meeting to be adjourned. If ever an oracle was required it was now, but evidently none was available.

The next day Nicias persuaded the Assembly to send a delegation to Sparta (which would include himself). It should tell them that, if they really meant well, they should give back Panactum intact – as will be remembered, Thucydides has previously told us that the Boeotians had already returned the frontier fortress to the Athenians, but only after demolishing the walls – hand over Amphipolis, and renounce their alliance with the Boeotians. On arriving, the Athenian delegation spoke as had been agreed, then reminded the Spartans that, so long as the Boeotians refused to recognise the peace settlement, Sparta was in breach of its terms through making an alliance with them. Under these circumstances, unless the Spartans renounced the alliance, Athens would be obliged to enter into one with Argos.

But the hardline Spartan ephors and their supporters refused to be moved, and so, in an attempt not to return completely empty-handed, Nicias got them to renew the treaty oaths that governed their relationship. It was a hollow concession on the part of the Spartans, which did nothing to alleviate Nicias' humiliation on returning from the commission he himself had proposed; nor did it placate the anger of the Athenians at what they regarded as Spartan perfidy and intransigence. As the Argive representatives were still in Athens, a treaty and an alliance were promptly concluded, the broad terms of which were: the Athenians, the Argives, the Mantineans and the Eleans, for themselves and for their allies, made a 100-year treaty, whereby (like the NATO alliance) an attack on one would be regarded as an attack on them all.

This treaty, which divided Athens and Sparta even further, while clearly enlarging the field of potential conflict, also introduced some less obvious complexities. Two of the new allies Athens had undertaken to defend were practically at war with Sparta already: Mantinea, because the previous year Sparta had driven them out of a disputed border town by a show of force; and Elis, as will be recalled, because of Lepreum, in which Sparta had now planted a military colony. These border disputes already posed a threat to peace, but by – wittingly or unwittingly – incorporating them into a formal alliance, the risk of the Greeks being engulfed in a renewal of the war had been greatly increased. Moreover, as we have repeatedly seen, allegiance to political parties extended beyond city walls and boundaries, and with this latest shake of the kaleidoscope Athens, Argos, Mantinea and Elis had shaped themselves into a democratic block, while those with oligarchic governments like Boeotia and Megara were gravitating back to Sparta. An isolated exception at this stage was Corinth, which rejected the blandishments of both blocks. Such was the situation at the end of 420 BC, and with it we have virtually come to the end of this involved period of diplomatic scheming. Those who find the political and geographic complexities of the Balkans bewildering need to put their confusion into perspective by looking at the situation in Greece during 421 and 420 BC.

The following year the Boeotians seized the Spartan colony of Heraclea, north-west of Thermopylae, justifying their strange behaviour towards a close ally on the grounds that, weakened by the defeat Heraclea had sustained at the hands of the neighbouring tribes, it was in danger of falling into the possession of the Athenians. Elsewhere, though there was some sabre-rattling by both Sparta and Athens, neither of them did anything to endanger the peace. But when fighting broke out between Argos and Epidaurus, allegedly over the latter's failure to pay Apollo his dues, it almost inevitably brought the danger of Spartan and Athenian intervention. Sparta was the first to move, mobilising her army and marching to help the Epidaurians, whereupon Alcibiades crossed the Saronic Gulf with 1000 hoplites.

The Spartans, however, seem to have had second thoughts, or perhaps the omens were not propitious, as they withdrew before crossing the frontier, so Alcibiades also returned home. For the time being the fighting remained localised, but in the winter the Spartans eluded the Athenian fleet and installed a garrison of 300 men in Epidaurus; so, in retaliation, the Athenians put a force of Messenians and Helots into Pylos, from where they could resume the raiding of the neighbouring Peloponnesian territory.

In the middle of 418 BC, seeing that the Epidaurians were getting into difficulty, and fearing the revolt of other states, Sparta decided to stamp out the fighting before it spread to other parts of the Peloponnese. She then arranged for her allies to send troops to Phlius, south-west of Corinth, where not only most of the Peloponnesian contingents assembled, but also 2000 Corinthian hoplites, together with the Boeotians, who sent 5000 hoplites, 5000 light troops, 500 cavalry and 500 dismounted troops specially trained to fight alongside the cavalry. When all was ready the Spartans under King Agis, with the Tegeans and some allies from Arcadia, set off for Phlius. But all these preparations had not gone unnoticed by the Argives, who, together with the Mantineans and 3000 hoplites from Elis, quickly moved to intercept them. Contact was made, and after a brief skirmish the two armies took up their positions for battle; but during the night the Spartans slipped away and joined up with their allies at Phlius. So yet again, through not keeping in close contact, an enemy force was allowed to elude battle; which, as will be remembered, is what occurred at Plataea in 479 BC.

When dawn broke and the Argives discovered that the Spartans had gone, they and their allies at once set off for Argos, from where they moved forward and took up a position on the plains at Nemea to block the road from Phlius, along which they expected the Spartans to advance. Agis, however, divided his army into three contingents. The Boeotians and Megarians were to wait until daylight, and then come down from the mountains, taking the direct route to Nemea across which the Argives lay. The two other contingents were to carry out a double envelopment, descending onto the plain during the night by two steep roads, which would bring them out behind or on the Argives' flanks. As soon as they realised what was happening, the Argives abandoned Nemea and, after a brief encounter with the smaller Corinthian contingent on a flank, they turned to confront Agis and his Spartans, who had got round behind them. Before the battle started, however, two of the Argive generals went forward and told Agis they were prepared to submit to arbitration any complaints that the Spartans might have, after which they wanted to make a treaty and live in peace. It was a startling initiative, as was Agis' acceptance of the proposals without any discussion amongst his Spartan and allied commanders; many of whom, though bound to accept his decision, felt bitter that, having trapped the Argives, the finest Hellenic army that had ever been assembled was then to retire instead of annihilating them. Thoroughly disgruntled at this turn of events, they reluctantly dispersed to their homes.

The Argives felt equally aggrieved. Thucydides says this was because they had many brave allies with them, and the battle would have been fought under the walls of their city, which – given their predicament – hardly justifies their optimism. Whatever the reasons, many of them felt they had been robbed of a victory, so they took their resentment out on one of the generals by stoning him. He was lucky to escape with his life by seeking sanctuary in a temple, but he lost all his property.

Shortly afterwards 1000 Athenian hoplites and 300 of their cavalry arrived, but they received a chilly welcome, at first being refused permission to speak in front of the Assembly. But under pressure from the Mantineans and Eleans, Alcibiades, who was present as an ambassador, was allowed to do so and immediately turned the tables against the Argives, accusing them of making an unlawful treaty without proper consultation. Won over by Alcibiades' eloquence, and still angry at having been let down by their generals, the Argives and their allies mounted an expedition into Arcadia, where the city of Orchomenus capitulated without offering resistance. A discussion then took place as to what they should do next: the Eleans wanted to attack Lepreum, while the Mantineans wanted to march against Tegea, probably because there were good grounds for believing that the city would be betrayed. The Athenians backed the Mantineans' proposal, whereupon the 3000 Elean hoplites departed in disgust.

In the meantime, when the Spartans had returned from Argos after making the four-month truce, there was considerable anger and indignation that King Agis had let slip an opportunity to win a notable victory – a mood that turned to fury when it was learned that

Orchomenus had fallen. Though Agis was fortunate not to have been sacked, have his house destroyed and a heavy fine imposed on him, his freedom of action was greatly curtailed: in future he was not empowered to lead an army out of the city without being accompanied by ten senior advisers. When news reached the Spartans that Tegea was on the point of being betrayed, they at once marched to its relief with all the troops they could muster, including the Helots, while telling the Arcadians to join them as quickly as possible. Once assured of Arcadian support, the Spartans then sent back their oldest and youngest troops, so as not to leave their homes completely undefended, while urging the Boeotians, Corinthians, Phocians and Locrians to come to their support. But though these allies mustered their forces as quickly as they could, they were too far away to arrive in time.

After some preliminary manoeuvring, the two armies finally clashed at Mantinea, some twenty miles north-west of Tegea. The Argives and their allies advanced rapidly, as though to break through the Spartan ranks by the sheer violence of their assault, while the Spartans came on more steadily, keeping in step with the flute-players so as not to lose formation. As will be remembered, because each man sought to obtain protection behind the shield of his neighbour, there was a tendency for the phalanx to extend to the right. So it was at Mantinea, with the Spartans overlapping the Athenians on the Argives' left flank, while the Mantineans stretched beyond the Sciritae – from Sciritis, a Laconian town some thirty miles north of Sparta – on the Spartan left flank. Because Agis feared he would be enveloped, he ordered the Sciritae to move to the left, intending that the gap would be filled with troops from his right wing, which would still maintain a numerical superiority. The two Spartan commanders, however, who should have filled the gap refused to do so and were later banished from Sparta for cowardice. It seems most improbable that both Spartan commanders would have refused to comply with such an important order: more probably it arrived too late for them to execute their instruction – not a failure that Agis and his ten advisers would wish to accept responsibility for in the subsequent inquiry.

As it was, a gap had opened up that resulted in the Spartans being attacked frontally and on their left flank. But although they are thought to have suffered some 300 casualties, as Thucydides says, 'they now showed that in courage they had no equals'. Hard-pressed and driven back to their wagons, they rallied and went on the offensive themselves, overlapping the Athenians' left wing to attack their exposed flank. Meanwhile, in the centre, King Agis with 300 picked troops broke through the Argives' line where it was held by some older men, and turned on the Athenians' exposed right wing. Had it not been for their cavalry, and the fact that Agis gave orders for the whole of the army to go to the assistance of his own left wing, the Athenians would probably have been annihilated. As it was, with both Agis himself and the Spartans calling off their attacks, they had plenty of time to escape. Seeing that their left wing had been defeated, and that the Spartans were bearing down on them, the Mantineans and the Argives fighting alongside them – instead of continuing to press forward – beat a hasty retreat. Thucydides says that, though the Spartans would fight tenaciously, once they had put their enemy to flight they did not press the pursuit. So the defeated Argives and their allies, who together had suffered more than 1000 casualties, escaped to fight again another day.

Tactically, the battle shows the need for flexibility in adapting to the unexpected, as when a gap opened up in the Spartan centre; and not having a cavalry arm, if only to be able to conduct an effective pursuit, displays a grave shortcoming in Spartan conceptual thinking after ten years of war. As for the Athenians, leaving aside the political situation, which will be addressed later, and looking at it purely from the military point of view: what was clearly going to be a battle of vital importance was entered into before there had been a proper concentration of force. If that had occurred, in all probability a decisive victory would have resulted, and Sparta's position as the dominant land power would have been irrevocably broken. As it was, the Spartans restored their prestige, which had been badly dented at Pylos, and it was twenty-four years before any Greeks ventured to face them again in the field.

To step back slightly in time. On the day before the battle of Mantinea, the Epidaurians took advantage of Argos being left only weakly defended by marching out in force and killing many of those who had been left behind. The Athenians, who had received 1000 reinforcements – being dribbled in once again – with their other allies, including the 3000 hoplites from Elis who had earlier gone off in a sulk, now marched to Epidaurus and started to build a containing wall round the city. But except for the Athenians, who completed their allotted section, the others lost interest and drifted off home. Not an incident of much interest in itself, but it showed the frailty of the alliance and the lack of Athenian will and leadership to hold it together; a situation that was to deteriorate even further almost at once. Having finished celebrating the Carnean festival, when the Dorians were required to refrain from military operations, the Spartans marched on Argos, where they offered the Argives a choice of war or peace.

The oligarchic party were now able to declare their pro-Spartan sympathies quite openly, and with the Spartans at the gates soon won over the people, persuading them to accept a settlement. In broad terms, this required Argos to repudiate her treaty with Athens, Mantinea and Elis, and to enter into a fifty-year alliance with Sparta. Other Peloponnesian states were free to join the alliance, and in a display of equal partnership, should it be necessary to mount an expeditionary force, it was agreed that the Spartans and the Argives would consult together to decide what forces each member should contribute.

As a consequence of this settlement the Athenians were forced to evacuate the Peloponnese, Mantinea made a thirty-year truce with Sparta, and Perdiccas of Macedonia was persuaded to take an oath of alliance. Though Perdiccas did not immediately break with Athens, this was his intention, and, seeing the way things were going, the Chalcidians also took oaths of allegiance. But what appeared to be the total disintegration of the Athenian position was abruptly halted when the democrats in Argos attacked the oligarchs during the summer of 417 BC. Because the Spartans had just begun celebrating the Gymnopaedic festival, they did not immediately make a move and, when they did, they had only got as far as Tegea before learning that the oligarchs had been defeated. In spite of the appeals of those who had escaped, the Spartans refused to go any further. Instead, they decided to return to complete the interrupted festival. Afterwards envoys arrived from the democratic party in Argos, together with representatives of the exiled oligarchs, both of whom stated their respective cases before the Spartans and their allies. After much discussion the Spartans found in favour of the oligarchs and decided to march on Argos, but for one reason or another the expedition was continually being put off.

Making the most of this breathing space, the Argives – men, women and slaves, together with Athenian masons and carpenters – started to extend the city's walls down to the sea, thereby ensuring that the Athenians could supply them by sea, should they be blockaded by land. In renewing her alliance with Athens and defying Sparta, Argos was not reviving her challenge to Sparta's leadership in the Peloponnese, but merely trying to preserve her independence.

Meanwhile Agis, on hearing about the building of the walls, and anticipating help from within the city, marched on Argos at the head of the Spartans and her Peloponnesian allies, though Corinth hung back. When there was no betrayal from within the city, the Spartans contented themselves with demolishing the as-yet-uncompleted extension walls; then, after massacring the inhabitants of Hysiae, a neighbouring Argive town, they returned home. In retaliation, the Argives mounted a raid against Phlius, some twenty miles north-west of Argos, and laid waste the surrounding countryside; the justification being that some of the exiles had settled there.

The reason for the Athenians not acting decisively in the Peloponnese, when the opportunity to gain a significant victory arose, was because of the political divide that existed between the war party and those seeking peace. Alcibiades wanted Athens to commit herself unreservedly, and to place the whole of her army under his command in support of her new Peloponnesian allies. In this way Sparta would be completely crushed. Nicias, on the other hand, saw the alliance as purely defensive. He wanted to avoid a confrontation with Sparta, which meant leaving unsatisfied both the territorial claims of Mantinea and Elis, and the aspirations of Argos for leadership in the Peloponnese. When Alcibiades went to foment trouble in the Peloponnese, he was thus only able to take a small Athenian contingent with him; hence the failure to achieve the necessary concentration of force at the battle of Mantinea, with reinforcements being dribbled in too late. The tragedy for Athens was that both Nicias and Alcibiades were right in their own ways; had the former got his way, the peace treaty might well have endured; had Alcibiades got his, in all probability Sparta would have been overwhelmed by the combined power of Argos and Athens. There would then have been no need to mount the disastrous expedition to Sicily. It was the dithering between these two clear-cut policies that was the root cause of Athens' ultimate downfall.

The Athenians undertook two final acts in 416 BC, before resuming the war openly. First, Alcibiades sailed to Argos with twenty ships and seized 300 Argive citizens, who were all suspected of still being pro-Spartan, and dispersed them amongst some nearby islands under their control. Then the Athenians mounted an expedition to Melos, a colony of Sparta's that was the only island that had refused to join the Delian League. As an account of what occurred has already been given, all that needs to be said now by way of a reminder is that there was a debate between the Athenians and the Melians, vividly recorded by Thucydides, in which the Athenian justification for their action was shown to be no more than an appeal to the absolute right of the stronger party. As Hilaire Belloc said of Roaring Bill in 'The Pacifist',

> Pale Ebenezer thought it wrong to fight,
> But Roaring Bill (who killed him) thought it right.

All the men were slaughtered, while the women and children were sold into slavery; the island was then repopulated with Athenian settlers. According to Xenophon, however, there must have been some survivors, as he says the Melians were resettled after the war. The treatment of Melos, however, was to remain a lasting blot on the history of Athens. As will be recalled from earlier in this chapter, the Athenians later behaved in much the same way at Scione in Thrace, but as Thucydides does not highlight the incident with an apologia, it is largely forgotten.

9

The Expedition to Sicily
415 BC

The Athenians, having failed to commit themselves to the defeat of Sparta when they had the opportunity to do so, now threw themselves into an undertaking of such magnitude and risk that their decision can only have been taken after a careful appreciation of the situation had disclosed a compelling reason. Or so one would have thought, but let us listen to what Thucydides has to say:

In the same winter [416 BC] the Athenians resolved to sail against Sicily with larger forces than those which Laches and Eurymedon had commanded [during the 427 BC expedition] and, if possible, to conquer it. They were for the most part ignorant of the size of the island and of the numbers of its inhabitants, both Hellenic and native, and they did not realise that they were taking on a war of almost the same magnitude as their war against the Peloponnesians.

Later Thucydides goes on to say: 'In fact they aimed to conquer the whole of Sicily, though they wanted at the same time to make it look as though they were sending help to their own kinsmen, and to their newly acquired allies there.'

As will be recalled, Thucydides said that though the expedition in 427 BC was ostensibly to help Leontini, a city with which Athens had a kinship, its real reason was to prevent corn being brought to the Peloponnese from the west, so it is surprising that he makes no mention of this being an objective now. Moreover, even during the protracted debate that took place in the assembly, no reference is made to cutting off the Peloponnesians' corn supplies from Sicily. A possible explanation for this seeming omission is that they were not solely dependent on Sicily, but had other sources of supply, such as Egypt, though why this should not also have applied eleven years earlier is unclear. But we must now look at the situation as it existed when the assembly held its debate.

At this stage the reader might find it helpful to glance back at the Historical Survey, to remind himself or herself of the island's background and ethnic divisions. That done, we can now jump to 416 BC, when a delegation from Egesta arrived at Athens to seek help in their war with Selinus, the most westerly Greek city on the south coast of Sicily. Though the cities were some thirty miles apart, their territories were contiguous, and a dispute had arisen over frontier and, to complicate matters, over marriage rights, which had led to fighting. Selinus had obtained the assistance of Syracuse, and Egesta was now being hard pressed on both land and sea, and so called upon Athens to honour the treaty that had been made between them during the expedition of 427 BC. The most telling argument the Egestaeans put forward was that Syracuse was seeking to dominate the whole island; once this had been achieved, being a Dorian city, at some time or other she would be bound to come to the aid of her fellow Dorians in the Peloponnese. Athens would thus be well advised to intervene while she still had some allies left in Sicily, especially as Egesta would finance the war. Before committing themselves, however, the Athenians sent a delegation to check that the Egestaeans did really have the money, and to report on the situation in regard to the war.

At the beginning of 415 BC the delegates returned from Sicily together with some Egestaeans, who brought with them enough uncoined silver to pay the crews of sixty triremes for a month; this was the number they were asking the Athenians to send. The Egestaeans and their own delegates were then invited to address the assembly, which they proceeded to do, giving an encouraging picture and, most importantly, assuring the Athenians that plenty of money was available in the treasury and the temples. On the basis of this information, the Athenians approved the despatch of sixty ships and appointed three commanders with full powers: Nicias, Alcibiades and Lamachus. Their instructions were to help Egesta, to pursue Athenian interests generally and, if possible, to free Leontini. Plutarch says that the reason why Nicias was elected as one of the commanders, against his wishes, was because the Athenians thought the war would be better managed if Alcibiades' rashness was diluted and blended with Nicias' caution. A seemingly wise precaution at the time, as Lamachus, the third commander, though an elderly man, had the reputation of being just as fiery and fond of taking military risks as Alcibiades. As will be seen, however, the blend was not maintained.

The task of trying to free Leontini had been given because, as will be remembered, during the expedition to Sicily in 427 BC a treaty of alliance had been made with the city; but after the Athenians withdrew in 424 BC, Leontini had been taken by Syracuse. Another assembly was held five days later to discuss how the preparations for the expedition could be hurried on, and to take a vote on any additional requirements the commanders had indicated. It was then that Nicias spoke against the expedition. He had not wanted to be appointed as a commander in the first place, thinking that a grave mistake was being made in using what looked like a reasonable pretext to mask an intention to conquer the whole island. He then went on to say that they were entering into a new, distant commitment, while leaving enemies behind who threatened the very existence of Athens. Finally, he launched a personal attack on Alcibiades, accusing him of putting Athens in the greatest danger she had ever known, just to satisfy his quest for personal glory and gain. Alcibiades then responded and, after replying to Nicias' accusations, extolling his own worth and listing his achievements, went on to deride the threat they would be leaving behind; he maintained that they were duty-bound to assist an ally, while holding out the prospect of increasing their own power by undertaking the expedition.

Plutarch, in his life of Alcibiades, tells a slightly different story and says that, even during Pericles' lifetime, the Athenians had coveted Sicily, from time to time sending out expeditions to 'relieve and reinforce the victims of Syracusan aggression'. But it was Alcibiades who persuaded them to overrun the island, though only as a stepping stone to annexing Carthage and Libya – the Greek name for the whole of Africa – and then taking over Italy and the Peloponnese. Perhaps this strange inversion of priorities was because he thought that, without first acquiring additional human and material resources through wider conquests, the Athenians would be unable to defeat the Peloponnese. Equally, he may just have been a romantic. Plutarch tells us that the young men were carried away by Alcibiades' ambitions, and that people could commonly be seen sitting and mapping out the shape of Sicily and the position of Carthage and Africa. But let us return to the debate in the assembly as related by Thucydides.

Nicias, seeing that he had no hope of winning the debate, urged that, if the assembly was determined to go ahead with this risky venture, at least it should do so in strength from the outset, and with the right sort of troops, so avoiding the dribbling in of reinforcements – *Klotzen nicht kleckern* ('clout, don't dribble'), as the Germans would say. Nicias thought that the sheer size of the requirement, which he put forward in very general terms, would cause second thoughts, but it had the opposite effect: his advice was considered to be excellent. Success was assured, and the scale of the enterprise only served to arouse even greater enthusiasm; those few who still maintained that a grave, and even fatal, mistake was being made were branded unpatriotic.

Nicias was now called upon to give the details of the forces he required, but he refused to do so before consulting his colleagues. He did, however, go so far as to say that they ought to sail with at least 100 triremes, together with the necessary transports, and at least 5000 hoplites, as well as light troops – mentioning archers from Athens and slingers from Crete. When it heard this, the assembly not only sanctioned his requirements, but voted to give him and his fellow generals full power to decide on the size and composition of the expeditionary force. There was now no turning back; so the preparations were put in hand, with the triremes and various contingents being called for from all the allies, while many of the light troops were recruited as mercenaries.

By midsummer the battle fleet lay ready for departure in the Piraeus. It was by far the most costly and best-equipped expeditionary force that Athens had ever raised. There had been equally large ones in the past, but they had not matched the quality of the one now riding at anchor, waiting for the signal to depart, in either human or material terms. The troops had all been hand-picked from amongst eager volunteers, while the fleet was in a high state of efficiency, magnificently equipped and manned by the best crews available. Neither public nor private money had been spared in making the expeditionary force the finest that could be raised. When all was ready, a trumpeter gave the signal for silence, whereupon the crews in every ship, and the thousands of spectators thronging the shore, followed the voice of the herald in praying to the gods for success, while libations were poured onto the water from gold and silver goblets. Then, when the religious ceremony was finished and the battle hymn had been sung, the fleet put to sea, filing out in a long column to race each other as far as Aegina, before settling down to the long haul that would take them to Corcyra.

Here the Athenians joined up with their allies and, after holding a review, the fleet was divided into three squadrons, each under command of one of the three generals. By organising the fleet in this manner, the need for it to sail as one cumbersome armada was avoided, as was congestion when coming ashore, while it also simplified the problem of resupply. Altogether there were 134 triremes, 100 of them Athenian, of which sixty were for fighting and forty for use as troop transports. Rhodes supplied two fifty-oared ships, and the other allies provided the remaining thirty-four triremes. There were also thirty requisitioned supply ships, some laden with corn, others carrying cooks, masons and carpenters, together with all the tools necessary for building fortifications; finally, there was a single ship carrying thirty horses. Providing further back-up were some 100 smaller boats, also requisitioned, and a considerable number of privately owned vessels: entrepreneurs, out to make what they could. On board were 5100 hoplites, 1500 of whom were Athenian citizens, with a further 700 who had been recruited from the lowest property classes to serve as marines. There were also 500 Argives and 250 Mantineans, who, like the eighty Cretan archers, were mercenaries. There were a further 400 archers and 700 slingers from Rhodes, together with 120 exiles from Megara serving as light troops.

After crossing the Ionian Gulf the fleet sailed down the Italian coast, but the cities of Magna Graecia gave it a chilly welcome: they were only prepared to provide water and grant permission to anchor. Even these modest requirements were refused by Tarentum and Locri. At Rhegium, though the Athenians were allowed to drag their ships ashore and could camp on some sacred ground where a small market was set up for them, they were not allowed into the city. This may appear a somewhat inhospitable reception by a former ally from the earlier expedition, but on hearing of the Athenians' intentions, all the Greeks in Italy had decided to remain neutral; so Rhegium, which was particularly exposed, was doing no more than look to her own security. The Athenians then turned their attention to Sicily, pondering what was the best course to take. If Thucydides is correct in what he tells us, either the Athenians had anticipated a very different situation on arriving, and so had been wrong-footed, or there had been a lamentable lack of forward planning. Either way, it reflects little credit on the three generals.

Three ships had been sent to Egesta, to check on the availability of the money that had been promised by the city's delegates while they were in Athens; when they returned to Rhegium, the Athenians learned that they had been duped. The promised money just did not exist; they were the victims of an elaborate hoax. The Athenians had been taken to the temple of Aphrodite at Eryx – a mountain on the north-west coast, which was the stronghold where Hamilcar Barca, Hannibal's father, would hold out against the Romans for the last four years of the First Punic War, between 244 and 240 BC. The temple stood on the mountain's flat top, and it was here that an imposing collection of silver bowls, goblets, censers and much else that glitters was laid up as offerings to Aphrodite. Thucydides says, however, that in spite of its appearance, the hoard was not of great value. But the Egestaeans had also collected together an impressive number of genuine cups of gold and silver, even borrowing them from neighbouring cities, both Hellenic and Phoenician. They had then been lent to selected households, where the ships' crews were royally entertained, leaving them astonished at the abundance of what they took to be private possessions. Once the Athenians were back home, stories about the prodigality of all they had seen soon became common currency, leaving no doubt about Egesta's ability to pay for the expedition; except, according to Thucydides, for Nicias, who had remained very sceptical. But he evidently kept his doubts to himself, since he made no mention of them.

The three commanders now met to consider what steps should be taken after this revelation of Egestaean duplicity. Nicias proposed that they should deal with Selinus, so fulfilling the main purpose of the expedition. After that, if it were found that the Egestaeans were in fact able to pay for the expedition, a decision could be taken as to their next move. If they could not, then Egesta should provide supplies for the sixty ships they had requested and, either by agreement or force, a settlement should be arrived at between Egesta and Selinus. This having been achieved, they should sail along the coast, demonstrating the power of Athens and her willingness to come to the assistance of her friends and allies. Unless they could find some quick way of serving Leontini's interests, they should then sail home. The last thing they should do was to endanger Athens by wasting her resources.

Alcibiades then spoke, claiming that it would be unacceptable to return home empty-handed after mounting such a formidable expedition; a course of action that would only lead to their disgrace. Instead they should send heralds to the various cities, except Selinus, urging them to revolt against Syracuse. Failing that, they should at least try and win their friendship, so that they could get supplies and troops from them. Their first step should be to gain the support of Messina, lying across the Straits, which, with its excellent harbour, was the gateway to Sicily. By then they would also know who was going to support them in an attack on Syracuse.

Lamachus said they ought to mount an immediate attack on Syracuse before she had completed her defensive preparations and had time to gather in all her property from outside the city walls. An early victory that established them in front of the city would win over more allies. He recommended using Megara, some ten miles north of Syracuse, as their naval base, from where the blockade of Syracuse could be conveniently maintained. Megara itself was in fact deserted, its inhabitants having been driven out at the time of Gelon's dictatorship of Syracuse some sixty years previously. Lamachus, however, eventually dropped his proposal and supported Alcibiades, who then sailed over to Messina and attempted to negotiate an alliance. But he met with a refusal: like Rhegium, all that Messina was prepared to do was establish a market outside the city. So Alcibiades' plan began to unravel with its first step.

Meanwhile in Syracuse, when news of the Athenians' approach had reached the city, the oligarchic party urged that precautionary measures be taken, but the idea that Athens should be considering an attack on them was at first met with general disbelief. Hermocrates, the leading democratic party politician, when addressing the assembly, expressed the view that the Athenians would not be so foolish as to start a new large-scale war, while leaving the Peloponnesians to menace their homeland; the tales doing the rounds were no more than alarmist fabrications. More probably, the Athenians must think themselves fortunate that a Sicilian army had not gone across to attack them. An acrimonious debate followed, during which much personal abuse was exchanged between the political opponents, obliging one of the generals to rise to his feet and tell them to stop such personal attacks. He went on to say that a number of defensive measures were already in hand. What was needed now was for everybody to play their part in dealing with the invaders. When the Athenian fleet reached Rhegium, the last doubts about Athenian intentions faded, and energetic steps were at once put in hand to prepare for the coming war. Garrisons were installed in a number of cities, fortified posts were manned, and in Syracuse itself everything from horses to personal arms was placed in a state of instant readiness.

After Alcibiades had failed to obtain support from Messina, he sailed with sixty ships to Naxos, some fifty miles north of Syracuse, where the Athenians were received into the city. They then went on to Catana, midway between Naxos and Syracuse, but here the people refused to admit them; so, after camping for the night, they sailed to Syracuse. Here ten ships were sent into the great harbour, and the Athenians proclaimed that, in accordance with their alliance and kinship with the Leontinians, they had come to restore them to their own land. Having made their proclamation, the Athenians made a reconnaissance of the city and its harbour, before sailing back to Catana.

At Catana, although no troops were admitted, Alcibiades was given the chance to address the assembly. While he was speaking, some of the Athenian soldiers managed to break down a badly maintained postern gate. On entering the city, they proceeded to stroll about the market place as though at home, causing consternation amongst the pro-Syracusan party members who, once they had come to believe their eyes, beat a hasty retreat. Those remaining at the assembly then voted to make a treaty with the Athenians and invited them to bring over the rest of their forces from Rhegium. When the whole Athenian expeditionary force had assembled at Catana, and work had begun on constructing a camp, news reached them from Camarina, on the south coast, that she too would like to join them. Camarina added the warning that the Syracusans were massing a fleet. The Athenians then put to sea with their whole fleet and sailed down to Syracuse, but after failing to find anything untoward, decided to continue on to Camarina. Here, if they were expecting a warm reception, they must have been disappointed. The Camarinaeans declared that, unless they specifically invited the Athenians into their city, they were bound by an oath not to admit more than one of their ships. Such strange behaviour suggests that the city was riven by the usual Greek party divide as to where their interests and loyalties lay. On their way back to Catana, the Athenians stopped off to raid Syracusan territory, and lost some of their light troops when they were caught by the Syracusan cavalry. So first blood had been drawn, and it was Athenian.

On arriving back at Catana, the Athenians found the *Salaminia* waiting for them with orders for Alcibiades to return to Athens immediately. As mentioned earlier, the *Salaminia* was one of the triremes kept in service throughout the year for special duties. Alcibiades was required to answer charges of sacrilege against Demeter, the corn-goddess, and her daughter Persephone (who, having been abducted by Pluto, king of the underworld, could only return to earth for the summer months). Alcibiades was also accused of having been involved in another sacrilege, the disfigurement of the Hermae, marble half-statues of the god Hermes (Mercury), the messenger of the gods, which were held in great veneration and conspicuously displayed throughout Athens. Both incidents had occurred before the expedition had set sail, and, though Alcibiades had come under attack from his political opponents, he had not been detained. Now, however, the public mood had swung against him, with the sacrileges he had committed being seen as part of a plot to overthrow the democracy and install an oligarchic government. He was then required to return and stand trial. From what Thucydides says, the stories told against Alcibiades seem to have been largely fabricated. Instead of the authorities checking up on the characters of their informers, there had been an atmosphere of panic, in which they had uncritically accepted the evidence of complete rogues. As a result, some of the best citizens had been arrested and imprisoned. Alcibiades jumped ship on his way home, at Thurii in Italy; so his trial proceeded without him, and he was found guilty *in absentia* and, according to Thucydides, sentenced to death. But Plutarch says he only had his property confiscated, as well as being publicly cursed by all the priests and priestesses in the city. It did not, however, seem to do Alcibiades much harm because, as we will see, he bounced back.

But to follow Alcibiades' movements a bit further. From Thurii he made his way to the Peloponnese. After spending some time in

Argos, he was granted asylum in Sparta, where he was made welcome, not only because of the traitorous advice he gave, but also for the way he adopted their lifestyle and mode of dress. As Plutarch says:

> the only difference between him and a chameleon was that, whereas a chameleon finds it totally impossible to assimilate itself to the colour white, whether Alcibiades found himself in the company of good men or bad, there was nothing he could not imitate and no habit he could not acquire. In Sparta he took exercise, lived frugally, and wore a frown on his face; in Ionia he was fastidious, companionable, and easy-living, in Thrace he went in for hard drinking and hard riding ... It was not that he actually changed personality so readily, or that his character was infinitely mutable ... he just assumed and took refuge in, whatever appearance and image was appropriate.

Here we must leave him for the moment, but we shall be meeting up with him again.

After the departure of Alcibiades, the Athenian expeditionary force was reorganised into two parts, each under the control of one of the two remaining commanders, and, as Nicias had first suggested, the Athenians contented themselves with assessing the situation at Selinus, while wringing some additional money out of Egesta. There was some scrappy fighting when the fleet stopped off at a number of places along the north coast, leaving the army to march across the centre of the island in a demonstration of strength to Catana. At the beginning of the winter in 415 BC, the Athenians were occupied with their preparations for attacking Syracuse, while the Syracusans – whose confidence had grown when they saw the Athenians occupied elsewhere on the island – were getting ready to give battle themselves.

Learning of the Syracusans' intentions, the Athenians wanted to lure them as far away from their city as they could, while avoiding having to make a long march themselves, which would expose them to attack by the Syracusan cavalry. So they sent a trusted agent from Catana to tell the Syracusans that if they came by night with their full force at an agreed date, the pro-Syracusan party in Catana would close the gates on the Athenians in the city and set fire to their ships. As the Syracusans had already decided to attack Catana, they at once agreed a date and sent the agent back to make the necessary arrangements. Once the Athenians heard that the enemy was on his way, they sailed by night to Syracuse and at dawn entered the grand harbour where, following the advice of some Syracusan exiles, they occupied a naturally strong defensive position opposite the Olympieum, the temple of Olympian Zeus. One flank was protected by walls, houses, trees and a marsh, and the other by steep cliffs. The River Anapus ran at right angles to the Athenian right flank, before curving round behind them to flow into the harbour; while the south–north road ran directly through the position, then over a bridge to the rear, which was now broken to prevent any interference from Syracuse. To protect the ships beached along the harbour shore, trees were felled and a stout stockade erected, while at Dascon, the inner bay, a small fort was hurriedly constructed, to which the southern extension of the stockade was probably fixed.

Meanwhile, the Syracusan cavalry had been the first to discover that the Athenians had left Catana. When the news was reported, the whole army was wheeled round and began the return march. Pushing on ahead, it was again the cavalry that gave news of the Athenians, whereupon the infantry closed up to them; but, when they made no move, the Syracusans withdrew and camped for the night. As has already been recounted, the following morning the Athenians prepared for battle: half the army occupied the defensive position, with the allies on the flanks and themselves in the centre, the whole phalanx being eight shields deep. The other half of the army formed a hollow square to the rear, also eight shields deep, tasked with protecting the tents and non-combatants, as well as providing a reserve.

After going along the line with words of encouragement, Nicias gave the order to advance, which came as something of a surprise to the Syracusans, who had not expected the action to begin quite so soon. But, forming up quickly, they went forward to meet the Athenians. First the light troops – stone-throwers, slingers and archers – engaged one another; then, after the soothsayers had made the usual sacrifices, the trumpeters sounded the charge and the two armies clashed. To begin with, the inexperienced Syracusans held their own, fighting courageously, until some sudden claps of thunder, accompanied by lightning and heavy rain, added to the fears of troops in action for the first time, and they started to give ground. First the Argives forced back the Syracusan left wing, then the Athenians burst through their centre to cut them in two, which brought about a general panic and put them to flight. The pursuit was not pressed home, largely because of the undefeated Syracusan cavalry, which restored some order and permitted their hoplites to form up again. But there was no further fighting, and after the Athenians had collected their own dead and placed them on a pyre, they camped for the night. The next morning they handed the Syracusans back their dead under a truce and, after recovering their fallen comrades' bones from the pyre, carried them and the captured weapons to their ships, then sailed back to Catana. The Athenians and their allies had lost about fifty men, and the Syracusans some 200.

The Athenians had done commendably well; first, in successfully executing a deception plan which, even though the Syracusans intended to attack Catana anyway, was well conceived; and second, in occupying a defensive position that negated the Syracusan cavalry. But it was the Syracusan exiles whom they had to thank for this, without whose advice they could have been gravely disadvantaged. Appreciating their own need for cavalry, they requested that some should be sent from Athens, together with money to buy corn and help win over new allies. They then passed the winter in Catana and Naxos preparing for an attack on Syracuse in the spring. It was all very leisurely.

It had been a serious omission not to have included cavalry in the first place. Seemingly the Athenians had learned nothing from their defeat at Delium in 424 BC when, as will be recalled, the Boeotian cavalry had taken them on a flank and, after they had broken and fled, had pursued them until darkness fell. That the Athenians had no cavalry of their own was no excuse. They should have obtained some from elsewhere, even as mercenaries. It was not a mistake the Carthaginians made. When they sent an expeditionary force to Sicily shortly after the outbreak of the First Punic War in 264 BC, it included a strong contingent of Numidian cavalry. Somewhat paradoxically, it was perhaps unfortunate for the Athenians that they won this first encounter outside Syracuse. Had they been defeated, and with Alcibiades out of play, they might well have abandoned the idea of trying to secure Sicily, so sparing themselves the infinitely greater losses that were to follow.

Looking back at the first four or five months of the campaign, although Nicias had finally turned his attention to Syracuse, much time had been wasted in a dispersal of effort elsewhere. It had always been quite clear that Syracuse was the main enemy, and Nicias had been given all the forces he had asked for to deal with them; yet both the fleet and the army had pursued the largely chimerical objective of rallying additional support, before the principal power had even come under attack. A tactical reverse had certainly been inflicted on the Syracusans, but it had not given the Athenians a decisive advantage. The lack of determination to get to grips with the Syracusans as quickly as possible had given them a breathing space which, through being extended over the winter months, was to cost the Athenians dear.

After the Syracusans had buried their dead, they held an assembly at which Hermocrates, who had brought peace to Sicily in 424 BC, once again displayed his high intelligence and clarity of mind. While he sought to lift them out of their despondency, he had no hesitation in exposing the causes of their defeat. Although they had been fighting against the most experienced troops in Hellas, they had fielded no fewer than fifteen generals. Consequently, too many orders were flying about, which had added to the disorganisation created by their own lack of discipline. He then went on to say that the Syracusans already had the necessary courage; what was needed now was fewer generals, compulsory training (which would put an end to the ill-discipline) and more hoplites. It was a courageous and clear-sighted analysis. The assembly agreed and voted to implement the necessary measures. Only three generals were elected, one of whom was Hermocrates himself, and representatives were sent to Sparta and Corinth asking for direct assistance; meanwhile Sparta was urged to attack Athens, so preventing her from sending reinforcements to Sicily.

The Syracusans also took a vitally important measure to secure their city. A new wall was constructed, which, by enclosing additional land to extend the city's fortifications, made it much more difficult for the Athenians to build a blockading wall. They also drove stakes into the ground at all the likely landing places, and built two new forts: one at the deserted town of Megara to the north, and another at the temple of Zeus, adjacent to the earlier battlefield. Meanwhile the Syracusan representatives who had gone to the Peloponnese found that, in spite of the Athenian intervention that had resulted in their defeat at Mantinea two years previously, Sparta was hesitant about conducting the war more openly, even when encouraged to do so by Corinth, which was quite prepared to provide whatever assistance she could. But Alcibiades gave one of his fiery speeches, presenting his own ambitions for conquest not only of Sicily, but also of Italy and Carthage, as being the Athenians' intentions. Then he went on to explain that the manpower and resources of these conquests would be marshalled for an assault on the Peloponnese. The key to all this was Syracuse: if she fell – as she would without Spartan help – Sicily would be lost and the rest would follow.

This fear was an early expression of the domino theory, the conventional wisdom in Washington during the 1950s: if Laos were lost, Cambodia would follow, then Vietnam would go, followed by Thailand, which would lead to the loss of Malaysia, and then Indonesia would go . . . and so on. This led to great pressure from the Pentagon to become involved, first in Laos (which Kennedy resisted), then in Vietnam (which he did not). But in the opinion of Sir Michael Howard, Britain's most eminent military historian, it is certainly arguable that American resistance in Vietnam did give time to shore up the other dominoes, especially Indonesia. If the whole of Vietnam had gone communist in 1964, rather than ten years later, the situation throughout South-East Asia would certainly have been very different. So the American effort in Vietnam was not entirely wasted.

But to return to Alcibiades. He continued to harangue the Spartans by saying that the war in Attica must also be pursued openly: Decelea, some thirty miles north-east of Athens, should be fortified, which would deter the Athenians from sending reinforcements to Sicily. Alcibiades concluded by telling them that if they followed his advice, Athens would be irreparably ruined, and the Spartans would be able to live in peace. His eloquence and unmeasured exaggerations incited them to action, so the decision to fortify Decelea and send support to Sicily was promptly taken. Possibly because of his family connections with Thurii, in Italy, the Spartan Gylippus was appointed as commander of the force, which was to be ready by the spring, and the Corinthians were asked to supply the necessary shipping. Though Alcibiades gained a high reputation amongst the Spartans, he imperilled his position by seducing Timaea, the wife of King Agis, so thoroughly that, as Plutarch says, not only did she get pregnant with his child, but she did not even deny it. With every reason to fear for his life, Alcibiades now fled from Sparta to Persia and took refuge with Tissaphernes, a satrap of the Persian king. Here we must leave him once more, but we shall hear of him again.

In the spring of 414 BC the Athenians sailed along the coast to Megara where, as has been mentioned, the Syracusans had just built a fort near the uninhabited town. Here the Athenians landed and, after devastating the countryside, and making an unsuccessful attack on the fort, continued further along the coast, wreaking as much devastation as they could before returning to Catana. They then advanced as far as Centoripa, a town belonging to the Sicels, approximately in the middle of the eastern part of Sicily; and, receiving its surrender, they marched back again, burning what they could on the way. Centoripa seems to have surrendered without offering any resistance, probably because the Sicels were unwilling to declare their support for either of the contestants: far better to end up on reasonably good terms with whoever was the victor. When the Athenians got back to Catana they found that the reinforcements had arrived: 250 cavalrymen, but without any horses, which were to be procured locally; thirty mounted archers; and a considerable amount of money. As it is only later that Thucydides relates how the horses were obtained, it seems that at this stage there were none; so the horsemen would still have been dismounted when embarking for Syracuse. A sense of urgency now seems to have gripped Nicias, for immediately after completing some essential preparations, the whole force set sail on the same morning as he had returned from Centoripa.

The Athenians faced a formidable task in attacking Syracuse, especially after having left time for the walls to be extended. A background review of Syracuse has already been given; but, to give a sharper focus, the city had been founded in the 8th century BC on the island of Ortygia (Quail Island) by the Corinthians. As what came to be known as the inner city grew, it had spread onto the adjacent mainland to form the outer city. Here a massive rocky outcrop (Achradina) butted into the sea, with its western edge leading onto the lower slopes of Epipolae (the Heights), the triangular-shaped plateau with its base running parallel to the shoreline. The Syracusans' chief concern was that the Athenians would try and gain Epipolae, which dominated the outer city. So, surprisingly late in the day for such an important measure, they selected 600 hoplites to guard the single route leading up Epipolae's precipitous outside face from the north. This guard force was not required to occupy its post; only to be immediately ready to do so.

Meanwhile the Athenians had disembarked unobserved at Thapsus, a narrow-necked peninsula that juts out into the sea just to the north of Syracuse. Here the sailors at once began erecting a stockade across the isthmus. The army went straight for Epipolae as fast as it could and, while the Syracusans were holding a review of their troops in the meadows below, gained the high ridge. Participating in the review was the guard force, which was hurriedly despatched to dislodge the Athenians, with the rest of the parade following. But after covering nearly three miles uphill, their attack was a disorganised affair and was easily repulsed. Severely mauled, and leaving some 300 of their dead on the battlefield, the Syracusans withdrew into the city.

The next day the Athenians marched down to the city walls, but when this drew no response, they went back again and started building a fort on some high ground called Labdalum at the western end of the Epipolae escarpment. The fort not only guarded this vital piece of ground, but served as a base from which the Athenians could fight or work on the encircling wall that they proposed to raise. Such an important outpost was something the Syracusans should have constructed long ago and kept manned at the first sign of danger.

It is now that Thucydides says that the Athenians had obtained the 250 horses needed to mount their horsemen, some of which had been purchased, while others came from Egesta and Catana. As he goes on to say that the Athenians now possessed 650 cavalry, it seems that the numbers must have made up from local sources, possibly Egesta. The Athenians' next step was to start raising another fort at Syca (the Circle), lower down on Epipolae towards the city. Thoroughly alarmed at the rapid fortification of this dominating feature, the Syracusans decided to put a stop to it, so they came out to give battle, but evidently had second thoughts and withdrew into the city again. They did, however, leave some cavalry behind to stop those Athenians who were collecting stone from doing so, beyond the protection of their main force. Thereupon the Athenian cavalry, supported by a detachment of hoplites, charged and routed them. Unless Thucydides omitted to mention other occasions, this is the only Athenian cavalry action he records, which suggests that they must have deterred the Syracusans from using theirs.

After this brief interruption, work on the encirclement of Syracuse resumed. The Circle fortress was completed, and was to act as a pivot from where one wall would reach down to the coast at Trogilus to the north, close to where the Athenians had landed, with a second one running south to the Grand Harbour. The Syracusans, recognising that their inferiority prevented them from interrupting this work by taking to the field, decided to counter the Athenian circumvallation by building a cross-wall, which would start from the city below the southern cliffs, then cut across the intended line of the Athenian wall at right angles. To protect the cross-wall while it was under construction, the Syracusans erected a stockade on its western side; they thought they would be able to hold this, as to attack it the Athenians would have to divide their force between the heights and the plains, something they would be loath to do. According to Thucydides, it was in fact because the Athenians thought it too risky to split their force, as well as not wanting to interrupt work on the northern wall, that they let the Syracusans complete their cross-wall.

Satisfied that they had foiled the Athenians, the Syracusans left a guard force behind to secure the wall, while the rest of them returned to the city. But in spite of Hermocrates identifying a lack of discipline as one of the causes of the Syracusan defeat in their first encounter with the Athenians, it had clearly not been sufficiently tightened up. Waiting until midday, when those Syracusans who were not actually on duty were taking a siesta in their tents, or had even gone into the city, 300 picked Athenian troops raced forward to the stockade, obtained complete surprise and quickly secured both it and the cross-wall. At the same time on the heights, what was probably the main part of the army advanced on the city to contain the troops in Achradina, while Lamachus led another *coup de main* against the postern gate leading into Temenites, lying directly to the west of the southern end of Achradina. But though some of the Athenians managed to get in, mingled with garrison troops fleeing from the cross-wall, they were overwhelmed or driven out. As in securing the cross-wall, the Athenians had achieved the main aim of their attack; after demolishing it and pulling up the stockade, they withdrew, carrying off the stakes for their own use. It had been a daring and well-executed operation – once again illustrating the battle-winning factor of surprise – which had probably been conceived by Lamachus, since it bore his hallmark and he had been entrusted with its execution.

The next day the Athenians, instead of first constructing the section of the wall that was to run from the Circle across the slope of Epipolae to the cliffs on its southern edge, began work afresh at the cliffs themselves: from where the wall was to run over the lower-lying land and the marsh, to the Great Harbour. To protect this work and form a pivot like the Circle, a fort was first constructed on the cliffs, which would also enhance security by providing all-round observation. To counter this latest project, the Syracusans began building another stockade, with a ditch running beside it, which extended from the city straight through the middle of the marsh, across the Athenians' intended path. As they had done on the previous occasion, the Athenians let this work continue until they were ready to make a move. Then, once the fortification of the cliffs had been completed and, as at the Circle, a garrison installed, Epipolae was considered to be secure; so they could now turn their attention to the Syracusan stockade.

The fleet was ordered to sail from Thapsus to the Great Harbour, and at dawn Lamachus led the Athenians down from Epipolae onto the plain. After laying planks across the marsh where the ground was firmest, they stormed the ditch and stockade, capturing both, except for one small section that was taken later. Seemingly taken by surprise again, the Syracusans abandoned their positions, with their right wing falling back to the city, while the left made for the bridge over the River Anapus to escape towards the Olympieum. Thereupon, 300 Athenian hoplites set off at the double to try and cut them off at the bridge, but they were caught on the way by the Syracusan cavalry and thrown back in confusion onto their own right wing. Seeing what was happening, Lamachus led forward the Argives and a few archers from the left wing to try and restore the situation; but, after crossing the ditch, he and five or six of his men became isolated and were killed.

Thucydides says that the Syracusans fleeing to the bridge had rallied before their cavalry had driven back the Athenian detachment trying to cut them off, but this sequence is questionable, if only because fleeing troops are difficult to stop without inspirational intervention. Whatever the sequence, the Athenian wing that had been thrown into confusion had somehow restored order in its ranks and now drove back the Syracusans, cavalry and all. Meanwhile, on the heights, an attack had been launched from the city against the Circle, where Nicias had remained because he was not feeling well.

The Syracusans were, however, beaten back by the Athenians, who set fire to the mechanical appliances and timbers and then threw them down to form a barrier of fire in front of the walls. With the Athenians from the plains now starting to arrive, and the sight of their fleet sailing into the Great Harbour, the Syracusans called it a day and withdrew into their city. According to Thucydides, they now became despondent, unable to see how they could prevent the Athenians from building their wall down to the sea with just their present forces.

After the fighting had died down, a temporary truce was declared and the bodies of the dead were exchanged; including that of Lamachus and those who had fallen with him. Lamachus probably died the way he would have wished, leading his men in a charge, and he would certainly have shared the view that, in Thomas Babington Macaulay's words, Horatius was later to express when defending the Tiber bridge and saving Rome from the Etruscans:

> To every man upon this earth
> Death cometh soon or late;
> And how can man die better
> Than facing fearful odds
> For the ashes of his fathers
> And the temples of his gods?

The Athenians now had nearly their entire force, naval and military, concentrated together, and they were ready to begin building a double wall that reached from the cliffs at Epipolae down to the Great Harbour. The Sicels now decided to come off the fence and ally themselves with the Athenians, whose supply problem was also eased by being able to obtain supplies from all over Italy. For their part, the Syracusans, having received no help from the Peloponnese, and now virtually cut off from any supplies by land or sea, began to despair of being able to win the war. Although nothing definite was decided, after discussing surrender amongst themselves, overtures were made to Nicias. Following the repeated reverses they had suffered, the Syracusans had also lost all confidence in their generals, thinking that they were either dogged by bad luck or – as they thought quite possible – even treacherous. So the generals were all summarily dismissed, and three new ones appointed in their place.

The Peloponnesian relief force under the Spartan Gylippus had not yet set sail when the misleading news was received that Syracuse was completely cut off by the blockading wall. Regarding Sicily as irretrievably lost, Gylippus turned his attention to saving Italy, and at once sailed with a part of his force across the Ionian Gulf to Tarentum, leaving the rest to follow him. On arriving off the coast of Italy, he attempted to get help from Thurii, which is where his father had settled after being exiled from Sparta. But the Thurians were unimpressed by the diminutive size of his force, so they refused, which obliged Gylippus to put to sea again. He then sailed further along the Italian coast, but was caught in a storm and had to return to Tarentum, where he beached his ships to carry out urgent repairs.

Meanwhile back in Greece where, even after the Athenian intervention in the Peloponnese and their defeat at Mantinea, the peace treaty was still regarded as being in force, low-level fighting had been resumed. The Athenians had mounted a number of raids against the coast of Laconia, and the Spartans had then invaded Argos, where they inflicted the usual devastation, which in turn caused the Athenians to send thirty ships to help her ally. All of which, the Spartans claimed, gave them reason for acting in self-defence.

While it is still fresh in our memories, let us now look back on the first year of the Sicilian campaign and, by considering it under the three levels of war, see what lessons and deductions can be drawn. Since the Syracusans were doing no more than defend their city and fight for their lives, except at the tactical level, it will inevitably be a one-sided analysis. So let us start by stating the Athenian strategic aim, which was: to defeat the Spartan Confederation, with a view to establishing Athenian supremacy over the Hellenic world. As will be remembered, the operational level of war is concerned with the implementation of the strategic aim, and here, as we have already seen, there was a wide divergence of opinion between Nicias and Alcibiades as to how this should be achieved.

Nicias wanted to confine the war to the direct defeat of Sparta and her allies. He considered that in attempting the conquest of Sicily they would be entering into a new and hazardous commitment, entailing a division of their resources, while leaving many enemies behind them. Athens was on the verge of the greatest danger she had ever known. All of what Nicias had to say in opposing an attack on Sicily was perfectly sound; but, without proposing an alternative operational-level concept for the defeat of the Peloponnesians, he was being purely negative.

Alcibiades' aim was to conquer, not just Sicily, but Italy, Carthage and Libya. Then, with these huge resources behind her, Athens could turn on Sparta and her allies and crush them. It was what today would be called taking an indirect approach: the defeat of the primary enemy through a preliminary achievement elsewhere. The debate between Nicias and Alcibiades has a remarkable similarity to the one that took place in the British War Cabinet during the First World War. On one side were the 'Westerners', headed by William Robertson, the Chief of Imperial General Staff; on the other side were the 'Easterners', headed by Lloyd George, the Prime Minister. Robertson maintained that Germany could only be defeated by fighting her on the Western Front. If this struggle were lost, so was France and everything else; only the essential minimum of resources should be allotted elsewhere. As seen by Lloyd George, the trouble with this concept was that Britain was being bled to death without achieving anything. He then argued that Turkey should first be knocked out of the war, thus tightening the iron ring round Germany herself and ending the stalemate on the Western Front. For the conservative realist William Robertson, read Nicias; for the imaginative romantic Lloyd George, read Alcibiades.

As Thucydides makes no mention of Lamachus, the third Athenian general taking part in the debate over Sicily, it would appear that he was not a great strategist or a deep military thinker, but a fine fighting soldier and an able tactician. Let us then begin our commentary on the tactical level, which deals with the implementation of the operational concept, by looking at what Lamachus said and did. As will be remembered, the expedition having been mounted, Lamachus advocated attacking Syracuse at once, whereas Alcibiades wanted to begin by winning over Messina, the gateway to Sicily, so wasting valuable time; meanwhile Nicias wanted to settle the Egesta–Selinus dispute and then sail along the coast, to demonstrate Athenian might, after which they should head for home. Lamachus was clearly right in his advocacy. The Athenians had no need of Messina, gateway or not, and, by failing to attack Syracuse at the earliest opportunity, time was given for the city to be put on a war footing.

How much the absence of cavalry really affected the outcome of battlefield encounters is hard to assess. The Athenians clearly saw no requirement for cavalry when assembling the expedition, nor are they mentioned as a factor when the generals put forward their three options. On the other hand, as has already been suggested, the omission of cavalry may show that the Athenians had no understanding of mobile warfare with its sudden, shock action; though, once the fighting had started, the need for cavalry was quickly recognised. But none of this negates the correctness of Lamachus' advocacy; it merely suggests that the whole expedition may have been mounted on a false premiss, so causing a fatal delay that eventually led to disaster. But, for the moment, this is carrying things a bit far. We must wait and see what occurs in the future before completing this assessment.

The tactical lessons from the actual fighting have already been drawn out, so they can be lightly touched upon now. Surprise stands out as a supreme battle-winning factor, and whenever possible it should be linked with its twin: deception. The Athenians achieved this twice. The first occasion was when they lured the Syracusans down to Catana and then sailed up to effect a landing at Syracuse itself. The second time was on the heights, when they advanced to the walls of Syracuse as though seeking battle, while in fact they were going to attack the cross-wall down on the plain. Then, when this attack went in, it achieved further surprise by its rapid and daring execution. Both were neat, well-implemented tactical operations that merit study. The next lesson of significance is the importance of security. This requirement was twice neglected by the Syracusans, and on both occasions they paid the price. By not guarding the track leading up the northern face of Epipolae, they lost the vitally important heights and endangered their city; then, through sloppy discipline, they were surprised and lost the cross-wall.

Finally, any military campaign must be entered into with a clear, consistent aim, together with a realistic assessment of the resources required for its fulfilment. As was demonstrated by the Athenians, when Alcibiades involved them in the half-hearted Peloponnesian campaign, a failure to meet these two fundamental requirements led to an extension of the aim – mission creep – which in turn led to the dribbling in of reinforcements. To avoid such a situation, the German exhortation *Klotzen nicht kleckern* should be strictly observed – a lesson that the Americans learned in Vietnam more than 2000 years later, but which, to their credit, they then successfully applied in the

Gulf War. But now we must return to Syracuse, and see how the tide turned to save the apparently doomed city.

10

Gylippus Turns the Tide
414–413 BC

As will be recalled, we left the Spartan Gylippus at Tarentum; where, having been caught in a storm, he had beached his ships to carry out some essential repairs. It was probably while Gylippus was undertaking this work that Nicias heard of his arrival. But, according to Thucydides, like the Thurians, he was so contemptuous of the small number of Corinthian ships that he took no precautions, dismissing them as being no more than privateers. Once his ships were seaworthy again, Gylippus put to sea and sailed along the coast to Locri, where he received more reliable news about the situation in Sicily. Learning that it was still possible to get into Syracuse, he considered two options: either he could sail directly to Syracuse and enter the city by way of Epipolae; or he could sail along the north coast to Himera, gather together what forces he could muster and then march on Syracuse.

Thucydides says that Gylippus decided to sail to Himera mainly because 'the four Athenian ships which Nicias in the end sent out when he heard they were at Locri, had not yet arrived at Rhegium'. A somewhat obscure explanation, but perhaps meaning that, by sailing to Himera, there would be less likelihood of encountering them.

Anyway, to Himera he went, where he persuaded the people to join him and to provide arms for those of the ships' crews who were unequipped. With the sailors now being employed as soldiers, there was no immediate requirement for the ships; so they were dragged ashore and, no doubt, safely secured in case of future need. Messengers were now sent to various cities asking them for help, and, in the case of Selinus, to send their whole army; in the event, probably because of their confrontation with Egesta, they provided only some light troops and cavalry. Meanwhile the Sicels, since their pro-Athenian king had just died, and since they were influenced by Gylippus' confident manner, began to change their minds about allying themselves with the Athenians, so that they provided a 1000-strong contingent. As for the others, Himera supplied 100 cavalry, and Gela sent a few individuals in token support. It was hardly an impressive response, but added to Gylippus' 1000 hoplites and light troops, together with his now fully equipped 700 sailors and marines, it had the makings of a force not to be lightly disregarded.

Even if the more distant of these contingents came by sea – it took about eight days for a merchant ship to sail round Sicily – a considerable amount of time would have had to be spent in collecting them together. Nicias had shown near-criminal neglect in not keeping Gylippus' movement to Himera under observation, especially as when he sailed along the southern coast of Italy his progress had been closely monitored. Even when Gylippus stopped on the way to capture a Sicel fort, he still remained unobserved, and then, through the near-unbelievable negligence of the Athenians, he was able to follow the same route as they had used to climb the escarpment and appear unannounced on the northern crest of Epipolae. Had Nicias not treated Gylippus' numbers so contemptuously, and instead kept him under close observation, he would have been able to eliminate Gylippus' small force as soon as it landed at Himera. As it was, Gylippus was able to make a timely arrival. The Syracusan assembly was about to decide how they could put an end to the war, but, on hearing that further help was on the way, and at the same time somehow learning that Gylippus was approaching, they took fresh heart and decided to march out in force to meet him.

The Athenians, having recovered from their surprise at Gylippus' sudden appearance, and at the sight of the Syracusans bearing down on them, formed up to give battle. For a moment Gylippus thought of attacking them; but, on seeing the disorderly manner in which the Syracusans were deploying, he thought better of it, and instead withdrew onto some more favourable ground to receive an Athenian attack. Thucydides says that Nicias, instead of leading his men forward, remained in a defensive position by the wall, so permitting Gylippus and his army to enter Syracuse. Maybe Nicias should have attacked; but as Thucydides does not tell us anything about the

Syracusans at this stage – disorganised or not – they could have threatened his rear or an exposed flank. As will be seen, however, with the death of Lamachus the Athenians had largely lost their aggressiveness, and from now on they virtually never took the offensive; so the initiative passed to their enemies, and they became reactive, chasing after events instead of determining them.

The next day Gylippus led out most of his force and, after drawing them up opposite the Athenian wall so as to hold them there, he sent a detachment to capture the fort at Labdalum. He then set to work building a cross-wall, which ran in a westerly direction from the city, across Epipolae to the edge of the plateau. By blocking the intended route of the Athenian encircling wall, he would prevent them from completing the investment of the city. As for Nicias, so as to make the southern area secure, he first finished the section of the wall reaching down to the Great Harbour, before moving up onto the heights. Though some sparring followed, Nicias made no attempt to prevent the cross-wall from being completed; instead, to stop the city from being supplied by sea, he occupied Plemmyrium, the blunt headland that narrowed the harbour mouth to about three-quarters of a mile. Here he built three forts and established a base for the fleet, which would now be more responsive if called upon to intercept enemy ships.

Moving the fleet to Plemmyrium, however, had created a major problem. As there was no water available on the headland, it all had to be fetched – a hazardous business. The Syracusans, to prevent the Athenians from coming out of their new base to plunder the neighbouring countryside, had moved one-third of their cavalry outside the city walls to the village of Olympieum. This cavalry detachment was now making it extremely difficult for the Athenian sailors to fetch water, and, as a result, they were frequently suffering casualties. Meanwhile, on the heights above, Gylippus was making good progress with the cross-wall across Epipolae; unwittingly helped by the Athenians, who had placed piles of stones along the intended line of their own wall.

Gylippus must also have been giving the Syracusans some hard training, since he now felt confident enough to march them out of the city and draw them up for battle outside its fortifications. Nicias accepted the provocative challenge and formed up opposite them, occupying a position between Syracuse itself and his own wall, thereby making it impossible for the Syracusans to use their cavalry. Not wishing to leave such a naturally strong defensive position, Nicias stood his ground and waited for the Syracusans to attack; but when they did, without the support of their cavalry, they were no match for the Athenians and withdrew back into the city. Gylippus later called them together, and told them that he was to blame: admitting that had fought the battle in too cramped an area where the cavalry could not be used. The next day, after a stirring address, he led them out into battle again, taking up a position so that their right wing was unimpeded by any fortifications. Nicias now faced a dilemma: if he did not attack, the cross-wall would be quickly completed; if he did attack, his left wing would be exposed to the Syracusan cavalry. Unfortunately, all that Thucydides tells us is that he chose to attack, apparently without taking any counter-measures, so the Athenian line was rolled up from left to right and they fled for protection behind their own fortifications. That night Gylippus finished the cross-wall, having been helped by the fortuitous arrival of twelve triremes (Corinthian and allied) whose crews had immediately been put to work. So ended all hope of the Athenians being able to invest the city.

By good leadership and professionalism, Gylippus had prised open the Athenian grip on Syracuse, and now he began making preparations to complete the task by challenging Athenian naval supremacy. While he was away touring the island to win over those cities that still remained uncommitted, he left the Syracusans busily occupied with raising and training a fleet. As for Nicias, though he had been sending regular reports to Athens, he now recognised that, unless the expedition was recalled or heavily reinforced, all would be lost; so he sent an urgent despatch back to Athens setting out the situation. While waiting for a reply, instead of trying to avert the looming disaster by taking vigorous action himself – such as attacking the Syracusans as they exercised their as yet untrained crews, or making a surprise night attack on their cavalry detachment at Olympieum – he sat on his backside and did nothing. As the Marquis of Montrose said:

> He either fears his fate too much
> Or his deserts are small
> That puts it not unto the touch
> To win or lose it all.

But let us hear what Nicias had to say in his despatch, which arrived in Athens in the winter of 414 BC, and then – perhaps rather unkindly, as the poor fellow cannot reply – raise some questions.

After putting himself in a favourable light by relating how he had defeated Gylippus in the first battle, Nicias went on to explain that the next day he was overpowered by the Syracusan cavalry and javelin-throwers, so that they (the Athenians) had been forced to retreat behind their fortifications. Now, because they lacked the troops both to defend their own lines and to complete the blockading wall, they had been forced to become inactive, and so were no longer the besiegers but the besieged, at least on land. He then warned the Athenians that Gylippus was trying to enlist the support of the hitherto neutral cities, while sending for reinforcements from the Peloponnese, and that he had nearly reached the stage where he could challenge them at sea. Maritime supremacy was being eroded, as their once-magnificent fleet had been at sea for too long and was now in a parlous state: the ships' timbers had rotted, and the crews were a shadow of their former selves. The triremes could not be hauled out of the water to be dried and cleaned, because the enemy had as many ships as, or more than, they did themselves; this kept them in constant expectation of being attacked.

Nicias then went on to say that the Syracusans now had the initiative; all the Athenians could do was maintain the blockade and guard against their own supplies being cut off. The slaves and foreigners were deserting, and whereas he could not get any replacements for his worn-out crews, the Syracusans had a number of sources on which they could draw for fresh manpower. Finally, Nicias issued a second, dire warning: if the Italian sources from which they obtained their supplies learned about the expeditionary force's deplorable condition, and that it was not going to be reinforced, they would change sides. Syracuse would then need to do no more than wait for him and his men to be starved into submission. If this was to be avoided, reinforcements must arrive by the very beginning of spring.

It was an inspired despatch, which put the Athenians on the hook. Either they reinforced Nicias, or they left him to his fate; which would so imperil their standing amongst their allies that they would probably desert them. As General James Wolfe was to comment some 2000 years later: 'War is an option of difficulties.'

But the key question is: how did this disastrous situation arise? By Nicias' own admission, the Syracusans now held the initiative. But how did this happen? The Syracusan fleet could not suddenly have appeared fully fledged and ready to challenge Athenian naval supremacy. Where was all the timber coming from to build this fleet, and why was the supply not halted? Why had the Syracusans not been attacked when putting to sea for training? And until the Syracusan fleet was fully trained, where did the threat to the Athenian supply lines to Italy come from? In the absence of such a threat, how was it that the ships had become water-logged? Whose fault was it that the situation ashore had deteriorated so drastically since Lamachus had been killed? Gylippus had certainly brought reinforcements with him, and the Syracusan cavalry still dominated the open battlefield; but why was the Athenian cavalry not patrolling the approaches to Syracuse and so giving early warning of Gylippus' intentions? And why was the route up to the Epipolae escarpment, which the Athenians had used themselves, not firmly secured? Finally, why was the Syracusan cavalry detachment at Olympieum, which was causing so much hardship for the ships' crews, not eliminated?

The answer to all these questions lies with Nicias. He just let things drift. Indecisive and too fearful of making a mistake, he lacked any initiative, whereas the Syracusans were led by an energetic, daring and enterprising commander. The truth of the old British Army adage that 'There are never bad battalions, just bad officers' could not be more starkly portrayed. But here we must leave Nicias with his self-inflicted woes, and see what was happening back in Greece.

Thucydides says that, after the Athenians had heard Nicias' report, they refused to relieve him of his command; which is hardly surprising, as they only knew the situation, and not how it had been arrived at. What is surprising is that, though they knew Nicias was sick, instead of recalling him, they merely appointed two temporary commanders so that he should not have to bear the whole weight of responsibility himself. The Athenians then voted to send out another expeditionary force, commanded by Demosthenes and Eurymedon, who, when they arrived, would take over from the two temporary commanders. Eurymedon was an experienced officer who, as will be recalled, had commanded a fleet in the Corcyraean civil war in 427 BC and had then taken over command of the expedition force in Sicily the following year. When, however, the Sicilian cities made peace with each other in 424 BC an Athenian presence became both unnecessary and undesirable; when the Athenians did withdraw, Eurymedon was arraigned on the spurious charge of having been bribed to leave Sicily. Now that he had been reinstated, he was to return to the island with an advance party of ten ships and 120 talents of silver and to inform the troops that help was on the way.

Demosthenes, who was to remain behind to organise the expedition, had even more operational experience. After a disastrously impetuous foray into Aetolia in 426 BC, he had redeemed himself by saving Naupactus, and then by defeating the Peloponnesian army when it invaded Acarnania. In 425 BC Demosthenes had been the brains behind the defeat of the Spartans at Pylos, and he had fought in Thrace the following year, and had participated in Alcibiades' Peloponnesian venture in 418 BC. Since he was tough, energetic and battle-hardened, there would have been justifiable hope that he would be able to restore the situation. In the meantime, apart from summoning troops and ships from the allies, he had to oversee the raising of money, the recruitment of hoplites, the collection of supplies, and the fitting out of the fleet for its many and varied tasks.

The Corinthians and Spartans were also intending to send out reinforcements, so twenty Athenian ships were sent round the Peloponnese to hinder them. The Spartans had been greatly encouraged by the fact that the Athenians now had two wars on their hands; and in response to the Syracusan appeal to deter the Athenians from sending out further forces, they were preparing to invade Attica once again. This time they intended to follow the advice Alcibiades had been continually pressing on them: to occupy and fortify Decelea, which lay some fifteen miles north-east of Athens and approximately the same distance from the Boeotian border. Early in the spring of 413 BC, the Spartans duly invaded Attica and headed for Decelea, marking their passage with the usual trail of devastation; then, on reaching the fort, they at once set about strengthening it.

Alcibiades could hardly have done his countrymen a greater injury than persuading the Spartans to fortify Decelea. From here they could dominate the rich plain, which stretched down to within sight of Athens, not just for a few summer months but throughout the year, and for as long as they chose. The Athenians were now deprived of the produce from this rich countryside, which included sheep and other farm animals; moreover, the supplies of food from Euboea, which had previously come overland, now had to be brought by sea. Then, as though this were not enough, some 20,000 slaves, the majority of whom were skilled workers, now deserted, while Athens' battlements had to be guarded by day and night. Thucydides says that the consequences stemming from the loss of Decelea were one of the chief reasons for the decline of Athenian power. This may well be the case, but it does seem that the military situation in Attica was not quite as desperate as he suggests.

In the summer 1300 mercenary peltasts from a Thracian tribe arrived in Athens; they should have sailed with Demosthenes to Sicily, but came too late. Instead of retaining them, however, to help deal with the threat from Decelea, the Athenians sent them back to save the expense of hiring them. But to get some value from the peltasts while travelling, they appointed one of their own generals to command them, giving him orders to do as much damage as he could along the Boeotian and Theban coastline – instructions that he diligently executed: first raiding Tanagra, and then unleashing the Thracians in the small unlocated town of Mycalessus, where they ran amok and perpetrated a general massacre, including the slaughter of all the children in the largest school in the town. This incident, recorded by Thucydides with controlled indignation, is an example of what can happen when a civilised army employs less civilised allies as mercenary troops.

Mycalessus was clearly so far inland that the inhabitants never thought they would be attacked from the sea. A Theban relief force, however, surprised and killed some of the Thracians while they were still at work, and then caught up with the remainder, driving them back to their boats. The Thracians clearly fought with considerable gallantry, standing up to the Theban cavalry by charging out in detachments, and then falling back again. On reaching the shoreline, however, things did not go so well. To avoid the shower of arrows falling on them, the ships' crews pulled out to sea, leaving the Thracians to swim for their lives; this was fine for those who knew how, but confronted the others with a stark choice: either they died where they stood, or drowned trying to escape. By all accounts they were fortunate only to lose 250 dead, while killing some twenty Theban cavalrymen and hoplites. For the sake of continuity, in recounting these events we have run ahead of what was happening in Sicily; so we must now step back to earlier in the year.

The relief force for Sicily had sailed at about the same time as Decelea had been lost, resulting in a strange juxtaposition of roles. While Athens was virtually under siege herself, she was besieging Syracuse, a city about as large as herself, some 100 miles away. No wonder that, as Thucydides euphemistically put it, Athens was becoming financially embarrassed. Fighting two wars simultaneously while revenue was declining had necessitated a tax being placed on all imports, but, as we have just seen with the Thracians, this was evidently insufficient to cover the enormous expenditure being incurred.

On his way to Corcyra, Demosthenes picked up some hoplites from the islands of Zacynthus and Cephallenia and then sailed up to Acarnania, where he met Eurymedon who, as has been mentioned, had gone ahead to tell the Athenians at Syracuse that help was on the way and, having done so, was now on his way back. Among other things, Eurymedon told Demosthenes that the Syracusans had captured Plemmyrium, the headland where the Athenians had built three forts to block the harbour entrance. While Demosthenes and Eurymedon were conferring about this reversal – which will be recounted shortly – they were joined by Conon, the commander at Naupactus, who asked them for assistance. Lying opposite him were twenty-five Corinthian ships, clearly seeking the opportunity for a naval battle; but as he had only eighteen ships himself, it would be too risky to take up the challenge, unless he was reinforced. So he was given ten of the fastest triremes available, and off he went back to Naupactus. Although the Corinthians wanted to engage Conon, this was not because they then wanted to attack Naupactus, but in order to prevent him from interfering with the Peloponnesian convoys carrying reinforcements to Syracuse.

Though Conon had been given ten additional triremes, the Corinthians had been able to man some extra ones themselves; so they were not greatly inferior in numbers when the Athenians decided to give battle. The Corinthians were anchored in a crescent-shaped bay, and since Thucydides says that their infantry were drawn up on the two headlands to give support, they must have had ample warning of Conon's approach. At first the Corinthians made no move, but then, choosing their moment, they sailed out into the attack. For some time neither side gained any advantage, but eventually the Corinthians gave way, losing three ships; the Athenians, though not losing any, had seven severely damaged. The Corinthians had widened and strengthened the bows of their ships, and so, by ramming those of the Athenians head-on, they stove in their prows and rendered them unseaworthy. When the action was broken off, the Athenians were able to sail back to Naupactus, taking their damaged triremes with them.

Now we must return to Sicily, and see how it was that Plemmyrium had been lost. After Gylippus had returned from the interior with fresh reinforcements, he decided to attack the fortified headland before Nicias himself was reinforced. In this way he would deprive the Athenians of their naval base, while gaining a significant tactical advantage in preparation for the great naval battle that lay ahead. For the attack on Plemmyrium, the Syracusans divided their eighty ships into two squadrons, and after sailing together during the night, at dawn they separated, to assault the Athenians on both sides of the headland; meanwhile, at about the same time, Gylippus led an attack by land from Olympieum. The Athenians received enough warning of the Syracusans' approach to man sixty ships, twenty-five of which engaged the thirty-five Syracusan ships assaulting the headland from within the harbour, while the remainder sailed against the squadron approaching from the sea.

There then occurred a near-unbelievable lack of security on the part of the Athenians. So engrossed were their troops with the naval battle that, when Gylippus launched his attack, they were caught completely off their guard and lost all three forts in quick succession. The result of the naval battle had now lost much of its significance, but the Syracusan squadron attacking from the sea drove the Athenians back inside the harbour. However, the Syracusans then lost formation and became hopelessly entangled; this provided the Athenians with time to recover, and then rout them. They next turned on the other Syracusan squadron, which was now heavily outnumbered and quickly scattered. The Athenians sank eleven Syracusan ships for the loss of three of their own, and, facing no further opposition, they were able to recover the Syracusan wrecks. Thucydides says that, in the opinion of the Syracusans, their defeat had been due to their own mistakes, not because of the Athenians'

innate superiority. Maybe; but in view of the changes they later made
to both their tactics and their ships, this seems a bit improbable.

But however much their fleet may have suffered, the Syracusans
had gained their main objective, the capture of Plemmyrium; this
brought consequences for the Athenians from which they never
recovered. More immediately, they now had to establish their naval
station on the narrow beach in front of their camp, the only stretch of
the shoreline remaining to them, while having to fight to clear a
passage whenever supply ships were being brought in. The Syracusans, on the other hand, besides controlling the harbour entrance,
were now able to intercept Athenian supply ships as far afield as Italy
– let it be noted, long after Nicias had claimed that this task had
water-logged his ships. But with the capture of Plemmyrium, it was
not just a tactical advantage that the Syracusans had gained. They had
also acquired three beached triremes, a huge quantity of stores and
corn, together with masts and other equipment for forty triremes.

Although Nicias tried to exploit his naval superiority by closing
with the Syracusans in the Great Harbour, he was thwarted in his
attempts. The Syracusans declined to give battle and instead anchored
their ships behind a stockade, made from large stakes that had been
driven into the seabed. In an endeavour to breach this obstacle, the
Athenians fitted out a large merchant ship with wooden towers, and a
protective screen along its sides. In the small hours, they rowed this
floating castle up to the stockade, fastened ropes around the stakes,
and dragged them up with windlasses. There was one particularly
difficult part, where the stakes had been driven below the water level
to create an artificial reef, so making it too hazardous to approach.
The Athenians dealt with this problem by sending down divers to
saw through the obstacle – an incredible feat. But it was all to no
avail; as soon as the Athenians withdrew, the stakes were immediately
replaced.

The Syracusans had drawn a number of conclusions from their
naval encounters and, quite possibly following the advice of the
Corinthians, they changed the design of their ships and devised new
tactics. Major engagements would be confined to the Great Harbour,
where, since the room to manoeuvre would be greatly restricted,
there would then be no need to try and match the skilled seamanship
and tactical dexterity of the Athenians. So, like the Corinthians before
them, the Syracusans shortened and strengthened the bows of their

ships, building in stout cross-timbers that projected out on either side for about nine feet. In this way, when they formed up for battle, they would present the Athenians with an impenetrable barrier. Restricted by the harbour, and unable to pass between gaps in the Syracusan line to encircle or ram them amidships, the Athenians would have no alternative but to stand and fight a head-on engagement. They could then be charged, and the bows of the Athenian ships shattered. Faced with the naval equivalent of a phalanx, the Athenians could then be driven back against the shore, the greater part of which was already in the possession of the Syracusans.

After the capture of Plemmyrium, and while these preparations for the naval battle were in hand, the Syracusans had also been busy strengthening their land component. Representatives had been sent out to raise further troops and having met with a good response, they were now on the point of returning with more than 2000 fresh recruits. Nicias, however, had been kept closely informed about all this activity; so he asked the Sicels, who controlled the route by which the Syracusans would be returning, to intercept them. Evidently still thinking they were backing the winning side, the Sicels complied with Nicias' request and set up an ambush. Falling upon the winding column of new troops, they killed at least 800 of them, together with the Syracusan representatives, except for one who managed to escape and lead back some 1500 survivors to Syracuse. But by now practically the whole of the rest of Sicily, except for Agrigentum which remained determinedly neutral, had sided with the Syracusans. Reinforcements then became far more plentiful and easier to acquire, with two south-coast cities, Gela and Camarina, between them providing 500 hoplites, 700 javelin-throwers, 300 archers, 300 cavalry and crews for five ships.

Thucydides says that after the disaster in the Sicel country, Gylippus gave up the idea of an immediate attack on the Athenians, which is slightly surprising, as shortly afterwards the reinforcements from Gela and Camarina arrived. As for the Athenian reinforcements, Demosthenes and Eurymedon had by now crossed the Ionian Gulf, picking up some javelin-throwers and a couple of triremes on the way. They then made their way along the Italian coast to Thurii, where they found the pro-Athenian party had seized power, so time was spent in trying to persuade them to join the expedition; which they evidently did, as Thucydides later names them as being amongst those joining the expedition. Meanwhile back at Syracuse, Gylippus, learning of Demosthenes' approach, decided to eradicate the Athenian base, which lay on the shore of the Great Harbour, where the encircling wall terminated just to the south of the city.

The intention was to mount a coordinated land and sea assault, with Gylippus and troops from Syracuse closing up to the Athenian wall, while those at Olympieum moved up to the wall from the other side. Immediately afterwards, the Syracusan fleet was to sail out and join in the attack. All went according to plan. The Athenians at first thought that they were only being attacked on land, but when they saw some eighty Syracusan ships bearing down on them, they quickly launched seventy-five of their own. Strangely, however, even though the tactical setting appears to have been exactly what they required, the Syracusans did not charge, but restricted themselves to making an occasional probing attack, and then withdrawing. Likewise, the Athenians seemed reluctant to commit themselves to a decisive engagement, and though the Syracusans sank a couple of their ships, nothing of consequence was achieved, and both sides eventually withdrew. Thucydides does not tell us what had happened on land, merely stating that, when the Syracusan fleet broke off the engagement, the troops also pulled back.

On the following day the Syracusans neither made a move nor gave any indication of what they were intending to do next. Nicias, however, anticipated another attack, so he ensured that repairs to his damaged ships were carried out at once and established a defensive screen by anchoring a line of merchant ships outside the artificial harbour. Like the Syracusan one they had tried to dismantle, the Athenian harbour had been created by erecting a stockade that extended out from the shoreline. The merchant ships that formed the screen were placed about 200 feet apart, so as to leave gaps between them through which the Athenian triremes could pass if hard-pressed. To prevent them being followed, beams – armed with what Thucydides describes as 'dolphins' – were suspended between the merchant ships; this suggests that some sort of spiked obstacle could be raised and lowered from their bows and sterns.

The next day, though rather earlier than before, the Syracusans repeated the same deployment and tactics: probing and withdrawing at sea, and apparently only mounting a holding operation on land. Towards midday, however, the Syracusans resorted to a ruse to try and achieve surprise. The market from the city was set up on the shore, whereupon the Syracusan fleet back-watered and disembarked, as though to have a meal. The Athenians, for their part, thought the Syracusans had broken off the engagement because they considered themselves beaten; so they too disembarked and began attending to their various jobs and preparing their own meal. The Syracusans waited until they were satisfied that the Athenians were off their guard, then quickly manned their ships and sailed out again.

But although Thucydides says that the Athenians were in great confusion, and only got their ships into formation with considerable difficulty, it was they who charged forward into the attack. Meeting head-on, the Syracusan ships with their strengthened bows stove in those of the Athenians, while javelin-throwers on small boats slipped in under the oars and, sailing close to the Athenian ships, hurled in their weapons through the oar holes. Badly shaken and suffering heavy casualties, the Athenians turned and made for the line of their merchant ships, closely pursued by the Syracusans, who lost two of their ships when, as Thucydides says, they went too close, presumably to the 'dolphins', which may then have been underwater. Seven Athenian ships were sunk, and many others disabled, while the crews were either taken prisoner or killed.

It is a strange, not altogether convincing story. What were the land forces doing? Why did the Syracusans' ships not charge? If the Athenians thought the Syracusans considered themselves to have been worsted, and so back-watered, why did they not press home their perceived advantage? Finally, the ruse sounds a bit naive. Anyway it gained the Syracusans no advantage; the Athenians may have had to scramble back into their ships, but it was they who then attacked. But there we must leave matters, for it is now that Demosthenes and Eurymedon arrive.

The relief force consisted of seventy-three ships, some hoplites, and a large number of light troops: javelin-throwers, slingers and archers – in fact everything that was required for the campaign. Such was the case with Nicias, but as we have seen, through not at once taking the offensive, he allowed time for Gylippus to reach Syracuse and then seize the initiative. A mistake that Thucydides says Demosthenes was determined not to repeat. It might be thought that Demosthenes had a great advantage over Nicias: the Athenians were already established ashore, their combined fleet was nearly twice the size of the

Syracusans' and their army was considerably larger. But against this must be set three important considerations: the Syracusans were now far better prepared and, with Gylippus, far better led; and whereas, before, the Sicilians were divided in their loyalties, they were now almost entirely behind the Syracusans. On balance, it seems that Demosthenes faced a far harder task. But in spite of this, he nearly won an early victory.

Demosthenes was quite clear about three things: first, the need to act at once while the fear caused by his arrival lasted; second, the capture of Syracuse would be the quickest way to end the war; and third, should he fail to take the city, to save the unnecessary squandering of both lives and resources, the expeditionary force should be withdrawn. In his opinion, the key to the capture of Syracuse lay with the cross-wall, which, as will be remembered, ran from east to west across Epipolae, so preventing the circumvallation of the city. The Athenians held the southern side of the cross-wall, and the Syracusans the northern side. The wall could either be taken by mounting a direct assault from the south, or by getting round behind it onto the Syracusan-held side. But since the latter course would entail climbing the steep escarpment up to Epipolae – as the original expeditionary force had done – in full view of the Syracusans, Demosthenes chose the direct approach. Siege engines were brought up to make a breach, and attacks were mounted at selected points along the wall; but the Syracusans burned the siege engines, and repulsed the attacks, so Demosthenes had to think again.

By day it would be impossible to get round the cross-wall onto Epipolae, but Demosthenes, ever resourceful and daring, proposed to do so at night. So, having obtained the agreement of Nicias and his fellow commanders, he set off at about midnight with Eurymedon and most of the army, which carried five days' provisions, together with all the masons and carpenters. Following the same route as the first Athenian army had done, they reached the top of the escarpment without being observed, and then captured the fort at its head, though they were unable to prevent most of the garrison escaping to the three Syracusan camps on Epipolae. The alarm having been raised, the 600-strong contingent responsible for the defence of this sector, who were attending a review on the previous occasion, now hastened forward, only to be routed for a second time. Maintaining the momentum of their attack, the main Athenian force pressed forward, while the contingent tasked with securing the cross-wall, having reached their objective without meeting any resistance, at once set about tearing it down.

At this stage Gylippus mounted a counter-attack with the troops who had been holding the outer fortifications, but they were bewildered by the novelty of night fighting, their attack lacked resolution and they were forced back. Up until now the Athenians had done magnificently, and victory seemed to be within their grasp; so quite rightly, to allow no time for the enemy to rally, there was no slackening of the attack. But through over-eagerness and lack of training for a night attack, they began to lose cohesion; in other words, they became disjointed and dispersed. They were then in no state to withstand a determined and well-directed counter-attack by the Boeotians, which burst them apart. Disorganised and unable to distinguish friend from foe, some of them started fighting one another; others continued to advance, while there were those who broke and ran. According to Thucydides, it was the Syracusans singing their paean, which was similar to that of the Athenians, that caused so much confusion and did as much harm as anything else. Moreover, when the Argives, Corcyraeans and other Dorian contingents on the Athenian side started singing their paeans, it produced as much panic amongst the Athenians as it was intended to cause amongst the enemy. While the Athenians were disintegrating into a state of near-chaos, the majority of the Syracusans managed to remain in a compact body; so they had less of a problem over identification, while they were familiar with the terrain, which, even at night, gave them an advantage.

As the route down from Epipolae was narrow and twisting, it soon became choked, causing many of those being pursued to cast themselves over the cliff without any hope of survival. Far better for them to have died facing the enemy in battle. But there is something incomprehensible about panic, in the way it drives human beings to choose a no less certain death than the one they are trying to escape. The terrible tragedy at New York's World Trade Center in September 2001, when a raging fire-storm followed the crashing of two aircraft into the twin towers, caused many of the trapped victims to jump to their death from unbelievable heights – in one recorded instance from the 104th floor of the North Tower. But to return to Syracuse: most of those who got down safely to the plain below escaped back to their camp, but others (especially those who had just arrived) lost their way and wandered off in the wrong direction; so when dawn broke they were rounded up and killed by the Syracusan cavalry. The battlefield on Epipolae was strewn with weapons, out of all proportion to the number of dead, especially at the edge of the cliffs, where those who intended to throw themselves over had discarded their shields. After such an unexpected victory the Syracusans recovered their confidence, and Gylippus, believing it would now be possible to drive the Athenians off their positions, felt able to set off on another recruiting tour to raise a further army.

Meanwhile the Athenian commanders discussed the situation following their defeat, and considered what their next move should be. The army was clearly in a bad way; badly shaken and depleted, while the sickness rate had risen, partly because of the time of the year, and partly because its camp was situated in low-lying, marshy ground.

Demosthenes held to his original view, that if their attack on Syracuse failed and they suffered a severe reverse, they should not delay any longer, but evacuate the expeditionary force while they still had naval superiority. Nicias held the opposite view. Admittedly, the situation was serious, but there were those in Syracuse who wanted to betray the city, and they were continually sending him messages not to abandon the siege. The Syracusans were also running short of money; they had incurred heavy expenditure in building a fleet, and soon they would not be able to continue paying all the mercenaries they had recruited. It would thus be wrong to despair; the Syracusan position could soon be worse than their own, so they should persevere and fight on. Nicias then went on to say that they should not abandon the expedition without the consent of the Athenian assembly, otherwise their political opponents would turn public opinion against them and impeach them. Nor should they pay attention to those soldiers who were now crying out so loudly about their desperate position, but who, as soon as they got back to Athens, would go round telling everybody that they had been let down by their generals, who had been bribed to withdraw. He himself would rather face death on the battlefield than disgrace and a sentence of death, should they return home at this stage.

Although Thucydides does not make the point, Nicias was truly hoist on his own petard. As will be remembered, to save his own political position, when Eurymedon withdrew from Sicily following the peace treaty in 424 BC, Nicias had brought trumped-up charges against him, and he had been unjustly convicted of accepting bribes to abandon the expedition. So it was from personal experience that Nicias knew what to expect; and it may well have been this consideration that he had in mind when he opposed Demosthenes' realistic assessment of the situation.

Demosthenes replied by saying that, if they could not discontinue the campaign without authority from Athens, then they should give up besieging Syracuse and move their base either to Thapsus or Catana, both further up the east coast. From either of these bases they could dominate most of Sicily and keep themselves well supplied, while laying waste the enemy's territory. Their fleet would also be able to fight in the open sea, where it would have freedom to manoeuvre, rather than having to do so under restrictive conditions that favoured the Syracusans. Although Eurymedon supported him, Nicias refused to consider abandoning the siege; so the Athenians stayed where they were.

In the meantime, Gylippus returned to Syracuse with substantial reinforcements, including some Peloponnesian hoplites, who had set off in the spring, but because of bad weather had made a somewhat circuitous journey via Cyrene and a number of other Libyan cities. When these reinforcements arrived, the Syracusans began planning to attack the Athenians both by land and sea; while the Athenians, for their part, had decided to abandon their positions. Having learned of the arrival of the Syracusan reinforcements, and because their army was suffering from sickness, Nicias had at last accepted that their position was untenable. In the greatest secrecy the Athenians then embarked, but just as they were on the point of setting sail, there was an eclipse of the moon. Interpreting this as an alarming portent of disaster, should they put to sea, the majority of the Athenians implored their commanders to let them remain where they were. So Nicias, who was always easily influenced by omens and the like, took counsel of his fears, consulted the soothsayers and ordered the troops to disembark. Thus irresolution and superstition imposed yet another delay, which this time was to prove fatal.

Somehow the Syracusans got to hear of the Athenian intentions; and not wishing them to establish themselves elsewhere on the island, they decided to bring them to battle as soon as possible. But first they

had to undertake some additional training before their fleet was ready
to fight what was going to be a major, and probably decisive, battle.
Thucydides, without stating the purpose of the Syracusan attack, or
being specific as to where exactly it took place, says that they
assaulted the 'Athenian walls'; when an inexplicably small force of
Athenian hoplites and cavalry came out to meet them, they drove
them back, inflicting a number of casualties. The next day the
Syracusans again advanced towards the Athenian walls, and at the
same time put to sea with seventy-six ships; which the Athenians
countered in slightly greater strength. Eurymedon, who commanded
the right wing, detached himself from the main body and attempted
to encircle the enemy; but the Syracusans defeated the Athenian
centre, then turned on Eurymedon, and trapped him in a shallow bay
where he was killed and his ships destroyed.

The rest of the Athenian fleet was then driven ashore and stranded,
just beyond the protection of their stockade and camp. Seeing their
plight, Gylippus led a contingent forward to kill the crews, and to
help with towing off the ships. But such was his eagerness and haste
that he lost formation, like the Athenians on Epipolae during their
night attack, and so, when counter-attacked by the Etruscans who
were responsible for this particular sector, his leading troops were
routed and the remainder driven back into some marshy ground.
Soon afterwards other Syracusans came to their assistance, but were
in turn driven off by the Athenians who, fearing for their ships, had
turned out in considerable force; but not before eighteen ships had
been captured, and all those aboard killed. Exploiting their remarkable achievement, and making use of the favourable wind, the
Syracusans next floated down a fire-ship; but it was intercepted by
the Athenians before it could do any harm.

The Syracusans had won a considerable tactical and moral victory:
the Athenian fleet had been severely mauled, and its vaunted
superiority shattered, while its troops and crews alike had been
thoroughly shaken. The situation had clearly become critical. The
Athenians had been unable to exploit their far greater superiority, and
now they had lost both the initiative and the ability to adopt different
tactics. But that was not all. According to Thucydides, though
Syracuse was a Dorian city, its ruling party was democratic. The
Athenians were thus fighting a fellow democracy; so, in spite of what
Nicias had claimed, there can never have been much hope of Syracuse

being betrayed from within. Now there was absolutely none. As for the Syracusans: quite apart from having gained both military and moral ascendancy, they were now no longer concerned about saving themselves, only determined to ensure that the Athenians could not escape total destruction. Moreover, there was the inspiring thought that, should they be able to defeat the Athenians on land and sea, they would win great glory throughout Hellas while gaining credit for having so weakened Athens that her eventual defeat would be inevitable. So, filled with confidence and enthusiasm, they set about the realisation of these beckoning aspirations.

It is now that Thucydides – as Herodotus did in naming Xerxes' host – gives a comprehensive list of all the Athenian and Syracusan contingents and allies. But as the details do not add anything to our understanding of the situation, they will be omitted; as will be remembered, the main participants have already been recorded in the Historical Survey. In order to contain the Athenians and destroy their fleet, the Syracusans now began anchoring a line of triremes and merchant ships across the harbour mouth. Seeing what was happening, the Athenians called a council of war to decide what their next move should be; and although the need for an early decision was apparent enough, it was lent greater urgency by the fact that their supplies were running low. This logistic crisis had arisen as a result of their earlier intention to abandon the siege of Syracuse and establish themselves at Catana. They had accordingly sent most of their provisions on ahead, with instructions not to send any more.

The decision was now taken to withdraw from the upper fortifications and construct a cross-wall close to the ships, so enclosing an area just large enough to accommodate the stores and the sick, which a relatively small garrison would be capable of defending. The rest of the army could then be taken on board and fill every ship, seaworthy or not, so as to fight it out at sea. If they were victorious, they would sail to Catana; if defeated, they would burn their ships and march in battle order to the nearest friendly city, Hellenic or not, from where the fight would be renewed.

The decision taken, the plan was acted upon without delay, and the entire force was concentrated ready for the coming action. It was then that Nicias made a last-minute attempt to raise morale: telling them all that if they wanted to save their lives and see their homes again, they must give their best in what was going to be a land battle fought at sea: the sort of battle they were well equipped and qualified to win. He then went on to explain the new tactics that had been devised to counter the modifications made to the Syracusan ships. When the enemy charged, they must be faced; there must be no backing water, since this would bring their ships up against the shore, which was mostly in Syracusan hands. Nor must the Syracusans be allowed to back-water, which would enable them to charge again; to prevent this from happening, grappling-irons had been fitted to all the ships. It was the duty of the soldiers to use them effectively, and afterwards to fight it out to the limits of their strength, when clearing the enemy decks of their hoplites.

While Nicias had been giving his address, Gylippus, seeing that a battle was imminent, had also assembled the Syracusans. After reminding them that the Athenians had come to enslave them, he encouraged them by saying that the enemy, through crowding their decks with troops, would impair the efficiency of their ships and so be unable to fight a coherent battle. Finally, he pointed out that the Athenians were thoroughly demoralised and desperate to escape; so the Syracusans and their allies should go into battle with anger in their hearts, seeking to revenge themselves on their aggressor.

Assuming that these exhortations could be heard in the first place, which seems highly improbable, it was also somewhat late for Nicias to be explaining the new tactics to be adopted. In recording them, Thucydides was probably doing no more than setting the scene and portraying the contestants' different attitudes towards the coming battle. But whether or not this was his intention, there can be little doubt that the Syracusans felt themselves to be superior to their enemy, possessing such a sense of moral and fighting ascendancy that the battle was already half won. Moreover (though Gylippus did not mention it when he spoke), unfortunately for the Athenians, their intention to use grappling-irons had been discovered by the Syracusans. So they had stretched hides over the prows and along much of the upper part of their ships, making it nearly impossible for the grappling-irons to get a hold.

The speeches over, the ships were manned and took up their battle positions. Part of the Syracusan fleet was sent to guard the harbour mouth, and the rest ringed the harbour, ready to charge the Athenians from every direction; meanwhile the hoplites occupied all the places along the shore where ships could put in. The battle scene set, the

Athenians made straight for the ships guarding the harbour mouth, and the impetus of their charge carried them through the Syracusans' screen of ships to the line of anchored vessels that they were covering. But as they were trying to break down this barrier and clear a passage, the rest of the Syracusan fleet bore down on them, and the fighting soon spread over the full extent of the harbour. There were nearly 200 ships engaged, so crowded together that there were frequent collisions between them, friend and foe alike.

But let us follow Thucydides' vivid and unmatchable account of this titanic battle, destined to seal the fate of the Athenians:

All the time that one ship was bearing down upon another, javelins, arrows and stones were shot or hurled on to it without cessation by the men on the decks; and once the ships met, the soldiers fought hand to hand, each trying to board the enemy. Because of the narrowness of the space, it often happened that a ship was ramming and being rammed at the same time, and that two, and sometimes more, ships found themselves jammed against one, so that the steersmen had to think of defence on one side, and attack on the other and, instead of being able to give their attention to one point at a time, had to deal with many different things in all directions; and the great din of all these ships crashing together was not only frightening in itself, but also made it impossible to hear the orders given by the boatswains. And indeed, in the ordinary course of duty and in the present excitement of battle, plenty of instructions were given, and plenty of shouting was done by the boatswain on either side ... Finally, after the battle had lasted a long time, the Syracusans and their allies broke the Athenian resistance, followed them up with great shouting and cheering, and chased them back, clearly and decisively, to the land.

While the battle at sea had been raging, those ashore – unable to see what was happening everywhere at once – shouted encouragement when they saw some of their own ships gaining the upper hand, while others, watching elsewhere, cried out in despair at the sight of them suffering defeat. Then there were those who, looking where no decision had yet been reached, mingled cries of elation and anguish as the battle ebbed and flowed. Thucydides portrays the Athenians eventually breaking, with the surviving ships making for the shore, where most of their crews and the troops, gripped with panic, fled in all directions. There were, however, some who kept their heads and tried to rally round the beached ships, while others hastened to man the fortifications. Somewhat despairingly, but not altogether accurately, Thucydides says that the Athenians were now in much the same state as the Spartans at Pylos, when, having lost their ships, they were stranded on the island of Sphacteria with no hope of getting away.

For some unknown reason the Syracusans did not exploit their success, but contented themselves with collecting up the wrecks and their dead, before returning to their city. As for the Athenians, somewhat surprisingly, we now learn that they still had about sixty serviceable ships left, which was more than the Syracusans; so Demosthenes tried to persuade Nicias to make another attempt to break out the following day. But even if they possessed a numerical superiority, Athenian morale was broken, and, in refusing to man their ships, they demonstrated the truth of Napoleon's dictum that: 'In war, moral considerations count for three-quarters, the balance of forces only for the other quarter.' So the Athenians abandoned all hope of escaping by sea, preferring instead to seek refuge elsewhere.

The Syracusans, having learned of the Athenians' earlier plan to abandon their positions and continue the war from elsewhere, had little doubt that this was still their intention. If it were to be prevented, it called for immediate action to block their escape routes. But they spent too long discussing the situation and so, by the time they had reached a decision, it was too late. The victory celebrations were under way, while a festival in honour of Heracles was being celebrated the same day. Orders to abandon them both would be unlikely to meet with ready compliance; so some other way of preventing the Athenians from eluding them had to be found. Once again, the Syracusans resorted to a ruse.

As soon as it began to grow dark, a cavalry detachment escorted some impostors, posing as friends of the Athenians, down to their camp; and proclaimed that, as the Syracusans were guarding all the escape routes, they should not attempt to withdraw during the night. Far better to get themselves properly organised, and to do so by day. Without making any attempt to check the identity of these shadowy individuals, Nicias naively accepted their authenticity and delayed his departure until all the necessary preparations had been completed.

Meanwhile, the celebrations over, and the festival sacrifices to Heracles completed, Gylippus galvanised the Syracusans into action: all the routes and river crossings were blocked, and the fleet was sent to recover all the Athenian ships that could be found from along the shoreline.

As for the Athenians, they spent two days after the great naval battle completing their preparations, before beginning their withdrawal towards Catana, which lay north of Syracuse on the east coast. On departing, the Athenians left behind them a terrible scene: their dead lay unburied in scattered heaps all over the battlefield, while the sick and wounded cried out for help as they recognised friends and relatives, clinging on to them, or dragging themselves along behind, imploring that they should not be abandoned. And when their strength finally failed, they lay down, crying out to the gods and raising their lamentations to heaven. But however distressing the able-bodied found it all, and however profound their sense of shame, they continued on their way, with each man carrying what he could; resembling a host of refugees, rather than a 40,000-strong army withdrawing in battle order to fight again.

Having painted this dismal picture, Thucydides then tells how Nicias and Demosthenes brought order to the ranks, while raising morale by addressing the various detachments, telling them how strong the army was, with many first-rate hoplites in the ranks. So the earlier rabble was miraculously transformed into a formed body of troops, marching in a hollow square, with Nicias' troops in front and those of Demosthenes, who amounted to more than half the total, bringing up the rear. The hoplites were placed on the outside, while the baggage carriers and general mass of the army were herded together in the middle.

It all leaves much to conjecture about. If, as Thucydides says, there really were 40,000 of them (or even only 10,000), if they were not properly organised to start with, how could order be imposed when once on the move? How did an army of that size manage to march in the manner described? It may seem unkind and unnecessary to spoil a good story with such questions, but if we are attempting to get at the truth so as to learn from history, they need to be asked.

For three days the Athenians fought their way forward; first clearing a passage across the River Anapus, and then, after repeated attacks, carrying a fortified pass; while all the time being assailed on the flanks and to the rear. On the night of the third day, Nicias and Demosthenes, realising that the army was being fought to a standstill, decided on a change of plan. Instead of trying to reach Catana, they would slip away during the night and march in the opposite direction, as though heading for Camarina and Gela, on the south coast. After lighting as many camp fires as possible, they then set off. Though there was considerable confusion, particularly amongst Demosthenes' troops who lost contact with one another, at dawn they reached the sea just south of Syracuse. From here they intended to continue as far as the River Cacyparis (Cassibili), then turn due west and follow its course up into the interior, where they hoped to join forces with the Sicels.

Meanwhile, when it was day and the Syracusans discovered that the Athenians had got away – another example of failing to maintain close contact – they set off after them. At midday they caught up with Demosthenes, and, using their cavalry, they cut him off from Nicias, who was by then some five miles ahead. Choosing to stand and fight rather than try and struggle on, Demosthenes and his troops were surrounded in a walled enclosure amongst olive trees. Here they were assailed by missiles throughout the day, until, exhausted and suffering heavy casualties, they eventually accepted a Syracusan call to surrender, made more acceptable by the assurance that no one would be put to death, either summarily or by imprisonment and starvation. Thucydides says that 6000 of them surrendered; but as he had earlier said that Demosthenes commanded rather more than half the 40,000-strong army, the numbers – even allowing for substantial casualties, earlier capitulations, desertions and stragglers – are hard to reconcile.

The next day Nicias had reached some high ground when the Syracusans caught up with him and told him that Demosthenes had surrendered, so called upon him to do the same. At first Nicias refused to believe them, but after he had been permitted to send a few of his cavalry to investigate, he tried to negotiate an agreement whereby his army would be allowed to go free. But his proposals were rejected, and the fighting was resumed for the rest of the day. After it was dark, Nicias tried to get away, but the Syracusans had at last learned to maintain contact, so only some 300 managed to escape. The next day Nicias resumed his march but, being under continuous attack from the flanks and rear, his army finally broke when trying to cross the River Assinarus (Tellaro or Atiddaru), where the enemy held the far bank.

Thucydides now describes another of the chaotic scenes he so relishes. Suffering agonies of thirst, the Athenians broke ranks and rushed into the river, where – largely oblivious to the enemy who held the far bank, or were closing up after them – they continued to drink greedily, even after the water had become muddy and stained with blood. Nicias finally put an end to the carnage by somehow managing to locate Gylippus and surrender to him personally. Most of the survivors were retained as personal possessions by their Syracusan captors; Thucydides says that they were to be found throughout Sicily, with only about 1000 being taken as official prisoners. As we will learn later, this apportionment is very suspect. Some of the Athenians managed to escape and make their way to Catana, but most of the army had been killed, either in this final slaughter or during the earlier, almost continuous fighting. Although Gylippus would have liked to have taken Nicias and Demosthenes back to Sparta with him, so as to parade them publicly, he could not prevent them being summarily executed.

The Syracusans gathered up all the spoils they could carry and then returned to Syracuse, where they put the prisoners in the stone quarries for safekeeping. Badly treated, suffering from hunger and thirst – the daily ration was half a pint of water and a pint of corn – with no cover from the weather, they were exposed to the heat of the sun by day, and then, as the autumnal nights set in, to a sharp fall in temperature. Crowded together with no sanitation amongst the piled heaps of the dead, it is a wonder that disease did not carry off not just the sick and wounded, but every living being. After ten weeks the surviving prisoners, except for the Athenians and those Greeks who had joined them from Italy and Sicily, were sold as slaves; the remainder were held for about a further six months. As will be remembered, Thucydides earlier said that there were only about 1000 official prisoners, but he now estimated that there must have been at least 7000. This is not in itself a matter of any consequence for us, but it does show that his figures need to be treated with reservation.

As Thucydides says, the victors won the most brilliant success, while the vanquished suffered the most calamitous of defeats; and out of the many, only a few ever returned home. According to Plutarch, in his *Life of Nicias*, quite a few of those who did make it back home owed it to the fact that the Greeks in Sicily were as keen on Euripides as those on the mainland. Some of the Athenian prisoners who had been employed as slaves had so endeared themselves to their Syracusan masters by teaching them snatches from the choruses of Euripides that they were eventually able to obtain their release.

During the two years that the Sicilian campaign had lasted, the three outstanding commanders – Gylippus, Demosthenes and Lamachus – all displayed the same qualities of leadership: decisiveness, determination, daring and drive. Gylippus, as a product of Sparta, was probably the most able and professional, turning what seemed like an inevitable Syracusan defeat into a resounding victory. It is a pity that Plutarch did not include him amongst his Greek *Lives*, though as he hardly features again, perhaps there was not enough material to make it possible. That said, in his *Life of Lysander*, Plutarch alleges that Gylippus stole money from Lysander which he had entrusted to him. But Plutarch does not attribute the story to anybody, and it is so out of character with what Thucydides has to say about him that it was probably no more than malicious gossip, spread by somebody jealous of his distinction. As for Demosthenes and Lamachus, they were never given the opportunity to show their true worth as independent commanders, but were hampered by the cautious, irresolute Nicias, who clearly had the last word in decision making. Had Lamachus' proposal to sail directly to Syracuse been accepted, there would have been no time to prepare for the city's defence; while the Athenians' sudden appearance might have caused such surprise and terror that resistance would have been minimal. There is no telling, but he who dares often wins, while he who prevaricates invariably loses.

As all the fighting was at the tactical level, most of the lessons have already been identified when recounting what took place, so only a few require more than a brief mention now. As will be recalled, when discussing the dilemma the Athenians faced after receiving Nicias' despatch asking for reinforcements, mention was made of General James Wolfe's observation that 'War is an option of difficulties' – a remark that requires no further comment. But the remarkable similarity between the way the Athenians secured Epipolae, and Wolfe the Heights of Abraham in Canada, deserves a mention, if only out of interest. James Wolfe was an 18th-century British general, who was appointed by Pitt the Elder to lead the expedition against Quebec in 1759. Like the Athenians before him, who, after landing from the sea, had scaled the escarpment unobserved to reach the crest of Epipolae, Wolfe sailed down the River Lawrence and then climbed the Heights of Abraham during the night. But here the similarity ends. Whereas the Athenians failed to defeat the Syracusans and capture their city, which would have led to the conquest of Sicily, Wolfe defeated the French and captured Quebec, which brought about the acquisition of Canada. Success or failure at the tactical level can have far-reaching consequences at both the operational and strategic levels.

Through failing to take the offensive, Nicias lost the initiative, so that he found himself reacting to events instead of dictating them. Surprise was achieved in many ways: through daring, as with the Athenians at Epipolae; through deception, as with the Syracusans in the Great Harbour; through new tactics, as with the Syracusans when they modified their ships; and through the unexpected, as with the Athenians when they attacked at night. Though their attack failed, it in no way discredits the attempt; rather it should be regarded as a bold tactical move, which, had it succeeded, could well have altered the outcome of the campaign, and so of the whole war. As will be remembered, an example of a successful night attack occurred when the Phocians, a few years before Darius' invasion in 490 BC, white-washed themselves and, attacking at night, so surprised and terrified the Thessalians that they broke and ran. Security is at least a partial antidote to surprise, and here both the Syracusans and the Athenians failed: the former in letting Nicias gain the summit of Epipolae unobserved, and the latter in letting Gylippus do exactly the same. Moreover, had Gylippus been kept under observation while still at sea, his small force could have been eliminated when it landed at Himera. Finally, mention must be made of morale. Although the Athenians still enjoyed a numerical superiority, they would not, as Demosthenes wanted, make a second attempt to break out of the Great Harbour.

11

Persian Intervention and Political Unrest in Athens 413–411 BC

Even when news of the disaster suffered in Sicily was brought to Athens by those who had escaped, it took time for the people to accept that it could possibly have occurred; the sheer magnitude of the loss was at first beyond their comprehension. Then, when they slowly started to come to terms with reality, their disbelief turned to anger. Maybe they had voted in favour of the expedition, but the fault lay with the public speakers whose advocacy had swayed them to do so; then there were the prophets and soothsayers, whose divinations had led them to believe that Sicily would be quickly conquered. But when the Athenians began to take stock of the situation, their mood changed yet again, this time giving way to fear and consternation. Their losses in triremes, ships' crews, hoplites and wealth were so overwhelming that there could be no hope of replacing them. Nothing now stood between them and defeat; they lay utterly exposed with no hope of survival; at any moment the triumphant Syracusan fleet would appear off Piraeus, intent on completing the destruction it had wrought in the Great Harbour. But as this grim spectre gradually faded with the passage of time, the Athenians' chameleon-like moods underwent another complete change.

As Thucydides perspicaciously comments: 'Like all democracies, once they have had a good fright, they get down to putting their house in order.' There was now no question of giving in: a new fleet would be built, more money raised, and their allies, particularly Euboea, upon whom they were so dependent for supplies, would be left in no doubt as to where their loyalties lay. Meanwhile in Athens itself strict economies would be introduced, amongst which was the withdrawal of the garrison from the island of Cythera opposite Laconia. They also concluded that responsibility for providing well-considered measures should be entrusted to a body of older men, selected by a general vote because of their special qualities. Among those appointed in this manner was Sophocles, the tragic poet. It was just as well that these resolute measures were promptly implemented, since practically the whole of Hellas now turned against Athens.

Those who had remained neutral, as had occurred with the cities in Sicily, quickly joined the winning side once they saw the way things were going, rationalising their decision by maintaining that, had Athens conquered Sicily, she would then have turned against them. Those who were already committed also started to shift their ground. Sparta's allies became even more eager to press home the advantage that had suddenly arisen; while Athens' allies, certain that she would not survive the coming summer, were ready to revolt. The Euboeans were the first to send representatives to King Agis of Sparta, who, early in 412 BC, had gone to Decelea to raise money and organise the building of 100 triremes. But having been authorised to do much as he chose, Agis decided to organise a revolt in Lesbos; his intention, however, was overtaken by the island of Chios and the city of Erythrae, on the Ionian coast due east of Chios, applying for assistance not to Agis, but to Sparta. Here we will leave this potentially tangled web for the moment, and take a look at the situation in the Peloponnese.

Spartan confidence had grown immeasurably: not only had Athens been gravely weakened but, with the prospect of being joined by the powerful Syracusan fleet, Sparta saw herself in possession of overwhelming force. The Athenians' loss of maritime supremacy made her defeat seem inevitable; after which, Sparta, with the resources of Sicily behind her, would be left to secure the leadership of Hellas. This was exactly what the Athenians had anticipated for themselves two years previously, when mounting their expedition to Sicily.

Acquiring the resources of Sicily was not dissimilar to America coming to redress the balance of power in Europe, and King Agis of Sparta must have felt much as Winston Churchill did, when the United States was brought into the war by the folly of Japan and Germany: 'So we had won after all. England would live; Britain would live; the Commonwealth of Nations and the Empire would live. How long the war would last, or in what fashion it would end, no man could tell, nor did I at this moment care . . . I went to bed and slept the sleep of the saved and thankful.' But, unlike the Americans, the Syracusans were in no state to play more than a minor role. Having born the brunt of the war against Athens for the last two years, they were exhausted – mentally, financially and materially. So it was not until late in the summer of 412 BC that twenty Syracusan ships arrived in the Aegean to help their Peloponnesian allies, while the other western states that had participated in the Sicilian war (Thurii, Locri and Tarentum) lent their support still later; though this hesitancy is likely to have arisen from a natural reluctance to become involved, rather than from their earlier exertions.

In fact, although they were not to know it at the time, both the Athenians and the Spartans were pursuing a chimera in thinking that the resources of Sicily would be available to them: there was another powerful predator about, the Carthaginians. To outline the situation: after the defeat of the Athenians at Syracuse, the Carthaginians had answered a call for assistance from Egesta, in the north-western corner of the island, and had occupied the south-coast cities of Selinus, Agrigentum and Gela, which had eventually drawn Syracuse into the conflict. But Dionysius, the tyrant of Syracuse, was obliged to accept a humiliating truce that left the Carthaginians in possession of their conquests. As soon as he was ready, however, Dionysius suddenly turned on them, and though the Carthaginians struck back and conquered the whole of Sicily except for Syracuse (greatly assisted by a plague), he finally defeated them. Fighting for their own survival, the Syracusans were then never in a position to provide the scale of assistance for which the Spartans had hoped.

We must now return to where we left the envoys from Chios and Erythrae, in Ionia, seeking Spartan assistance. They were accompanied by a representative from Tissaphernes, the Persian governor of the three Maritime Provinces (the Hellespont, Ionia and Caria), who supported Spartan intervention and undertook to maintain their army. A munificent gesture, but one inspired by necessity. When news of the Athenian catastrophe in Sicily reached Susa, King Darius II at once demanded that his two satraps, Tissaphernes and Pharnabazus (governor of the Hellespont) collect the tribute due from the Greek coastal cities – tribute that had not been levied ever since the Athenians, following the defeat of Xerxes in 480 BC, had extended their empire along the Asiatic coast. If Tissaphernes could induce the Spartans to help him break the hold of Athens, and detach the Greek cities from her, he would be able to extract the tribute, as well as being able to pay the Spartans for their assistance. Moreover, Tissaphernes thought this would bring Sparta into an alliance with the king, while enabling him to comply with the order he had received from Darius: to crush the revolt that had broken out in Caria, led by Amorges, whom we will be hearing more about later. Although Thucydides does not tell us so, it is clear from subsequent events that the Peloponnesians had acquired a fleet which, with that of the Athenians practically destroyed, enabled them for the first time to project power beyond Greece itself. This was a very significant development, giving the war a completely new dimension.

It was now that Persian financial power began proving decisive and, to nullify Pericles' original calculation, that Athens had the money to sustain a war, and Sparta did not. The situation was now being reversed, and as we will see, Athens could not compete with the wealth of Persia; and the liberation of the Greek cities from Persian rule was now being undone. The secessionist movement began to gain pace and manifest itself spontaneously in a number of areas, while Tissaphernes was joined by Pharnabazus, who also thought that the presence of a Spartan fleet would help him raise the tribute he had been ordered to collect. So Sparta had to decide whether its fleet and army should go to Ionia and Chios, or to the Hellespont. At this stage Alcibiades, who had taken refuge with Tissaphernes after seducing King Agis' wife, now makes another appearance: not altogether unexpectedly, to support the claim of his protector and benefactor. But what decided the issue was not Alcibiades and his silvery tongue, but the number of ships the two claimants had – and Chios, with sixty, had a clear lead. So the Spartans made an alliance with Chios and the Erythraeans, voting to send them forty ships, though in the event only five of them were actually fitted out and set sail under the command of Chalcideus.

At the very beginning of the summer of 411 BC, the Chians, fearing that the Athenians would get to hear of what was happening, sent an urgent appeal to Sparta for more than the token assistance of five ships. The need for urgency was particularly acute, since it was the oligarchic party that was masterminding the revolt, with the ordinary people knowing nothing about what was taking place. Appreciating the need for urgency, the Spartans arranged for twenty-one triremes to be dragged across the Isthmus from Corinth, after which they were to join up with those that Agis had equipped for Lesbos. The combined fleet of thirty-nine ships would then sail for Chios.

To decide on the priorities between the conflicting demands for Peloponnesian assistance, a commanders' conference was held at Corinth, when it was decided that after the fleet had settled matters in Ionia, it should then go to Lesbos and afterwards to the Hellespont. But as so often happens even with the best of plans, this one went badly astray. Further delay now arose because of the Isthmian festival, of particular importance to the Corinthians, who refused to begin any military operations until it had been completed. Although Agis offered to take personal responsibility for undertaking the operation, so as to elude Corinthian scruples, they would not agree. It was during the ensuing delay that the Athenians' suspicions were thoroughly aroused; so they sent one of their generals to present the Chians with the evidence and to demand that, as a token of good faith, they provide some ships to join their fleet. As the ordinary people knew nothing about all the scheming, and because there was still no sign of Peloponnesian support, the oligarchs had little choice but to comply, so they detailed seven ships to join the Athenians.

Meanwhile, back in Corinth, the Athenians who, like all the other Greeks, had attended the Isthmian festival, returned to Athens with a much clearer picture of the situation in Chios. Immediate steps were then taken to prevent the Peloponnesian ships from reaching the island. Having failed to draw the enemy fleet into the open sea, the Athenians forced it to take refuge in a deserted harbour near the border between Epidaurus and Corinth, just to the east of the Isthmus, in which they then blockaded them. To finish off this episode while it is fresh in our minds: the Peloponnesians later broke out and captured four of the Athenian ships. But before this occurred, and while the blockade was still in force, Alcibiades persuaded the Spartans to send another fleet to Chios, which he joined. To conceal the fleet's destination, Chalcideus, the commander, detained any ship they met and did not release it until reaching Asia Minor. In this way the fleet arrived undetected at Chios, where it caused much consternation amongst the democratic party. While making no mention of the blockaded fleet, Chalcideus and Alcibiades told the Chians that other ships were on the way; so first Chios and then

Erythrae revolted from Athens, followed shortly afterwards by Clazomenae.

The Chians then sailed to Teos, while the Erythraeans and Clazomenians marched to the city, which was quickly secured. To appreciate the significance of the Peloponnesians gaining the allegiance of these four cities, it is necessary to pause a moment and look at their geographical relationship. Clazomenae and Teos lay on either side of the narrow neck of a thirty-mile-long peninsula, which jutted out into the Aegean like a finger. On the western extremity of this peninsula lay Erythrae, facing the island of Chios across an irregular-shaped channel, some five miles wide at its narrowest point. The Peloponnesians had acquired a substantial and readily defensible foothold on the mainland, which was made all the more secure by demolishing the fortifications of Teos, a city which, having been forcibly incorporated into the revolt, remained of uncertain loyalty.

As for the Chians, having instigated the revolt to free themselves from Athens, their safety depended upon its success; so they joined with Alcibiades and sailed to Miletus, on the coast of Caria. Here Alcibiades had good relations with the leading citizens, so the city joined the revolt and refused to receive an Athenian fleet that arrived shortly afterwards. Directly after this revolt, the first alliance between the Persians and Spartans was concluded, whereby they committed themselves to carrying on the war jointly. Judging by other clauses in the treaty, the Spartans clearly had no imperialistic designs: they were on the Asiatic mainland to defeat Athens, not to replace her. Darius' right to all the territory and all the cities was fully recognised; and it was further agreed that the Athenians would be prevented from obtaining any money, or supplies, from their former possessions.

Thucydides says that the Chians, displaying the same energy and determination to spread the revolt as they had done initially, now acted alone to try and win over Lesbos. But in fact they were under the command of a Spartan admiral, and their operation was the maritime prong of a coordinated land/sea offensive intended to secure the Hellespont. The land prong consisted of Peloponnesian troops and local allies, who marched along the coast; but when, as we will see, the Chians failed to hold Lesbos, the army was embarked and the whole operation was called off. The Chians got off to a good start: thirteen of their triremes first went to Methymna, on the north coast, and brought it into the revolt. They then continued on to Mytilene, on the east coast, which also joined the insurrection. But the Athenians at Samos, who had been watching these developments, reacted vigorously and sailed straight into the harbour of Mytilene, where they seized nine Chian ships and, after landing, quickly recovered the city. They then took Methymna, and before long had gained possession of the whole island.

We will shortly be returning to earlier in the year to see what else the Athenians had been doing, but first we must take stock of the situation. In developing their operations, the Spartans had anticipated Epictetus by more than 400 years. One of the Stoic philosopher's rules was 'that we are not to lead events, but to follow them'. After Sicily, the Spartans had clearly not considered the courses open to them and then decided to shift the war's centre of gravity to Asia Minor; they had merely followed events. Sparta's strategic aim remained the defeat of Athens; which, at the operational level, was to be achieved opportunistically, by exploiting the uprisings in the East. If Athens were defeated there, as she had been in the West, she would be isolated. To achieve this at the tactical level, however, it was necessary to gain maritime supremacy, or at least equality; hence the decision to give Chios first priority, so winning her sixty triremes, which would be lost to Athens.

The Peloponnesian decision to make Lesbos their second priority would have been due to a number of considerations. King Agis had initially planned to go there, but had accepted the logic of giving priority to Chios. Lesbos was also conveniently near Chios, while providing a stepping stone to the Hellespont, Athens' jugular vein.

We can now turn our attention to the Athenians. We have seen the immediate naval response that the Athenians made when news of Chios' defection reached them; but if they were to prevent their other allies from also changing sides, they would have to display the military capability to intervene effectively throughout the Eastern Theatre. That meant restoring Athens' fleet to its previous pre-eminence, which would cost a lot of money. So great was their alarm, however, that they cancelled the strict rules safeguarding the last reserve of silver they had hoarded, and voted to spend it on the fleet. The seven ships they had obtained as a token of Chian loyalty were recalled from enforcing the blockade of the Peloponnesian fleet near the Epidamnus border; and while the slaves on board were given their freedom, the unfortunate freemen were imprisoned.

Not long afterwards the people of Samos, aided by the Athenians who were there with three ships, rose against the ruling classes, putting to death 200 of them, exiling a further 400 and seizing all their property and possessions. Although Thucydides does not say so, it is not improbable that oligarchs, like those in Chios, were plotting to betray Samos to the Spartans. In which case, the Athenians may well have considered it a desirable precautionary measure. But whatever the reasons, after this display of democratic fraternity the Athenians regarded the Samians as now being totally reliable, so they gave them their freedom. The city government then passed a law forbidding intermarriage between the landowners and the people – a ban that may already have been in force to preserve the purity of oligarchic blood, and which was now contemptuously flung back in their faces. Otherwise it would seem to hurt the people, by preventing them from bettering themselves, while sparing the landowners the opprobrium of misalliance.

It was now that the Athenians prevented the defection of Lesbos; which, for the time being, arrested the Peloponnesian operations against them in the Hellespont, while they were able to take the offensive themselves. A number of hoplites were called up and compelled to serve as marines; then, using Lesbos as their base, they undertook landings at several places along the coast, one of which was Chios. Here the Chians came out to repel them, but after losing three battles in quick succession they no longer took to the field, preferring to remain behind their fortifications and leaving the Athenians free to ravage the countryside. Thucydides tells us that, as far as he knew, the Chians were the only people, other than the Spartans, whose land had not been devastated since the Persian War. As a result, they had greatly increased both in prosperity and power, but in doing so they had become over-confident. After the disaster in Sicily, the Chians thought that Athens was on the point of collapse; like others, they were now paying the price of their misjudgement. Cut off from the sea, and with their well-stocked land being ravaged, there were a number of Chians who would have liked to betray their city to the Athenians. But the authorities, learning of the conspiracy, and in spite of being cut off from the sea, somehow managed to bring in four ships, thinking that this was the best way of checking an uprising, while avoiding such measures as taking hostages, which would have caused considerable disturbance.

Towards the end of the summer forty-eight ships, including transports carrying reinforcements, arrived from Athens, but shortly afterwards they crossed over to Miletus. Altogether there were 1000 Athenian hoplites, 1500 Argives – 500 of whom were light troops, but had been given heavy armour by the Athenians – and 1000 allied hoplites. The Milesians took up the challenge with 800 of their own hoplites, some Peloponnesians and a number of mercenaries in the pay of Tissaphernes. The Argives, thinking that they would quickly deal with mere Ionians, broke ranks and charged forward in some disarray; but they were repulsed by the Milesians and lost 300 men. The Athenians, however, routed the Peloponnesians and the mercenaries, whereupon the Milesians, seeing the rest of the army streaming back in defeat, withdrew into the city themselves. Thus the Ionians on both sides had defeated their Dorian opponents: the Athenians the Peloponnesians, and the Milesians the Argives. The Athenians then began preparing to blockade the city, which stands on an isthmus, but hardly had they started when news reached them that fifty-five ships from the Peloponnese and from Sicily were expected at any moment.

The ubiquitous Alcibiades, who had fought alongside the Milesians, now made his way on horseback to meet the Spartan admiral, Therimenes, and tell him that, unless he came as quickly as possible to prevent Miletus from being walled in, Ionia and the whole campaign would be lost. The decision was then taken to go to the relief of Miletus at first light.

The feeling amongst several of the Athenian commanders was that they should remain where they were and fight a decisive battle, maintaining that it would be disgraceful to withdraw. But their commander, Phrynichus, argued that there was nothing disgraceful about withdrawing, especially when the purpose was to delay fighting until they knew more about the enemy and had completed their own preparations. After the disasters that Athens had suffered, she was in no position to sustain another reverse, and for them to fight a battle now, under conditions not of their choosing, would be to put the city's very existence at risk. Phrynichus then outlined the concept of operations which he believed they should pursue: they should sail for Samos without delay and, when they had concentrated all their ships there, at a time and in a manner of their choosing, they should then use the island as a base for offensive operations. Accepting his view, the Athenians embarked all their troops, including the wounded; but to lighten their ships they abandoned everything they had captured. They then set sail for Samos the same evening. The Argives, however, smarting under the disgrace of their defeat, headed for home as soon as they reached Samos.

Shortly after dawn the Peloponnesians reached Miletus but, finding that the Athenians had gone, they only stayed for a day; then, taking with them some Chian ships that had previously been blockaded by the Athenians, they returned to Teichioussa, on the north coast of the Iasic Gulf, where they had left their masts and sails when stripping their ships for action. Here they found Tissaphernes waiting for them with an urgent request. He wanted the Peloponnesians to attack Iasus, at the head of the gulf, where Amorges was holding out. As will be recalled, Amorges was leading a revolt against Darius, and Tissaphernes had been ordered to take him, dead or alive. So the Peloponnesians mounted a sudden assault and, through being mistaken for Athenians, caught the garrison by surprise and captured the city, together with Amorges. Iasus was first thoroughly sacked before being handed over to Tissaphernes, together with Amorges and all the prisoners. The mercenary troops, however, who mostly came from the Peloponnese anyway, simply transferred their loyalties and sailed with their fellow countrymen to Miletus. There, after some haggling, the money promised by Tissaphernes for the Peloponnesians' assistance was finally paid.

It is an indication of the Athenians' astounding shipbuilding programme that by the winter of 411 BC, barely two years after the destruction of their fleet at Syracuse, they were able to concentrate some 100 triremes, as well as transport ships, at Samos. As Phrynichus had envisaged when insisting on withdrawing from Miletus, the Athenians were now ready to take the offensive. Thirty triremes and transport ships carrying hoplites were to mount an amphibious operation against Chios, while the remainder of the force was to blockade Miletus. For reasons that are not clear, the expedition against Chios was to use Lesbos as its base; so it was here that the Athenians began collecting together the necessary material to establish a fortified post on Chios. The place they chose was Delphinium, about nine miles from the city of Chios, which, according to Thucydides, could be easily defended from land and sea, and which possessed harbours; this makes it sound like a peninsula with a harbour on either side.

In order to complete the story of Delphinium, we will run ahead of events elsewhere. The Chians first tried to break the Athenian blockade by attacking the fortifications protecting the Athenian ships. But, though they managed to secure a section of the defences and gain possession of some of the ships that had been hauled up on land, they were counter-attacked and routed. Later, when clearly no help was forthcoming, they tried to break the Athenian blockade at sea; but, according to Thucydides, though they were gaining the upper hand, as it was getting late, they retired. Since they outnumbered the Athenians by thirty-six ships to thirty-two, this action, seemingly belated and then prematurely curtailed, hardly suggests that they were in a desperate situation. Chios, however, was eventually saved from being starved into submission, when the blockade had to be lifted because of a revolt in the Hellespont, started by the Spartan Dercyllidas, who had marched there from Miletus. In spite of this, the Athenians managed to hold Delphinium until their total defeat in 404 BC. Somewhat strangely, Thucydides does not tell us anything about the seventy ships sent to blockade Miletus; so it can only be assumed that they continued to mask the city until they, too, were required for service elsewhere.

Though the Peloponnesians had not been inactive during this period, they had been unable to agree a clear operational-level aim, but instead dissipated their resources in pursuit of a variety of tactical objectives. Some of them had wanted to raise a revolt in Lesbos; some crossed over to Chios; some tried to acquire more of the Greek coastal cities; others went to intercept trading vessels from Egypt; and, finally, there were those who raided the island of Cos, where they certainly did a lot of damage, but that was about all. It is hardly surprising that this dispersion of force and absence of any consistent objective contributed little to furthering the conduct of the war.

Eventually, however, the Peloponnesians concentrated their forces at Cnidus, at the tip of a peninsula protruding out towards the island of Cos, some sixty miles south of Miletus. Here they met up with Tissaphernes and held a conference, intended to resolve any problems that had arisen during the last year and to decide on a coherent operational plan. But they got no further than arguing about the various treaties which they had entered into, and they fell out in the process, which led to Tissaphernes leaving in a rage without anything having been decided.

While they were still in this state of disarray, an appeal for help was received from Rhodes. Here some of the leading citizens wanted to seize power themselves and revolt against Athens; so they invited the Peloponnesians to intervene. This was an alluring request. If Rhodes could be won over, they would acquire an island possessing a large seafaring population and a useful army. There was also the prospect of being able to obtain the resources to maintain their fleet, without having to rely on the unpredictable, and now aggrieved, Tissaphernes. So the Peloponnesians set sail with ninety-four ships and persuaded the Rhodians to revolt from Athens. From now on, they used Rhodes as their main naval base rather than Miletus; but, having established themselves there, they then did nothing for the next two or three months, even though, as will be remembered, Chios was under siege and appealing for help. The Peloponnesians had been lucky in gaining Rhodes. Although they did not know it at the time, it had been a close-run thing. The Athenians had been warned of the situation, and so they had sailed with their fleet from Samos, but had arrived just too late: the Peloponnesians had beaten them by a short head.

We must now leave military matters for the time being, and take a closer look at the economic and political situation in Athens. The Athenian propertied classes had continued to be particularly hard hit by the war. Their estates had been ruined; large numbers of their slaves had fled, forcing the closure of mines and factories; maritime trade had been greatly diminished, and tax after tax had been piled on them; while, as will be remembered, the last of Athens' carefully preserved financial reserves were being spent on replacing the fleet. The Athenian upper class, and the city itself, were practically broke; meanwhile the war, though being prosecuted with considerable skill, showed no sign of being brought to a satisfactory conclusion. So economic pressures began to bring demands for political change. Those paying for the war wanted a greater voice in decision making, which necessitated fundamental changes to the existing democratic system. With the smell of intrigue in the air, the time had come for Alcibiades to play a leading role.

After their defeat at Miletus, the Peloponnesians had become suspicious of Alcibiades, and a letter was sent from Sparta with instructions to put him to death. Alcibiades was now in a position to appreciate the difference between Athenian and Spartan procedures: whereas the Athenians had wanted him to return to face trial, the

Spartans wanted him dead on the grounds of suspicion, no doubt fortified by the fact that he had cuckolded King Agis. Forewarned, he sought refuge with Tissaphernes again and, having become his adviser, did all he could to harm the Peloponnesians: persuading the satrap to reduce the amount he had undertaken to pay their sailors, while bribing the captains of the triremes and the commanders to secure their agreement. Only Hermocrates, who had brought peace to Sicily in 424 BC, and who was now in command of the Syracusan fleet, protested. In so doing, he made an enemy of Tissaphernes, which was later to lead to his being removed from command and exiled.

Tissaphernes now had something of a stranglehold on the Peloponnesians. As Alcibiades pointed out, by paying or withholding subsidies he could manipulate policy for his own ends. He need not be in too much of a hurry to end the war; far better to let the Greeks go on fighting and wear themselves out than to have one dominant power that was master of both land and sea. In this way Darius would incur only a fraction of the expense and none of the risk, but, if he had to make a choice, the Athenians were the better people with whom to share power: they were not as interested in acquiring possessions on land as in ruling the sea. The Spartans, on the other hand, after liberating their fellow Hellenes from Athens, would hardly be willing to hand them over to foreign domination. But, according to Thucydides, Alcibiades then changed these priorities by recommending that, while leaving the Greeks to wear themselves out, the power of Athens should be weakened as much as possible. After this the Phoenician fleet, which the Persians were raising, would be strong enough to deal with the Peloponnesians.

As for the Greek cities, especially the prosperous island of Chios, Alcibiades said they should be made to help financially. Hitherto they had been compelled to pay tribute to Athens, so there was absolutely no reason why they should not now have to pay for their own defence. But at the same time the subtle Alcibiades saw that there was a danger in treating the Peloponnesians and Greek cities too harshly, for they might be driven into opposition; so some blanket inducement must be offered. They should be told that, because Tissaphernes was having to pay for the entire cost of the war, there was no avoiding these measures; but, should subsidies be received from

Darius, then of course the full rate of pay would be promptly resumed and aid provided to the Grecian cities.

Until now Alcibiades had pursued a broadly anti-Hellenic policy, but at this stage he shifted his ground and began looking for ways to be recalled to his own country, where he would be able to wield direct power. This ambition, he concluded, would be best achieved if he were seen to be able to influence Tissaphernes for the benefit of Athens. So this was the card he played. He sent messages to the commanders of the fleet and army in Samos, many of whom were men of power and influence, to say that if there were an oligarchy in Athens, instead of the corrupt democracy that had expelled him, he was ready to return and to use his influence with Tissaphernes to obtain his support for Athens. Perhaps as an indication of how urgent the need was to end the war, Alcibiades' proposals gained quick acceptance. The agitation for political change that now began amongst the forces in Samos was soon to converge with the economic pressures for change in Athens. But before this occurred, a delegation was sent to make contact with Alcibiades, who claimed that an oligarchy would be far more likely to gain the confidence and support of a despotic monarch like Darius than would a democracy where the rabble held sway. When those who had been in contact with Alcibiades returned thoroughly convinced, they formed their own party and started to try and win over the seamen and soldiers; explaining that they would receive their full pay from Darius, if Alcibiades was recalled and the democratic party in Athens removed from office. The proposal was at first received with indignation; but, as Thucydides says, the agreeable prospect of getting pay from the king soon calmed them down and won them over.

After they had secured the support of the troops, those who were leading the intrigue held another meeting to give further consideration to Alcibiades' proposals, at which the general view emerged that his plan was perfectly feasible and could be confidently accepted. Phrynichus, however, who had persuaded the Athenians to withdraw from Miletus to Samos, was strongly opposed. Alcibiades cared for an oligarchy no more than for a democracy; all that he was after was to change the constitution so that he could get back to Athens. As for Darius, now that the Peloponnesians were in control of his most important cities and were a match for the Athenians on the sea, he had nothing to gain by supporting the Athenians, whom he did not trust anyway. He was far more likely to want to remain friendly with the Peloponnesians, who had never done him any harm. Athens' allies were deserting her, not because she was a democracy, but because she dominated them; they wanted to be free, under whatever kind of government they happened to have. The one thing the Athenians should avoid was disrupting their constitution by revolt, so Darius was totally opposed to the ideas of Alcibiades and the intrigues he was fermenting.

Phrynichus had already shown himself to be an able commander, and now he had displayed the qualities of a statesman. But such was the indispensable need of Persian money, and such too were personal ambitions, that his advice was ignored. The conspirators thus nominated Pisander to lead a delegation to Athens, where they were to negotiate for the recall of Alcibiades, get rid of the democrats and have Tissaphernes recognised as a friend. Phrynichus, seeing that he had no chance of influencing events by open negotiation, and fearing for his own safety from a revengeful Alcibiades, now resorted to intrigue himself, and in doing so lost a lot of his lustre. He sent a secret message to Astyochus, the Spartan admiral at Miletus, in which he told how Alcibiades was betraying Spartan interests by making Tissaphernes Athens' friend. His message also contained a plea that his own action, in plotting against a personal enemy, even at the cost of his country's interests, should be understood. If that is really what he wrote, then it was an admission that he was prepared to betray his country in order to get even with Alcibiades.

But Phrynichus was betrayed in turn by Astyochus, who passed on this information to Tissaphernes and Alcibiades. According to Thucydides, Astyochus was already being bribed by Tissaphernes to act as an informer, which is why he had not made a stand when the troops' pay was not produced in full. As for Alcibiades, he at once wrote to the authorities in Samos asking that Phrynichus be put to death. It seems, however, that his accusation was not believed, since Phrynichus wrote to Astyochus again, complaining about him disclosing the contents of his first letter, but then telling him how he could destroy the whole Athenian force in Samos. All of which was again passed on by Astyochus. But somehow Phrynichus received warning that Alcibiades was writing another letter, informing the authorities of this latest act of betrayal. So some quick footwork was called for, which Phrynichus was agile enough to achieve. He told the commanders he was quite sure that, as the island was unfortified and the ships not at anchor in the harbour ready for immediate action, the enemy would make an attack. It was therefore imperative that Samos was fortified as quickly as possible, and a high degree of alert maintained. His advice was followed, and when Alcibiades' letter arrived, telling the authorities that they had been betrayed and should expect an attack, they thought Alcibiades – knowing of the enemies' intentions – was trying to use this to implicate Phrynichus. So, instead of doing him any harm, he was esteemed for his wise advice.

The agitation that had started in Samos was now being spread to Athens. Pisander, who was leading the delegation, on arrival spoke in front of the public assembly, setting out the arguments for changing the constitution. The proposals were indignantly rejected by the opponents of Alcibiades, who refused to countenance breaking the law in this manner, while the priestly families of the Eumolpidae and Ceryces, connected with the Eleusinian mysteries that Alcibiades had profaned, wished to prohibit his return in the name of the gods. In the face of this violent opposition, Pisander called upon each of those who had spoken against the proposals to answer the following question: 'Now that the Peloponnesians have as many ships as we have ready to fight us at sea, now that they have more cities as their allies, and now that the King and Tissaphernes are supplying them with money, while ours is all gone, have you any hope that Athens can survive unless someone can persuade the King to change sides and come over to us?' When they replied that they had not, he then said to them: 'Well, then, that is impossible, unless we have more integrated government, with the power in fewer hands, so that the King may trust us. At the moment what we have to think about is our survival, not the form of our constitution; so we must bring Alcibiades back, as he is the only person who can arrange this for us.'

At first there was angry opposition by the people to the idea of an oligarchy, but they gradually came to accept there was no other way out, especially as they expected to be able to change the constitution back again later, if they did not like it. Having gained his main point, Pisander now called for the replacement of Phrynichus and his close colleague Scironides, as they were not the right people to undertake the sensitive negotiations with Alcibiades. While his name is still fresh in our memories, Phrynichus' fate will be related now. As will be remembered, he had at first stoutly opposed undermining the

Athenian constitution by installing an oligarchic government. After being recalled, however, he became one of the leaders of the oligarchy of Four Hundred and was sent to try and negotiate peace with Sparta; but on his return he was assassinated in the market place by an unknown assailant.

But to return to the moment when Pisander's request for the recall of Phrynichus was approved. Two new commanders were appointed, Leon and Diomedon; though, as will be seen, Pisander would not have been so satisfied with the Assembly's selection, had he been able to anticipate the consequences. More immediately, he spent some time making certain that the various political associations and clubs in Athens followed a common policy in getting rid of the democrats. Having assured himself that all was in order, and the necessary arrangements completed, Pisander and the ten delegates appointed to accompany him then left Athens, to begin negotiations with Tissaphernes.

By the time Pisander reached Ionia at the beginning of 411 BC, the Peloponnesian fleet had already moved from Miletus to Rhodes, and the two new Athenian commanders at Samos, Leon and Diomedon, had not only taken up their appointments but had mounted a surprise attack on Rhodes. Here they found the Peloponnesian ships drawn up on the shore but, for some unknown reason, they did no more than defeat the Rhodians who came out to oppose them, before retiring to Chalce. This is an unlocated island, which must have been near Rhodes, since Thucydides says that Leon and Diomedon preferred it to Cos as a forward operating base, because they were better placed to keep the Peloponnesian fleet under observation. These events were taking place at about the same time as the Athenians began laying siege to the city of Chios and, as has been related, were fortifying Delphinium, an adjacent peninsula on the island.

When the negotiations between Pisander, Alcibiades and Tissaphernes got under way, Alcibiades quickly realised that Tissaphernes was going to follow the earlier advice he had given him: to play off the Greeks one against the other, so wearing out both sides. Confronted with this predicament, and wishing to conceal from Pisander and the other delegates that he was incapable of producing what he had promised, Alcibiades resorted to a stratagem: claiming to speak for Tissaphernes, he would place such extravagant demands on them that an agreement was impossible. In this way, the Athenians would think the talks had broken down, not because Tissaphernes was unwilling to help them, but because they were not prepared to compromise.

Thucydides says that, in his opinion, Alcibiades was in fact expressing Tissaphernes' inner thoughts; which were largely brought about by his fear of the Peloponnesians. So demand was piled on demand. He first claimed for Tissaphernes the whole of Ionia, then the islands off the coast, together with a number of other concessions, all of which the Athenians accepted. Finally, in the third session, he claimed that the king should be allowed to build ships and sail along his coastline wherever, and with as large a fleet, as he chose. This was too much for the Athenians. Such a measure would not only spell an end to Athens' maritime empire, but also inevitably lead to a renewal of Persian expansion to the west; all of which evoked painful memories of Darius I and Xerxes. So the talks were broken off, and the Athenians returned to Samos. They were under no illusions, however, as to why the negotiations had failed: they had been deceived by Alcibiades. For the sake of continuity, we will again run ahead of events elsewhere and follow through this tragicomedy. ·

Far from Pisander and the ten delegates recognising that a grave error of judgement had been made, and that their policy needed reassessing, they instead compromised. Motivated by personal ambitions, they ploughed ahead. Pisander was despatched to Athens with five of the delegates, to make certain that the establishment of an oligarchy was progressing as planned. On the way, he was to install oligarchies in all the subject states at which he called; and, at the same time, the other five delegates were sent in different directions, to do the same elsewhere. Meanwhile the conspirators in Samos, in spite of the recent democratic revolt that had resulted in the assassination or exiling of the aristocrats, approached the most important people on the island, with a view to setting up an oligarchy. Three hundred of them agreed to collaborate, but their intentions were discovered by the democrats, who appealed to Leon and Diomedon for help. In spite of having been appointed when Pisander had persuaded the Assembly to select two new commanders, who would work more harmoniously with Alcibiades, they were both sincere democrats. They now took a number of precautionary measures, so that when the conspirators struck, they were overpowered. As we will see, by preserving democracy in Samos, Leon and Diomedon were the means whereby democracy was also preserved in Athens – a development that Pisander had not anticipated, any more than he anticipated the behaviour of the oligarchic governments he had installed in the subject states. When he left to continue on his way to Athens, they promptly declared themselves to be independent. At Thasos, for example, as soon as power was concentrated in the hands of the government, the island went straight to freedom, showing no interest in what the Athenians called 'reform'. Now, before we see what happened when Pisander arrived in Athens, we must return to Ionia to look at what Tissaphernes and the Peloponnesians had been doing.

After the breakdown of negotiations with the Athenians, Tissa-phernes went down to Caunus, on the south coast of Caria. He wanted to try and persuade the Peloponnesians to come back to Miletus for three reasons. First, they would clearly be better placed to serve his own purposes. Second, he was afraid that, if they were left without any pay, they might turn hostile, or feel it necessary to reach an early decision in the war against Athens; in which case there was the risk of their being defeated. Third, the crews might desert, thus leaving the Athenians free to achieve their objectives without his assistance; and under no obligations to him. So Tissaphernes made another treaty with the Peloponnesians. He undertook to pay for their continuing support, and when the king's Phoenician ships were ready, the two fleets would prosecute the war together. Finally, should either of the two parties wish to make peace with the Athenians, they would only do so after consulting together. The treaty concluded, Tissaphernes started preparing to move up the Phoenician fleet, while carrying out other measures, which made it appear as though he were fulfilling his side of the bargain.

It was shortly after this that the Spartan Dercyllidas marched overland from Miletus and started a revolt in the Hellespont; which, as will be remembered, forced the Athenians to raise the blockade at Chios. They then sailed to the Hellespont with twenty-four ships, including some transports carrying hoplites, where Lampsacus was regained, and the secessionist movement confined to Abydos. Finally, to complete this jigsaw puzzle of movement by jumping ahead of events, when Astyochus sailed from Miletus to engage the Athenian fleet at Samos, it was the arrival of this Athenian squadron from the

Hellespont that made him decide not to risk fighting a battle. But here we must leave Ionia and see what was happening in Athens.

When Pisander arrived in Athens, he found that good progress had been made towards getting rid of the democrats. Several undesirable individuals, who had been opposing the changes, had been assassinated, and the first steps had been taken towards concentrating power in fewer hands. In future, those involved in government would be limited to 5000, all of whom should be those best qualified to serve the state. But this was just a propaganda exercise, designed for the general public. In the same way, though the Assembly and the Council (ostensibly chosen by lot) continued to meet, they had been infiltrated by the oligarchic party and merely served to give an air of respectability to decisions that had already been taken. According to Thucydides, intimidation was rife, and those who did speak out mysteriously disappeared, without any subsequent investigation being undertaken. So everyone kept quiet, even fearing to discuss matters amongst themselves in case of betrayal. As in a communist state, fear and mutual suspicion amongst the majority kept a despotic minority in power.

Two things, however, should be borne in mind. First, not all oligarchic governments were so tyrannous as the embryo one Thucydides portrays. As will be remembered, the Athenian Pisistratus, in the 6th century BC, often put the interests of the ordinary citizens before those of the oligarchs. Second, we have seen how Thucydides relishes depicting a near-calamitous scene and then staging a remarkable recovery. Nicias' decision to abandon the siege of Syracuse serves as an earlier example. So perhaps the situation in Athens was not quite as bad as he would have us believe. Certainly, Aristophanes, the comic dramatist, felt free to satirise the futility of the war in his play *Lysistrata*, produced at the beginning of 411 BC, in which the women withheld conjugal rights until the men came to their senses and recognised where their true interests lay: in friendship with Sparta and not Persia. Lysistrata, the leader of the movement for sexual abstinence, is seen making her neighbour, Calonice, repeat an oath of compliance; to which all the other women nod their heads to show their assent:

Lysistrata: I will not allow either boyfriend or husband –
Calonice: I will not allow either boyfriend or husband –

Lysistrata: to approach me in an erect condition. – Go on!
Calonice: to approach me in an – erect – condition – help,
     Lysistrata, my knees are giving way!
Lysistrata: And I will live at home without any sexual activity –
Calonice: And I will live at home without any sexual activity –
Lysistrata: I will not raise my legs towards the ceiling.
Calonice: I will not raise my legs towards the ceiling.

And so it goes on. Later, the Spartan and Athenian ambassadors take their place on either side of Lysistrata, who tells them:

Now listen both:
Hard will my words be, but not undeserved,
You worship the same gods at the same shrines,
Use the same lustral water, just as if
You were a single family – which you are –
Delphi, Olympia, Thermopylae –
How many other Panhellenic shrines
Could I make mention of, if it were needed!
And yet, although the Mede is at our gate,
You ruin Greece with intestine wars.

That Aristophanes could write in this vein, even under a pro-Spartan government, suggests that conditions for the individual were not as oppressive as Thucydides portrays. Meanwhile, the subversion of democracy had been gathering pace, and it was now to take another substantial step forward.

Pisander called for an assembly not, as usual, to be held within the city walls, but in the sanctuary of Poseidon at Colonus, about a mile outside the fortifications. (In Sophocles' play, first performed ten years later in 401 BC, Colonus was also the grove of the Furies, to which Oedipus was led by his daughter Antigone.) Since the amount of space at Colonus was limited, and the ordinary people lacked any protection, the fear of being caught by marauding Spartans from Decelea was very real. So attendance was conveniently restricted. Three proposals were brought forward. First, every Athenian should be allowed to make whatever suggestion he liked with impunity; while heavy penalties would be imposed on anyone who tried to prosecute him for violating the law, in making a proposal illegal under the democratic constitution. Second, a programme of austerity should be implemented, whereby only members of the armed forces would be paid. At a stroke, all those who administered the Council, ran the courts and organised the religious festivals were struck off the public payroll. Third, instead of the Council of Five Hundred and the Assembly, an oligarchy of Four Hundred self-appointed individuals should be established. The Assembly, after ratifying all three proposals without a dissenting voice, was then dissolved.

The next step was to get the Four Hundred into the Council chamber. So, after unobtrusively positioning some of their supporters around the Council chamber in case things went wrong, they just walked in, each of them carrying a concealed dagger, accompanied by 120 thugs. They then approached the legitimate Council members and, after giving them the pay due to them for the rest of their term in office, told them to get out; an order which they had little alternative but to comply with. The Four Hundred then took their places in the Council chamber and, after deciding their respective tasks by lot, got on with the business of governing. One of the first things they did was to make overtures to King Agis, who was at Decelea, telling him that they were ready to come to terms, and reminding him that he now had an opportunity to do business with fellow oligarchs, rather than with the untrustworthy democrats.

Agis, however, was thoroughly sceptical. He did not believe that the situation in Athens was stable enough to permit negotiations; so he came to have a look for himself and advanced right up the city walls, hoping to exacerbate the disturbances he imagined to be taking place. Athens would then be more likely to submit to terms dictated by Sparta, or even to surrender without a fight. But instead of finding a divided city ready to receive him, he came under attack and, after losing a number of his men, led his army back to Decelea. The Four Hundred continued to make overtures to Agis, but they were advised to send a delegation to Sparta to negotiate a settlement.

The Four Hundred also sent a ten-man delegation to Samos, where they were supposed to whip up support for the oligarchs; but when they reached Delos, they heard disturbing news. Leon and Diomedon had suppressed the oligarchs' attempt to seize power on Samos, and the democrats, with the wholehearted support of the army, were firmly in control. With both the Samians and the armed forces determined to carry on the war, regardless of what Athens chose to do, it seemed only prudent not to proceed; so the delegates decided to remain at Delos.

But not all was going well for the Peloponnesians, either. There were disturbances in the fleet, which had moved to Miletus as Tissaphernes had wanted. The feeling was that Astyochus and Tissaphernes had thrown away the opportunity to defeat the Athenians: instead of fighting when the fleet had been at the peak of efficiency, they had kept it waiting for a Phoenician fleet that never materialised. Moreover, Tissaphernes was undermining morale in the fleet by not paying the crews regularly, and then, when he did eventually pay them, not doing so in full. The Syracusans, in particular, were insistent that a decisive naval battle must be fought. So when Astyochus received news of the disturbances at Samos, he put to sea with 112 ships; but, as will be remembered, on hearing that the Athenians had been reinforced by their squadron from the Hellespont, he promptly sailed back to Miletus. Astyochus was a prototype of Fabius Maximus, who after the Roman defeat by Hannibal at Lake Trasimene in 217 BC was firmly resolved to avoid fighting a pitched battle in which he risked defeat. So it was with Astyochus: when the Athenian fleet was divided, he was prepared to give battle; but once it was united, though he still possessed a small numerical superiority (112 to 108), he drew back. On the other hand, being in receipt of bribes from Tissaphernes, he could have been complying with instructions not to hazard his fleet, and so risk the Athenians gaining the upper hand without being indebted to the satrap.

There now occurred an unanticipated development. Without offering any explanation, Thucydides says that the leading men in Samos, with the agreement of the army, brought Alcibiades over to the island. Here he once again greatly exaggerated his influence over Tissaphernes, so raising expectations in Samos, while hoping to alarm the oligarchy in Athens. Once again he had switched his support, this time from the oligarchs in Athens to the democrats in Samos. He then went on to say that Tissaphernes had assured him that, so long as he could trust the Athenians, he would never leave them short of supplies, and he would bring the Phoenician fleet now at Aspendus – on the coast, about 100 miles east of Rhodes – to the Athenians instead of to the Peloponnesians.

The only condition Tissaphernes had stipulated was that Alcibiades should be reinstated and then return to him as a guarantee of Athenian good faith. Seemingly either out of gullibility or as a desperate last throw, the army immediately decided to put everything into Alcibiades' hands, and elected him to be a general. When the Peloponnesians at Miletus got to know of the recall of Alcibiades, their mistrust of Tissaphernes grew even further, as did his unpopularity for still withholding pay for the fleet. Unable to lay hands on him, the sailors turned on Astyochus, who narrowly escaped being stoned to death by seeking refuge at an altar. After such a mutinous incident, it is hardly surprising that Astyochus was recalled and replaced by another Spartan admiral, Mindarus. At the same time the able and honourable Syracusan commander, Hermocrates, who was on bad terms with Tissaphernes after accusing him of playing a double game, was exiled from Syracuse and replaced by three new commanders.

By now Alcibiades had returned from Tissaphernes, and shortly afterwards the ten oligarchic delegates from Athens, who had been lurking at Delos, appeared on the scene. They tried to put the oligarchs' case, but met with no support from the assembled troops, who put forward a number of their own proposals. Amongst these, the most popular one was to sail against Piraeus; and according to Thucydides, it was at this point that Alcibiades did his first great act of service to his country. He dissuaded them from sailing against their own countrymen, as this would have resulted in the immediate occupation of Ionia and the Hellespont by the Peloponnesians.

Though this seems an obvious enough consequence, emotion must have been running high, as Thucydides goes on to say that 'There was not another man in existence who could have controlled the mob at that time.' Alcibiades then addressed himself to the Athenian delegates, telling them that he was not opposed to the governing Five Thousand, but they should get rid of the Four Hundred, and reinstate the original Council of Five Hundred. He was entirely in favour of any measures of economy that would result in better pay for the armed forces; and he urged them to fight on, making no concessions to the enemy, since if either Athens or Samos fell there would be nobody left to make a settlement with.

In the same summer Tissaphernes, who by now was considered to be openly collaborating with the Athenians, sailed to Aspendus, claiming that he was going to fetch the Phoenician fleet. Once again,

however, the fleet failed to materialise, which caused much specula-
tion as to Tissaphernes' motives; though Thucydides was convinced
that he was keeping the two sides evenly balanced and so had
no desire to commit the fleet to either of them. When Alcibiades
heard that Tissaphernes was going to Aspendus, he went there
himself with thirteen ships, telling the Athenians at Samos that he
would either bring the Phoenicians back with him or prevent them
joining the Peloponnesians. For Alcibiades to have committed himself
to such an undertaking must have meant that he, like Thucydides,
knew what Tissaphernes was doing. After all, it had been his original
advice to play the Greeks off against one another. According to
Plutarch, the Phoenician ships were sighted off Aspendus ready to
sail, and Alcibiades was credited by both sides with having got them
to turn back.

Meanwhile in Athens, from what Thucydides tells us, the oligarchs
were clearly not as wholehearted in their support for ending
democracy as, until now, he has given us to believe. Even before the
Athenian representatives had returned, most of them, including some
of the principal leaders, would gladly have got out of the whole
business, and Alcibiades' message stiffened their resolve. They did not
like to go as far as to suggest getting rid of the oligarchy completely,
but as a first step they proposed that the Five Thousand should
actually be appointed. Thucydides, rather bewilderingly in view of
what he had just said, then tells us that what really motivated them
was the strength of Alcibiades' position in Samos, and the fact that
they did not believe the oligarchy would last. While some of the Four
Hundred were wavering in this manner, the more radical amongst
them had sent another delegation to try and make peace with Sparta;
but they came back empty-handed. It was shortly after their return, as
has been recounted, that Phrynichus was struck down in the market
place by an unknown assassin.

At the same time, the more dedicated members of the Four
Hundred speeded up the work they had put in hand to fortify
Eetionia, the mole that narrowed the entrance into Piraeus. Ostensibly the construction of a wall along the mole, with a tower at the end
facing its land-based counterpart, was to protect the harbour against
the fleet and army in Samos. In reality, however, the oligarchs
intended to take possession of Eetionia, so that they could admit the
Spartans whenever they chose. But when a Peloponnesian fleet sailed

into the gulf and, after seizing Aegina, went on to Megara, Theramenes, one of the principal oligarchs, who had become disillusioned, realised what was afoot. He and his associates then denounced the plot and, after gaining the support of the hoplites working on the fortification of Eetionia, got them – helped by the people of Piraeus – to tear down their own work. The hoplites next proclaimed their support for the government of the Five Thousand, which the Four Hundred had little option but to approve.

As for the Peloponnesian fleet, when it was reported to be sailing along the coast of Salamis, the Athenians thought that an attack on Piraeus was still intended; but, possibly because the Peloponnesians did not receive an agreed signal, it sailed past and went on to Oropus, on the mainland opposite the island of Euboea. As will be remembered, after the virtual loss of Attica, Athens had become dependent upon Euboea for most of her food supplies. So a fleet was hastily assembled, partly manned by men who had never trained together as crews, and despatched as reinforcements for their squadron at Eretria, across the channel from Oropus. Here the sailors disembarked at Eretria to go in search of provisions; but they were betrayed by the Eretrians, who signalled to the Peloponnesian fleet, which at once sailed into the attack. Thucydides says that the Athenians put out to fight in front of the harbour; so they were not caught totally unprepared, though perhaps not all their thirty-six ships were manned. Whatever the situation, they at first managed to hold off the Peloponnesians, but were eventually defeated and most of their ships driven ashore. Although about fourteen Athenian ships managed to escape, the Peloponnesians captured twenty-two of them, either killing the crews or taking them prisoner.

When news of what had happened reached Athens, Thucydides indulges in one of his disaster scenarios, saying that it caused the greatest panic that had ever been known there, surpassing even what had occurred after the annihilation of the Sicilian expedition. There was, in his opinion, every reason for despondency: the army in Samos was in revolt; they had no more ships, or crews; civil disturbances divided them to such an extent that it might lead to actual fighting; and, worst of all, they had lost Euboea, which was more useful to them than Attica itself. The Peloponnesians could have sailed into Piraeus, which was undefended, or just blockaded the city, so forcing the fleet at Samos to come to their rescue: this would have left Ionia, the Hellespont and the Aegean islands unguarded. As Thucydides drily comments when reviewing the situation: 'The Spartans proved to be quite the most helpful enemies that the Athenians could have had. For Athens, particularly, as a naval power, was enormously helped by the very great difference in the national characters – her speed as against their slowness, her enterprise as against their lack of initiative.'

We now, however, again hear of a near-miraculous recovery on the part of the Athenians. Somehow they managed to find and man twenty ships, and in a series of assemblies, at which the voice of moderation prevailed, a number of political decisions and constitutional changes were made. The Four Hundred were deposed, and power handed over to the Five Thousand; amongst whom were to number all those who could provide a hoplite's equipment. To enable so large a body to transact business, it was divided into four councils. Later, a number of other assemblies were held, when legal advisers were elected and the necessary steps taken for drawing up a new constitution. 'Indeed,' says Thucydides, 'during the first period of this new regime, the Athenians appear to have had a better government than ever before, at any rate in my time.' There was then a blending of conflicting interests, when the minority and the majority saw that their very survival depended upon subordinating self-interest and working together. Fear always concentrates the mind wonderfully, and in the case of Athens, it made it possible to stage a recovery and continue the war.

Pisander, and the more extreme members of the oligarchic party, fled to Decelea; so their short usurpation of power came to a humiliating end. This was a period of such intense political manoeuvring and infighting that military operations were largely overshadowed. The military in Samos, however, played a cardinal role in opposing the oligarchs, and it was the failure of the Four Hundred to gain the support of the sailors and soldiers that undermined their authority and, ultimately, their hold on power. The obvious lesson to be drawn is that a clear political objective, devoid of party strife, is an essential pre-requisite for the conduct of sustained operations.

The Struggle for the Hellespont and the Fall of Athens 411–404 BC

While Athens had been racked with political disputes, the position of the Peloponnesians at Miletus was not much better. The Phoenician fleet had not appeared, Tissaphernes was still down at Aspendus, and the pay of the sailors and troops had fallen into arrears. As will be remembered, Pharnabazus, the governor of the Hellespont, had been asking for assistance since he (like Tissaphernes) wanted the Greek cities in his province to revolt against Athens, thus enabling him to raise the tribute demanded by Darius. So Mindarus, the Spartan admiral for 411 and 410 BC who had replaced Astyochus, decided to shift the centre of gravity for naval operations to the Hellespont. After making careful preparations and disguising his intentions from the Athenians at Samos, Mindarus left Miletus with seventy-three ships and set off for the Hellespont, where he joined up with the sixteen Peloponnesian ships that had been sent there the previous summer.

Mindarus' decision to base his fleet in the Hellespont heralded a new dimension to the war. Until now Persian policy, as practised by Tissaphernes, had been to weaken the Greeks so that they were no longer capable of playing a major role in Asia Minor. In this way seventy years of Greek imperialism would be ended, and the situation, both politically and militarily, would revert to what it had been before Xerxes had so disastrously gone to war with Greece. With policy now increasingly determined by Pharnabazus, Persian support for the Peloponnesians became a reality. While the Athenians were practically destitute and forced to raise money from wherever they could, the Peloponnesians would receive regular payment and active military assistance. But to get back to earlier events.

When Thrasyllus, the Athenian admiral at Samos, heard that the Peloponnesians had left Miletus, he at once put to sea with fifty-five ships in an attempt to reach the Hellespont first. But when he found that Mindarus had been delayed by bad weather for five or six days and had got no further than Chios, he placed observation posts on Lesbos and the mainland, with instructions to watch the Peloponnesians and report any movement they made. Thrasyllus then sailed round to lay siege to Eresus on the seaward side of the island, which had revolted; this left Mindarus free to slip away and, by hugging the mainland shore, to reach the Hellespont. Here he had a brush with the Athenian squadron stationed there which, after losing four ships, escaped to Imbros and Lemnos. Mindarus then concentrated the Peloponnesian fleet at Abydos, on the Asiatic coast opposite the Gallipoli peninsula.

As the Athenian observation posts had not detected the Peloponnesians when they had passed through the Lesbos straits, Thrasyllus was still carrying on with his siege operations in ignorance of what had happened. But as soon as he heard that Mindarus had flown, he abandoned the siege and hurried to the Hellespont. While it is fresh in our memories, let us draw a lesson from this incident. Thrasyllus' task was to prevent the Peloponnesians from reaching the Hellespont. This he failed to do, through not adhering to his aim; choosing instead to besiege an inconsequential city on the far side of the island. Having decided on this folly, he then made inadequate arrangements to keep the Peloponnesian fleet under observation. The importance of sticking to the task one has been given, and not letting oneself get blown off course in pursuit of secondary objectives, is the lesson. As will be remembered, the need to adhere to this principle has already been illustrated, when in 460 BC the Athenians abandoned their campaign against Persian-held Cyprus to undertake one of little relevance in Egypt. But to return to what was happening in 411 BC.

After reaching the Hellespont, the Athenians anchored off Elaeus, near the tip of the Gallipoli peninsula, and spent the next five days preparing for the coming battle, which, in the event, took place off the headland of Cynossema. When all was ready, they sailed up the straits towards Abydos, from where the Peloponnesians came out to meet them. Mindarus had eighty-six ships to the Athenians' seventy-six, which may have been the reason for his seizing the initiative and attacking first. By placing his fastest ships on his left flank under his personal command, he planned to out-flank the Athenian right wing and cut them off from the open sea, while driving their centre onto the shore. Anticipating Mindarus' intentions, the Athenians extended their right wing and succeeded in out-flanking Mindarus, by which time their left wing had rounded the headland of Cynossema. These two movements had so stretched the Athenian centre that when the Peloponnesians bore down on them, as Mindarus had planned, they were driven onto the shore, where, abandoning their ships, they fled inland hotly pursued by the Peloponnesians.

At this stage the battle became uncoordinated: those on the Athenian left wing, once they had rounded the headland of Cynossema, were unable to see what was happening elsewhere, while those on the right were too heavily engaged to notice. As for the Peloponnesians, according to Thucydides, believing that victory was theirs, they started to scatter in pursuit of individual ships and so lost formation. Whereupon the Athenian right wing turned about and routed their opponents, before falling upon the rest of the disorganised Peloponnesian fleet and putting them to flight. Plutarch says that at the end of the day the Athenians captured thirty ships and recovered the ones they had lost. He gives, however, a rather different account of the battle, saying that it was the arrival of Alcibiades with thirteen triremes that tipped the scales. Hoisting the Athenian standard on his flagship, he charged into the thick of the fighting, scattering the Peloponnesians and driving them ashore.

But as Thucydides tells us that it was about this time that Alcibiades returned to Samos from Aspendus, we will discount Plutarch's story, and see what had resulted from his meeting with Tissaphernes. Alcibiades claimed that he had been able to prevent the Phoenician fleet from joining the Peloponnesians, and had also made Tissaphernes far more friendly to the Athenians than before. But in the improbable event of Tissaphernes having ever felt any friendship towards the Athenians, it proved to be a fleeting fancy. On learning that the Peloponnesian fleet had left Miletus, Tissaphernes moved from Aspendus to Ionia, from where he intended to go to the Hellespont, in an attempt to improve his relations with the Peloponnesians; who, Thucydides says, he feared might do him more harm. He was also aggrieved that Pharnabazus was receiving their help and, at the cost of less time and money, perhaps doing better against the Athenians than he had done. Here we must regrettably take leave of Thucydides, whose text breaks off in mid-sentence with the words, 'he [Tissaphernes] went first to Ephesus where he made a sacrifice to Artemis . . .'

As a small testimony to Thucydides, it seems appropriate to quote his own account of how he went about his writing:

> I have made it a principle not to write down the first story that came my way, and not even to be guided by my own general impressions; either I was present myself at the events which I have described, or else I heard them from eye-witnesses whose reports I have checked with as much thoroughness as is possible. Though not even then was the truth easy to discover: different eye-witnesses gave different accounts of the same events, speaking out of partiality for one side or the other, or else from imperfect memories.

From now on, the story will be carried forward mainly by Xenophon, a fine soldier and an acute observer of his fellow men, though not of the intricacies of politics, who was born about the time Pericles died in 429 BC. He begins by saying that, following the Athenian victory at Cynossema, a number of smaller, inconclusive engagements were fought in the straits, before the Athenians divided their fleet. Forty ships remained at Sestos, in the middle of the Gallipoli peninsula, directly north of the main Peloponnesian base at Abydos, while the remainder went off on a variety of missions, including raising money.

By this time Tissaphernes had arrived at the Hellespont, and Alcibiades went to see him, bearing gifts and tokens of friendship. But on arriving he was told it was the king's order that the Athenians were to be treated as enemies; so Alcibiades was arrested for his trouble and imprisoned at Sardis. Being the fellow he was, his time in prison was short-lived. Barely a month later he escaped on horseback to Clazomenae; which, as will be remembered, lay on the neck of the long peninsula pointing out to the island of Chios. Plutarch says that there may have been a different reason for Tissaphernes' imprisonment of Alcibiades. The Spartans had been highly critical of Tissaphernes for a long time, and he had become afraid that if Darius listened to them he would lose the king's confidence. So, to placate the Spartans, he arrested Alcibiades and then, to keep the Athenians in play, let him escape. Plutarch, however, says that this story was only a rumour, spread by Alcibiades to make things worse for Tissaphernes; he ought to know, but it does not sound altogether improbable.

Shortly after these events, in early 410 BC, a crisis arose in the Hellespont that required the Athenians to concentrate their entire fleet there again. The forty ships which they had left at Sestos had felt themselves so threatened by the superior Peloponnesian fleet at Abydos that they had moved to Cardia, high up on the west coast of the Gallipoli peninsula. Here they were joined by Alcibiades, as well as two squadrons, each of twenty ships, which had been collecting money from Macedonia and the island of Thasos. All eighty-six ships now sailed back into the Hellespont under the command of Alcibiades, where they learned that Mindarus had left Abydos and, assisted by Pharnabazus, was besieging Cyzicus, about seventy miles along the south coast of the Propontis (Sea of Marmara).

Alcibiades had followed Mindarus through the Hellespont and was on his way to Cyzicus when he heard that the city had fallen; so he hove to for the night at the island of Proconnesus, north-west of the Cyzicus, from where he set sail the next day in a heavy rainstorm. As the Athenians approached Cyzicus, the weather suddenly cleared, and they found themselves between the harbour and sixty Peloponnesian ships training out at sea. Unable to reach port and heavily outnumbered, Mindarus made for the shore, where he beached his ships and prepared to defend them. Alcibiades, with twenty ships, then sailed a short distance beyond them, before disembarking and attacking along the shoreline. Seeing the Athenians coming, Mindarus went ashore to repel them, but fell in the fighting, whereupon the Peloponnesians abandoned their ships and fled, with only the Syracusans staying long enough to burn theirs. Altogether some sixty Peloponnesian ships were either destroyed or captured, so restoring to the Athenians their naval supremacy, and with it, their operational freedom.

The next day the Athenians prepared to attack Cyzicus. They found it had been evacuated by the Peloponnesians and Pharnabazus, so were admitted into the city; where, according to Xenophon, though no harm was done, the inhabitants had to raise a substantial amount of money. But considering that Cyzicus had been besieged and then forcibly taken by the Peloponnesians, it was only to be expected that no harm would be done, though extorting a large sum would not have cemented feelings of loyalty. After leaving Cyzicus, Alcibiades spent the rest of the summer re-establishing Athenian authority, as well as collecting money, along the north coast of the Sea of Marmara. Here two cities, Perinthus and Selymbria, made direct payments, while at Chrysopolis, the port of Calchedon to the east of the Bosphorus, a customs post was established, and a 10 per cent tax was levied on all cargoes passing through the straits.

Though Calchedon itself could not be brought back under Athenian authority, Chrysopolis was fortified, and thirty triremes were left there to enforce this levy and to keep the Bosphorus open. Nine triremes were considered sufficient to guard the Hellespont; though, as we will see, they did not prevent a Peloponnesian squadron passing through the straits later in the year. These matters may not seem of great significance, but they illustrate the Athenians' growing awareness of the vital importance of keeping open their supply line to the Black Sea. Until the spring of 412 BC, Athens had remained in undisputed control of both straits; but during the following year, with the revolt of Abydos in the Hellespont and those of the cities around the Bosphorus, her pre-eminence had been challenged and her supply line threatened. We have also been able to gain a better understanding of how Athens managed to sustain the cost of the war.

The consequences of the Peloponnesian defeat at Cyzicus were also felt in Athens and Sparta. Amongst the Athenians, confidence in final victory rose when a captured letter, addressed to the Spartans by Hippocrates, Mindarus' secretary, laconically reported: 'Ships lost. Mindarus dead. Men starving. Don't know what to do.' If the report of the Peloponnesian defeat that finally reached Sparta was as stark, their reaction was understandable. According to Diodorus, a delegation was sent to Athens with an offer of peace on the basis of the *status quo*: Decelea would be given up in exchange for Pylos, but Athens would lose the important islands of Euboea, Rhodes, Chios and Thasos, together with a number of other places. So, not altogether surprisingly, the offer was rejected. Since, however, neither Xenophon nor Plutarch mentions this Spartan initiative, there must be some doubt as to whether it ever really took place. Alternatively, it may just have been an unofficial peace feeler which, lacking any official backing, was not generally known.

Meanwhile, Pharnabazus showed himself to be a consistent friend and a leader of distinction in adversity. He did his best to restore the shaken morale of his own army, as well as that of the Peloponnesians; telling them that what mattered was that they were alive to fight on. He then went on to say that, since timber was readily available in the king's domains, the loss of their ships was no cause for discouragement; they could easily be replaced. He summoned the Persian commanders from the various cities and told them go to Antandrus, near the head of the gulf opposite the island of Lesbos where, at his expense and taking the wood from Mount Ida, they were to replace all the triremes they had lost.

Meanwhile back at Decelea, though Agis still dominated Attica, he had become frustrated at watching the flow of Athenian grain ships destined for Piraeus. What was gained by cutting the Athenians off from their land, when they could bring in all they wanted by sea? In an attempt to stem these supplies he sent fifteen ships, crewed by the Megarians, to Byzantium and Calchedon; but other than Xenophon telling us that three of them were sunk by the Athenians when passing through the Hellespont, we hear no more of them. The failure of the Spartans – and for that matter of the Athenians – to recognise the supreme importance of the Hellespont and the Bosphorus has already been commented upon several times.

In the following year, 409 BC, the Athenians seem to have reached two conclusions. First, that the threat from Agis at Decelea could be largely discounted; he had approached the walls of Athens again but, as on the previous occasion, had beaten a hasty retreat when they showed themselves ready for a fight. Second, having re-established their hold on the Bosphorus and the Hellespont, the supply line to the Black Sea was no longer threatened. Confident that their city was secure from both attack and starvation, it seems that the Athenians may have decided to re-establish their position in Ionia. A fine operational concept, but as we will shortly see, too ambitious to be executed at the tactical level.

Thrasyllus sailed from Athens to Samos with fifty triremes, 5000 of the sailors being equipped as peltasts, so that they could also serve as light troops; together with transports carrying 1000 hoplites and 100 cavalry. When Alcibiades had been plotting to impose an oligarchy in

Athens, Thrasyllus was serving as a hoplite in Samos, and he had been one of Alcibiades' strongest opponents. He had later commanded the Athenian left wing at the battle of Cynossema in the Hellespont; and now here he was, two years later, in command of this substantial expedition.

After spending three days at Samos, Thrasyllus landed near Phygela, south of Ephesus, where he met and virtually annihilated some 200 Milesians, who were attempting to prevent him from laying waste the countryside. Leaving Phygela, he then landed north of Ephesus and captured Colophon, before turning his attention to Ephesus itself. But near here he was defeated by a strong force sent by Tissaphernes to defend the city, losing 300 men and being forced to withdraw through the port of Notium, where, rather unusually, Xenophon says they buried their dead. So ended the Athenian excursion to Asia Minor. If it was an endeavour to re-establish themselves in Ionia, then, given the relatively small size of the force, it was over-ambitious. If it was intended to be no more than a raid, it was an extravagant use of resources. The Athenians were in no position to do more than adhere to the principle of minimum force. Either way, it was a hazardous and pointless undertaking.

Whether on his own initiative, or because he had been ordered to do so, Thrasyllus now headed north to the Hellespont, where he joined Alcibiades at Sestos, halfway up the Gallipoli peninsula. From here they crossed over the straits to Lampsacus, where they spent the winter fortifying the town, raiding the surrounding countryside, and fighting a couple of battles with Pharnabazus, which, other than demonstrating the satrap's commitment to the Peloponnesians, were of little significance. It is difficult to understand what the Athenians were trying to achieve in the Hellespont. They made, for example, no attempt to take Abydos, which would probably have forced Pharnabazus to come to its assistance and so fight a major battle. The only conclusion to be drawn is that they were preparing for the major operation to be undertaken the following year.

In 408 BC Alcibiades concentrated his whole force on the capture of Byzantium, ostensibly to ensure the free passage of Athenian shipping through the Bosphorus. But what was the threat? Without the backing of a Peloponnesian fleet, Byzantium and Chalcedon were in no position to challenge the Athenians – even assuming that they wanted to do so in the first place. Certainly, twenty-two of the twenty-five ships sent by Agis had escaped being sunk by the Athenians, so they were at large somewhere. But according to Xenophon they were more akin to merchant ships than warships, so they would hardly have been a match for the thirty Athenian triremes stationed at Chrysopolis. Moreover, as we have just seen, the Hellespont and Bosphorus being quiescent, the Athenians had felt confident enough to send a considerable force to Ionia. So it looks as though the capture of Byzantium was undertaken to satisfy Alcibiades' thirst for personal glory, rather than to fulfil a pressing operational need. But whatever the reasons, in the beginning of spring, the whole Athenian force sailed to the island of Proconnesus, where, it will be remembered, the Athenians had spent the night before sailing to Cyzicus.

After leaving Proconnesus, the Athenians established their camp near Chalcedon, on the east bank of the Bosphorus opposite Byzantium. Alcibiades then put the army to work constructing a wooden stockade, which ran from the sea, across a river, then on to the Bosphorus. Hardly had this blockading wall been completed when Pharnabazus made a determined attempt to relieve the city, while the Spartan governor, Hippocrates, tried to break out and join him. But the Athenian defences held, Hippocrates was killed and Pharnabazus was forced to withdraw. Alcibiades now went off to raise money from around the Hellespont. While he was away, the Athenian commanders came to an agreement with Pharnabazus. Chalcedon would capitulate and, in return for not being sacked, would resume paying the same amount of tribute as it had done before revolting, together with the arrears. Additionally, Pharnabazus undertook to make a substantial payment on behalf of the city himself, and to conduct Athenian envoys to Darius, with whom they would try and negotiate a settlement. Meanwhile, until the envoys returned, the Athenians would take no further hostile action against Chalcedon.

Pharnabazus then left, to meet up with the Athenian envoys at Cyzicus, before accompanying them to see Darius, who (though Xenophon does not specifically say so) must have been at Susa, some 1200 miles away. To make such a journey just to settle the affairs of a single city does not seem very probable, so there must have been wider issues at stake. But we will leave Pharnabazus for the moment, and see what Alcibiades was doing.

On his return from raising money, Alcibiades had at once set about capturing Byzantium; siege works were constructed round the city and, according to Xenophon, the fortifications were assaulted 'both at long range and at close quarters', which presumably means with missiles and direct assault. Rather surprisingly, while all this was going on, the governor, Clearchus, somehow managed to get out of the city and cross the straits to meet Pharnabazus – which would have been difficult if he were on his way to Susa, so it may have been a deputy. But whoever it was that Clearchus was meeting, while he was away Byzantium was betrayed to the Athenians. The conspirators opened the gates at night, thus enabling the Athenians to occupy all the key positions before the alarm was raised. Resistance clearly being hopeless, the garrison surrendered.

News of the capture of Byzantium reached Pharnabazus and the Athenian envoys while they were spending the winter at Gordium, the Phrygian capital; so they still had some 200 miles to go, if Susa was their destination. It was at Gordium in 334 BC that Alexander the Great, who was on his way to Cappadocia, was to create the legend of 'cutting the Gordian knot'. Having been told of the oracular prediction that the man who unfastened the elaborate knot tying the yoke to the chariot of King Gordius would rule all Asia, Alexander hurried to the citadel where the chariot was kept and sought the ends of the strap. Not finding them, he lost patience, drew his sword and solved the problem by cutting through the obstinate knot.

Nothing as dramatic as that happened to Pharnabazus and the envoys; but, when they resumed their journey in the spring of 407 BC, they met another party on its way back. These were Spartan envoys, from whose Boeotian companions they learned that the Spartans had got everything they wanted from the king. They were also told that Cyrus, the king's son, had been given command of the whole coastal area, with instructions to give the Spartans all the assistance they required. So, just when it looked as though the Athenians were in the ascendancy, the resources of the Persian empire were thrown behind the Spartans, to bring them down to earth. Financially secure, all the Spartans needed now was an able commander; and he was already waiting in the wings to be called forward.

After the Athenian envoys had heard this devastating news, they wanted to continue their journey and see Darius himself, or, if this were not possible, to turn back and warn Alcibiades. Cyrus, however, had no intention of letting the Athenians know what was going on; so Pharnabazus was ordered to detain them, which he did for the next three years. In an ironic twist of fortune, Alcibiades, unaware of these developments, and little thinking that the war was about to enter its final phase, returned to Athens to receive a hero's welcome. Dense crowds thronged Piraeus as the ships sailed in, with everybody pressing forward to see the great Alcibiades, the noblest citizen they had. There were a few, however, who remembered his duplicity in the past and remained fearful of what he might do in the future. But there was nothing they could do to stem the flood of popular adoration, which reached its peak when Alcibiades was proclaimed supreme commander. Satiated with glory, Alcibiades returned to Samos to face reality in the prosecution of the war.

The Athens that Alcibiades left behind was still suffering from the constitutional upheaval brought about by the oligarchic government. To counter the disintegration of the body politic, extreme measures had been introduced, resulting in what was little more than a democratic tyranny. The killing of political opponents was not murder, but a necessary means of preventing another revolution; while the sole guardians of the law were the people's courts, which were ready to give credence to any charge brought against aristocrats, or men of prominence. As a result, judicial corruption was rife, prosecutors were bought off, and even whole juries bribed. Small wonder that Plato, who came of age during this period, inverted the political responsibilities of the classes when he wrote the *Republic*, the earliest of Utopias. The common people were placed firmly at the bottom; the soldiers, who kept them there, were firmly under political control; that left the guardians – a small, secure elite – free to wield political power. But the age-old question then arises: who watches the guardians? And in the absence of an interfering God, it can only be the people. So round and round it goes. It is time, however, to get back to the war and military matters.

Two events had occurred during this period. First, the Athenians had sailed along the Thracian coast and reduced all the cities and places that had revolted. Amongst these was the island of Thasos, which, Xenophon says, 'what with war, revolution and famine, was in a very miserable condition'. So the Athenians had regained control not only of the Hellespont, but of the whole of the Northern Theatre. Second, the able commander the Spartans needed had arrived:

Lysander, who, with Brasidas and Gylippus, made up the trio of outstanding Spartans to emerge during the war. Lysander, the admiral who brought the war to a successful conclusion for his country, here requires an introduction.

Lysander's date of birth is not recorded; we know only that he died in 393 BC. He was brought up in penury, and from early childhood he was trained for war in the traditional Spartan fashion. Like his contemporaries, he would have been hardy, indifferent to pain or pleasure, and submissive to discipline; trained to honour the exploits of his forebears, and to be ambitious and competitive, since to be otherwise was, according to Plutarch, to be despised by the Spartans as a spiritless clod. On the other hand, he allegedly displayed an inborn obsequiousness to the great, which was unusual in a Spartan, and he was prepared to put up with the arrogance of those in authority to achieve his own ends.

In Plutarch's opinion, the most peculiar fact about his character was that, although he uncomplainingly endured poverty and was never corrupted by money, as a result of flooding Sparta with the spoils of war Lysander whetted his countrymen's taste for riches; so that they lost their indifference to wealth, for which they were held in such admiration. As will be related more fully later, when Lysander's successor arrived to take over the fleet in Asia Minor, Lysander did all he could to make things difficult for him, which suggests a certain meanness of spirit. If Plutarch is correct, fame seems to have gone to his head. Though wielding greater power than any Greek before him, he gave the impression that it still trailed his ambition and sense of superiority; while his administration of the former Athenian territories and cities became increasingly harsh and dictatorial. Lysander had also become abrupt and aggressive towards people, as though wishing to intimidate anyone who opposed him, while his cruelty in unhesitatingly putting people to death left a legacy of hatred that gravely tarnished his own and his associates' image. As he got older, he became increasingly melancholy, which sounds as though he may have suffered from bouts of depression, and perhaps even guilt. Hearing all these disquieting reports, the ephors eventually stepped in and recalled him. But we will leave him, as his story has already extended beyond the period with which we are concerned and contains little of interest anyway. Except for his years in command during the closing years of the Peloponnesian War, Lysander does not appear to have had a very happy life; and it probably came as a relief when he found himself leading the simple life of a fighting man again, this time as a soldier, in the Boeotian War. Leading his army from Phocis, he was killed outside the walls of Thebes in 393 BC. But we must now return to early 407 BC, when he was on his way to Ephesus.

Lysander first went to Rhodes to collect the ships stationed there, before sailing to Cos, then to Miletus and finally to Ephesus, where he remained until Cyrus arrived at Sardis. He then went with the Spartan envoys to call on Cyrus, taking the opportunity to denounce Tissaphernes and express the hope that Cyrus would play an energetic part in the war, doing all he could to help defeat the Athenians. Cyrus told him that these were exactly the instructions he had received from his father, and what he intended to do. Having reassured Lysander on that point, Cyrus next gave him the money he had brought with him, telling him that if it was not enough, he would use his own; and if that ran out, he would break up his throne of gold and silver.

Greatly encouraged, Lysander tried to persuade Cyrus to pay the Peloponnesian crews above the going rate, thus encouraging the Athenian sailors to desert. Cyrus at first refused, claiming that he had no authority to pay more than the amount his father had stipulated. But, after a well-provisioned dinner, he eventually agreed to a 25 per cent pay rise, to the settling of arrears and to provide a month's pay in advance. As for the Athenians, Cyrus refused to see their envoys and rejected Tissaphernes' intervention on their behalf, so they can have been left in little doubt about Persian intentions. There now followed a period of naval sparring, during which Antiochus, whom Alcibiades had left in command while away raising money, lost fifteen triremes in an ill-conducted engagement off Ephesus. On his return, Alcibiades tried to settle the score by drawing Lysander into the open sea to accept battle, but he, being considerably inferior in numbers, refused the challenge.

Plutarch gives an insight into Alcibiades' position at this time. In his opinion, Alcibiades was being destroyed by his own reputation: people had begun to expect nothing but success from him, and if he suffered a reverse, he was suspected of not trying hard enough. They did not stop to consider that he was short of funds and frequently had to leave off fighting to raise money. His absence on these occasions led to accusations that he was drinking and womanising, while the enemy fleet rode at anchor nearby. So it was decided to replace him.

Alcibiades' fall from grace was certainly precipitous; which suggests that, in spite of the hero's welcome he had been given on returning to Athens, his enemies were more numerous and powerful than was realised at the time. Now, when he learned that he was being replaced, he left Samos and, after raising a force of mercenaries, enriched himself by waging a private war against the Thracian tribes that had remained outside the Persian Empire. Alcibiades then went to the Hellespont, where he advised the Athenian fleet commanders at Aegospotami to tighten up on their discipline and to move to a safer anchorage. But his advice was ignored.

As the Spartan hold tightened, Alcibiades first moved back to Thrace, but shortly afterwards went to Pharnabazus in Phrygia, where he was welcomed as an honoured member of his court. While he was there, Lysander received instructions from Sparta to get rid of Alcibiades, as he was causing too much trouble; or perhaps because the authorities wanted to gratify King Agis. Plutarch gives a vivid and striking image of his death:

> The men who were sent to kill him did not dare to enter his home, but surrounded it and set it on fire. When Alcibiades discovered this, he collected most of the clothes and bedding in the house and threw them on the fire. Then he wrapped his cloak about his left arm, and with the sword in the right dashed through the flames untouched before his clothes could catch alight, and scattered the barbarians, who fled at the sight of him. None of them stood their ground nor attempted to close with him, but kept out of reach and shot at him with javelins and arrows. So Alcibiades fell, and when the barbarians had gone, Timandra took up his body, covered it, and wrapped it in her own clothes and gave it as sumptuous and honourable burial as she could provide.

There is, however, another version that Plutarch mentions; which, though he appears not to give it much credence, is much in keeping with Alcibiades' character. According to this story, it was neither the Spartan authorities nor Lysander who was responsible for Alcibiades' death. He had seduced a woman from a noble family, and it was her brothers who killed him in the way described. So that was the end of a man gifted with enormous ability, which – had it been properly directed – would have earned him an honourable place in a pantheon dedicated to great statesman and warriors. As it was, he lived a life of such duplicity that he could have had nothing to learn from Machiavelli, with his advocacy to princes that they should keep faith when it pays to do so, but not otherwise. But in following Alcibiades we have run ahead of events again, so we must step back some three years.

When Conon, who had succeeded Alcibiades when he fled to Thrace, arrived at Samos in late 407 BC, he found the crews so dispirited that he withdrew more than thirty of the triremes from service. He then put to sea with the remaining seventy ships to plunder the enemy coast; probably to raise morale and supplement his sailors' pay. He was perhaps fortunate that the Peloponnesian fleet was also in some disarray. Lysander's time in command had expired in 406 BC, so he had been recalled and replaced by Callicratidas, an as yet unproven Spartan admiral. The system of replacing commanders in this manner had been devised so as to ensure that control of operations abroad remained in the hands of the home authorities. But apart from the inevitable disruption caused by the arrival of a new commander, who needed time to take stock of the situation, Callicratidas did not endear himself to the crews with his Doric simplicity and candour. But the most harm was caused by Lysander himself who, aggrieved at being recalled, did all he could to make life difficult for his successor. He handed back to Cyrus the balance of the money he had been given to pay the fleet, telling Callicratidas that, since he was now in command, he would have to make his own arrangements. Lysander must also have turned Cyrus against him, since when he went to try and recover the money, Callicratidas was kept hanging around until he lost patience and, furious at such insulting treatment, left without receiving an interview.

Callicratidas then managed to persuade the Milesians and Chians to cover his immediate expenses, a sum that he augmented by capturing and plundering Methymna, in Lesbos. The 170-strong Peloponnesian fleet next moved round the coast to Mytilene, where Conon was trapped with his seventy ships in the harbour entrance and, after losing thirty of them, sought refuge with the remainder under the city's fortifications. To complete the encirclement of Mytilene,

Callicratidas ordered the Methymnaeans to block the land approach until he had brought over his army from Chios. Cyrus, perhaps because he was impressed by Callicratidas' vigorous and successful offensive, now sent him the money that he had tried to obtain when first seeking an interview.

When news of Conon's plight reached them, the Athenians displayed the same remarkable resilience and defiance which they had shown after the loss of their fleet and army at Syracuse in 413 BC. The Assembly voted to send 110 ships to his relief, putting aboard all the men of military age, irrespective of whether they were aristocrats, cavalrymen, citizens or slaves. To pay for them and the ships, taxes were raised, and the silver plate in the temples was converted into currency, which itself was debased by minting a form of token money made from copper. Thirty days later the fleet sailed to Samos, where another forty ships were collected, and from there it continued on its way to Lesbos. Admirable as all this sounds, it does raise a number of questions. How could such a large number of ships be constructed, fitted out and the crews trained in such a short time? On the other hand, if many of them were already in commission, what were they all doing at Athens? We have been told that Conon, when he took over command of the fleet at Samos, had to withdraw some thirty triremes from service. If there were replacements and crews available at Athens, why did he not send for them? How could a veritable armada, manned by such an ill-assorted collection of individuals, be handled without an extensive period of training? Perhaps, as with both Herodotus and Thucydides, the numbers have become exaggerated; but even then the questions remain, though in a less acute form. So, bearing in mind this reservation about numbers, and applying it to both combatants, let us continue to follow Conon's progress.

When nearing Lesbos, the Athenians went ashore for their midday meal on the Arginousae islands, between Mytilene and the mainland. Meanwhile Callicratidas, on learning that an Athenian relief force was at Samos, had left fifty triremes to continue the blockade at Mytilene, and sailed with the other 120 to just west of Cape Malea, on the south-east corner of Lesbos. Separated by the cape, the two fleets apparently remained unaware of one another's presence until it grew dark, when Callicratidas saw the Athenian fires. He accordingly planned to sail at midnight and mount a surprise attack, but was detained by bad weather, so he did not get away until dawn. By then the Athenians had also left Arginousae and had completed their deployment, with their right wing close to the shore. Though Xenophon does not tell us where this shore was, it must have been Lesbos.

The Athenian commanders were fully aware that capabilities had been reversed: it was now the Peloponnesians who were the more skilled seamen, able to manoeuvre at speed, break through, then turn and ram. So the Athenians had deployed in depth, with four squadrons of fifteen ships on each wing; two squadrons were in the front line, with the other two directly behind them. Although the centre was weaker, with only three squadrons of ten ships (two in the front line, and the third to the rear), it still had depth. This meant that, should the Peloponnesians break through the first line of ships and then turn to ram them, they would expose their sides to the Athenian ships in the second line.

The Peloponnesians deployed in a single line, which would have meant their 120 ships were facing an Athenian front-line strength of eighty; this enabled them to overlap the enemy's left wing, which extended out into the open sea. Xenophon, however, does not mention this, and devotes only a few cursory words to the actual battle. 'The fighting went on for a very long time, at first the ships were in close order, but later they became separated. Finally, Callicratidas, as his ship was ramming an enemy ship, fell overboard and disappeared in the water.' The outcome was a victory for the Athenians, who lost twenty-five ships, including most of their crews, while the Peloponnesians, who fled back to Chios, lost nine out of the ten Spartan ships, and more than sixty allied ones. When the Peloponnesians blockading Mytilene heard of this heavy defeat, the squadron slipped quietly away, and the troops marched back to Methymna. Conon was then free to join the main Athenian fleet and return with it to Samos.

In Athens there was elation at their sailors regaining mastery of the sea. The slaves who had served with the fleet, as had been promised to them when they enlisted, were given their liberty and citizenship. But when details of the battle started to filter back, the generals were accused of having made no attempt to recover the disabled triremes, so saving the lives of those aboard them, while deserting those struggling to reach the shore and abandoning their dead like so much flotsam and jetsam. On hearing of the charges, two of the generals chose not to return to Athens, but the other six presented themselves for trial. In such cases it was the Council that inaugurated proceedings, and the Assembly that passed judgement. When the generals appeared before the Council to see whether they had a case to answer, they limited their statements to saying it was the storm and high sea that had prevented them from recovering the damaged triremes or saving the crews. When they were arraigned before the Assembly, they also pointed out that they had detailed off some of the captains to do the job, but they too had found the task impossible, and produced some of the steersmen to testify to the violence of the storm. But their account was contradicted by others, one man claiming he had been saved by clinging to a barrel, and those drowning around him had called out that he should tell the people the generals had done nothing to try and save them. This sounds a somewhat improbable request to have come from men drowning in a high sea, who would not have been able to see very far anyway.

The whole business was a sordid, rabble-rousing affair, largely motivated by political and personal interests, with Theramenes, who had been one of the captains detailed off to carry out the rescue operation, defending himself by pressing the charge of criminal negligence against the generals. We need not concern ourselves with any more of the details, which differ between Xenophon and Diodorus anyway. Suffice to say that the six generals, who included Pericles' son and Diomedon (who had done so much to save democracy in Samos and Athens in 411 BC), were found guilty and put to death. Perhaps they did fail in their duty, but in a chaotic post-battle scene, with command fragmented between eight of them, it is doubtful if anybody really knew who was supposed to be doing what and where.

As for the Peloponnesians, following the death of Callicratidas when he fell overboard, the surviving commanders held a conference at Ephesus. Here it was decided to ask the Spartans for Lysander to return and take command again, a request that was backed separately by Cyrus, but which put the Spartans on the spot. On the one hand, they did not want to offend their allies and Cyrus by refusing; on the other hand, they were tied by the law that restricted an overseas commander to one tour of duty. To get round the problem, they selected a new commander who was to be no more than a figurehead and appointed Lysander with full powers of command as his deputy.

So in the spring of 405 BC, in all but name, Lysander was back as the commander-in-chief of the Eastern Theatre.

Once Lysander had established himself at Ephesus he sent for the fleet at Chios, together with any other ships he could lay hands on, and started refitting them, while arranging for the construction of new ones at Antandrus, north-east of Lesbos at the head of the gulf. He also went to see Cyrus, to raise more money; only to be told that everything Darius had supplied had already been spent, and a great deal more besides. But after this unpropitious start Lysander eventually got what he had asked for, so that he was able to resume paying the crews. Not long afterwards, Cyrus sent for Lysander and told him that his father, who was seriously ill at Susa, wanted to see Cyrus. He then advised Lysander not to seek a battle with the Athenians until he had a convincing numerical superiority; precipitate action was quite unnecessary, and there was plenty of money available to maintain the fleet until the right moment had come. Then, as though to make the point, Cyrus gave Lysander all the tribute he had received, with any surplus funds he had at his disposal. As was mentioned earlier, the wealth of Persia had been increasingly committed to the Spartan cause, and now we see it being lavished on a scale that made an ultimate Athenian defeat almost inevitable.

Meanwhile, the Athenian fleet at Samos, which had been placed under the command of Conon, had also been refitting after the battle of Arginousae and preparing for another major engagement; so naval activity had been restricted to coastal raiding. This period of comparative calm was now broken by Lysander, who, in spite of Cyrus' cautionary advice, seems to have recognised that the quickest way of defeating Athens was to cut off her supplies coming through the Hellespont. Defeated there, the Athenian position in Asia Minor would be untenable, and Athens itself placed in the gravest danger. But if Lysander had at last come round to Agis' way of thinking, apparently the Athenians had still not fully appreciated the danger. It was probably when seeking to relieve Conon, after he had been bottled up in Mytilene, that the two squadrons guarding the Bosphorus and the Hellespont had been withdrawn. At the time, in order to achieve a concentration of force for a major battle, this was probably necessary; but not to have replaced them afterwards looks inexcusable. So when Lysander sailed to the Hellespont, he found it unguarded.

Supported by troops from Abydos and other cities, Lysander sailed further up the straits and attacked Lampsacus, an ally of Athens, and took it by storm. It was a rich city, well stocked with supplies, including grain and wine, and though all the prisoners who were free men were released, the city was sacked. Lysander now had control of the Asiatic side of the narrows, so when the Athenian fleet that had been following him arrived, it first anchored at Elaeus, near the southern tip of the Gallipoli peninsula. It was here it heard that Lampsacus had fallen, so after picking up provisions at Sestos, the fleet sailed to Aegospotami, barely two miles across the straits from Lampsacus.

At dawn the next day Lysander embarked his men, and ordered the side-screens to be erected and the ships prepared for battle. As soon as the sun rose, the Athenians came up to the harbour mouth and deployed in line; but getting no response to their challenge, they returned to Aegospotami late in the day. Whereupon Lysander ordered a few of his ships to follow them and to report on what the Athenians did after they had disembarked; meanwhile, the rest of the fleet was kept at battle stations until they returned. For the next four or five days, the Athenians and the Peloponnesians behaved in exactly the same way, with the Athenians becoming increasingly contemptuous and careless, scattering further and further inland in search of food. It was during this period that Alcibiades advised the Athenian generals to move to Sestos, from where they were drawing most of their supplies anyway; it had a good harbour, with the city affording protection behind them, whereas at Aegospotami they were moored on an exposed beach. But his advice was scornfully rejected and, having been unkindly reminded that he was no longer in command, he departed.

On the fifth day Lysander instructed the ships that were to follow the Athenians to return as soon as they had seen them disembark, and then to signal with a shield when they were back in sight. These orders were duly carried out and, once Lysander had received the signal, he ordered the fleet to sail at best speed for Aegospotami. As soon as the Athenians saw them approaching, they attempted to return to their ships; but it was too late. Some ships never left the shore, some put to sea with just one bank of oars manned, others with two; only the eight triremes accompanying Conon were fully manned, but they made no attempt to fight, fleeing instead to Cyprus.

The entire Athenian fleet was either captured or destroyed, and the crews slaughtered or taken prisoner. It was not the end of the story, but it was the end of Athens' ability to wage war effectively. Through neglecting the need for security, the Athenian generals had brought about a defeat from which there could be no recovery. Athens' vital supply line had been irreparably severed.

When Conon had fled to Cyprus, the special-duties trireme, the *Paralus*, had escaped from Aegospotami with him, but had then sailed directly to Athens bearing the appalling tidings. It was night when the *Paralus* arrived, and as news of the disaster was passed from mouth to mouth, the sound of wailing could be heard, beginning at Piraeus, then extending along the walls to the city itself. There was no sleep for anybody that night. Wakeful and fearful, the Athenians were haunted by the memory of what they had done at places like Melos, where all the adult males had been slaughtered, and the women and children sold into slavery: treatment which they could now expect to be repaid in kind. But the next day their thoughts turned to survival. An assembly was held, where it was decided to block up all the harbour entrances, except for one; to man the walls; and to prepare the city to resist a prolonged siege.

Meanwhile, back in the Hellespont, Lysander had called a meeting to decide the fate of the 3000 prisoners they had taken. In the speeches that followed, bitter accusations were made against the Athenians: they had thrown the crews of two captured triremes overboard and had threatened to cut off the right hand of any prisoners they took in naval actions. Many other such stories were told, and in the end it was decided to put all the Athenians amongst the prisoners to death, starting with Philocles, who had ordered the trireme crews to be thrown overboard. So he was led forward, and after being unable to give a satisfactory explanation as to why he had behaved like a common criminal to his fellow Greeks, had his throat cut. The question of the prisoners having been settled, Lysander sailed to Byzantium and Chalcedon, both of which submitted to him, together with their Athenian garrisons. But unlike the prisoners taken at Aegospotami, the Athenian troops from the two cities, and all the others that capitulated, as well as the colonists and traders, instead of being put to death were sent back to Athens under safe conduct. Lysander's humane treatment, however, was intended to serve a purpose: the more people who flocked into Athens, the quicker the city would be starved into submission.

Lysander now mounted a two-pronged mopping-up operation. While he sailed out of the Hellespont with 200 ships to Lesbos – where, as Xenophon puts it, 'he settled matters in Mytilene and the other cities' – Eteonicus with ten triremes brought all the Thracian cities over to Sparta. With the collapse of the Athenian Empire, Lysander now turned his attention to Athens itself. Messages were sent to the two Spartan kings, Agis at Decelea and Pausanias in Sparta, that he was sailing to Athens with 200 ships to blockade the city by sea. Whether at Lysander's prompting or on their own initiative, Agis and Pausanias then marched on Athens to complete its encirclement on the land side. At the same time Lysander restored Aegina to its exiled inhabitants, then did the same for the Melians and all the others who had been forced to leave their homes.

In the unseemly stampede to be seen fighting alongside Sparta when Athens clearly faced defeat, only Samos and Argos remained loyal. The Samians fought on until, as will be recounted, they were finally forced to capitulate; while the Argives, though not actively supporting Athens in the field, refused to join the other Peloponnesian states when they marched with Pausanias to share in her downfall. The Athenians were now cut off by land and sea with no hope of relief, and yet, according to Xenophon, they held out through fear. They were still haunted by the atrocities they had committed when driven by the arrogance of power; though hoping for a miracle may also have played a not unimportant part. Seemingly as an act of propitiation, the Athenians gave back their rights to all those who had been disenfranchised.

Eventually, however (again according to Xenophon), when the Athenian food supplies were completely exhausted, they sent envoys to Agis saying that they were willing to join the Spartan alliance, so long as they could keep their walls and Piraeus. But Agis told them he had no authority to negotiate, and that they should instead go to Sparta. However, as the envoys approached the Laconian border, the ephors, who had been informed of their proposals, told them that, if they really wanted peace, they should think again and come up with something more realistic. When the envoys returned to Athens and the matter was discussed in the Council, one unfortunate senator was flung into prison for suggesting that they should accept the Spartan terms. Xenophon does not tell us how these terms came to be known, but they involved dismantling some 1200 yards of the wall. To prevent a weakening of resolve, the Council at once passed a decree forbidding anybody to consider such a proposal. Thus, as so often occurred with Thucydides, the situation cannot have been as critical as Xenophon has portrayed, especially when we learn what happened next.

Theramenes, who had pressed the charge of criminal negligence against the generals after the battle of Arginousae, now proposed to the Assembly that he should go and see Lysander, and try to discover the reason for Spartan insistence on the demolition of the walls. Did they want this so that they would be able to enter the city and enslave the population? Or was it just a pledge of Athenian good faith? His proposal was accepted and off he went; only to be detained by Lysander for more than three months, in the hope that by then the Athenians' plight would be so desperate that they would agree to any terms. When Theramenes was finally released and returned to Athens, he told the Assembly that Lysander had said it was only the ephors who could answer his question. So Theramenes, accompanied by nine envoys, was sent to Sparta with full powers to negotiate a peace settlement. Once they had been admitted into Sparta, the Spartans convened an assembly of the Peloponnesian Confederacy. During the debate that followed, many of the Greek states, in particular Corinth and Thebes, were opposed to making peace with Athens under any conditions; she had been defeated and should be dealt with harshly, with the city razed and her population being sold into slavery.

The Spartans, however, unequivocally declared that they would never consent to enslave the Athenians, who had done so much to save them all from the Persians. They then offered to make peace on the following terms: the Long Walls and the fortifications of Piraeus must be dismantled; all ships except for twelve to be surrendered; and the exiles to be recalled. Finally, Athens was to have the same enemies and the same friends as Sparta and was to follow Spartan leadership in any expedition that Sparta might make by land or sea. When Theramenes returned to Athens, the people crowded round him, fearful that he might have failed in his mission and all they could expect was enslavement. Evidently Theramenes was in no hurry to relieve the people's anxiety. It was not until the next day that the envoys made their report to the Assembly, when they recommended that the Spartan peace terms should be accepted. There were a few dissenting voices, but the great majority were thankful to have been spared a worse fate; so they voted in support of Theramenes' recommendation.

Lysander then sailed into Piraeus to supervise the implementation of the Spartan conditions, and from the accounts that Xenophon and Plutarch give – with some variations – his arrival was the cause of a celebratory festival: the walls were pulled down amid scenes of great enthusiasm and to the music of flute girls, whom Lysander had rounded up from the city and his own camp. Sparta's allies garlanded themselves with flowers, rejoiced together and hailed the day as the beginning of freedom for Greece. If that is really what they thought, it was unfortunate that there was no diviner present to warn them about Alexander of Macedon, who, barely seventy years later, was to subjugate Greece.

The last flicker of Athenian resistance came from Samos, which at first resisted Lysander's blockade; but just as he was about to mount an all-out assault, the Samians came to terms. The free men were allowed to leave, though they had to surrender all their possessions except for a single cloak. The exiled party then returned, and Lysander gave them back the island with everything it contained. Their work completed, Lysander then dismissed the allies' naval contingents and returned to Sparta. Here he handed over everything he had acquired during the war: the triremes from Piraeus, the trophies, the gifts, and the balance of the money given to him by Cyrus for the prosecution of the war.

So ended the twenty-eight-year-long war that had set Greek against Greek, broken proud Athens and destroyed her empire, restored Persia to her pre-eminent position in Asia Minor, and left Sparta as the predominant power in Greece. But after all the tragic loss of human life, untold suffering and squandered wealth, little had been learned. Athenian political infighting was resumed almost immediately, soon leading to a civil war; fighting broke out once more in Asia Minor; and within a decade the Greeks were at one another's throats again. But all that is another story.

Epilogue

Since what I wrote in the opening paragraphs of the Epilogue for my book on *The Punic Wars* is equally relevant to the Peloponnesian War, I will repeat them now, with some slight modification so as to put them into context. The Persian and Peloponnesian Wars provide such a wide diversity of political and military experience that for me to have withheld all comment to the end would have resulted in a confusing loss of textual relevance. The purpose of this chapter is then to draw together earlier comments and put them into perspective. As Polybius pointed out, the study of history provides a means of learning from the experience of others, so avoiding some of the mistakes of our predecessors. Let me reinforce this opening statement by quoting Captain Mahan, of the United States Navy, who wrote at the end of the 19th century: 'History both suggests strategic study and illustrates the principles of war by the facts which it transmits. But if these lessons are to be of any value, they must be shown to have a practical application.'

Because we live in a material world that has changed immensely from the days of early Greece and Persia, we tend to measure our differences from them in terms of such developments as aircraft, nuclear power, the exploration of space, and the host of everyday things with which we are surrounded, inevitably making events that occurred more than 2000 years ago appear irrelevantly remote. But the fundamentals of life remain unchanged, and to judge historical relevance through purely material comparisons is to take a somewhat superficial view of history and what it can teach us. In spite of the deterministic theories we have developed, providence remains as fickle as ever.

We can at least introduce an element of predictability in assessing the likely consequences of our actions by applying the lessons of the past, although care must be taken that those lessons are not reduced to dogma. They should be regarded only as signposts, or guidelines, for future action, which can then be formulated into policy through debate. But before looking to the future, I will summarise the main lessons that can be drawn from the wars between Greece and Persia, and then from those of Greek against Greek.

As will be remembered, the cause of the first major clash between East and West had its origins in the Ionian revolt against Persian domination, which took place in 499–494 BC. The Athenians responded to an appeal for help from the city of Miletus and, after joining up with the Ionian forces there, marched to the Persian provincial capital at Sardis, which they burned to the ground. They then withdrew to Ephesus, where they were defeated by an advancing Persian army after which they deserted the Ionians and returned to Athens. It was this incident that Darius I set out to avenge in 490 when he sent an army to Marathon, but after being decisively defeated he was forced to call off his campaign.

The Athenian decision to intervene on behalf of Miletus had been taken by the Assembly, where high emotion prevailed over a rational assessment of Athenian interests and capabilities. Athens was a maritime power, yet here she was, sending an expeditionary force of fifty triremes to participate in an uncoordinated revolt against a massive continental power. To have then gratuitously enraged the Persians by burning Sardis served only to compound her folly. It may be thought that today, with such decisions being taken by an inner coterie of ministers, there is no danger of such an inanity being repeated. That, however, would be making a very dangerous assumption. For the Assembly read the media, with its emotive calls for *something to be done* to put a stop to some distant conflict or atrocity; the demand is given a sense of intimacy and urgency by being displayed in our homes. Then add a politician seeking to be seen playing a role on the world stage; next subtract the Americans; and you have all the makings of a potential disaster.

As all the other lessons from the Persian War have already been drawn together at the end of Chapter 4, they do not need repeating now, so we can turn our attention to the Peloponnesian War itself. As will be remembered, with the rise of Pericles, Athens' strategy was declared to be one of consolidation. Her commitments were extensive enough already; they were not to be enlarged. Though this policy was applied to overseas theatres, it was contradicted in Greece by Pericles himself. He was continually trying to wrong-foot Sparta, driving her to break the Thirty Years Truce and open hostilities. His strategic aim must have been to side-line Sparta as a major power, or to subordinate her to Athens, so enabling Athens to become the capital of a pan-Hellenic empire, a role for which he had already adorned her. Why should he have done this?

Pericles was certainly not burning with such democratic zeal that he wanted to bring its benefits to oligarchic Sparta; especially as his form of administration was characterised by Thucydides as being 'democracy in name, but in practice government by the first citizen'. He was then no evangelist leading a moral crusade, but an autocrat wanting to impose government by the first city. The wealth of Athens, its empire, its fleet, its intellectual and cultural superiority, its constitution, and the splendour of its buildings – all gave the city a self-evident right to be the Hellenic imperial capital. From there it is but a short step to hubris, to an arrogant intolerance of rivalry. None of this distracts from Pericles' outstanding achievements during the thirty or so years that he governed the city, but it does provide an early illustration of the danger resulting from one man exercising too much power for too long.

When war did break out, Athens' strategic aim was clear enough: to subordinate Sparta. At the operational level this was to be achieved by remaining on the defensive behind her fortifications, and ... ? This was the trouble: there was nothing else she could do at the operational level; she did not have the capability to undertake a land campaign, while she had no means of applying her maritime supremacy offensively. Pericles and those who supported him in seeking a war with Sparta had not thought through how it was to be conducted offensively. The result was an immediate descent to the tactical level: raiding the Peloponnesian coastline, possibly with the aim of wearing her down and forcing her to abandon the war. But if this really was the Athenian intention, the raids were on far too small a scale to have any hope of attaining their objective.

As for Sparta, her strategic aim was also clear enough: to defeat

Athens; which was to be achieved at the operational level by invading and devastating Attica. But since Athens was secure behind her fortifications and could be supplied by sea, which the Spartans had no means of preventing, just plundering and incinerating Attica was also not achieving anything of consequence. So there was a stalemate – an elephant versus a whale – with neither of the protagonists being able to bring about a decisive encounter.

After the death of Pericles in 429 BC, Nicias and the majority of the Athenians wanted peace, while most Spartans had never wanted war in the first place, and ever since had been ready to bring it to an end. So King Pleistoanax, with the support of the majority of the Spartans, remained ready to reach a negotiated settlement. Nor should it be overlooked that when Athens was finally starved into surrender, it was the Spartans who refused to accede to the demands of the Boeotians and Corinthians that the Athenians should be enslaved and their city razed to the ground. Magnanimity in victory had not always been an Athenian characteristic. But to return to the winter of 422: peace negotiations were opened, and an agreement was reached the following year. Through a combination of factors, however – not least Athenian and Spartan active support for rival factions in the Peloponnese – the truce was hardly holding, and it collapsed completely when Athens mounted an expedition against Sicily in 415 BC. How this decision was arrived at has already been related, and so, other than to repeat that the venture was undertaken with only the scantiest understanding of what it involved, nothing further will be said. What concerns us is: was the decision correct, in that it would further the war against Sparta?

Because the expedition ended in disaster, it is all too easy to condemn it; but before doing so, let us try and determine what the consequences might have been, had it been successful. We will discount the kite-flying of Alcibiades, who visualised the conquest of Sicily as a stepping stone to the annexation of Carthage and Libya, thus drawing the Athenians into war with a great maritime power. So we will confine our inquiry to considering the consequences for the conduct of the war against Sparta.

In the short term, since, as has been discussed, the Peloponnesians were not dependent upon Sicily for their grain supplies, no early advantage would have resulted. In the medium term, the resources of Magna Graecia would also have become available to Athens, but again with no immediate consequences for Sparta. In the longer term, the question is: would the Athenian acquisition of substantial additional resources, both human and material, have eventually overwhelmed the Spartan Confederation? But before any attempt can be made to answer that question, another one has to be addressed: would these resources (especially the human) have been available, or would the Athenians have found themselves having to hold down a resentful population, probably aided by the Spartans?

There is no telling, but it should not be forgotten that there was another powerful predator about: the Carthaginians, who, within a few years of the Athenians' defeat at Syracuse, started to try and restore their position on the island. Had the Athenians been successful, then they might also have had to contend with Carthage. If, however, it is assumed that garrisoning Sicily would not have prevented the island's resources being available to the Athenians, then it is probable that the Peloponnesians would not have been able to sustain the war, any more than Athens could have done after the wealth of the Persian Empire became available to the Spartans.

In summary, the Sicilian expedition was a gamble. Practically nothing was known about what to expect, the outcome could thus not be assessed, and the ultimate benefits were open to question. Two currents seem to have converged and brought about the irrational decision to go ahead: frustration at the stalemate in the conduct of the war, and the expectation, aroused by Alcibiades, of being able to accomplish great things.

The Spartans for their part, because they too had unbalanced forces, were initially unable to conduct the war at the operational level. Being a land power, when they could not draw the Athenians out into the field and were incapable of assaulting their city's fortifications, they were at a loss as to what they should do. Even during the two years in which the Athenians were committed to the Sicilian campaign, the Spartans were apparently unable to exploit the opportunity this presented. During this period, however, they must have greatly enlarged the size of their fleet, which enabled them to project power and so give a new dimension to the war. But instead of developing a positive operational concept, they just followed events, only becoming involved in Asia Minor by responding to the requests for help from cities in revolt against Athens. It was only with the arrival of Lysander that the Spartans advanced beyond not just opportunistically exploiting events, but dictating them by going for Athens' jugular vein, the Hellespont.

Since the various lessons that can be drawn from the actual conduct of the fighting have already been brought out, they will only be briefly mentioned here. A clear, consistent aim must be established from the start, backed by the necessary resources. It was the Athenians' failure to meet these two fundamental requirements that led to what is known as mission creep: the extension of the original aim, which leads to the dribbling in of reinforcements, usually too few and too late. Or, as the Germans would say, *Klotzen nicht kleckern*; in other words, give the fellow a jolly good clout, don't just pussyfoot around licking him.

As the other lessons require little explanation, they will be listed as principles: Surprise, which can be obtained, for example, by deception, rapid reaction or technological innovation; Security, measures to prevent the enemy achieving surprise; Offensive action, to gain the initiative; Logistics, to ensure that operations can be sustained; and Morale, which can overcome both numerical and material shortcomings. Some of these lessons are also brought out in the last two chapters, which illustrate their importance. There is, however, one additional and important lesson that has not previously been mentioned: Maintenance of the Aim – having been given a task, adhere to it and do not, like the Athenian admiral Thrasyllus at Lesbos, go wandering off in pursuit of a secondary objective.

So much for the past; what deductions can we make for the future? The need for balanced forces could not have been more clearly portrayed. If the Romans and the Carthaginians had studied the Peloponnesian War, they would not have made the same mistake in the First Punic War. Getting the balance between capabilities right, especially when defence spending is under constant pressure, is extremely difficult. On the one hand, there is the old lesson not to go on trying to fight the last war; on the other hand, it is equally mistaken to tailor force structures to closely defined assumptions about the future. The only certain thing about the future is that it will be full of surprises.

The importance of training cannot be overrated; the Spartans produced a series of professional, competent commanders, while the Athenian higher commanders were singularly undistinguished. Care then must be taken that commanders are selected for their professional ability and not for reasons that will prove to be of no account when the going gets rough. With today's conflicts calling for near-instant readiness, there will be no time to replace them.

Once a commitment has been decided upon, the national aim must be clearly defined at the strategic level. If this is not done, or if it subsequently lacks consistency, then its prosecution at the operational level becomes virtually impossible. Finally, the Peloponnesian War brings out many lessons, some of which I have probably missed, but they are all there for the finding; which, as Polybius observed about history generally, enables us to learn from the experience of others and so avoid repeating their mistakes.

Selected Further Reading

de Ste. Croix, G.E.M., *The Origins of the Peloponnesian War*, London and Ithaca, 1972

Forrest, W.G., *A History of Sparta 950–192 BC*, New York, 1968

Grundy, G.B., *Thucydides and the History of His Age*, Oxford, 1948

Hansen, V.D., *The Western Way of War*, New York, 1989

Kagan, D., *The Outbreak of the Peloponnesian War*, Ithaca, 1969

Kagan, D., *The Archidamian War*, Ithaca, 1974

Lewis, D.M., Boardman, J., Davies, J.K., and Ostwald, M., *The Cambridge Ancient History, Vol. 5: The Fifth Century BC*, Cambridge, 1992

Meier, C., *Athens: A Portrait of the City in Its Golden Age*, London, 1999

Meiggs, R., *The Athenian Empire*, Oxford, 1972

Strassler, R.B. (ed.), *The Landmark Thucydides: A Comprehensive Guide to the Peloponnesian War*, New York, 1996

Index